STUDIENKURS POLITIKWISSENSCHAFT

Textbook series for students of political science at universities

Scientifically profound and written in understandable language, the volumes of this series introduce the central research areas, theories and methods used in political science and convey the knowledge that is fundamental for prospective academics. The consistent problem orientation and the didactic preparation of the individual chapters facilitate access to the series's specialist content. This series is ideally suited for exam preparation, e.g. through summaries, questions that test knowledge and understanding, as well as charts and thematic cross-references.

Nele Noesselt

Chinese Politics

National and Global Dimensions

 **Nomos**

Onlineversion
Nomos eLibrary

The Deutsche Nationalbibliothek lists this publication in the
Deutsche Nationalbibliografie; detailed bibliographic data
are available on the Internet at http://dnb.d-nb.de

ISBN   978-3-8487-4673-6 (Print)
         978-3-8452-8900-7 (ePDF)

British Library Cataloguing-in-Publication Data
A catalogue record for this book is available from the British Library.

ISBN   978-3-8487-4673-6 (Print)
         978-3-8452-8900-7 (ePDF)

Library of Congress Cataloging-in-Publication Data
Noesselt, Nele
Chinese Politics
National and Global Dimensions
Nele Noesselt
290 pp.
Includes bibliographic references.

ISBN   978-3-8487-4673-6 (Print)
         978-3-8452-8900-7 (ePDF)

1st Edition 2021
© Nomos Verlagsgesellschaft, Baden-Baden, Germany 2021. Overall responsibility
for manufacturing (printing and production) lies with Nomos Verlagsgesellschaft mbH
& Co. KG.

为政以德，譬如北辰，居其所，而众星共之

Contents

List of Figures

List of Tables

List of Boxes

List of Acronyms

ACFTU	All-China Federation of Trade Unions
ADIZ	Air Defence Identification Zone
ANC	African National Congress
AI	Artificial Intelligence
AIIB	Asian Infrastructure Investment Bank
ALBA	Alianza Bolivariana para los Pueblos de nuestro América
APEC	Asia-Pacific Economic Cooperation
ARATS	Association for Relations Across the Taiwan Straits
BRI	Belt and Road Initiative
BRICS	Brazil, Russia, India, China, South Africa
CAC	Central Advisory Commission
CAN	Comunidad Andina de Naciones
CARICOM	Caribbean Community and Common Market
CASCF	China-Arab States Cooperation Forum
CASETF	China-Arab States Economic and Trade Forum
CBDR	Common But Differentiated Responsibilities
CCDI	Central Commission for Discipline Inspection
CCF	China-CELAC Forum
CCP	Chinese Communist Party
CCTV	Central China Television
CDB	China Development Bank
CFAU	China Foreign Affairs University
CELAC	Comunidad de Estados Latinoamericanos y Caribeños
CIC	China Investment Corporation
CICA	Conference on Interactions and Confidence-Building Measures in Asia
CIIS	China Institute of International Studies
CNOOC	China National Offshore Oil Company
CNR (Group)	China Northern Locomotive and Rolling Stock (Industry)(Group)
CNSA	China National Space Administration
CPPCC	Chinese People's Political Consultative Conference
CRCC	China Railway Construction Corporation
CSSTA	Cross-Strait Service Trade Agreement
DABP	Democratic Alliance for the Betterment and Progress of Hong Kong
DPP	Democratic Progressive Party
EC	European Community/European Communities
ECFA	Economic Cooperation Framework Agreement
EETO	European Economic and Trade Office
EIA	Energy Information Administration
ENGO	Environmental NGO
EPL	Environmental Protection Law
ESA	European Space Agency
EU	European Union
EUR	euro
EXIM (Bank)	Export-Import Bank
FALG	Foreign Affairs Leading Group
FDI	Foreign Direct Investment

FOCAC	Forum on China-Africa Cooperation
FPA	Foreign Policy Analysis
GATT	General Agreement on Tariffs and Trade
GDP	Gross Domestic Product
GMD	Guomindang (or: KMT, Kuomintang)
(GO)NGO	(Government-Organized) NGO
ICBC	Industrial and Commercial Bank of China
ICANN	Internet Corporation for Assigned Names and Numbers
ICU	International Clearing Union
IDB	Inter-American Development Bank
IGF	Internet Governance Forum
IMF	International Monetary Fund
INF	Intermediate-Range Nuclear Forces Treaty
IR	International Relations
IS	Islamic State
ISD	Integrated Surveillance Decision
ISS	International Space Station
IT	Information Technology
KMT	Kuomintang (or, in Hanyu Pinyin, Guomindang)
MEE	Ministry of Ecological Environment
MNR	Ministry of Natural Resources
MOOTW	Military Operations Other Than War
NATO	North Atlantic Treaty Organization
NDB	New Development Bank
NDRC	National Development and Reform Commission
NGO	Non-Governmental Organisation
NIMBY	Not In My Backyard
NPC	National People's Congress
OBOR	One Belt, One Road
OFDI	Outward FDI
OPEC	Organisation of the Petroleum Exporting Countries
PAC	Pan African Congress
PBoC	People's Bank of China
PFP	People First Party
PLA	People's Liberation Army
PRC	People's Republic of China
PRICS	Polar Research Institute of China
RATS	Regional Anti-Terrorist Structure
R2P	Responsibility to Protect
RP	Responsible Protection
RwP	Responsibility while Protecting
SAFE	State Administration of Foreign Exchange
SAR	Special Administrative Region
SASAC	State-owned Assets Supervision and Administration Commission
SCO	Shanghai Cooperation Organisation
SDR	Special Drawing Right
SEF	Straits' Exchange Foundation
SEPA	State Environmental Protection Agency
SOE	State-Owned Enterprise
SU	Soviet Union
THAAD	Terminal High Altitude Area Defense

UN	United Nations
UNASUR	Union of South American Nations
UNCCC	UN Climate Change Conference
UNCTAD	UN Conference on Trade and Development
US	United States
USD	US dollar
VoC	Variety of Capitalism
WGIG	Working Group of Internet Governance
WHO	World Health Organisation
WTO	World Trade Organisation

1. Introduction

The People's Republic of China (PRC) has risen to global power status. Its new role as investor in Europe and the US, as architect of the globe-spanning New Silk Road, and as advocate of major reforms of existing international institutions in the name of the so-called Global South has refuelled the "old" debate about the uniqueness and singularity of the Chinese case: is it possible to analyse Chinese politics based on theoretical frameworks inspired by European history and developed by scholars based in Western democracies? Or do non-Western states display patterns of (domestic) governance and international relations rooted in their distinct historical-philosophical foundations and cultural traditions? If so, this would imply that one would have to resort to alternative analytical frameworks to understand the hidden drivers and determinants of these countries' deviation from the "universal" model.

Regarding the causal nexus between domestic system patterns and the PRC's position as an actor on the global stage, two (opposing) theory-guided approaches can be identified:

The first approach starts from the assumption of a direct causal relation between a state's political regime patterns and domestic economic structures, as well as philosophical-cultural foundations, and its foreign strategy and global positioning. A socialist state-actor would accordingly display behavioural patterns different from those of a pluralist, liberal democratic system. For example, Democratic Peace Theory postulates that democracies would not fight each other. Non-democratic systems, by contrast, are expected to pursue an assertive, expansionist foreign policy and to oppose the liberal international order.

The second approach postulates that the inclusion of the PRC into international institutions and organisations would cause an internalisation of international values and compliance with international rules and regulations. Over time, the integration of a socialist state into a capitalist world (trade) system was expected to trigger a transformation towards capitalism and democracy. The currently observable development – that a rising non-democratic system might climb within the existing international institutions and participate in the reform and restructuring of the international order, but not necessarily plot its overthrow – has initially not been reflected by studies subscribing to this second approach.

The signals sent by the PRC often appear slightly contradictory, at least when viewed from the perspective of an outside observer. The Chinese leadership resolutely rejects and denies pursuing any hegemonial power ambitions or striving for supreme global leadership (*bu dang tou*). Nonetheless, at a working meeting of the Commission for National Security in February 2017, Xi Jinping framed the concept of "twofold guidance" (*liang'ge yindao*): to "guide the international community to jointly build a more just new world order" and to "guide the international community to jointly maintain international security". In terms of terminology, this is in line with the PRC's axiomatic foreign policy principles, as it draws a clear divisive line between the concept of "guiding" (*yindao*) and the notion of "leading" (*lingdao*). Nonetheless, the PRC's global role conception has undergone some internal revisions: China is actively participating in multilateral bargaining rounds on global trade and finance as well as on global politics and (non-traditional) security.

This textbook introduces the reader to the basic patterns and guiding principles of Chinese politics, covering both the domestic and the global level. It discusses the interplay between formal and informal dimensions and includes the political psychological level of Chinese politics through images, perceptions, and role claims. The textbook summarises the existing English-language state of the art, complemented by select streams of contemporary inner-Chinese debates and theory models. These debates amongst Chinese scholars and frameworks developed by Chinese political scientists are often excluded from textbook introductions to the political system of the PRC. They are, however, essential for understanding the concepts and calculations underlying the dynamic institutional adjustments and policy innovation in China. When institutional change becomes visible, this is normally the outcome of an internally discussed re-steering process that has been prepared over a long time. By decrypting the debates amongst scholars and think tanks advising the government, one might be able to identify these shifts before they are ultimately proclaimed. It goes without saying that during these phases of internal institutional restructuring China's visible political actions might appear irrational, as they are not in line with previous practices.

The PRC is a dynamically learning system, permanently adapting itself to changes in its domestic and global environment. A textbook which provides the tools and techniques to analyse Chinese politics can, therefore, only pinpoint current basic features and core patterns of Chinese politics and tentatively sketch potential future development trajectories. A multitude of governance concepts and ways of positioning China at the global stage are being discussed amongst Chinese scholars and policy practitioners – out of which the decision-making elite can cherry-pick and amend the official model accordingly. As the following chapters will show, the Chinese political system has never been an ideologically ossified, monolithic system – with the Mao years being no exception. Novel structures and instruments are experimentally tested, informal mechanisms and practices dominate formal system settings. Knowledge of the PRC's formal institutional order and administrative structures is generally important, but one should not forget that in a (Communist) one-party state the party has the final say and stands above the law and the state apparatus. To understand the functional mechanisms of Chinese politics and to assess their current transformations, one has to wear both structure- and agency-focused analytical lenses and to reflect on the ideas and policy paradigms underlying the system's ordering principles.

This textbook is located at the intersection of political science research and modern China studies. To allow the reader to go deeper into the details of the topics addressed, each chapter ends with a list of recommended reading. The textbook employs illustrative case studies to point out recent transformations, often not yet covered in English-language secondary literature. For these specific case studies, Chinese primary sources are referenced. Over the past few years, these illustrations have proven useful in seminars taught in Vienna, Göttingen, Hamburg, Duisburg-Essen and Zurich: they put flesh on the bones of the often rather abstract and blurry concepts of Chinese governance, and illustrate the variations and flexible (re-)interpretations of key concepts. The in-depth decryption of Chinese political science debates and governance innovation by the fourth and the fifth generation of Chinese political leaders was kindly sponsored and supported by the German National Research Foundation (DFG Project NO 1041/2–1). In this textbook, the results of my project-related fieldwork trips to China are not dealt with in full detail, but they are referenced whenever the internal scholarly debates seem crucial for understanding the most recent transformations of Chinese politics.

The audience addressed by this textbook includes undergraduate and graduate university students and scholars from the fields of political science, international relations, law, economy and China studies. It might also serve as policy consulting material for governmental and political institutions in this field.

The textbook is composed of six topical sections that reflect the historical and philosophical foundations of the PRC's political system, taking a closer look at the interplay between formal and informal system structures. Moreover, it looks at the causal relations between the national and global dimension of Chinese politics. The main contents of each chapter are summarized below to guide the reader through this book:

Chapter II starts with political philosophy and governance theory that determines and shapes Chinese politics. Knowledge of these historical-philosophical foundations is not just relevant to historians but is of crucial importance for being able to read and decrypt official political statements by the PRC's political elites. When drafting new policies, the political elites and their team of advisers debate not only the lessons to be drawn from policy experimentations in other systems but often undertake a retrospect evaluation of governance solutions documented in China's historical records. When proclaiming a new policy, the framing often borrows from China's (pre-modern) political philosophy or creates related neologisms (such as the Harmonious Society *hexie shehui*). The formula *yi shi wei jian*, to take history as a mirror, is almost omnipresent in these internal debates. Along these lines, in 2008 Wen Jiabao, in his role as premier, stressed that there would never be a relaunch of the Cultural Revolution in China – thus framing this episode of the PRC's history as a negative counter-image to the fourth generation's quest for harmony. The dissolution of the Soviet Union (SU), amongst others, is another cautionary historical example quoted to justify policy innovation and institutional reforms as the only way to avoid a state collapse. Recent studies by Chinese scholars come to the conclusion that the big-bang transformation of the Soviet economy and the neglect of ideology, in combination with a loss of control over the military, were the main drivers and causes of the SU's decay. Immediately after his appointment as General Secretary of the Chinese Communist Party (CCP), Xi Jinping undertook steps to secure the army's loyalty to the party and started to redefine the PRC's core socialist values (inscribed as Xi Jinping Thought into the CCP's constitution at the 19th Party Congress). The Chinese Empire's dynastical records, and the reasons reported for the previous dynasty's decline therein, present the ruling dynasty as the one restoring order, fixing the reported aberrations of their predecessors. Political historiography hence forms part of the PRC's official narrative to justify and legitimise reforms. One lesson from the Tang dynasty, for instance, was that empty talk causes the decline of the empire; this has been quoted to explain and justify the top-down enforcement of reforms (and the sanctioning of local officials in case of underperformance) under Xi Jinping. Operating with a symbolic path-dependent development narrative, the Hu–Wen administration (2002/2003–2012/2013) introduced novel political formula inspired by Confucian traditions. Likewise, Xi Jinping's speeches are full of direct and indirect quotes from the Chinese classics and pre-modern (political) philosophy. In addition to Xi Jinping's collected core speeches (available in English under the title *The Governance of China*) compilations of his quotations from the Chinese classics can be purchased in Chinese bookstores. These compilations list both the original quote as well as the context of Xi Jinping's speech in which this reference was made. They thus offer important clues to delve below the surface of Xi's official speeches and statements. English-language translations of Xi's speeches generally include the translation of the quote but do not provide the reader with any background information about the original quote's context and its exegesis by Chinese scholars and political scientists. In some cases, small deviations from the original quote imply that the formula has been adjusted slightly to fit into Xi's speech and send a decrypted message to some members of the audience (in some cases, this adjustment is done by using homophones, i.e., by replacing one character for another that is pronounced the same way – these messages are only visible in the printed version of the speech). The quotations from the Chinese classics serve the construction of a unified "Chinese" value and reference scheme that presents Chinese governance concepts as unique and sui generis. In addition, Xi Jinping has also reconfirmed Maoist concepts both in political debate and political practice – e.g., the "mass line" and campaigns to "rectify cadres' work style".

Likewise, groups of Chinese intellectuals look at contemporary developments against the backdrop of China's historical past and argue that any denial of the country's distinct (political) history would equal the end of China's political system. Liang Zhu's (Peking University) pamphlet against "historical nihilism" fuelled an emotional debate on the Chinese Internet, during which the fragmentation of China's scholarly community and the incompatible positions of competing factions within the CCP became visible once again. The bone of intellectual contention was the parallel that Liang Zhu outlined between the de-Stalinisation and historical nihilism under Khrushchev and the developments in the contemporary PRC (Liang 2012).

The official governance model coined by the fourth and the fifth generation of the PRC's political leaders should not be mistaken as a unified monolithic model, synthesizing the various sources of Chinese governance philosophy. Instead, these philosophical reference systems (Confucianism; Daoism; Buddhism; Marxism/Maoism; and Western values) coexist and are only loosely combined under one overarching roof. Depending on political developments, some frames and elements might be (temporarily) deactivated or removed from the official governance canon.

A clear line of demarcation has been drawn rhetorically between the Maoist era of revolution and class struggle and the post-Maoist era of reform (of the economic system). However, the debate on "historical nihilism" and the concept of "permanent, continued class struggle", initiated by the Chinese Academy of Social Sciences in Beijing, demonstrates the persistence and the legacy of Maoist concepts and terminology in the 21st century.

Chapter III provides the reader with an overview of China's institutional order and the operative mechanisms of the Chinese party-state. The notion of the "party-state" illustrates the close intertwined relationship between the CCP and the PRC's state apparatus. This parallel, mirror structure of party and state is re-duplicated at all levels of the administration, down to the level of the county. However, in the PRC's political history there have been periods of radical restructuring or abrogation of China's state institutions – as, for example, during the Maoist mass campaigns. The post-Maoist generations of China's political leaders are guided by the proclaimed goal of setting up a modern, transparent administration with robust checks and balances. After internal turbulences and interruption of these reforms, the fourth and the fifth generation have undertaken efforts to enforce the implementation of these restructuring measures. However, any institutional reforms or adjustments of the governance process can be expected to generate resistance of the bureaucratic state apparatus and groups of state officials whose (institutional) power would be curbed by these reform measures. Mass mobilisation or anti-corruption campaigns are one possible way to enforce the employment of new political personnel and to ensure compliance with the central authorities' reform agenda. The anti-corruption campaign initiated by Xi Jinping persecutes "tigers and flies", i.e., cadres at all ranks and levels of the party-state (including the military) (Noesselt 2014). Anti-corruption campaigns might have multiple goals and drivers. They can be deemed necessary to restore the efficiency and performance of the state apparatus – and they can be used to get rid of counter-elites and opposition movements. On the other hand, they can be an attempt to win back people's trust in the political regime and to generate symbolic support for the CCP and its governance approach. Corruption and power abuse by local party cadres and state officials have shaken people's trust in the system. In the perception of Chinese (local) society, the family members of high-ranked cadres are seen as enjoying multiple privileges. The lawsuits against "tigers" (and "flies") have accordingly been publicly documented by Chinese state media.

Another Achilles' heel of the one-party state is the phenomenon of so-called "naked cadres", i.e., cadres who managed to transfer their family and fortune to other countries and are the only ones of their family staying on. At internal meetings, Chinese analysts have remarked that a similar phenomenon of capital flight occurred in the final years of the Soviet Union. Before this background Xi's anti-corruption campaign goes far beyond those launched by his precursors in terms of scope and range. Operation Fox Hunt (*da liehu*) targeted Chinese officials who had escaped abroad (Xinhua 2015). Until 2017, this operation was coordinated by Wang Qishan, a close ally and companion of Xi Jinping, in his function as head of the CCP's Commission for Discipline Inspection. Whilst, with the PRC's entrance into the period of reform and opening, this commission did not attract much attention, the role and power of this party organ have been reinforced from 2012 onwards. Operation Fox Hunt was succeeded by Operation Skynet which persecuted Chinese nationals in the US and Great Britain accused of having committed economic crimes. In March 2018, the National People's Congress passed a revision of the Chinese state constitution that included the establishment of a National Supervisory Commission (*Guojia Jiancha Weiyuanhui*) with regional sub-branches. In 2019, a second investigation round of Operation Skynet was launched (*Renmin Ribao* 2019).

The fine-tuning and modifications to the PRC's state apparatus also imply a re-distribution of power and responsibilities between the party and the state as well as amongst the central ministries. Super-ministries have been reorganised and sub-divided into smaller units. Additional mechanisms of internal supervision and checks and balances have been introduced. The fifth generation's governance model follows a "top-level design" (*dingceng sheji*): power has become recentralised. Albeit in political practice, the central party-state still relies on cooperation with the lower levels of administration instead of enforcing top-down decisions without prior consultation. It also continues to cooperate with local (civil) society; formats of local self-administration are regarded as essential for the successful implementation of central level regulations (and their adaptation to local conditions).

The formal institutional order of the state apparatus, as documented in the PRC's constitution, is hardly revealing when analysing the complex interactions between central and local levels as well as between party and state, and regarding the PRC's special administrative units. Hong Kong and Macao are parts of China but – under the formula of "one country, two systems" (*yi guo, liang zhi*) – are allowed to have their own multi-party system structures. Likewise, Taiwan is de jure treated as a province of China – even though the CCP government in Beijing never exerted direct power and control over the island. Chapter III concludes with an assessment of the political history of Hong Kong and Taiwan and discusses the outcome of recent elections and their implications for Beijing.

Chapter IV starts from the Fourth Plenum's (2014) announcement to strengthen legal reforms and the legal system. This chapter places these developments in the historical context of China's past processes of state-building and constitutionalisation. It outlines the parallels between Xi Jinping's proclamation of rule-based governance (*yi fa zhi guo*), complemented by the idea of constitution-based governance (*yi xian zhi guo*), and the intellectual debates and initiatives in the late 19th century to transform China into a constitutional monarchy. In the 20th and 21st centuries, the PRC's ruling elites repeatedly discussed the function of legal frameworks and institutionalised modes of governance to stabilise the one-party state. The Fourth Plenum in 2014 was, however, the first of its kind to formally highlight the importance of rule-based governance. The concept of constitution-based governance, which was discussed simultaneously, was later dropped. This points at internal controversies within the CCP. In January 2013, the Guangdong-based weekly newspaper *Nanfang*

Zhoumo (*Southern Weekend*) reported that the new year editorial, originally entitled as "Chinese Dream, Dream of Constitutional Governance" (*Zhongguo meng, xianzheng meng*), had been censored. Other newspapers and journals also elaborated on this notion – including *Yanhuang Chunqiu* (English title: *China through the Ages*), whose webpage was down after an essay had been posted that identified constitution-based governance as a necessary prerequisite for a general restructuring of the political system (Yuen 2013). The official party organ, *Renmin Ribao* (*People's Daily*), intervened in this dispute and published three editorials that documented the official definition of the Chinese governance model and rule-based governance. Since August 2013, constitutionalism and democracy, as well as Western values, have obviously been put on a blacklist.

The internal controversy back in 2013 over the concept of constitutionalism insinuates that one should not look at the Chinese configurations of the law (and law-based governance) separately, but in connection with the concepts of democracy, socialism and capitalism. In Western political science, democracy and rule of law are widely seen as causally interrelated. In the Chinese debate, these concepts have been redefined and adapted to the political reality of the one-party state.

In principle, the strengthening of rule-based governance accompanies the recent modifications of the PRC's economic development strategy and its institutionalisation. Chapter IV thus concludes with some reflections on the transformation of the Chinese economy and the debate about a distinct "Chinese" variety of capitalism.

With **Chapter V** the textbook turns to the visible pluralisation of actors directly or indirectly involved in Chinese politics (and policymaking). During the Maoist years, tensions between factions – competing interest groups within the CCP – had reached their peak in the "struggle between two lines", i.e., between those labelled as "revolutionary-proletarian" and those falling into the category of "capitalist-bourgeois" forces. These cleavages have survived and continue to erupt from time to time. Tensions and conflicts also occur amongst China's economic elites – between the state-owned sector and the private economy, between advocates of a neo-Maoist development approach and those favouring a neo-liberal agenda. One of the CCP government's central tasks is to restore and maintain social harmony and cohesion and to mediate between the competing socio-economic actor groups. In 2018, the PRC's Gini coefficient, describing the inequal distribution of income, reached 46.8 (down from 49.1 in 2008, but up from 46.2 in 2015).[1] This indicates a severe imbalance that could threaten social harmony and regime survival.

The economic reforms initiated in 2013 aim at reducing state subsidies for state-owned companies and to strengthen market-based competition. The National Development and Reform Commission (NDRC), an agency under the State Council, outlined some basic reform ideas in its 383 Plan. This plan proposes the simultaneous expansion of market economy principles, the reform of administrative

---

1 https://www.statista.com/statistics/250400/inequality-of-income-distribution-in-china-based-on-the-gini-index/.

system structures and the strengthening of rule-based governance. To foster competition, the NDRC recommends a further opening of the market for private and foreign investors, especially the sectors of banking and finance – and to further internationalise the Chinese renminbi. The plan also includes the liberalisation of the energy and telecommunication sectors. With regard to the situation of Chinese peasants, the 383 Plan devises the strategy of reforming land use rights regulations. The prospective legalisation of rural–urban labour migration also requires the establishment of (private) social insurance systems. Access to social security and welfare systems should no longer depend on people's original *hukou* registration.[2] The Third Plenum (2013) finally passed a 60-points reform package that remained far more abstract than the original NDRC reform proposal.

The reform package of the Third Plenum formally stands for a top-down imposed re-steering of China's economy. Indirectly, the reform proposal reflects the positions and demands of relevant societal actor groups. Under certain conditions – outlined in Chapter V – mass protests and contestation movements are tolerated, as they serve as seismographs that provide the central government with information about local (mis)developments and allow the formulation of policies designed to pre-empt people's demands. The CCP has undergone a transformation from a revolutionary party of workers, soldiers and peasant to a ruling party that represents the Chinese "people" in its entirety. This also includes the group of the so-called "red capitalists" – private entrepreneurs maintaining a symbiotic relationship with the party. But the CCP also pays special attention to rural areas, maybe also due to historical legacies, as the revolution that brought the CCP to power heavily relied on its power bases in the countryside. Furthermore, as historical records reporting on the decay of several Chinese dynasties highlight, religious movements and peasant rebellions were the main reasons for the fall of the ruling dynasty and the instalment of a new – sometimes local only – government led by the revolutionary forces.

Chapters **VI** and **VII** turn to the global dimensions of Chinese politics and assess the links and dependencies between the PRC's global positioning and reforms and developments at the domestic level. **Chapter VI** begins with a short overview of the international perceptions and views on China's role as an actor in international politics, contrasting them with the PRC's officially proclaimed national and global role conceptions. In international political science, as well as in debates amongst Chinese academic communities, one central topic is the modes and effects of the rise of a state to global power status. Whilst neorealist scholars categorically deny that such a process could occur peacefully, the political and political science debate in China operates with the paradigm of Peaceful Rise (*heping jueqi*) and postulates that the PRC is cooperatively rising within the existing international system structures. The Peaceful Rise (also framed as Peaceful Development Road (*heping fazhan zhi daolu*)) is – like the Harmonious World (*hexie shijie*) – one of the PRC's magic formulas to defuse threat perceptions and to counter scenarios of an inevitable conflict between rising powers (China) and the old gravitational centres of world

---

2 The 383 NDRC document is available online: http://www.xatdj.com/article/11003.html.

politics (the US). Chapter VI moves beyond the official narratives of China and the US by assessing concrete actions and developments in select sub-fields of global politics – especially in those characterised by under-regulation and seen as emerging fields of global power competition: outer space, cyberspace and the Artic region. To assess global power shifts, the chapter examines the PRC's refined approach to Africa and Latin America – the latter being historically regarded as the strategic backyard of the US. The expansion of Chinese economic (and political) activities is an undeniable fact – as the emergence of the PRC as an investor in Europe and the US, also covered in Chapter VI, corroborates. The exploration of global markets and the PRC's infrastructure and investment in other world regions have led to a readjustment of China's security strategy. China did not only modernise its army – the annually announced increase of its military spending adds fuel to the debate on Beijing's "new assertiveness" – but also set up a blue water navy and special forces trained for global missions. The PRC participates in UN peacekeeping missions and, under Xi Jinping, for the first time in its history, also contributed combat forces. This indicates that crises and conflicts in other world regions are seen as detrimental to Chinese economic development interests – and, clearly, Beijing seeks to position itself as a responsible global power contributing to the resolution of global challenges. These image campaigns might also explain the PRC's new positioning in the fields of global climate change and global finance. Whilst, over the past few decades, the PRC refused to sign any contracts that would include binding quota for emission reduction, since the Paris Summit (2015) the PRC actively advocates the re-steering of national and global economies towards green and sustainable development. Two developments might lie behind this strategic turn: firstly, the PRC enforces a more sustainable, low-emission growth model at home and heavily invests in the development of green technologies – which could be exported to other regions undergoing a similar re-steering process. Secondly, the PRC's positioning as an advocate of combatting climate change happened when the Trump administration withdrew from the Paris protocol. At the World Economic Forum and at G20 meetings, the PRC also pushed for "green finance" and put forward its own concepts to stabilise the global financial system.

Chapter VII takes a closer look at recent power shifts and transformations of world politics that are still at an early stage but have the potential to trigger additional modifications in China's foreign and security strategy (this already happened in some cases). With the New Silk Road (also known as One Belt, One Road (OBOR) or Belt(s) and Road(s) Initiative), the PRC has put forward the idea of constructing a globe-spanning network of trade corridors managed and coordinated by Beijing. This New Silk Road also means that the PRC's relations with the Arab world will be deepened and expanded. This diversification of the PRC's foreign relations and its reaching out to "new" world regions has implications for the Chinese-imagined cartography of the world as composed of major power centres. The Chinese term *duojihua* (multipolarisation) stands for a transition from the US-centred world system to one in which China would play an important role but not act as supreme leader. In the Chinese political debate of the 1970s/1980s, the rather broad concept of multipolarity was broken down to pentapolarity, a world composed of China, Europe, Japan, Russia and the

US. Chapter VII re-assesses these four bilateral relationships by looking at their historical evolution and most recent transformations in the 21st century.

A retrospect view on the theories and paradigms guiding research on Chinese politics evidences that scenarios and interpretations tend to be overshadowed by the researcher's position in time and space and impacted by global power constellations and power competition. Sometimes, analyses might have also been inspired by normative views and thus do not document facts but provide the reader with an *ex cathedra* interpretation of Chinese politics.

The evaluation and classification of Xi Jinping's leadership style by international analysts illustrates that the interpretation of Chinese politics is subject to rapid changes of views and opinions (of course, reflecting unexpected shifts and turns of Chinese politics). Initially hailed as liberal reformer, Xi Jinping, for example, activated slogans and steering mechanisms of the Mao era. In official party terminology, he is referred to as core leader (*hexin lingdao*), his theory on Chinese socialism – Xi Jinping Thought – was inscribed into the CCP constitution at the 19th Party Congress. At this congress, Xi was also reconfirmed as CCP General Secretary. In March 2018, the National People's Congress passed a revision of the state constitution that would allow him to remain in his position as State President for life (before the revision of the constitution, this had been formally limited to two consecutive office terms). Hence, international observers now see him more as charismatic-authoritarian leader and conservative defender of one-party rule than as a liberal reformer (see, inter alia, Economy 2014).

Even the cult of personality appears to have been restored. There has been no second red book or wide-spread launch of propaganda posters (though wall slogans and posters carrying core political statements can be found across the country). But one should not forget that Xi Jinping's speeches have been compiled and translated into various languages; the third volume was released in 2020. Additionally, short video clips and animated cartoons on the PRC's reform policies are being circulated on the (Chinese) Internet. Some of them address the Chinese audience, others are reaching out to the English-language community (such as one cartoon on the advantage of Chinese meritocracy as compared to Western democracy, and one music cartoon clip on the PRC's 13th Five-Year Plan). The analysis of visual documents – images, graphs and maps printed in Chinese newspapers; posters; animated cartoons; videos and documentaries broadcast by Chinese state media – offer additional ways to get access to the "hidden" dimensions of Chinese politics. Whilst the official political narrative operates with rather obscure frames and concepts that are open to definition, the visualisation of these frames by the state media hints at some of the content elements linked to these frames which are currently being discussed. Regarding the fifth generation of Chinese political leaders, these visual dimensions of Chinese politics have remained rather under-theorized and under-explored. Given the opaqueness of the Chinese political system and the partial self-censoring of the public (intellectual) debate, visual documents provide the analyst not only with the official narrative of the party-state but might reflect elements of the various competing policy images and reflections on China's future developments that are neither publicly displayed nor documented in official political statements or official journal publications.

These contemplations on the dynamic fluidity of Chinese politics imply that a textbook written to provide the reader with the knowledge and skills needed to identify and interpret contemporary developments of Chinese politics can only document the basic patterns and facts and outline views and interpretations documenting the state of Chinese governance at the moment of the conclusion of the textbook manuscript. This textbook aims at raising the reader's awareness of the importance of the informal dimensions of Chinese politics and the temporary oscillations of the system (which should *not* prematurely be read as indicators of a lurking regime collapse).

In order to allow the reader to "jump" between the chapters and to use this book also as reference book to look up basic definitions and core facts, some definitions and episodes mentioned in the opening parts of this book are taken up again at a later point – so that each (sub-)chapter can also be read as independent (learning) unit.

In addition to the list of references and the list of recommended literature at the end of each chapter, this textbook includes a list of central databases and online portals on Chinese politics. Throughout the manuscript Hanyu Pinyin is used for romanising Chinese characters – unless an older (e.g., Wade Giles) transcription is commonly used for certain names of people or places in the English-language literature.[3]

References

Economy, Elizabeth (2014), "China's Imperial President", *Foreign Affairs*, 93, 80–91.

Liang, Zhu (2012), *Lishi xuwuzhuyi pingxi* (Critical Review of Historical Nihilism). Peking: CASS.

Noesselt, Nele (2014), "Staatlich-zivile Interaktionsmuster im Wandel. Governance-Konzepte der neuen chinesischen Führungselite" (Changing Patterns of State-Society Interactions: Governance Concepts of the New Chinese Leadership Elite), in: Heinelt, Hubert (ed.) (2014), *Modernes Regieren in China*. Baden-Baden: Nomos, 137–157.

Renmin Ribao (2019), "'Tianwang 2019' xingdong zhengshi qidong" (Official Launching of "Skynet 2019"), 29 January 2019, http://djy.people.com.cn/n1/2019/0129/c117092-3 0595504.html.

Xinhua (2015), "'Tianwang' rang tan guan xiao yao meng mie" ("Skynet" Destroys the Happy-go-lucky-Dreams of Corrupt Cadres), 2 April 2015, http://news.xinhuanet.com/ world/2015-04/02/c_1114851117.htm.

Xinhua (2015b), "Beijing ziliao: Jinnian lai Zhongguo haiwai zhui tao zhui zang zhuyao chengguo" (Background material: The most important results of hunting Chinese nationals who have fled abroad and of recovering ill-gotten gains), http://news.xinhuanet.c om/legal/2015-04/02/c_1114851199.htm.

Yuen, Samson (2013), "Debating Constitutionalism in China: Dreaming of a Liberal Turn?", *Perspectives Chinoises*, 4, 67–72.

---

3 E.g., Chiang Kai-shek is used instead of the pinyin transcription as Jiang Jieshi; Sun Yat-sen instead of Sun Yixian.

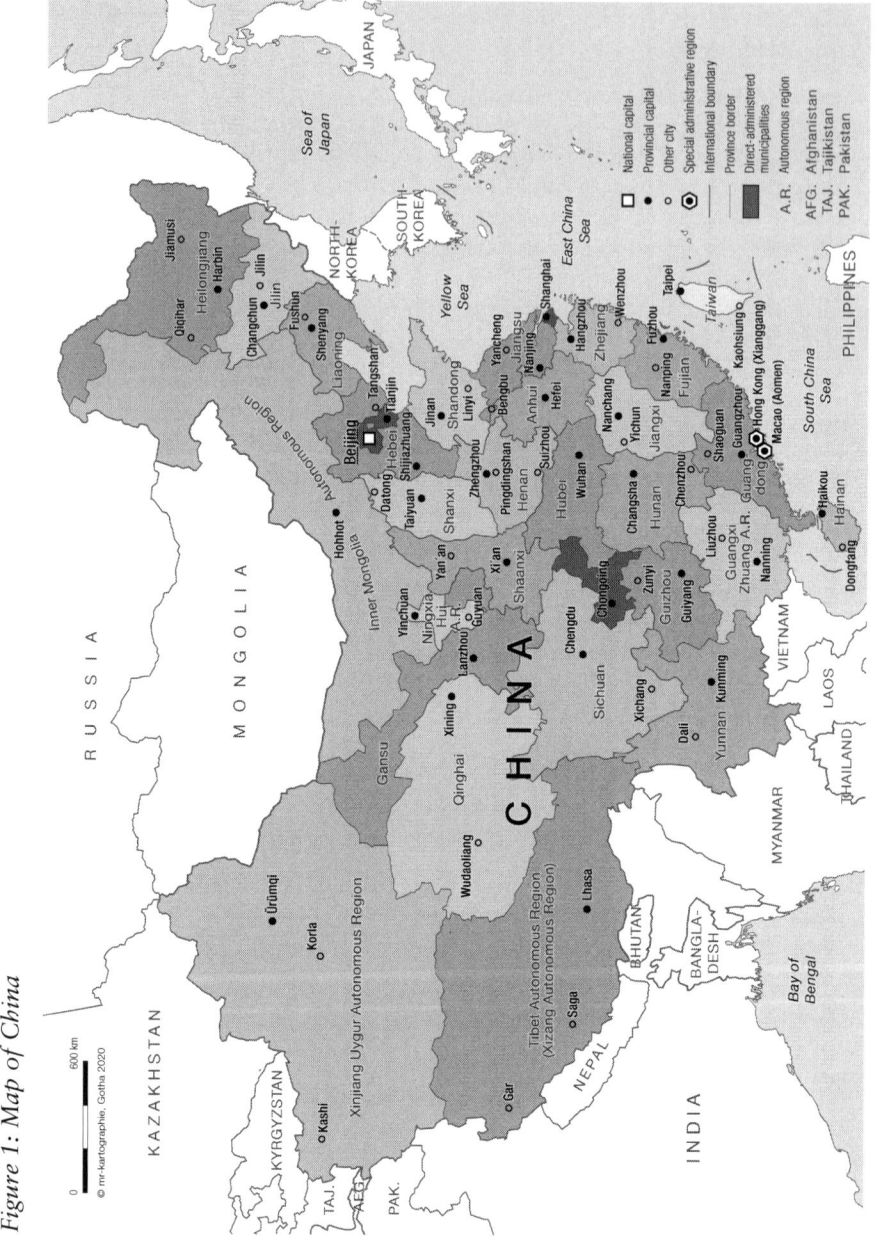

Figure 1: Map of China

2. Philosophical and Ideational Foundations of Chinese Politics

Key Content and Learning Goals

- Overview of typologies of political systems and their legitimation strategies
- General knowledge of the various philosophical streams and governance ideas guiding Chinese politics: reinventions of Marxism and Confucianism in the 21st century
- Differentiation between symbolic-rhetorical and operational levels of Chinese politics, between (strategic) particularity claims and universal patterns of political theory

This chapter introduces the reader to the issue of political legitimacy and legitimation strategies, and sheds light both on the theory-based configuration of legitimacy in the context of the Chinese one-party state as well as on the system's concrete justificatory legitimation instruments in the post-Mao era. Contrary to the widely voiced belief that politics after 1978 would be characterised by pragmatism and a farewell to ideology, ideas (and "ideology") are still playing a decisive role in the making of Chinese politics. This chapter sketches the plurality of ideas and philosophical traditions shaping and influencing the Chinese concepts of political rule and legitimate order. Although it seems nigh on impossible to reduce these multiple traditions of thought to just one single unified concept, the chapter will provide the reader with an overview of those ideas that serve as the reference system and conceptual yardstick upon which the Chinese one-party state builds its legitimacy. Whilst some ordering principles might serve as the justification for and as the symbolic consolidation of the existing system structures, others might inspire (and legitimate) future-oriented institutional reforms. However, not all reference elements originate from China itself. The chapter thus addresses both the re-activation as well as the reinvention of Chinese traditions.

The "Chinese" political system is often associated with the concepts of Socialism and Maoism, standing in sharp contrast to the apparently increasingly capitalist production modes of the Chinese economy. Simultaneously, there has been a re-emergence of religious and spiritual traditions – especially Buddhism and Daoism – within Chinese society. In addition to this "religious renaissance", *Guoxue* Studies, as a more academic response, turn back to the reading of pre-modern philosophical texts and discuss the meaning of Chinese cultural traditions for a post-industrial society. Again, the official political debate quotes Mao and Marx to stress the system's unique identity and particular features. This raises the tantalising question of whether a system can, all at the same time, be Confucian, Maoist and capitalist, or whether these ideational streams are mutually exclusive and only become dominant during distinct stages of development.

The concept of "imagined communities", as developed by Benedict Anderson (1983), implies that the formation of any political community requires the existence of joint narratives and ideational reference systems. In this case, the plurality and fragmentation of China's "ideological" canon directly leads to the question of how the modern one-party state manages to govern its multi-ethnic, multi-religious society – and, indeed, to balance the related competing specific group interests.

The PRC repudiates external criticism of its "socialist" system identity, and proudly stresses the uniqueness and particularity of its own developmental path. The claim to practise an independent, unprecedented model of governance is, however, not restricted to the domestic level of Chinese politics. The Chinese Dream, articulated by Xi Jinping in 2012, underlines the PRC's claim to possess its own world order views and ordering principles – ones incompatible with Western standards. Seen from a "Chinese" perspective, the international system is not determined by anarchy, but dominated by the United States as the solitary global superpower. China's visionary ideas of world order seek to overcome US predominance and undertake an indirect, hidden positioning of China embedded in abstract configurations of global order.

In order to enable the reader to decrypt official positioning statements and the strategic calculations underlying the framing of Chinese governance and institutional reforms, this chapter assesses the basic patterns of the PRC's ideational reference schemes – as well as their most recent re-interpretations and re-configurations under the CCP's fifth generation of political leaders.

2.1. Confucian State Philosophy and Maoist Ideology

Confucianism is the top reference scheme for Chinese state philosophy. For more than a thousand years, Confucianism served as official state doctrine. The selection of officials for the first unified Chinese Empire under the Qin dynasty (221 BC) followed aristocratic principles. The Sui and Tang dynasties, by contrast, switched to a formalised examination system (*keju*) requiring in-depth knowledge of the Confucian classics and their correct interpretation. Starting from the county level, successful candidates could qualify for the next rounds of the examination system – and finally serve as officials in the imperial capital (Twitchett 1976). The Song dynasty introduced the additional palace exam, leaving the selection of highest officials to the emperor and reducing the power of the Ministry of Rites (*Libu*) – one of the six ministries of the Chinese imperial administration.[4] Although the examination system generated an ideological streamlining of the intellectual elites, disappointed Confucian scholars turned away from the system, formed secret societies or supported local rebellions. Many of them were highly dissatisfied and lost faith in the imperial system due to the fact that many successful applicants were not appointed to a leading position and a huge number never managed to pass the required exams, despite years wasted on intense preparation. Nonetheless, the Confucian examination system remained the main instrument of personnel recruitment until 1904/1905.[5]

---

4 On the examination system during the Song dynasty, see Chaffee (1985). For an overview of the basic organisation of the state bureaucracy and its core ministries, see: Hucker (1985).
5 For a comprehensive overview, see Elman (2013); see also the annotated bibliography composed by Wang (2013).

Even though the Confucian canon – the Four Books (*si shu*) and the Five Classics (*wu jing*) – hardly provided any directly applicable manual for governing the Chinese Empire, the examination system facilitated the ideological unification of the administrative elites and their willing internalisation of the Confucian ideas of hierarchical order and ethical norms. The idea of the moral, ethical self-cultivation of the individual was connected to the order of the state and the harmony of the cosmos. Only if all sub-systems are harmoniously organised can the balance of the cosmological order be maintained. Even the figure of the ruler was included into this cosmological-ideological Confucian world order. The traditional concept of legitimate rule was based on the "mandate of heaven" (*tianming*), which the emperor, in case of misconduct, could all too easily lose. In such a case – that is, if the emperor did not comply with the ritual norms – impeachment and the overthrow of the ruling dynasty was, according to Mencius, regarded as justified and legitimate action. Manifestations of chaos – natural disasters, rebellions – were read as indicators of a lurking decline in legitimacy and a loss of the ruling mandate.[6]

In the aftermath of the disaster of the Opium Wars, Confucianism was regarded as one potential cause of the Chinese Empire's ossification, weakness and technological inferiority. This was an even more traumatic experience as the Chinese Empire had previously been known and admired for its inventions and technological discoveries, such as printing with moveable letters, porcelain and gunpowder. The tremendous loss of self-confidence after 1840 fuelled debates displaying a plurality of governance ideas, ranging from complete Westernization (advocated by Hu Shi) over imported anarchism to various varieties of Marxist thought (Chang 1980). In the late imperial times, many of those ideas were imported from abroad. Seeking refuge in Japan, Chinese reformist intellectuals translated key works of Western philosophy and social sciences from Japanese into Chinese. Other liberal-minded Chinese scholars (and political activists) spent some years in Europe or the US. This is how ideas such as nation/nation-state, constitutionalism and Social Darwinism found their way into the formerly hermetically isolated realms of the Chinese Empire.

Amongst the few engaged advocates favouring an affirmation of Confucian ideas as the core governance reference scheme of China was Kang Youwei (1858–1927). In his essays, he described Confucius as a reformer and argued that the original Confucian ideas had been distorted and misinterpreted. According to his writings, the Confucian state doctrines, heavily criticised by liberal reformers at the end of the Qing dynasty, had been rooted in unrepresentative versions of the original Confucian state philosophy. These fakes had once been created so as to justify an illegal throne occupation in China's dynastical history (here, Kang Youwei refers to the controversy between the Old Text School and the New

---

6 On the socio-cognitive, ideational dimensions of legitimacy in the Chinese context, see Guo (2003). These archetypal patterns of legitimacy continue to shape Chinese politics up to present times: the successful solution of crises increases the people's trust in the government and support for the political system. Major crises testing the management capacities of China's 21st century elites have included SARS, the earthquake in Sichuan and the spill-over effects of the global financial crisis of 2007/2008.

Text School). Further elaborating on his reading of Confucianism, Kang Youwei drafted his *Book of Great Unity* (*Datongshu*) – referring herein to the Confucian "golden age" of unity and harmony as outlined in the Confucian *Classics of Rites* (*Liji*). "Globalising" the idea of a society without any borders, Kang Youwei even constructed a "Chinese" world system vision based on unity and inclusion (Thompson 1958; Xiao 1975).

In 1898 a reform-oriented group of Confucian literati, led by Kang Youwei and his disciple Liang Qichao, managed to convince the Guangxu emperor to engage in reforms aimed at transforming China into a constitutional monarchy. The Meiji Restoration in Japan, which had catalysed the establishment of a Japan-style constitutional Tenno-cracy, served as the external blueprint of inspiration. After a symbolic period of one hundred days (hence the label Hundred Days' Reforms, or, according to the traditional Chinese calendar, *Wuxu* [=1898] Reforms), the emperor's dowager Cixi ordered an end to these governance experiments and, furthermore, launched a persecution of the reform's main protagonists.

In 1904/1905, the official restructuring of the state bureaucracy and the introduction of a modern curriculum for the examination system signalled farewell to Confucian state doctrines. Access to the state apparatus required professional management skills. The rather reluctant and hesitant implementation of the announced (institutional, especially constitutional) reforms finally triggered a radicalisation of Chinese society, sparking the New Cultural Movement asking for (cultural) renewal and (political and institutional) change. Instead of evolutionary adjustments of the Chinese state apparatus, more radical reformers went as far as to demand a substitution of Chinese characters for Latin ones and a clear-cut negation of traditional Chinese Confucian norms and values. The eruption of radical iconoclasm with the May Fourth Movement (1919) stood for a fundamental distancing from the old Confucian reference texts. During the Cultural Revolution (1966–1976), Confucius – jointly with Lin Biao, Mao's previously designated successor who had by then fallen from grace – once again was attacked as the ultimate personification of everything evil.

BOX I: ANTI-CONFUCIANISM

May Fourth Movement

On 4 May 1919, the streets of Beijing were filled with people venting their disappointment and anger about the outcome of the peace negotiations at Versailles. The Chinese Republic had entered the First World War siding with the Allied forces, guided by the hope of seeing the territories transferred back to China that had been ceded by the Unequal Treaties of the Opium Wars to the jurisdiction of Germany. The interests and positions put forward by the Chinese delegation remained, however, unheard. In reality, informal secret treaties had already prepared for the transfer of these territories to Japan. Beyond the protests of the year 1919, seen in a broader context, the May Fourth Movement symbolises the peak of the Chinese New Cultural Movement striving for renewal and modernisation. The latter movement took off around 1915 and, depending on whose historiographical records one decides to rely on, ended in the mid-1920s (consolidation of the GMD government), in the early 1920s (formation of the Chinese Communist Party) or in 1949 (proclamation of the People's Republic of China). The ultimate goal was to "renew" Chinese society; Mr

Democracy and Mr Science were the allegorised icons of this early Chinese modernisation movement.

Critic Campaign against Lin Biao and Confucius (pi Lin, pi Kong) (1973–1976)

At the First Plenum of the 10th Central Committee (1973), Mao called for public criticism of Confucius and Confucian values and encouraged people to undertake a critical re-evaluation of Chinese history from a Maoist-Marxist perspective. This campaign, which was initiated two years after the ousting of Lin Biao, was targeting Mao's inner-party opponents and dissidents. It was, however, playing with the famous formula of "using history as a mirror", as it was allegorically equated with the ancient antagonism between Legalism and Confucianism. According to official Chinese historiography, Qin Shihuang, the founder of the legendary Qin dynasty, is reported to have turned against Confucian scholars – ordering to bury them alive and banning their writings. The Legalist camp, advocating a societal order based on legal regulation and draconic punishment, was hence promoted. Mao (and the Gang of Four) metaphorically continued the role of the Legalists and turned against the followers of the Confucian "feudal slave-holder aristocracy", addressing Lin Biao and, in the longer-term perspective, Zhou Enlai.

The abolition of the Confucian examination system in 1904/1905 and the occasionally exploding hyper-modernisation movements nonetheless did not cause a final elimination of Confucian norms and moral values. The PRC named its body for promoting the Chinese language and culture abroad Confucius Institute; Confucius temples – including the core place of Confucian worship alongside the Confucian academy in Qufu, hometown of Confucius' ancestors – have likewise been renovated and refurbished. This reactivation and commemoration of Confucius as a figurehead of a distinct "Chinese" culture illustrates the strategic fine-tuning of the party-state's legitimation strategy in the 21st century.

BOX II: Legitimacy – Basic Definitions

"[L]egitimacy is the capacity of the system to engender and maintain the belief that the existing political institutions are the most appropriate ones for the society" (Lipset 1959).

"[T]he belief that in spite of shortcomings and failures, the political institutions are better than any other that might be established, and therefore can demand obedience" (Linz 1988).

"Political authority is legitimate [...] to the extent that it is acquired and exercised according to established rules (legality); the rules are justifiable according to socially accepted beliefs about (i) the rightful source of authority, and (ii) the proper ends and standards of government (normative justifiability); positions of authority are confirmed by express consent or affirmation of appropriate subordinates, and by recognition from other legitimate authorities (legitimation)" (Beetham 2001).

"[This] power relationship is not legitimate because people believe in its legitimacy, but because it can be justified in terms of their beliefs" (Beetham 1991).

"[A] government is legitimate if and only if the results of governmental output are compatible with the value pattern of the society" (Stillman 1974).

The legitimacy of any political system can be further broken down into legitimacy beliefs and legitimacy claims.[7] Immediately after the PRC's entrance into the post-Maoist reform era, international China pundits initially assumed a transition from ideology- to output-based legitimacy (economic growth, stability). Since the mid-1990s scholars have, however, highlighted the pertinence of the ideational – if not "ideological" – dimensions of legitimacy for the stabilisation of the Chinese one-party state (Zeng 2014). Especially in times of economic turbulence and crisis, any exclusively output-oriented legitimation strategy would be bound to fail. Chen Feng (1997), drawing on pre-modern ideas of Confucian "parental" governance in combination with Max Weber's typology[8] of legitimate modes of political rule, classified this specific configuration of legitimation as "eudaemonic legitimacy": the system provides certain goods for the people, whilst the political elites present themselves as caring and benevolent public servants and wholeheartedly committed coordinators of the state apparatus.

Another model formulating a synthesis between the main categories of Western political science and Chinese state philosophy has been developed by Guo Bao-gang. He differentiates between "original justification" and "utilitarian justification". Original justification consists of the mandate of heaven (*tian ming*), rule by virtue (*ren zhi*), popular consent (*min ben*) and legality (*he fa*). Whilst the mandate of heaven is generally not referenced in official speeches by China's post-Tian'anmen leadership generations, the formula of "putting people first" (*yi ren wei ben*), inspired by Mencius and often abbreviated as *min ben*, is almost omnipresent. The same applies to the elites' rhetorical commitment to practise a "rule-based" mode of governance. Anti-corruption campaigns and the efforts to correct the working style of party cadres are presented as being in line with Confucian ideas of benevolent governance, based on moral values and virtue (referenced as *ren zhi*). To these symbolic elements of legitimation, Guo adds the aforementioned utilitarian justification (Guo 2003: 6).

Contrary to Easton's dynamic input-output model, the "Chinese" idea of legitimacy focuses on indirect input channels and canalised, orchestrated feedback loops rather than an input based on elections or the open articulation of interests and demands. The Chinese party-state conducts politics "for" the people (remember the Maoist slogan "serving the people" (*wei renmin fuwu*)) not "by" the people, and links its governance approach to reactivated, rewritten patterns and archetypal images of an inherited "Chinese" governance model (Tong 2011).

After the founding of the PRC, the philosophical-historical debates on Chinese Confucianism and modern reinterpretations were continued amongst epistemic communities in Hong Kong, Taiwan and the Chinese diaspora in the US. The resultant New Confucianism – connected with the philosophical work by Mou Zongshan (1909–1995), Tang Junyi (1909–1978), Xu Fuguan (1902–1982) and Tu Wei-ming (*1940) – is, however, not a mere recapitulation of "old" Confucian

---

7 On the theoretical conceptualisation of legitimacy, see Beetham (1991, 2001); Easton (1965); Lipset (1960).
8 Max Weber differentiates between three modes of political rule which all possess their specific features and patterns of legitimacy: traditional, charismatic, legal-rational.

ideas. It is rather an eclectic reinterpretation of Confucianism merging select streams of Daoism, Buddhism and Western philosophy.

On the post-Maoist Chinese mainland, Confucian norms have become part of so-called *Guoxue* Studies, which seek to excavate and reactivate pre-modern "Chinese" philosophical traditions. *Guoxue* ("national, cultural studies"), once again, display a strong instrumentalist connection to the system's identity and justification discourses, stressing the "particularities" of the Chinese model of development and rejecting all demands for an emulation of Western-style democratic values.

Beyond the reference to Confucianism as a source of moral philosophy and "Chinese" identity, the essays by Jiang Qing (*1953), published under the title of Political Confucianism (*zhengzhi Ruxue*), present a concrete blueprint for a "Confucian" institutional order and state bureaucracy. Together with Fang Keli, Jiang counts as one of the PRC's main protagonists of New Confucianism.

Jiang Qing suggests an institutional setting – as an alternative to the basic patterns of Marxist-Leninist state administration borrowed from the Soviet Union – that is based on three "houses". He does not present this tripartite system as an import of the Western threefold separation into legislative, executive and judicative powers, but claims to reactivate elements of Chinese state philosophy. Jiang, however, quotes the famous five *yuan* (chamber/house) model put forward by Sun Yat-sen, who suggested adding two "Chinese" institutions to the triad of legislative, executive, judicative powers – namely the examination *yuan* and a control *yuan*. This separation into five constitutive institutions inspired the Republic of China and is still upheld in Taiwan to this day. Jiang Qing, by contrast, constructs a house of educated Confucian scholars (*tongruyuan*), a house of the people (*shuminyuan*) and a house of the Chinese nation (*guotiyuan*). The head of the Confucian house should be a distinct Confucian scholar, and is to be appointed by their peers. His period in office would be about 15–20 years (until the fifth amendment of the Chinese state constitution in 2018, the PRC's highest officials were only allowed to serve for two consecutive legislative periods – a maximum of ten years!). Whilst the training and recruitment of the members of the Confucian house should be organised by the Confucian Academy, the representatives of the people should be selected and appointed according to principles also used by parliaments in Western democracies. The house of the Chinese nation, finally, should be headed by one direct heir of Confucius (Jiang 2013: 41). Jiang Qing's model is far beyond the concessions voiced by the Chinese party-state authorities regarding institutional reforms and restructuring of the state administration. Nevertheless, it is representative of a novel stream of reactivated Confucianism – one that is far more than just an abstract philosophical debate bearing certain religious, spiritual features.

The core leaders of the Chinese party-state present their new policies and political agendas by borrowing frameworks and symbols from the debates prevailing amongst China's epistemic communities and within domestic society. Some of these frameworks are not directly taken from the Confucian classics, but are rather neologisms disguised as Confucian-style governance patterns such as the fourth generation's Harmonious Society and Harmonious World.

In addition, Xi Jinping undertook several media-covered visits to the historical sites of Confucianism – including Qufu and its archives and research institutes on Confucian culture. In a speech delivered during his stay in Qufu, Xi Jinping stressed that the CCP had always been a defender of ancient Chinese traditions and would refuse all kinds of "historical nihilism". Likewise, when visiting Beijing Normal University in 2014, Xi Jinping reportedly stressed the importance of studying the Chinese classics and philosophical canon as these were the DNA of Chinese identity and Chinese culture (Sina 2014). This official rehabilitation of Confucian values culminated in Xi's speech commemorating the 2,565th anniversary of Confucius, delivered in the Great Hall of the People in Beijing (Xinhua 2014b), which symbolically highlights the meaning ascribed to Confucian values for the modern Chinese (nation-)state.

> **BOX III: Xi Jinping on the CCP as "Defender" of Traditional Chinese Values**
>
> "De-Sinicization is not something to celebrate. Classics should be embedded into students' minds, and become the 'genes' of Chinese culture [...]." (Xi 2014)
>
> "Members of the Communist Party of China are Marxists, who uphold the scientific theories of Marxism, and adhere to and develop socialism with Chinese characteristics. But Chinese communists are neither historical nihilists nor cultural nihilists. We always believe that the basic principles of Marxism must be closely married to the concrete reality of China, and that we should approach traditional native culture and cultures of all countries in a scientific manner, and arm ourselves with all outstanding cultural achievements humanity has created [...]." (Xi 2014)

Xi's kowtowing with respect to a highly politicised modern reading of Confucianism, or, more precisely, a fusion of pre-modern state philosophy with select retrospective reimaginations of Marxist thought, does not, however, represent a U-turn in Chinese politics under the fifth generation of China's political leaders. In 2011, the Hu-Wen administration, China's fourth leadership generation, had presented a declaration on socialist core values at the Sixth Plenum of the 17th Central Committee, merging Mao–Marxist concepts with pre-modern Chinese state philosophy.[9]

2.2. MarXism in the 21st Century

The CCP tries to avoid any formal deviation from its official ideological canon and operates with a constructed narrative of uninterrupted, path-dependent development. Every leadership generation usually adds its own slogans to the CCP's official ideological canon but does not relinquish any of the former elements. Novel ideas and frameworks are presented as updates on previous, inherited ideological elements.

Mao and Marxism are at the top echelons of the party-state's ideology. Whilst the CCP first copied Marxism-Leninism and modelled the Chinese party-state as

---

9 The declaration is available online at: http://www.gov.cn/jrzg/2011-10/25/content_1978202.htm.

a carbon copy of the Soviet Union, Mao Zedong instead undertook a reinterpretation and modification of Marxist ideas – adapting them to the socio-economic conditions of the early PRC. Whilst the Soviet version focused on the working class and proletarian masses, China – according to Mao a "semi-colonial, semi-feudal" system – had to rely contrariwise on its peasants, as the level of modern industrialisation was still comparatively low. Furthermore, instead of pursuing gradual collectivisation, Mao favoured a "Great Leap" approach, starting with the high-speed collectivisation of the rural economy. Mao's Sinification of Marxism, canonised as Mao Zedong Thought, hence marks a clear distancing from the doctrines of the Soviet Union.

The fourth generation under Hu Jintao claimed that the PRC was the only socialist country not only using Marxist ideas as guidance for political practice, but also contributing to the permanent conceptual embellishment of core Marxist ideas based on China's own "socialist" experience. Major research projects conducted in China are dedicated to the contemporary theorisation of Marxist ideas, developing a (Sinicized) global Marxist theory for the 21st century. They do not refer to the Russian (Soviet) translations of the collected works of Marx and Engels, but to a modern Chinese translation of the original German text version.

The CCP's Party Constitution confirms its adherence to Marxism-Leninism, Mao Zedong Thought, Deng Xiaoping Theory, the Three Representations (ascribed to Jiang Zemin), the Scientific Outlook on Development (associated with Hu Jintao) and, since 2017, Xi Jinping Thought on "Socialism with Chinese Characteristics for the New Era". This list includes a clear ranking of the contributions made by the various leadership generations: the starting point is the "isms" (zhuyi), Marxism and Leninism, whilst China's major contributions to Marxist theory innovation are classified as "ideas/thought" (sixiang). The add-ons associated with the second, third and fourth generation thus do not carry the same power as the renewal of Chinese socialism by Xi Jinping, whose concepts are ranked on a par with Mao's original Sinification of Marxism(-Leninism). Mao Zedong and Xi Jinping are the only ones directly mentioned as creators of core Chinese Marxist ideas; the other ideological concepts are listed without any official mention of the respective founders.

Nonetheless, Xi Jinping's ideas are officially linked to Deng Xiaoping's formula of Socialism with Chinese Characteristics and indirectly continue the division of China's development path into stages by stressing the entrance into a "new era" – thus following the general pattern of drafting a linear, continued evolution of Chinese Marxism. In addition, Xi Jinping not only follows the concepts formulated by his predecessors but is also directly turning back to core theory reflections put forward by Mao on different types of contradiction and the correct way to solve them. Whilst Mao, following the paradigm of class struggle, saw the main contradiction as being between the proletariat and the bourgeoisie, Xi Jinping, in his report to the 19th Party Congress (October 2017), identified the new main contradiction being between current unequal development and people's demand for a better life (Xi 2017). The CCP's efforts to secure sustainable development and to establish a modern responsive and efficient state administration are thus presented in line with the identified "main contradictions" that the PRC is facing in the 21st century.

Xi has also reactivated the Maoist "mass line". In 2013, he officially announced a Mass Line Campaign, limited to one year, to overcome the alienation and rising gap between the Chinese people and (local) party cadres. The original Maoist mass line consisted of the idea of listening to the masses and formulating policies that are played back to them. This is designed as a never-ending, indirect feedback loop – one that should prevent the doctrinal ossification of Chinese politics. Critics of the Maoist period state that the mass line was instead used as a transmission belt serving top-down control and did not empower the Chinese (peasant) masses at all. Whilst Xi Jinping's 2013 campaign borrows the Maoist term, the content of the campaign instead targets corruption and mismanagement. The focus lies on combatting the "four winds" of formalism, bureaucracy, hedonism and extravagance (Xinhua 2013). The mass line campaign entered a second round in 2014, being further expanded at the grass-roots level (Xinhua 2014a).

Xi's mass-line formula "from the masses to the masses" is taken from Mao's essay "On Practice" (1937). Therein, Mao explains the necessity of a dynamic linking between theory and practice to avoid a stalemate of the socialist state-building process. Additional frameworks of Xi's campaign originate from Mao's text "On the Correct Handling of Contradictions Among the People", in which Mao (1957) differentiates between antagonist and non-antagonist contradictions.

When applying these frameworks to the evaluation of China's domestic constellations and/or those of world politics, the idea is to identify the primary and secondary contradictions of the given stage of development – and to coin corresponding, context-sensitive political answers. As the primary contradiction can turn into a secondary one, or vice versa, modifications of Chinese policy principles are not only legitimate but also inevitable. This also implies that policies and steering instruments, such as the One-Child Policy or the *hukou* system introduced under Mao, have to be partially replaced to fit the needs of China's development in the 21st century.

China is not, however, turning back to the original concepts and instruments of the Mao era. Wen Jiabao's reform statements left no doubt that a renewal of the Cultural Revolution would be categorically rejected. In this vein, the 21st century governance reforms do not operate on the basis of the concept of (permanent) class struggle. Given the aggravating socio-economic stratification of Chinese society, the CCP is instead trying to find a serene way to balance rising tensions and to prevent the sparking of a new revolution fuelled by expanding protests and contestation movements from China's less-privileged, lower-income classes. In 2014 an article authored by Wang Weiguang, the President of the Chinese Academy of Social Sciences in Beijing, thus caused severe concerns amongst the party elite: one of the leading CCP journals usually known for its close ties to the regime, *Red Flag (Hongqi)*, proclaimed the persistence and continuation of class struggle in China. This was immediately refuted by articles published in other high-ranking party journals and newspapers, denouncing Maoist class struggle as a radicalisation and expression of leftist extremism during the times of the Cultural Revolution (*South China Morning Post* 2014). Wang Weiguang also pleaded for an elimination of Western ideas, especially "constitutional democracy" and "universal (Western) values". Additionally, quoting Mao's typology of contradictions, he asked for a new dictatorship cracking down on the "enemies of the people".

In addition to the 2013/2014 mass line initiative, Xi Jinping inaugurated a campaign against Western values – reaching out in the process to Chinese academia and the country's universities. An internally circulated paper, Document No. 9, mentioned seven sensitive (and hence "banned") issues regarded as destabilising China's political system: Western constitutional democracy, universal values, civil society (as opposed to the state), neo-liberalism, free media and freedom of speech, historical nihilism (meaning the negation of the positive effects of reform and opening), and the Chinese version of socialism.[10]

Document No. 9 clearly continues the path originally taken by the fourth generation of Chinese leaders. In late 2008, the government intervened against the circulation of the Charter 08, drafted by Liu Xiaobo and a group of liberal scholars asking for a major restructuring of the Chinese party-state. The Charter 08 sought to use the historical legacy of the Czech Charter 77, clearly hoping to secure international backing for it. The initiator of China's Charter 08, however, was imprisoned (and, finally, passed away) whilst his wife was put under house arrest until finally being allowed to leave the country in 2018, for Germany.

As these two episodes – Document No. 9 and Charter 08 – illustrate, terminology and framing play a crucial role in Chinese politics. The Chinese party-state has launched nationwide reforms and has modified China's general development and growth strategy. Hence it is not the general identification of reform needs, but the way that this criticism is articulated which decides subsequent official backing or persecution. Current authorised reform debates even go as far as to discuss the possibility of transforming Chinese socialism into a new variety of social(ist) democracy. Xie Tao outlined these ideas in his widely quoted essay "The Model of Democratic Socialism and the Future of China" (Ma 2015: 102).

The party elites' reference to Maoist slogans and the returning glorification of Mao are, however, a double-edged sword and could easily trigger unexpected, uncontrollable dynamics. Mao is officially judged as 70 % good, 30 % evil – as the responsibility for the violent excesses of the Cultural Revolution has been ascribed to the infamous Gang of Four grouped around Mao's wife Jiang Qing. Nevertheless, the crimes and atrocities of the Cultural Revolution have not yet been forgotten but persist as unspoken traumatic memories, haunting the minds of those who were involved.

The erection of a gigantic golden Mao statue in Henan Province (January 2016) consequently attracted much attention both in China and abroad, given that this province had been severely afflicted by the Maoist mass campaigns, the Great

---

10   For a translation hereof, see: https://www.chinafile.com/document-9-chinafile-translation.

Leap Forward and the resultant Great Famine. Almost immediately after related pictures and comments had gone viral on the Chinese Internet, the statue was demolished without any official explanation. This silent process of erection and removal reminds one of an earlier episode: the instalment of a Confucius statue in Tian'anmen Square in the heart of Beijing in January 2011. In both cases it is most likely that there had been an informal agreement between influential factions or patron–client networks, which was later revoked given people's critical and emotionally charged reactions.

It is clearly evident that the CCP claims a monopoly over the "correct" interpretation of the ideational/ideological foundations of the Chinese party-state. The controversy between two Chinese blueprints of modernisation and political-economic development – the Chongqing Model favoured by the New Left versus the Guangdong Model promoted by China's neo-liberal camp – in the run up to the changing of the guard in autumn 2012 ended with the imprisonment of Bo Xilai (party secretary of Chongqing) and a crackdown on the new left online fora (Freeman/Yuan 2011). Whilst new left ideas have found their way into the fifth generation's reform agenda, the CCP opposes any ideological radicalisation – such as the singing of Maoist red songs and the reactivation of Mao-style mass mobilisation – by local units of administration.

In order to stress that the CCP's support for market-economy elements and capitalist competition does not stand in opposition to the PRC's socialist system identity, the CCP officially proclaimed the Four Cardinal Principles when initiating the reform and opening strategy. These principles – to maintain the socialist path, democratic dictatorship, leadership by the CCP and to uphold Marxism-Leninism and Mao Zedong Thought – have also been reconfirmed by the fifth generation headed by Xi Jinping.

In 2018, during the preparations for the 200th anniversary of Karl Marx's birth, Xi Jinping asked all CCP cadres to study the *Communist Manifesto*. The worship of Confucius, in connection with moral ethics and China's cultural identity, is thus complemented by the iconographic appraisal of Marx. When delivering the official anniversary speech at the Great Hall of the People on 4 May 2018, Xi Jinping underlined that the adoption of Marxism as the guiding ideological framework – as well as its Sinification and adaption – had been "completely right" (Xinhua 2018). Xi's speech did not reflect the tensions and contradictions between Mao's critique of capitalism and the current Chinese stage of state-led hyper-capitalism. The celebrations of Karl Marx and his writings were accompanied by television documentaries depicting his life and main ideas. An internationally disputed act, however, was the donation of a Marx statue, crafted by a Chinese artist, to the city of Trier in Germany. Trier is on the main travel route of China's "red" tourism, guiding Chinese travellers to the centres of (Western) Marxism.

The CCP has clearly fine-tuned the ideology-based dimensions of its legitimation strategy. It responded to the aforementioned visible religious renaissance and return of ancient Chinese ideas within Chinese society by coining a new narrative, one presenting the CCP as both advocate and defender of "Chinese" culture. In addition, to prevent internal sceptics from using Marxism to criticise the PRC's current socio-economic conditions and Manchester-style capitalism, the fifth generation developed an official reinterpretation of Marxism and Maoism, presented as Xi Jinping Thought. Whilst certain streams of Western values are, once again, banned, on the operational level the system integrates select elements of Western administration skills into its revised governance strategy.

To preserve the system's unity, all these modifications are presented as a continuation of inherited principles. This is done by:

(1) ascribing new content to an "old" framework (e.g., the partial reconfiguration of the mass line under Xi Jinping);

(2) deactivating select sub-streams of the ideological canon (rejection of the Cultural Revolution and class struggle; reconfirmation of Mao Zedong Thought);

(3) introducing novel terms and frameworks that are claimed to be taken from China's ancient state philosophy (although these are actually neologisms).

The PRC's oscillation between periods of openness and internationalisation versus years of isolation – between learning from abroad and the elites' focusing on particularly "Chinese" ideas and political philosophy, between radical iconoclasm and the self-confident reactivation of "Chinese" culture and traditions – implies that the ratio of ingredients in China's official state philosophy (Marxism/Maoism; imported Western ideas; pre-modern Chinese state philosophy) is dynamically changing.

With the Four Comprehensives (*si ge quanmian*) – (1) comprehensively building a moderately prosperous society; (2) comprehensively deepening reform; (3) comprehensively governing the nation according to law; (4) comprehensively but strictly governing the Party – alongside the formula of the Chinese Dream, Xi Jinping has presented a new equation of existing party ideologemes enhanced by his own slogans and flagship concepts.

2.3. "Chinese Dream" and "American Dream": Competing Visions of Ideal Modes of Political Rule and Social Order?

The formalisation of the official political discourse in the PRC, the circumspect coining of key terms and the reference to select streams and elements of pre-modern Chinese state philosophy imply that the reading of official speeches and statements becomes a decryption process – one necessitating etymological knowledge of core ideas of state philosophy and their evolution over time.

Due to the perceived gaps or even contradictions between the PRC's official positions, as documented in political declarations and visible political actions, the speeches and positioning papers of the Chinese party-state are often classified as empty slogans or "propaganda" that exclusively serve to justify Chinese politics. Another function associated with the PRC's official slogans is the devaluation of neo-realist threat perceptions, as well as the rejection of demands voiced by the international community regarding the future transformation of the Chinese party-state or the PRC's role in global affairs. When coining foreign policy terms, the PRC's political elites (and their advisers) carefully observe what the perceptions and interpretations of its concepts by the outside world are – as the history of the formula Peaceful Rise (*heping jueqi*) clearly evidences. Identifying the outside world's distrust and unease with this slogan, the term was eventually silently substituted with Peaceful Development (*heping fazhan*) instead.

Both of these terms counter negative (threat) scenarios developed to assess the potential implications of China's ascent to global power, doing so by providing a positive scenario of win-win and common, inclusive global development. China's official political slogans and concepts should, however, not be taken as concrete guidance for political action and determinants of China's actual global positioning. Chinese politics follow an incremental, experimental approach – pragmatically responding to changes and emerging challenges in domestic, regional and global contexts. The narratives clustered around a specific policy field ascribe meaning to visible (fragmentary) political actions, seeking to embed single events into a linear storyline of a path-dependent, uninterrupted modernisation process under the guidance of the CCP. The frameworks and narratives coined are presented as being derived from Chinese political culture and traditions, hence creating a unified, collective identity and joint reference system.

The growing diversity in and socio-economic fragmentation of Chinese society means that the concepts and slogans formulated by the political elites must be abstract and vague enough to integrate the specific policy preferences of the different societal actor groups. Rather than providing one unified top-down definition of key terms, the ruling elites operate with frames that can be interpreted in a variety of ways – thus allowing different actors to project their specific notions on ideal political rule and institutional order onto them.

The fourth generation (Hu Jintao/Wen Jiabao) discovered sustainability and social justice as necessary cornerstones of the PRC's refined development and modernisation strategy. The two novel concepts associated with Hu Jintao's leadership – the Scientific View on Development (*kexue fazhan guan*) and the formula of the Harmonious Society – were later complemented by the Harmonious World so as to encompass global affairs. Shortly after being appointed as new General Secretary of the CCP, Xi Jinping reportedly put forward the notion of the Chinese Dream (*Zhongguo meng*), mentioned above. Following the official chronology of the concept's genesis, Xi Jinping elaborated on the idea of a Chinese Dream when visiting the "The Road to Revival" exhibition hosted by the National Museum in Beijing in November 2012. The idea of restoring the Golden Age and utopian pre-modern harmonious order, as described in the Confucian Classic of Rites (*Liji*), has inspired all previous generations of Chinese leaders, in dynastic times as well as under Mao; all of them quote the Confucian passages on harmony and "great unity" (*datong*). Xi Jinping's notion of a Chinese Dream seems to have contributed to these never-ending commemorations of a paradise lost but has also become significantly more concretised as it defines a roadmap and clear-cut timeline for implementation. According to Xi Jinping's Two One-Hundred (*liang'ge yi bai nian*), by 2021 – which marks the 100th anniversary of the CCP's founding – the installation of a "well-off society" (*xiaokang shehui*) should have been completed. And by the year 2049, when the PRC will celebrate its centennial birthday, China should have reached the status of a global great power. China should then be a modern socialist, economically prosperous state with a powerful army and significant global influence. However, being a socialist state, the PRC will pursue its own vision of "democracy"– leading to harmony and stability at the domestic system level (Xi 2014 [2012]: 37–39).

All of these reflections are embedded in the narrative of national rejuvenation and restoration of the old centre position that the Chinese Empire had once held before being defeated by the colonial powers in the Opium Wars. Whilst Xi Jinping's first public mentioning of the Chinese Dream had targeted specific party cadres, his speech at the annual session of the National People's Congress in March 2013 delegated the implementation of the Chinese Dream to state organs and institutions. Xi Jinping stressed that the Chinese Dream would represent a continuation of the cardinal idea of "Socialism with Chinese characteristics" and stand for a particular "Chinese" development path paying attention to the country's specific development needs. Xi also highlighted the meaning of national unity and territorial integrity (Xi 2014 [2013]: 40–46). At the 19th Party Congress (2017), Xi further called for a pragmatic adaptation and reinterpretation of socialism based on China's historical development. He also set the years 2020, 2035 and 2050 as end points/starting points for core stages of modernisation in the PRC's socialist development path.

One defining characteristic of Xi Jinping's speeches on the Chinese Dream is the commemoration of pre-modern state philosophy and the historical records of the rise and fall of the various Chinese dynasties. An oft-quoted formula is the statement that "empty" speech without any actual action being taken leads to the downfall and ruin of empires. This insight has been paraphrased in connection with the issue of rampant corruption, which might – in the terminology used by the CCP itself – cause "the decay of the state and the decline of the party" (*wang dang, wang guo*). This serves to illustrate the inherent function of political terminology and symbolism: the fifth generation seeks to establish a governance model that claims to continue basic patterns of "Chinese" benevolent rule in line with core Confucian values and, at the same time, determined by socialist ideas. This, however, is the rhetoric-justificatory level of Chinese politics, and should not be confused with concrete political actions.

As the Chinese party-state is a learning system responding to changes and shifts in its external environment, it is caught in a mode of permanent restructuring and readjustment. Major corrections and changes in China's official development path – such as the proclaimed entrance into the era of "new normal" in 2014, dedicated to sustainable green growth and social development – imply changes to previously existing power structures. China's (business) elites, especially those who had so far profited from the flourishing of unconditional Manchester-style capitalism, will have to give up some of their former privileges. In this vein, the coining of the Chinese Dream notion is an attempt to win diffuse support from various (competing) actor groups, but ones united by ideas of culturalism and patriotism. Xi Jinping's formula of the Chinese Dream also draws a red line that no one will be allowed to cross: the Chinese Dream remains a "socialist" concept managed and coordinated only by the CCP's core leaders.

Whilst the fourth generation created terminology wrapped in pre-modern Chinese state philosophy, the fifth generation's Chinese Dream seems to directly counter the American Dream – the primary allegory of Western liberalism and pluralist democracy. This appears to be a Chinese reply to the assumed black-and-white antagonism between the Washington Consensus and the Beijing Consensus – the latter being a classification of China's unconditional investment and cooperation with other nation-states, including so-called rogue and failed ones, as put forward by a think tank based in London. The underlying view, as expressed by this constructed inevitable antagonism, was that China would practise and export a governance model incompatible with Western norms and values. Likewise, some observers of China introduced the notion, mentioned previously, of a Chinese Model – also complemented by the typology of a "Chinese Variety of Capitalism", relating to the PRC's hybrid economy – so as to highlight the particularities of China's governance approach as a model sui generis. The Chinese Dream, if read as a "Chinese" invention and reaction to debates on the country articulated from outside perspectives, stresses the procedural, dynamic dimension of Chinese governance – as opposed to the idea of an integrated, stable single "model". Furthermore, it expresses the demand voiced by China's fifth generation to be accepted as a global player on a par with the US – practising its own governance approach that is, if evaluated according to "Chinese" norms and values, a legitimate one.

Whether or not the *Zhongguo Meng* can be read as the counter model to the American Dream remains, however, highly contested, even amongst Chinese political scientists. Some parts seem to overlap, whilst a few conceptual differences are more than evident: the *Zhongguo Meng* seeks to convince all actors to contribute to the collective goal of China's rejuvenation and rise to global power status. The American Dream, meanwhile, allows everyone to pursue their own "rise" and therein stresses individual freedom. "Liberty" and the "pursuit of happiness" are eternally guaranteed in the US Constitution. The Chinese Constitution, being a socialist one, fixes stages of development leading to the realisation of Chinese "Socialism". However, the PRC's strategies of development and modernisation are based on the in-depth observation and theory-guided analysis of the determinants facilitating the rise (or causing the decline) of previous great powers, starting with the Roman Empire. As one lesson to be learnt from these retrospective interpretations, the PRC focuses on balancing competing interests and seeks to pursue a sustainable rise instead of a short-lived power peak with a sharp decline immediately afterwards. One prerequisite for becoming a global empire, as identified in studies by Chinese historians and political scientists, is the capacity of a state (and its national economy) to develop innovative technologies. The PRC's "Made in China 2025"[11] initiative prioritises innovation over the imitation

---

11 "Made in China 2025" is available online (in Chinese) at: http://www.gov.cn/zhengce/content/2015-05/19
   /content_9784.htm.

of "Western" technologies and seeks to position China as a new leader in the fields of green technologies.

The distancing from other systems and the coining of a Chinese "socialist" exceptionalism is not a novel phenomenon of 21st-century Chinese politics. The external world is constructed as a counter model, one opposed to "Chinese" ideals of political rule and world order. The early PRC opposed Soviet socialism by setting up Mao Zedong Thought as a unique "Chinese" reference scheme. With the Great Leap Forward, the PRC sought to surpass Great Britain in terms of coal and steel production and to catapult itself to the level of the world's leading industrialised economies. Its 21st-century sparring partner to "surpass" is the US, as evidenced by the claim formulated under Xi Jinping to be treated as an equal partner and to establish a "new type of relations between great powers" (*xin xing daguo guanxi*) with Washington. Under Xi Jinping, the PRC has thus started to redefine its own position and to re-evaluate the power distribution at the level of world politics. Whilst the long-term demand put forward by the PRC is to strive for a multi-polar world order, it has so far classified the structures emerging after the end of the Cold War and the dissolution of the Soviet Union as those of "one superpower, many great powers". Since 2007/2008 more and more Chinese scholars have referenced this formula as "many great powers, one superpower", thus stressing the vulnerability and weakness of US-style capitalism and the increasing clout of the rising powers (headed by the PRC, which has become the world's second-largest economy).

Whilst the PRC officially rejects any Western-style democratisation of its domestic system structures, it refers to the US definition of pluralist, liberal democracy in order to demand a "democratisation of international relations" – thus fighting the West with its own normative "weapons". Beijing positions itself as an advocate of the Global South and the rising economies to demand more voting rights and access to participation in the reform of the post-World War II international institutional order.

2.4. Summary

"Ideas matter"[12] – ideas do indeed play an important role in the formulation and implementation of domestic and international politics. Nonetheless, the analysis of Chinese politics is often reduced to the visible dimensions of concrete actions, whilst political statements and concepts are devaluated as mere ideology and propaganda. A closer look at the ideational reference scheme of Chinese elite politics allows one to gain insight into the hidden dynamics of the PRC's ongoing reforms as well as its permanent gradual learning processes. On the one hand, political elites and their advisers are searching for policy solutions to cope with the negative socio-ecological side effects of high-speed, resource-intense economic growth. The 2013 reform package reflects the best practices found in other political systems. There are, however, ongoing factional struggles within the CCP as well as controversies between the party(-state) and the various influential

---

12 On the causal interplay between ideas and policymaking, see Goldstein/Keohane (eds.) (1993).

socio-economic actor groups over what the "best" mode of governance might look like.

To justify the refined Chinese governance model, the fifth generation with Xi Jinping nominated as its "core leader" has had to redefine the PRC's ideational reference systems to present the new development roadmap as standing in line with the main principles of Chinese-inherited socialism and Sino-Marxism. Furthermore, the political elites have reinforced symbolic levels of legitimacy and legitimation by referring to Confucianism as the basic fundament of a "Chinese" political identity.

In this vein, to decipher the multiple visible and hidden dimensions of Chinese politics one must differentiate between an operational level guided by the principle of pragmatism and an ideational-rhetorical level fulfilling a justificatory function and contributing to the creation of a "Chinese" identity. The decryption of the PRC's official political slogans requires in-depth knowledge of Chinese history and philosophy: under the fifth generation, most political concepts and frames are not presented as novel ideas but as path-dependent development and a reactivation of ancient Chinese thought. A closer look at the operational level reveals that the content associated with the new policies is based on a thoughtful combination of best practices of local policy experimentation and learning through observation of the success and failures of others – including democratic-liberal political systems.

In sum, however, these policy solutions are sold as a "distinct" Chinese governance approach, even though they might contain certain recycled Western ideas. Xi Jinping has launched a campaign against Western values and officially seeks to base the Chinese governance model on "Chinese" culture and traditions – including the chimera of Sino-Marxism (it is worthwhile to note that, despite the ongoing campaign and censorship of Western values, the collected works of Marx and Engels have not been banned).

As a learning autocracy, the PRC responds to the multiple ideas put forward by its various socio-economic interest groups and epistemic communities. The visible contradictions in China's bundle of reform policies are, then, the outcome of the efforts to find a new balance between the contradictory demands and expectations voiced by this new plurality of domestic actors.

Questions for Discussion

- Are the PRC's political norms and values based on a single state philosophy? What are its main ideas and components? Is this ideational reference scheme a monolithic, stable one? Under what conditions does it change?
- What are the main instruments and strategies used by the Chinese government to maintain the system's unity and to re-stabilise the one-party regime?
- How is good governance defined in the Chinese case? Is there only one unified definition?
- What role do pre-modern philosophy and cultural traditions play in the coining of the PRC's official "socialist" development model?
- What are the main differences between the American Dream and the *Zhongguo Meng*, the Chinese Dream, as introduced by Xi Jinping?

References

Anderson, Benedict (1983), *Imagined Communities: Reflections on the Origin and Spread of Nationalism.* London: Verso.

Beetham, David (1991), *The Legitimation of Power.* New York: Palgrave Macmillan.

Beetham, David (2001), "Political Legitimacy", in: Nash, Kate / Scott, Alan (eds.) (2001), *The Blackwell Companion to Political Sociology*, 107–116.

Chaffee, John W. (1985), *The Thorny Gates of Learning in Sung China: A Social History of Examinations.* Cambridge: Cambridge UP.

Chang, Hao (1980), "Intellectual Change and the Reform Movement, 1890–8", in: Fairbank, John K./Liu, Kwang-Ching (eds.) (1980), *The Cambridge History of China* (Vol. 11, Part 2). Cambridge: Cambridge University Press, 274–338.

Chen, Feng (1997), "The Dilemma of Eudaemonic Legitimacy in Post-Mao China", *Polity*, 29:3, 421–439.

Easton, David (1965), *A Systems Analysis of Political Life.* New York: Wiley.

Elman, Benjamin A. (2013), *Civil Examinations and Meritocracy in Late Imperial China.* Cambridge: Harvard UP.

Freeman, Charles W./Yuan, Wen Jing (2011), *China's New Leftist and the China Model Debate after the Financial Crisis.* Washington: CSIS.

Goldstein, Judith/Keohane, Robert (eds.) (1993), *Ideas and Foreign Policy: Beliefs, Institutions, and Political Change.* Ithaca: Cornell UP.

Guo, Baogang (2003), "Political Legitimacy and China's Transition", *Journal of Chinese Political Science*, 1–2 (Fall 2003), 1–25.

Hucker, Charles O. (1985), *A Dictionary of Official Titles in Imperial China.* Stanford: Stanford UP.

Jiang, Qing (2013), "The Way of the Humane Authority: A Theoretical Basis for Confucian Constitutionalism and a Tricameral Parliament", in: Bell, Daniel/Fan, Ruiping (ed.) (2013), *A Confucian Constitutional Order.* Princeton: Princeton UP, 27–43.

Lipset, Seymour Martin (1960), *Political Man: The Social Bases of Politics.* Garden City, NY: Double Day.

Ma, Licheng (2015), *Leading Schools of Thought in Contemporary China.* Singapore: World Scientific.

Mao, Zedong (1937), "On Practice", https://www.marxists.org/reference/archive/mao/selected-works/volume-1/mswv1_16.htm.

Mao, Zedong (1957), "On the Correct Handling of Contradictions Among the People", https://www.marxists.org/reference/archive/mao/selected-works/volume-5/mswv5_58.htm.

Noesselt, Nele (2012), *Governance-Formen in China: Theorie und Praxis des chinesischen Modells (Governance Modes in China: Theory and Practice of the Chinese Model)*. Wiesbaden: Springer VS.

Sina (2014), "Xi Marks Confucius Anniversary", 24 September 2014, http://english.sina.co m/china/2014/0924/739843.html.

South China Morning Post (2014), "Abandoning 'Class Struggle' Central to China's Achievements, Paper Says in Rebuke to Leftists", 29 September 2014, http://www.sc mp.com/news/china/article/1603924/abandoning-class-struggle-central-chinas-achieve me nts-paper-says-rebuke.

South China Morning Post (2018), "A New Class Struggle: Chinese Party Members Get Back to Communist Manifesto Basics", 29 April 2014, http://www.scmp.com/news/chin a/policies-politics/article/2143841/new-class-struggle-chinese-party-members-get-back.

Thompson, Laurence G. (transl.) (1958), *Ta T'ung Shu: The One-world Philosophy of K'ang Yu-Wei*. London: Allen & Unwin.

Tong, Yanqi (2011), "Morality, Benevolence and Responsibility: Regime Legitimacy in China from Past to the Present", *Journal of Chinese Political Science*, 16, 141–159.

Twitchett, Denis (1976), *The Birth of the Chinese Meritocracy: Bureaucrats and Examinations in T'ang China*. London: China Society.

Wang, Rui (2013), *The Chinese Imperial Examination System: An Annotated Bibliography*. Lanham: Scarecrow Press.

Xi, Jinping (2012), "Achieving Rejuvenation is the Dream of the Chinese People", in: Xi, Jinping (2014), *The Governance of China*. Beijing: Foreign Languages Press, 37–39.

Xi, Jinping (2013), "Address to the First Session of the 12th National People's Congress", in: Xi, Jinping (2014), *The Governance of China*. Beijing: Foreign Languages Press, 40–46.

Xi, Jinping (2017), "Secure a Decisive Victory in Building a Moderately Prosperous Society in All Respects and Strive for the Great Success of Socialism with Chinese Characteristics for a New Era",http://www.xinhuanet.com/english/download/Xi_Jinping's_report_a t_19th_CPC_National_Congress.pdf.

Xiao, Gongjuan (1975), *A Modern China and a New World: K'ang Yu-Wei, Reformer and Utopian, 1858–1927*. Seattle: University of Washington Press.

Xinhua (2013), "Xi Demands Implementation of 'Mass Line' Campaign", 10 December 2013, http://en.people.cn/90785/8479207.html.

Xinhua (2014a), "CPC Rolls Out 'Mass Line' Rules", 23 January 2014 http://english.cntv.c n/20140123/105451.shtml.

Xinhua (2014b), "Xi Jinping: Zai jinian Kongzi danchen 2565 zhounian guoji xueshu yantaohui shang de jianghua" (Xi Jinping's Speech at the International Conference Celebrating the 2565th Anniversary of Confucius), 24 September 2014, http://news.xinh uanet.com/politics/2014-09/24/c_1112612018.htm.

Xinhua (2018), "Xi Jinping: Zai jinian Makesi danchen 200 zhounian dahui shang de jianghua" (Xi Jinping's Speech Commemorating the 200th Anniversary of Karl Marx), 4 May 2018, http://www.xinhuanet.com/politics/2018-05/04/c_1122783997.htm.

Zeng, Jinghan (2014), "The Debate on Regime Legitimacy in China: Bridging the Wide Gulf between Western and Chinese Scholarship", *Journal of Contemporary China*, 23:88, 612–635.

Recommended Reading

Hundred Days' Reform

Karl, Rebecca E./Zarrow, Peter (eds.) (2002), *Rethinking the 1898 Reform Period: Political and Cultural Change in Late Qing China*. Cambridge; London: Harvard UP.

May Fourth Movement

Dolezelova-Velingerova, Milena (ed.) (2001), *The Appropriation of Cultural Capital: China's May Fourth Project.* Cambridge: Harvard UP.
Schwarcz, Vera (1986), *The Chinese Enlightenment: Intellectuals and the Legacy of the May Fourth Movement of 1919.* Berkeley: University of California Press.
Wang, Q. Edward (2001), *Inventing China Through History: The May Fourth Approach to Historiography.* Albany, NY: State University of New York Press.
Zhou, Cezong (1967), *The May Fourth Movement: Intellectual Revolution in Modern China.* Stanford: Stanford UP.

Great Leap Forward

Chan, Alfred L. (2001), *Mao's Crusade: Politics and Policy Implementation in China's Great Leap Forward.* Oxford: Oxford UP.
Teiwes, Frederick C./Sun, Warren (1999), *China's Road to Disaster: Mao, Central Politicians, and Provincial Leaders in the Unfolding of the Great Leap Forward.* Armonk: M.E. Sharpe.
Thaxton, Ralph (2008), *Catastrophe and Contention in Rural China: Mao's Great Leap Forward Famine and the Origins of Righteous Resistance in Da Fo Village.* Cambridge: Cambridge UP.

Cultural Revolution

MacFarquhar, Roderick/Schoenhals, Michael (2006), *Mao's Last Revolution.* Cambridge: Belknap Press of Harvard UP.
Schoenhals, Michael (1997), *China's Cultural Revolution, 1966–1969: Not a Dinner Party.* Armonk: Sharpe.

Political Leaders

Mao Zedong

Karl, Rebecca E. (2010), *Mao Zedong and China in the Twentieth-century World.* Durham: Duke UP.
Meisner, Maurice J. (2007), *Mao Zedong: A Political and Intellectual Portrait.* Cambridge: Polity.
Schram, Stuart R. (1963), *The Political Thought of Mao Tse-tung.* New York: Praeger.
Spence, Jonathan (1999), *Mao Zedong.* New York: Viking.

Deng Xiaoping

Dillon, Michael (2015), *Deng Xiaoping: The Man Who Made Modern China.* London: Tauris.
Pantsov, Alexander V./Levine, Stephen (2015), *Deng Xiaoping: A Revolutionary Life.* Oxford; New York: Oxford UP.
Vogel, Ezra F. (2011), *Deng Xiaoping and the Transformation of China.* Cambridge: Harvard UP.

Jiang Zemin

Kuhn, Robert Lawrence (2004), *The Man Who Changed China: The Life and Legacy of Jiang Zemin.* New York: Crown.
Gilley, Bruce (1998), *Tiger on the Brink: Jiang Zemin and China's New Elite.* Berkeley: University of California Press.
Lam, Willy (1999), *The Era of Jiang Zemin.* Singapore: Prentice Hall.

Tien, Hungmao/Chu, Yun-han (ed.) (2000), *China under Jiang Zemin*. Boulder: Rienner.
Wang, Gungwu (ed.) (2003), *Damage Control: The Chinese Communist Party in the Jiang Zemin Era*. Singapore: Eastern UP.

Hu Jintao

Cheng, Tun-jen (ed.) (2006), *China under Hu Jintao*. New Jersey: World Scientific.
Lam, Willy (2006), *Chinese Politics in the Hu Jintao Era: New Leaders, New Challenges*. Armonk: Sharpe.

Xi Jinping

Economy, Elizabeth (2018), *The Third Revolution: Xi Jinping and the New Chinese State*. New York: Oxford UP.
Lam, Willy Wo-Lap (2015), *Chinese Politics in the Era of Xi Jinping: Renaissance, Reform or Retrogression?* New York; London: Routledge.
Li, Cheng (2016), *Chinese Politics in the Xi Jinping Era: Reassessing Collective Leadership*. Washington: Brookings Institution Press.
Shao, Binhong (ed.) (2015), *China under Xi Jinping: Its Economic Challenges and Foreign Policy Initiatives*. Leiden: Brill.
Zheng, Yongnian/Gore, Lance L. P. (eds.) (2015), *China Entering the Xi Jinping Era*. London; New York: Routledge.

Political Elites

Bo, Zhiyue (2010), *China's Elite Politics: Governance and Democratization*. Singapore u.a.: World Scientific.
Fewsmith, Joseph (2001), *Elite Politics in Contemporary China*. Armonk; New York: M.E.Sharpe.
Fewsmith, Joseph (2008), *China since Tiananmen: From Deng Xiaoping to Hu Jintao*. Cambridge: Cambridge UP.

Political Ideas/Ideology

Chang, Hao (1980), "Intellectual Change and the Reform Movement, 1890–8", in: Fairbank, John K./Liu, Kwang-Ching (eds.) (1980), *The Cambridge History of China* (Vol. 11, Part 2). Cambridge: Cambridge University Press, 274–338.
Furth, Charlotte (1980), "Intellectual Change: From the Reform Movement to the May Fourth Movement", 1895–1920, in: Fairbank, John K. (ed.) (1980), *The Cambridge History of China* (Vol. 12, Part 1). Cambridge: Cambridge UP, 322–405.
Misra, Kalpana (1998), *From Post-Maoism to Post-Marxism: The Erosion of Official Ideology in Deng's China*. New York; London: Routledge.

Legitimacy

Chen, Feng (1995), *Economic Transition and Political Legitimacy in Post-Mao China*. Albany; New York: State University of New York Press.
Guo, Baogang (2007), "Beyond Technocracy: China's Quest for Legitimacy in the Era of Hu Jintao", in: Hua, Shiping/Guo, Sujian (eds.) (2007), *China in the Twenty-first Century: Challenges and Opportunities*. New York: Palgrave MacMillan, 25–47.
Guo, Baogang (2010), *China's Quest for Political Legitimacy*. Lanham: Lexington Books.
Zhao, Suisheng (ed.) (2017), *Debating Regime Legitimacy in Contemporary China: Popular Protests and Regime Performances*. London; New York: Routledge.

3. Political Institutions and Operational Foundations of the Chinese Party-State

Key Content and Learning Goals

■ Overview of political institutions and organs of the Chinese party-state
■ One Country, Two Systems: introduction to the historical and constitutional foundations of the PRC's special administrative region Hong Kong and the multi-party landscape in Taiwan
■ Critical assessment of the complex interplay between formal and informal dimensions and mechanisms of Chinese politics
■ Overview of the evolving debate on the PRC's pragmatic (authoritarian) resilience

PRC politics include two levels: the institutional settings and the official roles and functions of state institutions, as outlined in the (state) constitution, stand for the formal level of Chinese politics. As the PRC is organised as a Leninist one-party state, the CCP and its party organs are closely connected to the state apparatus, resulting in a "mirror structure" of party organs and state institutions. The "real" power hierarchy within the bureaucratic state apparatus deviates from the formally prescribed structures and policy-making procedures. Party decisions precede reform decisions by state organs. This (often invisible) informal dimension of PRC politics is often far more relevant than the formal (legal and constitutional) frameworks.

This chapter starts with a short overview of the formal institutional foundations of the Chinese party-state and assesses the transformation of these structures over time, including efforts to modernise and professionalise the bureaucratic state apparatus via administrative reforms within the given regime structures.

3.1. Political Institutions

The basic patterns and principles of the PRC's political-administrative state organs are outlined in the 1982 (state) constitution. Since 1982, this post-Maoist reform constitution has undergone five major rounds of revisions and amendments. Given the predominant position of the party in PRC politics, the formal state organs have often been regarded as rather weak window-dressing institutions for the ex post transposing of party directives into national policy regulations (and, hence, for the ex post re-justification of party decisions). If this were the case, one could just ignore the (formal) state constitution and the (formal) domestic institutional order, and instead focus exclusively on the informal dimension of Chinese politics. However, a closer look at current political processes clearly evidences that the PRC's state-building efforts of the post-Maoist reform period did lead to the partial empowering of state organs and the strengthening of rule-based governance.

In times of major (administrative) reforms, the complex multifaceted network structure of the power matrix of the Chinese (party-)state becomes visible. This multidimensional network structure includes a horizontal dimension (state institutions and party organs at the same level of the state administration) and a vertical dimension (state institutions and party organs at the central, provincial, municipal and village level). To understand the dynamic transformation of the Chinese party-state, one must thus also reflect on the power competition between the central government and local level governments (and party organs). Furthermore, the 1978 decisions on reform and opening paved the way for local policy experimentation and the establishment of special economic zones, followed by special pilot zones for free trade in 2013. These special zones are governed by more liberal regulations; the nation-wide reproduction of these local incubator experimentations can be expected to augment liberalisation and decentralisation trends. Even though the core organs and institutions of the Chinese party-state have formally remained unchanged, the integration of market capitalist elements has triggered a pragmatic modification of the informal power matrix of central-local relations added by procedural readjustments that reflect the constellations at the local level of administration.

The Chinese system is characterised by an interlocking instead of a separation and division of power between legislative, executive and judicative branches. Nonetheless, in the course of the reform and opening process, and the professionalisation of the administrative system patterns, the party-state witnessed a partial decoupling of powers and legal formalisation. This development should, however, not be mistaken as a democratisation in the tradition of Western liberalism. All efforts undertaken to increase the efficiency of the administrative system generally serve the (re-)legitimation of the one-party system. As a side effect, the re-steering of the Chinese economy after 1978 caused a de-ideologisation and pragmatic reconfiguration of Chinese politics. As part of these restructuring processes, the Chinese government introduced reforms to increase the system's transparency and responsivity in order to combat corruption and inefficiency. The social stratification and fragmentation of Chinese society and the emergence of competing socio-economic actor groups cause a major steering dilemma. Totalitarian top-down steering has already been supplemented by indirect modes of deliberation and participation. The idea is to generate people's support via co-optation and consultation, including local deliberation (such as bargaining rounds on local budget spending), to respond to and to pre-empt people's demands.

This chapter introduces the reader to the formal organs and institutions of the Chinese party-state and explains their formal role and function in the PRC's political system. This system is composed of three interrelated pillars: the party, the state and the military. The organs and institutions of the party and of the state bureaucracy display an interwoven "mirror" structure of units with the same (or at least largely overlapping) functions and responsibilities. China's top politicians are wearing two hats at the same time, as they hold a position in one of the core organs of the CCP and, simultaneously, also hold a key position in central party organs, securing the control of the state apparatus by the CCP. Small party cells within state institutions, companies – as well as within the military – secure adherence to the party line. At the apex of this three-pillar structure – or, given the multidimensional interdependencies, three-sided pyramid – of the Chinese party-state resides the General Secretary of the CCP, at the same time serving as State President and head of the Central Military Commission.

Figure 2: Formal Organisational Structure of the Chinese Party-State at the Central Level

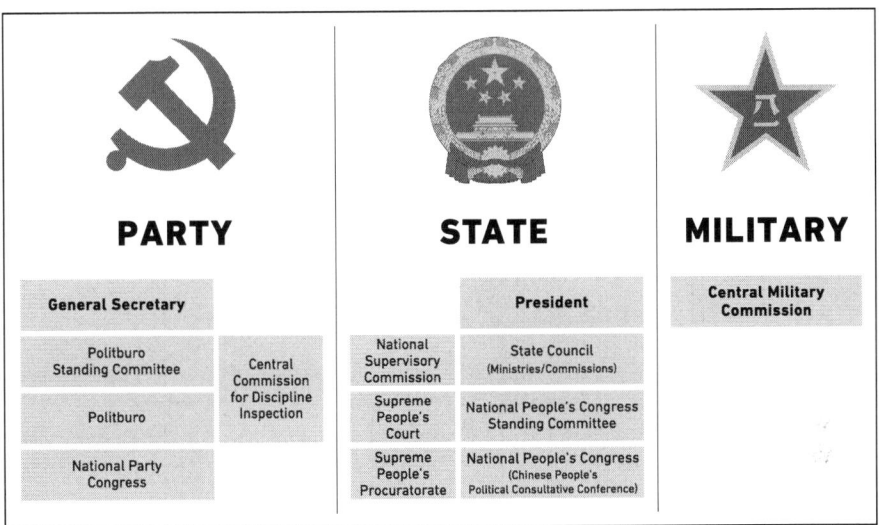

Graphic design: Harald Krähe (2020).

These mirror structures at the central level are reduplicated at all lower levels of the state administration. At the central level, the state apparatus is composed of the National People's Congress (NPC), the Chinese People's Political Consultative Conference (CPPCC), the Standing Committee of the National People's Congress, the State Council (and its ministries/commissions) and the State President. According to the Chinese (state) constitution, the organ with the largest number of (selected) representatives – the National People's Congress – should be the most powerful organ in China's political decision-making process. Informally, the final authority and control lies in the hands of the top party elites. Meetings of the party organs precede the meetings of the state institutions. The socio-economic development targets and development guidelines – summarised in the country's five-year plans upon which the Chinese economy is (still) formally based – are first debated at the plenary sessions of the CCP's Central Committee (in the late autumn months), before they are finally passed at the annual meeting of the National People's Congress scheduled for the following year (normally taking place in March).

Nonetheless, in the course of the modernisation and professionalisation processes of the Chinese bureaucracy, the NPC's room for manoeuvre and decision-making "autonomy" has increased. It is no longer unanimously rubber-stamping party decisions.

→ The "Two Sessions" (*liang hui*)

The Chinese parliament falls into the category of unicameral legislatures. Contrary to bi- or tricameral systems, unicameral legislatures are immune to intra-parliamentary deadlocks. Advocates of bicameralism, i.e., the division of the legislative system into two chambers, argue that the second chamber mainly exerts a representative and supervisory function. The inclusion of more groups of political representatives would generate trust and increase the political regime's legitimacy, thus ultimately stabilising the existing institutions. Informally, the PRC does have a second organ that is formally included in the Chinese state constitution and is ascribed a consultative, deliberative function: the Chinese People's Political Consultative Conference, which convenes annually parallel to the annual meeting of the NPC. The annual meeting in March is thus referred to in the Chinese debate as the "two sessions" (of the NPC and the CPPCC).[13] The focus, however, rests on the final reports and documents – including the annual budget planning – passed by the NPC.

→ Chinese People's Political Consultative Conference (CPPCC)[14]

The Political Consultative Conference is an advisory body of the Chinese state bureaucracy. The CPPCC's and the NPC's annual plenary meetings are held as "parallel" sessions. Apart from CCP cadres, members of the CPPCC include representatives of the formally legalised eight democratic Chinese parties, Chinese mass organisations, civil society organisations, representatives of the Chinese Special Administrative Regions (SARs) (Hong Kong, Macao) and "special" provinces (Taiwan, Tibet, Xinjiang), overseas Chinese (though a comparatively small share of the CPPCC), as well as foreign advisers. The CPPCC collects policy ideas as well as views and specific interests of its various member groups. These views and recommendations are then fed into the official political decision-making process. The CPPCC has no formal power to initiate laws or to launch policy reforms. The Political Consultative Conference thus does not fulfil the formal role of a second chamber or house. However, it serves as a platform for China's multi-party cooperation and, via deliberation, integrates the demands, expectations and recommendations of system-relevant actor groups.

The origins of the Political Consultative Conference date back to the year 1945/46, when it was established as a forum for negotiation and coordination between the GMD and the CCP during the times of the Second United Front. The PRC's Political Consultative Conference was formed in 1949, as an interim institution preceding the formal establishment of the PRC's state organs and state institutions. At the first meeting of the PRC's "new" Political Consultative Conference, in September 1949, a Joint Programme – the forerunner of the PRC's

---

13 As part of the Chinese government's efforts to establish an efficient and transparent state bureaucracy, reports, speeches, as well as background documents of the two sessions are archived online. Chinese version (2020): http://www.gov.cn/zhuanti/2020qglh/index.htm; English summary: http://en.people.cn/n3/2020/0525/c90000-9694258.html.

14 This part is based on the CPPCC's official webpage: http://www.cppcc.gov.cn. For the English version: http://en.cppcc.gov.cn.

(state) constitution – was passed. In 1954, the CPPCC decided that the Joint Programme should be substituted by the new constitution of the (Maoist) PRC, and, implicitly, transferred its own functions and responsibilities to the NPC.

The CPPCC consists of a central committee and local (regional) committees. One legislative term is five years (corresponding with the legislative term of the NPC delegates).

Table 1: CPPCC

Chairman of the CPPCC	Term of Office
Mao Zedong	1949–1954
Zhou Enlai	1954–1976
Deng Xiaoping	1978–1983
Deng Yingchao	1983–1988
Li Xiannian	1988–1992
Li Ruihuan	1993–2003
Jia Qinglin	2003–2013
Yu Zhengsheng	2013–2018
Wang Yang	2018–

The 1982 (state) constitution describes the role of the CPPCC as follows:

> "The Chinese People's Political Consultative Conference, a broadly based representative organization of the united front which has played a significant historical role, will play a still more important role in the country's political and social life, in promoting friendship with other countries and in the struggle for socialist modernization and for the reunification and unity of the country. The system of the multi-party cooperation and political consultation led by the Communist Party of China will exist and develop for a long time to come".[15]

The above statement is part of the constitution's preamble. Chapter III of the constitution, dealing with the "structure of the state" and the state organs, does not mention the CPPCC. The only legislative organ addressed is the NPC.

→ **The National People's Congress (NPC)**[16]

The National People's Congress, formally established as the PRC's national legislative body by the first Mao constitution in 1954, is the largest parliament

---

15   An English translation of the Chinese state constitution (including the 2018 revision) can be found online: https://npcobserver.files.wordpress.com/2018/12/PRC-Constitution-2018.pdf.
16   The following overview is based on the official webpage of the NPC (in Chinese): http://www.npc.gov.cn. For the English version: http://www.npc.gov.cn/englishnpc/news/.

worldwide (composed of almost 3,000 delegates). Regarding the formation of Chinese politics and policy formulation in the PRC, it is, however, regarded as a rather weak and toothless body. It has been classified by international observers as a rubber-stamp institution, ex post legitimising (and formalising) policies and decisions made by the CCP.

Its composition, office term, and its role and duties are outlined in Chapter III of the Chinese (state) constitution. The delegates of the NPC are elected from the provinces, China's autonomous regions, directly governed municipalities, Special Administrative Regions and the armed forces. Furthermore, all national minorities are represented (Article 59). The term of office is five years (Article 60). In general, the NPC convenes for its annual plenary meeting at the Great Hall of the Chinese People in March. Additional sessions of the NPC can be convened upon initiative of the NPC's Standing Committee or if voted for by one-fifth of all NPC delegates (Article 61). In 2020, the corona pandemic caused a postponement of the meeting – which was finally held in late May 2020.

According to Article 62 of the Chinese constitution, the NPC has the power to...

- amend and oversee the implementation of the constitution,
- to enact and amend basic criminal and civil laws (as well as basic laws governing the state organs),
- to elect the State President and the Vice-president as well as the Chairman of the Central Military Commission, the Chairman of the National Supervisory Commission, the President of the Supreme People's Court, the Procurator General of the Supreme People's Procuratorate,
- to (formally) decide on the choice of the prime minister, ministers, members of state commissions nominated by the state president,
- to review and approve the state budget,
- to approve the establishment of Chinas provinces, autonomous regions, and directly governed municipalities and to decide upon the instalment of special administrative regions,
- and, finally, to decide on questions of war and peace.

Amendments of the state constitution – as of March 2018, the Chinese constitution has undergone five major revisions – can be proposed by the NPC's Standing Committee or by more than one-fifth of the NPC's delegates. The adoption of constitutional amendments requires a majority of more than two-thirds of all votes (Article 64). However, all past revisions of the Chinese (state) constitution had been initiated and designed by the National Party Congress, preceding the March meeting of the NPC.

In between the annual plenary sessions of the NPC, legislative work is delegated to the NPC's Standing Committee and the NPC committees. Six permanent committees are established by the constitution; additional commissions can be created if deemed necessary (Article 70). The permanent committees cover the following fields:

- ethnic affairs
- constitution and law
- finance and economic affairs
- education, science, culture, public health
- foreign affairs,
- overseas Chinese affairs.

The 13th NPC set up a total number of 10 committees, including additional ones responsible for:

- supervisory and judicial affairs,
- environmental protection and resource conservation,
- agriculture and rural affairs,
- soci(et)al development.

The establishment of these new committees reflects the PRC's unsolved developmental challenges and the aggravating socio-economic tensions between the different strata of society as well as the disparities and imbalances between the urban and the rural sector.

On 21 March 2018 the NPC released its "Plan to Deepen Reform of Party and State Institutions". Its annual March meeting concluded with a major restructuring of state ministries. Some ministries were abolished, others were merged, eight new ministries were created. The ministries are as follows:

- agriculture and rural affairs,
- culture and tourism,
- ecological environment,
- veteran affairs,
- natural resources,
- emergence management,
- national health (commission).

The newly established Ministry of Ecological Environment (MEE) (in Chinese: *Shengtai Huanjingbu*) replaced the former Ministry of Environmental Protection, continuing its work with a much broader agenda as duties and responsibilities formerly ascribed to other ministries or the NDRC were merged under the MEE's roof. This makes the MEE the central unit of the PRC's "war against environmental pollution", targeting air, water, and soil pollution as caused by China's high-speed, resource- and emission-intense growth model of the past three decades. The Ministry of Natural Resources (MNR) (in Chinese: *Ziran Ziyuanbu*) is a similar example of merging formerly separate commissions and ministries into one super-ministry. The MNR is expected to guarantee a more efficient and sustainable exploitation and use of natural resources. The mergers launched by the NPC are not limited to the environmental sector – as the creation of the National Health Commission (*Guojia Weisheng Jiankang Weiyuanhui*) exemplifies.

Moreover, the March 2018 reforms also strengthened supervision and checks and balances of governance processes, including the sectors of banking, finance, and insurance. Ultimate supervisory power has been assigned to the newly created National Supervisory Commission (*Guojia Jiancha Weiyuanhui*). Adding this body to the list of Chinese state institutions required a general revision of the 1982 constitution (March 2018).

By launching these institutional reforms and restructuring processes, the NPC responded to the reform needs already identified under the fourth generation of Chinese political leaders. The reform ideas sketched in the 12th Five-Year Plan, in the work report of the Chinese prime minister, as well as in the general secretary's report at the National Party Congress, however, evidently did not lead to the expected results. The reform initiative under the fifth generation does not operate with short-term institutional modifications but seeks to redefine China's development model and to back this re-steering process by a novel round of institution-building.

In addition to the special committees listed above, the NPC's administrative body further includes the NPC General Office and the commission for legislative affairs, the commission for budgetary affairs, the committee for Hong Kong SAR Basic Law, and the committee for Macao SAR Basic Law.

At all lower levels of the state administration – provinces, directly-governed municipalities, counties, cities, municipal districts, townships and ethnic townships – local people's congresses are set up (Article 95); they are guided by the NPC but officially preserve their local "autonomy".

In the aftermath of the PRC's entrance into the post-Maoist era of modern state-building and reform, the NPC (and local people's congresses) are no longer simply obeying the party line. In 1992, only 67 % of all delegates voted for the construction of the (heavily disputed) Three-Gorges Dam. In other cases, bills submitted to the NPC by the State Council did not get through. Even the (s)election or appointment of China's state personnel did not always take place in unison (though dissenting votes and abstentions never transgressed the symbolic 10 % threshold).

Regarding the formal (s)election of core politicians, party discipline still seems to work. In 2008, the NPC confirmed the re-(s)election of Hu Jintao as state president for his second term. Hu Jintao got 2,956 positive votes, 3 negative votes and 5 abstentions. In 2013, Xi Jinping only got one dissenting vote and 3 abstentions. In March 2018, Xi was unanimously re-confirmed as state president and chairman of the Central Military Commission.

The first election law of the PRC was passed in March 1953. Between 1953 and 1979, three rounds of (s)elections were held to fill government and parliamentary positions. The CCP, however, had the ultimate right to nominate candidates, meaning that these elections were neither competitive nor open and transparent. As the number of nominated candidates exactly matched the number of seats available, political participation via elections was reduced to (forced) acclamation and confirmation of top-down selected candidates (in times of political radicalisation and mass mobilisation, any protest vote – a blank, spoiled, or "non-of-the-proposed-candidates" vote – would have had severe, maybe even lethal consequences). On 1 July 1979, some years after the end of the Cultural Revolution (1966–1976), a revised election law was passed. Additional revisions followed in 1982, 1986, 1995 and 2004. Village chiefs and delegates of local people's congresses are (s)elected via direct elections, whilst the members of the NPC are (s)elected by the people's congress one level down. As part of the reforms of the election law, the right to nominate candidates has also been modified. Apart from the CCP, China's democratic parties, mass organisations and civil (society) actor groups are permitted to propose candidates. Finally, the list of eligible candidates should include more than one candidate for each position available in order to allow for "real" elections.

→ **State Council[17]**

The NPC elects (or confirms) the State Council, the government of the PRC. According to the constitution, the State Council is "the executive body of the highest organ of state power and (…) the highest organ of state administration" (Article 85). The State Council comprises the premier, several vice premiers (2013; 2018: four), several state councillors, ministers, chairmen of commissions, the auditor general and the secretary general (Article 86). The "executive meeting" of the State Council, the most powerful sub-unit, involves the premier, the vice premiers, as well as the state councillors.

Table 2: Inner Core of the State Council (since 2018)

Function	Name
Premier	Li Keqiang
Vice Premier	Han Zheng
	Hu Chunhua
	Sun Chunlan
	Liu He
State Councillors	Wei Fenghe
	Wang Yong
	Wang Yi
	Xiao Jie
	Zhao Kezhi

---

17 This passage is based on the webpage of the State Council (in Chinese): http://www.gov.cn. For the English version: http://english.gov.cn.

The functions and powers of the State Council are listed in Article 89 of the (state) constitution.

3.2. Organisational Foundations of the CCP

→ Formation and Consolidation of the CCP

According to official party historiography, the CCP was founded in Shanghai in July 1921 as a "revolutionary" party, copying the Leninist "vanguard" party, representing workers, peasants and soldiers. The origins of the CCP date back to the late imperial period when Marxist ideas entered China. The Soviet Union's Communist International (Comintern) sent advisers to spread the idea of a socialist world revolution and to support the formation of Communist cells in China (the Soviet advisers simultaneously provided assistance to the GMD and supported its reorganisation as a Leninist cadre party (Zarrow 2005: 196–197)). This dual support of these two competing Chinese party groupings – the Chinese Marxists as well as Sun Yat-sen's GMD – by the Comintern formed part of the SU's promotion of worldwide national, anti-capitalist liberation movements. With the founding congress of the CCP convened in the French concession of Shanghai, the Chinese underground cells and Marxist circles were finally merged into one integrated party.

Mao Zedong did not play a major role in this founding period of the CCP. He reportedly came into close contact with Marxist ideas when working as an assistant librarian at Peking University, where the later "founding fathers" of the CCP, Chen Duxiu (1879–1942) and Li Dazhao (1889–1927), had promoted the formation of Marxist study groups. China's Marxist pioneers were deeply inspired by the October Revolution and sought to follow Moscow's socialist path (Pantsov 2000). Chen Duxiu, however, was rather hesitant to accept direct orders from the SU and only reluctantly joined the First United Front between the CCP and the GMD – advocated by the SU. When Chiang Kai-shek unilaterally ended the collaboration with the CCP and launched the nation-wide purge of Communist and Marxist forces, Chen Duxiu was held responsible for this traumatic defeat of the Chinese communists. In 1927, Chen was labelled as a rightist and forced to resign from all party offices; in 1929, he was formally expelled from the CCP.[18]

From 1927 onwards, the CCP re-launched its guerrilla war against Chiang Kai-shek's GMD government. As the Autumn Harvest Uprising led by Mao faced a severe defeat, the CCP's Red Army retreated to the Jinggang mountains, where they set up the Jiangxi Soviet. Chiang Kai-shek started the military encirclement of Communist soviets. In October 1934, when the Jiangxi Soviet could no longer be defended against these attacks, the Communist troops embarked on their legendary Long March, finally setting up their new base in Yan'an (October 1935). During this Long March, at the enlarged meeting of the Politburo in Zunyi (Guizhou province) in January 1935, Mao successfully managed to reduce the direct control of the Comintern by expelling their members and followers from

---

18 Chen Duxiu then turned to Trotsky's ideas on Marxism and thus opted for a development model not supported by Mao and the partly restructured "new" CCP. On Chen and Trotsky, see: Kuhfus (1985).

the party, paving his ascent to the top echelons of the CCP. He continued securing his power base during the Yan'an period, when he promoted the Sinicization of Marxism(-Leninism). The focus of the Marxist theory of class struggle and revolution was shifted from the urban industrial workers and proletarian class to the Chinese peasants. Mao also launched several ideological streamlining campaigns to establish his own ideas as guiding ideology and to get rid of opposition within the ranks of the CCP.[19]

The GMD's encirclement crusades were only suspended when two GMD generals forced Chiang Kai-shek to enter into a Second United Front, collaborating with the CCP in the War of Resistance to counter the invasion of China by Japanese forces (Xi'an Incident, December 1936). During the War of Resistance, the Chinese Communists managed to expand their spheres of control beyond their base in Yan'an by setting up "liberated zones" (under Communist control). The power struggle between the GMD and the CCP thus continued even whilst fighting the Japanese invasion. In 1941 GMD troops launched an attack on the headquarters of the CCP's New Fourth Army; with the US entrance into the Pacific War after the Japanese attack on Pearl Harbor, the intra-Chinese armistice was finally over. Following the capitulation of Japan, China (re-)entered into a civil war and open military power struggle, concluding with the final victory of the CCP. The defeated GMD retreated to the island of Taiwan, where they installed their temporary administration of the Republic of China (claiming to be the only legitimate government of "China", including the mainland as well as Taiwan). The CCP set up its government in Beijing; on 1 October 1949, Mao Zedong proclaimed the founding of the People's Republic of China.

The political history of the CCP as a "ruling" party can be divided into two periods: the Maoist era (1949–1976/78) and the post-Maoist reform era, associated with the Third Plenum's decisions on reform and opening (1978).

In the Mao era, the Chinese state was reorganised with the formation of a people's republic, guided by the idea of "people's democratic dictatorship" (as opposed to the Soviet formula of "dictatorship of the proletariat"). In the early Maoist period – the transition period from the old feudalist to the CCP-ruled socialist order – the administrative system structures and the economy, which had been eroded by the Japanese attacks and the Chinese civil war, had to be restored. As a first step, the CCP initiated a land reform (1950–1952), designed as a mass campaign that fuelled large-scale socio-economic class struggle. In 1951, the CCP started a campaign against counterrevolutionaries to reduce the risk of a counter-movement by GMD supporters or by those socio-economic ("feudalist") classes targeted by the land reform. These Maoist mass campaigns cracked down on China's old clan and gentry structures and allowed the CCP to consolidate its power base amongst the lower socio-economic strata as well as in rural areas. Additional campaigns were launched to secure loyalty and compliance of state bureaucracy:

---

19 In his "Talks at the Yan'an Forum on Literature and Art", Mao proclaimed that literature and art would have to serve the Chinese (socialist) Revolution, encouraging writers to engage in "proletarian" literature. For a translation and interpretation of Mao's "Talks at the Yan'an Forum on Literature and Art", see: McDougall (1980).

the Three-Anti Campaign was started in Manchuria in 1951 and targeted the three evils: "corruption, waste, bureaucracy". The Five-Anti Campaign, following in January 1952, turned against Chinese urban entrepreneurs and business elites, persecuting "bribery, theft of state property, tax evasion, cheating on government contracts, stealing state economic intelligence". China's intellectuals were forced into line by a campaign on "thought reform" (1951–1952). The interim stage of the "new democracy" – legitimising cooperation with the "national bourgeoisie" in order to overcome imperialist, foreign domination and to stabilise the Chinese domestic economy – was substituted by a new phase of socialist reconstruction and state building. The PRC's First Five-Year Plan (1953–1957) mainly borrowed from the Soviet blueprint and prioritised the further development of the heavy industry sector, and advocated that the restructuring of the rural agricultural sector into producers' cooperatives should be steadily implemented. Starting in 1955, however, Mao initiated a "great leap" collectivisation of the agricultural sector. Khrushchev and the Leninist wing of the CCP heavily criticised this move.

Developments in the communist one-party systems in Eastern Europe – especially the uprisings in Hungary – factional tensions within the CCP as well as the growing distance between Moscow and Beijing finally triggered another Maoist mass campaign in the second half of the 1950s. The Hundred Flowers Movement (1956/1957) encouraged Chinese intellectuals (and the wider Chinese civil society) to openly voice their views on the one-party regime. Retrospective assessments of this dark episode in the PRC's history assume that this campaign might have served to identify opposition networks and critics amongst China's intellectuals. Others have argued that Mao believed that the CCP power monopoly would be backed by the overarching majority of the Chinese people and thus did not expect to encounter such a viral wave of criticism. When public criticism threatened to get out of control, Mao responded with sharp repression and launched the Anti-Rightist Campaign.

Despite all these setbacks, Mao perpetuated his modernisation strategy that, contrary to the development path chosen by the Soviet Union, focused on Chinese peasants and rural industrialisation. His Great Leap Forward (1958–1961) aimed at catapulting China to the ranks of the world's industrialized nations. The collectivisation campaign started with mutual aid teams and continued with setting up agricultural cooperatives. In 1958, the first people's commune was opened in Henan province (inspired by the Paris Commune). Mao's proclaimed idea was that the PRC should surpass the UK in terms of steel production within 15 years after the formal initiation of the Great Leap Forward. To enforce China's steel production, people's communes operated with backyard steel furnaces, which were of rather poor quality. To formally fulfil the official quota (for grain and steel production), local cadres submitted false reports with inflated figures. Information about the disastrous development in rural areas was not directly communicated. Grain deliveries to the big cities continued, even though this meant that granaries were emptied, leaving local people starving. The Great Leap Forward caused a catastrophic famine (1959–1961). Mao retreated to the second row and left the reconsolidation of the one-party state and the Chinese economy to

Liu Shaoqi and Deng Xiaoping. The failure of Mao's great leap approach was taken up by Chinese writers in the early 1960s, reflecting on these events via allegoric essays and parables.[20] Mao answered by initiating a Socialist Education Movement (1962–1966), which, however, did not restore his pre-1960s authority. This movement, also known as a the Four Clean-ups, set out to "clean" the four fields of politics, economy, organisation and ideology. Via this campaign, Mao sought to silence critical voices and enforce compliance with the party's official ideology. A much more radical attempt of ideological streamlining and mass mobilisation followed with the Cultural Revolution (1966–1976). To eliminate his critics and factions opposing Mao's socialist modernisation roadmap, Mao relied on the People's Liberation Army, controlled by Lin Biao, and the Red Guards. Lin Biao compiled and edited the *Little Red Book: Quotations from Chairman Mao*, published from 1964 onwards and sent to select units of the PLA before being distributed to the wider public with the goal to have 99 % of the Chinese people read Mao's core ideas. Political radicalisation only ended with the death of Mao Zedong (9 September 1976) and the imprisonment of the Gang of Four.[21]

The post-Mao reform era was driven by the idea of pragmatic economic reforms and proclaimed a farewell to Mao's permanent revolution and class struggle. Deng Xiaoping coined the formula of "Socialism with Chinese characteristics", implying the integration of market capitalist elements into the PRC's centrally planned "socialist" economy.

BOX IV: Rise and Fall of Mao's Designated Successors

Peng Dehuai (1898–1974)

Peng Dehuai, trained as a professional soldier, participated in Chiang Kai-shek's Northern Expedition. He supported the attempt by the GMD's left wing to install an alternative (GMD) government in Wuhan. When this attempt had failed, Peng joined the Chinese Communists (1928). During the Long March, he got promoted to the position of vice commander in chief of the Communist forces (with Zhu De serving as official commander in chief). In 1934, Peng became a member of the CCP's Central Committee and, at the 7th National Party Congress in Yan'an, was nominated as vice chairman of the Central Military Commission, finally becoming defence minister in 1954. Peng had passionately backed Mao's rise to power at the Zunyi Conference. Nonetheless, he did not keep silent on the disastrous effects of the Great Leap Forward and openly criticised Mao's mismanagement of socialist state-building at the Lushan Conference. He was dismissed from office and

---

20 One of the most famous is the Peking Opera *Hai Rui Dismissed from Office* (1959) composed by Wu Han, a Chinese writer and vice mayor of Peking. Hai Rui served as a scholar-official under the Ming emperor Jiajing. According to historic records, he criticised the emperor for not fulfilling his (ritual) duties and was sentenced to death. The emperor passed away before the sentence was executed, and Hai Rui was reinstalled as adviser by the emperor's successor. Hai Rui is commemorated as a model official known for his integrity. Wu Han's opera tells the story of Hai Rui informing the emperor about illegal land confiscations by local officials. His complaint leads to his political demotion. Chinese readers immediately noticed the parallels to the land collectivisation and instalment of people's communes under Mao, as well as the demotion of Peng Dehuai. Peng openly criticised Mao's Great Leap Forward at the Lushan Conference (July/August 1957). Another example voicing political criticism via allegoric essays are the "Evening Talks at Yanshan", written by Deng Tuo, municipal party secretary of Beijing. These were published as short essays in the *Beijing Evening News* in the early 1960s.

21 For a lucid overview of China's political history in the Mao era: Fenby (2013 [2008]).

replaced by **Lin Biao**. During the Cultural Revolution, Peng was persecuted and tortured by radicalised Red Guards and finally passed away in jail.

Liu Shaoqi (1898–1969)

Liu Shaoqi received part of his academic (and ideological) education in Moscow (1920–1922) and, inspired by Marxist ideology, joined the Chinese Communist Party (1921). Immediately after his return to China, Liu took part in the organisation of labour strikes and political campaigns and coordinated the formation of labour unions. In 1927, Liu became a member of the CCP's Central Committee and head of the CCP's Labour Department. He experienced the Long March and actively supported the ideological reorientation of the CCP at the Zunyi Conference. During the Yan'an years, Liu served as head of the Institute for Marxism-Leninism and published political essays, including his treatise on "How to be a Good Communist" (1939). When Mao (temporarily) retreated to the second row, Liu Shaoqi took over the position as state president (1959). He had, however, expressed some concerns regarding the negative outcome of Mao's Great Leap Forward and got attacked by Mao's Red Guard sympathisers during the Cultural Revolution. Liu Shaoqi (and Deng Xiaoping) was denounced as a "capitalist roader" and came under direct violent attack by the Red Guards. Liu was posthumously rehabilitated by a decision of the Fifth Plenum of the 11th Central Committee (1980).

Lin Biao (1907–1971)

After his graduation from the Whampoa Military Academy in Guangzhou, Lin Biao joined the CCP and rose to high ranks in the Communist Red Army during the Long March. He spent the years 1938 to 1942 in the Soviet Union (he had been wounded in the Second Sino-Japanese War and reportedly suffered from tuberculosis, receiving medical treatment in Moscow). In 1945, Lin became a member of the CCP's Central Committee and was appointed to a core position in the Communist army. Having served as vice premier and having become a member of the Politburo Standing Committee, in 1959, Lin was nominated as the successor of the PRC's Defence Minister **Peng Dehuai** (who had fallen out of Mao's grace at the Lushan Conference). Lin Biao is known as the initiator of the red Mao "bible" (*Quotations from Chairman Mao*). During the Cultural Revolution, Lin positioned himself as one of Mao's strongest supporters. With the demotion of **Liu Shaoqi**, Lin became Mao's only remaining "designated" successor. In 1971, Lin Biao died in a plane crash in Mongolia – according to the CCP's official party historiography, he was trying to flee and defect to the Soviet Union after a failed plot (571 conspiracy) to assassinate Mao. International scholars have questioned this official narrative, pointing at contradictions in this conspiracy story.

Hua Guofeng (1921–2008)

When Mao died in September 1976, he was succeeded by Hua Guofeng. In 1969, Hua became a member of the Central Committee and in 1973 he joined the Politburo. In 1975, he took over the position of the PRC's minister for public security. After the death of Zhou Enlai, Mao appointed Hua as premier and first vice chairman *ad interim*. Hua was the only "designated" successor who "safely" survived the turbulent years of the Maoist mass campaigns and the Cultural Revolution. He ordered the arrest of the Gang of Four (a group of Communists centred around Mao's wife Jiang Qing). In 1980, the Gang of Four was subjected to a (show) trial and found guilty of leftist extremism and violence during the Cultural Revolution. Hua Guofeng coined the legendary formula of the "Two Whatevers" (*liang ge fanshi*): to uphold "whatever policy decisions Mao made" and to follow "whatever instructions Mao gave". In the long run, the pro-reform circles of the CCP took over, replacing this resolute dedication to Maoist ideology by the formula "seeking truth from facts" (*shi shi qiu shi*). Hua's idea of a continuation of Mao's collectivisation à la Dazhai and permanent class-struggle were no longer backed by the CCP. In 1980, Hua Guofeng was replaced by Zhao Ziyang as premier of the PRC and Hu Yaobang as head of the CCP (Deng Xiaoping, the intellectual architect of China's economic reforms, took over control of the Central Military Commission in 1981).

→ Transformation from a Revolutionary Party to a Ruling Party

Originally established in 1921 as a revolutionary cadre party representing workers, peasants and soldiers, following the decisions on reform and opening (1978), the CCP has transformed itself into a ruling party that represents the interests of the "Chinese people". This refined definition of the Chinese "people" also includes those groups classified, in the Mao era, as "enemies of the people", i.e., private capitalist entrepreneurs as well as intellectuals. This integrative representation claim has been summarised by the formula of the Three Represents/Three Representations (*san ge daibiao*), a concept associated with the governance paradigms developed by (or under) Jiang Zemin. This formula states that the CCP "represents the developmental demands of China's advanced productive forces" (i.e., the economic elites), "the orientation for China's advanced culture" (i.e., intellectuals) as well as the "fundamental interests of the greatest possible majority of the Chinese people".[22]

The CCP's ideological canon has continuously been updated and amended. Every generation of Chinese political leaders added a novel frame to the Chinese version and interpretation of Marxism. Deng Xiaoping Theory and the Three Represents have thus become listed as a continuation of Marxism-Leninism and Mao Zedong Thought. Later, revisions of the party constitution also added the Scientific Outlook on Development (Hu Jintao). In general, these updates and amendments are added ex post, i.e., after the ascent of a new generation that will still have to coin its own slogans and formula. However, already in 2017, when Xi Jinping was reconfirmed for a second period in office, the CCP decided to add "Xi Jinping Thought on Socialism with Chinese Characteristics for the New Era" to the party constitution. The official canon of CCP ideology has not been supplanted, as these frameworks and concepts are presented as upholding and continuing the legacy of Mao Zedong Thought.

In September 2004, the CCP's Fourth Plenum of the 16th Central Committee passed the "Resolution on Strengthening the Party's Governance Capacities", a document perceived as having paved the way towards the reinvention of the CCP as a modern (Communist) "catch-all" people's party. For the CCP, having redefined itself as a "ruling party" (*zhizheng dang*), the utmost priority is the instalment of an efficient state bureaucracy and the coordination of the competing interests of various Chinese socio-economic actor groups.

---

22 These excerpts are taken from the CCP's Party Constitution, revised and amended in 2017: http://www.xin huanet.com/english/download/Constitution_of_the_Communist_Party_of_China.pdf.

The 2004 resolution highlighted the need to practise rule-based governance (*yi fa zhi zheng*) and to strengthen inner-party democracy (Womack 2005). In 2014, the Fourth Plenum of the 18th Central Committee (Xi–Li administration) once again addressed the issue of legal-rational rule and rule-based governance

Table 3: Number of CCP Party Members

Year	CCP Members (in million people)
2004	69.6
2005	70.8
2006	72.39
2007	74.15
2008	75.93
2009	78
2010	80.27
2011	82.6
2012	85.13
2013	86.69
2014	87.79
2015	88.76
2016	89.45
2017	89.56
2018	90.59

Source: Statista 2018; *China Daily* 2017.

The Chinese one-party state is aware of the theories and models of modernisation and transformation theories that predict that the formation of a middle class and the rise of the private economy will trigger a transition towards democracy. In 2002, the CCP formally ruled that capitalists can apply for CCP membership. By including and co-opting the PRC's private economic sector, the CCP seeks to secure compliance. Given the symbiotic relationship between the party-state and the business sector, counter-movements by this actor group are unlikely to happen (at least as long as party membership implies certain securities and privileges).

This might explain why the number of party members has continuously increased, even after the PRC had entered the post-Maoist reform era. From 2004 to 2014, 13 million new party members were recruited. In 2014, however, official statistics documented a decrease in the total number of party members of about 351,000 people as compared to 2013 figures. This temporary decline has neither been commented on nor publicly explained. Some scholars speculate that the anti-corruption campaign could have created an atmosphere of fear, causing an interim break in party recruitment campaigns. Overall, the CCP has, however, remained an elitist circle, as party members account for less than 7 % of China's populace.

Table 4: Demographics of CCP Members by Employment

Employment Sector	Number of CCP members (in million people)
Farmers, herders, fishermen	25.44
Industrial workers	6.51
Managerial staff	9.1
Management	12.5
Party/Government/State agencies	7.6
Retirees	18.15
College students	1.81

©Noesselt 2020, based on Statista 2018; SCMP 2015

Since the PRC's entrance into the reform era, the CCP has actively recruited new members from the younger generation, especially from groups with a university degree. The percentage of female party members has also increased, accounting for roughly one quarter of CCP members. As a response to the perceived "counter-elite" formation of 1989, the CCP has intensified its campaign to co-opt and incorporate China's intellectual and business elites.

Party schools, especially the Central Party School, function as "talent incubators" of the Chinese party-state. In the 1920s, the Comintern and Soviet advisers had urged the PRC to set up a country-wide network of party schools. The CCP's earliest party schools date back to the years of the Jiangxi Soviet, where a School for Marxist Studies was established. When, at the end of their Long March, the remaining Communist troops reached Yan'an, they opened a follow-up school, called the University of Anti-Japanese Resistance. In 1948, in the final year of the "civil war" and military struggle for control over "China" between the Nationalists and the Communists, the CCP set up the Marxist-Leninist Academy in Anhui headed by Liu Shaoqi.

In August 1955, just a couple of years after the proclamation and founding of the PRC, the Central Party School was established in Beijing. During the years of the Cultural Revolution, the Central Party School – like most organs and institutions – was closed. It was relaunched under Hua Guofeng, who served as the school's president from 1977 to 1982. He was succeeded by Hu Yaobang in 1982. Party schools exist at all levels of the Chinese administration and in all Chinese provinces; their total number is estimated at 2,600 to 2,700 schools (Liu 2009).

The Central Party School in Beijing not only functioned as a training centre in issues of party ideology, but, under Hu Jintao, became quite an influential think tank advising the Chinese ruling elite. The school became known as an incubator for policy innovation and the coining of the PRC's political flagship slogans. The Three Represents as well as the concepts of Scientific Development and the Peaceful Rise have, reportedly, all been developed or assisted by scholars affiliated with the PRC's Central Party School.

In 2005, during the course of the Central Committee's efforts to strengthen the CCP's governance capacities, three cadre schools for training the core elite were set up under direct control of the CCP's organisation department: located in Pudong (the special economic zone in Shanghai) as well in Jinggangshan and Yan'an – all central sites of the CCP's revolutionary history (Shambaugh 2008b).

For cadre recruitment, the CCP continues to rely on the Communist Youth League. Hu Yaobang (CCP chairman/CCP general secretary 1981–1987), Hu Jintao (general secretary 2002–2012) and Li Keqiang (member of the Politburo Standing Committee since 2012 and, since 2013, premier of the PRC) rose to the top echelons of the Chinese party-state via the Youth League (*tuanpai*).

3.2.1. Party Organs[23]

According to the CCP's party constitution, and in terms of absolute numbers of participants, the highest CCP organ is the National Party Congress, which convenes every five years. The Party Congress debates and (ex post) justifies ideological readjustments by passing formal revisions or amendments of the party constitution. The Party Congress (s)elects the CCP's Central Committee, which meets once or twice a year to hold its plenary session(s). The Central Committee includes two types of (s)selected members: full members equipped with voting rights and "reserve" members participating in CCP meetings without voting rights. Since the 13th National Party Congress, the number of eligible candidates has been higher than the number of seats available – hence implying a turn to "competitive" (s)elections (Li, Cheng 2012). Amongst the organs administered by the Central Committee is the Central Military Commission, the control centre of the PRC's armed forces, headed by the general secretary (and state president).

The (informal) control centre of the CCP (and of Chinese politics) is the Politburo (since 2012 composed of 25 members) and the Politburo Standing Committee (since 2012 comprising 7 members).

Party discipline is enforced by the Central Committee's Central Commission for Discipline Inspection (CCDI). The CCDI was set up in connection with the Third Plenum's decisions on reform and opening in 1978; precursor institutions of internal party control and supervision include the rather short-lived Central Control Commission. The CCDI is not only charged with enforcing compliance with

---

23 See the CCP's official web portal: http://cpc.people.com.cn (Chinese version); http://english.cpc.people.co m.cn (English version).

party regulations and party ideology but also with investigating and persecuting corruption and malfeasance of party cadres.

The Central Committee includes four core institutions: The Organisation Department of the CCP, controlling and coordinating personnel assignments based on the nomenklatura system; the CCP's Propaganda/Publicity Department; the CCP's United Front Work Department, coordinating contacts with non-Communist parties and elites "outside" the CCP (including the Chinese overseas community); the CCP's Central Foreign Affairs Commission (also known as the Foreign Affairs Leading Group, FALG), which manages the party's foreign affairs (since the PRC's turn to a pragmatic foreign diplomacy, the FALG is no longer involved in providing support for national, anti-imperialist and anti-colonial liberation movements). Again, these structures are reproduced at all levels of the Chinese party-state administration down to the township level.

For a short interim period, spanning the years from 1982 to 1992, the Central Advisory Commission (CAC) was established, led by Deng Xiaoping (1982–1987) and Chen Yun (1987–1992). The core of this additional advisory body, composed of elderly party members, had become known as the "eight great eminent CCP officials", also referred to as the "eight immortals", i.e., the eight deities of Chinese Daoism. This body allowed Deng Xiaoping and his political supporters to conduct high party politics without holding any of the party-state's top positions. The "eight eminent officials" were reportedly involved in the demotion of several high-ranked party officials, including Hua Guofeng, Hu Yaobang and Zhao Ziyang. In the early 1990s, the CAC – somehow functioning as the CPPCC's mirror organ within the party pillar – was finally abolished.

Internal revision and correction campaigns – such as the correction of party cadre's leadership style or measures to combat corruption – temporarily empower the CCDI and reshuffle the informal hierarchy of party organs and institutions (Guo 2014). Given that the head of the CCDI has to be a member of the Politburo Standing Committee and given the CCDI's direct organisational ties with the Central Committee, its "real" power turned out to be rather limited. Once again, the fourth generation of Chinese leaders set out to reform the CCDI by increasing its powers, but, again, scholars and analysts state that the commission mainly followed party guidelines and did not initiate "independent" investigations. The ousting of Chen Liangyu, serving as CCP secretary in Shanghai (2002–2006), during the Shanghai pension scandal in 2006 and his final trial (2008) are thus regarded as a strategic move to disempower the "Shanghai clique", a faction closely related with Jiang Zemin (Gong 2008). Under Xi Jinping, the CCDI underwent a major restructuring and all-encompassing institutional reorganisation: the Third Plenum (2018) announced to decouple the CCDI and local CDIs from (local) party politics. Local CDIs should, according to the reform proposal, report to higher level CDIs and act "independently" from local party units. Furthermore, the 18th National Party Congress established a CCDI Organisation Department, allowing the CCDI to recruit its investigators independently from the CCP Organisation Department. Moreover, in 2014, a CCDI office for the supervision of officials involved in discipline inspection was opened as an additional layer of internal checks and balances. Xi Jinping also recruited cadres with work experience in discipline inspection for top positions in organs and commissions of the party-state. Out of the 39 members of the Leading Group for Comprehensively Deepening Reforms – later upgraded to the Central Commission for Comprehensively Deepening Reforms in 2018 – 5 had a background in discipline control.

Additionally, (former) members of the commission(s) for discipline control joined local government bodies at the provincial level of the state bureaucracy. The delegation of these "special" cadres mainly targeted those provinces and regions where either a rising number of social unrest and upheavals had been reported or where there was an increase in local counter-elites (e.g., the network of Neo-Maoist factions in connection with Bo Xilai's local governance reforms in Chongqing) (Lam 2015).

Within the course of following a "law- and rule-based" governance model, as formalised and institutionalised by the decisions of the Fourth Plenum of the 18th Central Committee (2014), the CCP's core elites also found an answer to the question "who guards the guardians?" (quis custodit custodes). This includes the setting-up of the CCDI supervision commission, mentioned above (Xinhua 2014). The Fourth Plenum also underlined that party orders and basic principles of party discipline rank higher than laws and regulations of the state apparatus. The party's regulations on good governance and correct (moral) behaviour, as these statements stressed, were more rigid than "normal" laws and legal frameworks (*Renmin Ribao* 2014). These statements demonstrate that the Xi–Li administration links the success of establishing a transparent and clean government to the efficient restauration of party discipline. The main lines of conflicts and cleavages evidently do not run between the party and (civil) society, but between competing factions within the party as well as between elites and counter-elites.

Table 5: Members of the Politburo Standing Committee (2018–)

Name	Position in the Party-State Apparatus
Xi Jinping	General Secretary; State President; Chairman of the Central Military Commission
Li Keqiang	Premier
Li Zhanshu	Chairman of the Standing Committee of the NPC
Wang Yang	Chairman of the CPPCC
Wang Huning	(First) Secretary of the Central Secretariat
Zhao Leji	Secretary of the CCDI
Han Zheng	Vice Premier

The party pyramid is headed by the general secretary of the CCP, who simultaneously functions as state president and chairman of the Central Military Commission. The principle of collective leadership, introduced in the early post-Maoist reform era, implies that the general secretary acts as *primus inter pares* and must secure strategic majorities for his governance solutions. With the initiation of the "top-level design", this formula seems to have been informally replaced by the concept of *princeps inter pares*.

As part of the post-1978 state-building process in the reform era, a set of legal and institutional elements to limit and control political power was introduced. The position of the CCP chairman was replaced by the position of the general secretary.

Xi Jinping was able to consolidate his power and authority within the first few years of his first term of office. He managed to establish his own set of political slogans and ideas and to have them inscribed into the party constitution before being re-(s)elected for a second legislative period. The recentralisation and re-personalisation of Chinese politics under Xi followed a course that deviated from Maoist patterns of violent suppression of the party opposition and state bureaucracy. Xi's rapid power consolidation mainly relied on ad hoc established, informal, parallel institutions: the (central and small) leading groups. Via these leading groups, institutional reform agendas were developed and implemented – bypassing the inherited bureaucratic state apparatus.

Table 6: CCP Chairmen

Name	Period in Office
Mao Zedong	1943–1976 (interrupted)
Hua Guofeng	1976–1981
Hu Yaobang	1981–1982

Table 7: CCP General Secretaries

Name	Period in Office
Hu Yaobang	1982–1987
Zhao Ziyang	1987–1989
Jiang Zemin	1989–2002
Hu Jintao	2002–2012
Xi Jinping	2012–

The CCP's control over politics, the economy, as well as society and its ultimate leadership are outlined in the Four Cardinal Principles.[24] Furthermore, the CCP's leadership role is stated in the PRC's state constitution. The organs of the Central

---

24 These Four Cardinal Principles, formulated by Deng Xiaoping, state that despite economic relaxation and capitalist experimentation, the "socialist path", "people's democratic dictatorship", the "leadership of the CCP", and "Mao Zedong Thought and Marxism-Leninism" would be upheld.

Committee secure the operationalisation and enforcement of the party's leadership claim: the selection, appointment and demotion of party cadres falls into the responsibilities of the Central Committee's Organisation Department. Party organs and party cells permeate all levels and layers of the state administration and the military. Party units are also present within Chinese companies and businesses; party groups even exist at the village level. This implies that the central party authorities secure their control and influence over regions and administrative units that are formally self-administered.

3.2.2. Informal Leading Circles

The "small leading groups" (lingdao xiaozu) are a special unit of extra-institutional policy formulation whose origins date back to the Maoist era. They design policy guidelines and roadmaps to secure the accomplishment of the system's overarching political-economic (reform) goals. In most cases, these (central) small leading groups are headed by core figures of the CCP's Politburo Standing Committee. In the Maoist years, especially during the high tide of political-ideological radicalisation during the Cultural Revolution, official state organs were disempowered and substituted by revolutionary leading groups. The internal checks and balances of the Chinese state administration were deactivated; Chinese politics were centralised in the hands of the charismatic CCP Chairman Mao Zedong – who, via his leading groups, enforced absolute loyalty and compliance with his revolutionary Great Leap development agenda (Miller 2008).

Even in the post-Maoist reform period, the party-state continues to operate with ad hoc established (small) leading groups that allow a bypassing of deadlocked structures and inefficient procedures. However, these leading groups do not formulate concrete policies but can only come up with new policy paradigms and policy recommendations. The new generation of small leading groups is not guided by ideology but seeks to design efficient solutions for complex governance challenges. By mid-2015, CSIS researchers counted 18 small leading groups belonging to the central party apparatus and 21 coordinated by the State Council (Johnson/Kennedy 2015). When reassessing the field in October 2017, they reported a doubling of small leading groups during Xi's first period in office.

At the Third Plenum of the 18th Central Committee (2013), the Central Leading Group for Comprehensively Deepening Reform was set up, directly headed by Xi Jinping. In addition, Xi also took the lead of the (central) leading groups for Taiwan Affairs, for Cybersecurity and Informatisation, as well as the one for National Defence and Troop Reform.[25] In November 2013, Xi became head of the newly established National Security Commission. The CSIS 2017 report counts seven small leading groups under Xi's direct control (Johnson/Kennedy/Qiu 2017).

The Central Leading Group for Comprehensively Deepening Reform coordinated six sub-fields (and sub-groups): economy and ecological civilisation; democracy and the legal system; culture; social system(s); party-building; discipline inspec-

---

25   For an overview of China's small leading groups under the fourth and the fifth generation of political leaders: Miller (2014).

tion. Zhang Gaoli, who coordinated the development of the PRC's special economic zone in Shenzhen from 1997 to 2001; the PRC's premier Li Keqiang; and Liu Yunshan, in charge of the Central Propaganda Department from 2002 to 2012, joined the group as vice leaders. Further members included the PRC's vice premier Liu Yandong; Ma Kai, the former head of China's National Development and Reform Commission; and Wang Yang, the former party secretary of Guangdong Province and known for his liberal, pro-reform orientation. The composition of this team clearly illustrated the Central Leading Group's focus on economic reform and the development of measures to balance the aggravating developmental disparities and disbalances across China. Key reform topics included the legalisation of rural-urban migration via a combination of readjustments of the *hukou* system, reforms of land-use rights and the strengthening of the private economy sector (Naughton 2014). The inclusion of Meng Jianzhu, head of the Central Committee's Politics and Law Commission; Zhou Qiang, president of China's Supreme People's Court; and Cao Jiangming, procurator general of the Supreme People's Procuratorate, evidences a turn towards constitutionalisation and formalisation of China's governance reforms. The Central Leading Group also involved high-ranked party cadres from the fields of party organisation, inter alia Zhao Leji, secretary of the Central Commission for Discipline Inspection, a unit also charged with securing the implementation of central reform policy by local cadres. Furthermore, Zhou Xiaochuan, governor of the People's Bank of China, reportedly also participated in the leading group's meetings.

At the annual meeting of the NPC in March 2018, several small leading groups were finally abolished and some of their duties and responsibilities were delegated to formal state organs (and their mirroring party units). Other leading groups – including the Central Leading Groups for Comprehensively Deepening Reform, for Cybersecurity, and for Finance and Economy – were transformed into central commissions (Xinhua 2018a). At the end of March 2018, the Central Commission for Comprehensively Deepening Reform, again headed by Xi Jinping, convened for its first meeting. Li Keqiang, Wang Huning and Han Zheng functioned as vice leaders. Concrete reform ideas on the commission's new agenda included pilot projects to open free trade zones in Guangdong, Tianjin and Fujian. General measures to reform and restructure the financial sector were also discussed (Xinhua 2018b).

In the Hu–Wen era, informal structures beyond the formal party-state organs and institutions had been reduced to a minimum. The annual meetings in Beidaihe, a seaside town where Mao initiated informal party summer retreats, were paused in 2003 and only reactivated in 2007 when preparing for the 17th Party Congress. In summer 2015, commentaries published in Chinese (state) media initially seemed to indicate a continued suspension of the summer retreat. One article published by the Chinese weekly newspaper *Caijing* argued that two summits had already been held in July 2015, discussing the preparation of the 13th Five-Year Plan and issues of party organisation – such as the correction of cadres' working style, the fight against corruption, and the nomination and promotion of the incoming core group of political leaders (*Sina* 2015). Rumours spread that the glamorous Beidaihe retreats would be incompatible with Xi Jinping's governance style, which stressed a cutback of banquets and luxury events. The two meetings in July were interpreted as an alternative format to replace the informal retreat with a formalised and more transparent meeting (*Global Times* 2015). Other Chinese state-owned media articles, however, reported that preparations for the Beidaihe summer summit in August 2015 were under way. Speculations ran high that factional struggles continued and were expected to be settled during the 2015 Beidaihe summit. Finally, the meeting took place.

3.3. Territorial Levels and Layers of the Chinese Administration

According to the PRC's state constitution,

(1) The country is divided into provinces, autonomous regions, and municipalities directly under the central government;

(2) Provinces and autonomous regions are divided into autonomous prefectures, counties, autonomous counties, and cities;

(3) Counties and autonomous counties are divided into townships, nationality townships, and towns (...) (Article 30).

Below the level of the central government, there are 34 provincial level administrative units that can be further subdivided into 23 provinces, 4 municipalities (Beijing, Shanghai, Chongqing, Tianjin) and 5 autonomous regions (Guangxi, Inner Mongolia, Ningxia, Tibet, Xinjiang), complemented by the 2 special administrative regions Hong Kong and Macao. The direct reach of the state ends at the county level, lower levels are "self-administered" and "self-organised", but permeated by local party cells.

The decisions on reform and opening (in 1978), and the following integration of China into international trade and the country's active positioning in world affairs, initiated processes of decentralisation. This caused a major informal reshuffling of the entangled power structure of China's multi-layered administration and had spill-over effects on the interlacing of party organs and state institutions. In the early 1980s, trade liberalisation and the participation in international trade and finance agreements required a restructuring and professionalisation of the PRC's state bureaucracy. These institutional adjustments implied a hollowing out of the monolithic one-party state. Consequently, the image of the party-state as a powerful, centralised leviathan was substituted by the concept of "fragmented authoritarianism" (Lieberthal/Oksenberg 1988; Lieberthal 1992; Lieberthal/Lampton 1992) that highlighted the plurality of actors involved in China's multi-layered governance process and accentuated the limited power and control of the central government in Beijing. The main assumption of the fragmented authoritarianism model is that China's provinces and local units of administration are far more powerful than standard models of authoritarianism – guided by the idea of iron-hand top-down control – would suggest. Nonetheless, Lieberthal's definition of fragmented authoritarianism operates within a multi-player matrix in which the central government is still a core actor, even though it has to interact with increasingly powerful provinces (Lieberthal 1992: 10). Since the mid-1990s, the process of institutional fragmentation and actor pluralisation has gained momentum. Local projects – such as the construction of dams and hydropower plants – can, as Mertha (2009) has shown, not be designed and imposed by the central-level administration. Local actor groups, involving (GO)NGOs and local media, interfere in the implementation process and, in some cases, even organize local contestation against the implementation of central (or local) government decisions. The outsourcing and the delegation of certain duties and responsibilities from the central to the local government level made them feel and act as partially sovereign and independent players. And, as a side effect of the internal cadre evaluation system that allows local society to express their level of content and discontent regarding local cadres' performance, the latter are willing to choose unconventional methods and proceed beyond established methods in order to overfulfil the official central plan quota and expectations. Assessing developments under the fourth generation, Mertha further argued that the formal democratisation via grass-root, village level elections would never result in an all-encompassing transition towards democracy. The informal pluralisation of actors and the self-organisation of local society could, however, be seen as an incremental bottom-up "democratic participation" trend (Mertha 2009).

Empirical analyses based on the concept of fragmented authoritarianism illustrate that the local adaptation and enforcement of central guidelines by local actors and their local reform experimentations did significantly contribute to economic growth and, thus, helped to stabilise the (autocratic) one-party state (Yang 2013). This seems to disprove the general assumption of early-stage modernisation and transformation theories which predicted that the empowering of local actors would result in the formation of a counter-elite contesting the power and authority of the central government.

The central government, especially since the recentralisation of political power under Xi, is still regarded as possessing the power capacities to implement reforms and central decisions even against the will of local groups. Nonetheless, coercion is still seen as a measure of last resort, and as a steering mode that the central government is trying to avoid. Local governance experimentation is actually the preferred modus operandi as this allows local governments to design solutions that reflect China's regional diversity and specific local conditions.

The daily operations and activities of the overlapping, redoubling mirror structure of party organs and state institutions that is reproduced at all levels of the Chinese bureaucracy have been described by a multi-layer *tiao–kuai* matrix. *Tiao* stands for the vertical relations between organs and institutions located at two different levels of the administration. *Kuai* means the horizontal relations between organs and institutions at the same level (Mertha 2005). The power relations between the *tiao* and *kuai* structures are not formalised but emerge and develop dynamically, resulting from the bargaining processes and interactions of the actors – organs and institutions – involved. Depending on the topic, context constellations and the composition of the actor groups, *tiao–kuai* networks can end up in a multitude of highly diversified power constellations. These constellations include the option of a restrengthening of the higher level party (or state) organ, equalling a return to top-down, centralised steering.

At the 19th Party Congress in 2017, party positions were indirectly distributed according to a silent contract between the party's central level authorities and the Chinese provinces: all members of the (incoming) Politburo Standing Committee had served in core positions at the provincial level of the Chinese party-state, either as party secretary or as head of the provincial government. Other qualification criteria were ranked second to this new balancing strategy between central and local authorities. This new co-optation approach was also silently applied to the re-composition of the Central Committee. Only half of the total number of members of the 14th Central Committee, formed in 1992, had a background in the party-state's provincial administration; for the 16th Central Committee (2002), this number already amounted to 66.7 %. For the 17th Central Committee (2007), there was a 10 % increase, i.e., with the ratio reaching 76 % (Li 2008). This clearly shows that the central party-state authorities hope to fight centrifugal tendencies and to counter some powerful regions' attempts to increase their autonomy via a new strategy of inclusion and co-optation. Simultaneously, central level power capacities have been re-strengthened, especially in connection with the system's proclamation of a "top-level design" (*dingceng sheji*) by Xi Jinping.

3.3.1. Taiwan's Party Landscape

De facto, the island of Taiwan has its distinct administrative, institutional settings with institutions beyond Beijing's direct reach. Taiwan/the Republic of China is governed by a multi-party parliament and a locally elected president. De jure, Taiwan has the status of a Chinese province – as also outlined in Beijing's One-China formula. The concept of One Country, Two Systems (*yi guo, liang zhi*), coined also to pave the way for a reintegration of Taiwan under the direct control and coordination of the Communist government in Beijing, served as the guiding principle for the hand-over of Hong Kong, the former British Crown Colony, in 1997, and the re-transferal of the Portuguese protectorate Macao (in 1999). The One Country, Two Systems formula guarantees the continuation of these special administrative areas' liberal values and specific socio-economic system patterns for a duration of 50 years. The Taiwanese side unremittingly expressed its doubts and concerns regarding the trustworthiness of Beijing's offer and its self-proclaimed dedication to a strategy of peaceful coexistence and non-interference into these special administrative settings.

For the past few decades, the status quo of cross-strait relations was associated with the 1992 Consensus, dating back to a meeting of representatives of mainland China and of Taiwan in Hong Kong, when the latter was still under British administration. The written minutes of this meeting – it should be noted that only the summary of the Taiwanese delegation is publicly available – states that there is only "one China" but that both sides of the Taiwan Strait would have their own views on and interpretation of it. The Taiwanese meeting minutes also contain a passage that states that the Republic of China – albeit claiming a broader territory

– did, de facto, exert its political power only over the islands of Taiwan, Penghu, Kinmen and Matsu.[26]

With the initiation of Taiwan's transition to democracy in the late 1980s and early 1990s, four decades of authoritarian one-party rule and martial law came to an end. Since then, the party landscape is mainly composed of two camps: the Pan-Blue camp clustered around the Guomindang/Kuomintang (Chinese Nationalist Party), the ruling party of the early Chinese Republic that fled to Taiwan during its defeat by Communist troops in the 1940s. It also comprises the New Party (*Xindang*), founded by former GMD members, the People First Party (*Qinmindang*) established in the year 2000, and the Non-Partisan Solidarity Union. The opposition coalition, the Pan-Green camp, is centred on the Democratic Progressive Party (DPP) and involves the Taiwanese Solidarity Union as well as a number of smaller political parties and political movements that, in majority, opt for Taiwanese autonomy and/or independence. The Pan-Blue camp, by contrast, favours the status quo, meaning that, de jure, Taiwan has the status of a Chinese province, but, de facto, is self-administered by local democratic institutions.[27]

Up until the transfer of the permanent seat of China in the United Nations Security Council from the Republic of China to the People's Republic of China, the internationally recognised representation of "China" had been the GMD government with its "interim" power base on Taiwan, officially claiming to represent all of China. This territorial claim covered mainland China, with the Republic of China's capital city Nanking (in Pinyin: Nanjing), as well as the province of Taiwan. The GMD pursued the idea of a liberation of the mainland from Communist control, reduced, a couple of decades later, to the concept of a reunification of both sides of the Taiwan Strait after the end of Communist rule.

Chiang Ching-kuo, Chiang Kai-shek's son and successor, commenced to initiate incremental political reforms in the second half of the 1980s, including the legalisation of opposition parties. In 1986, the Democratic Progressive Party was founded and started to compete with the KMT in parliamentary elections. In 1988, when Chiang Ching-kuo died, Lee Teng-hui became his successor. In 1991, he abolished martial law; in 1996 the first direct presidential elections were held. Even though the opposition parties were allowed to participate and to present their own candidates, it was the KMT candidate Lee Teng-hui who finally won the elections. Scholars and analysts have argued that the reconfirmation of the KMT government was based on the party's successful suppression and elimination of counter-elites during the decades of authoritarian one-party rule and the formation of a new business elite closely connected to the party. One

---

26 "Both sides of the Taiwan Strait agree that there is only one China. However, the two sides of the Strait have different opinions as to the meaning of "one China." To Peking, "one China" means the "People's Republic of China (PRC)," with Taiwan to become a "Special Administration Region" after unification. Taipei, on the other hand, considers "one China" to mean the Republic of China (ROC), founded in 1911 and with de jure sovereignty over all of China. The ROC, however, currently has jurisdiction only over Taiwan, Penghu, Kinmen, and Matsu. Taiwan is part of China, and the Chinese mainland is part of China as well". Cited from: Kan (2014).

27 For an overview of Taiwan's political parties and their agendas – preservation of the status quo versus autonomy and independence – see: Huang/James (2014).

should also keep in mind that even though Lee Teng-hui was a KMT member, he did not belong to the group of *waishengren* (people from outside Taiwan, i.e., the mainland) but was born in Taiwan and did thus stand for a new generation of KMT politicians with a "Taiwanese" identity. As Lee did gradually distance himself from the KMT's "old" paradigm of liberation of the Chinese mainland and instead created the formula of state-to-state relations between the two sides of the Taiwan Strait, he was also able to win votes from the Pan-Green camp. His "Taiwanisation" of the KMT, however, triggered an internal fragmentation of the KMT and fuelled the old rivalry between KMT members from the mainland (*waishengren*) and KMT members from Taiwan (*neishengren*). In 1993, KMT members favouring the idea of reunification with the mainland and those upholding their "mainland" identity formed their own party – the *New Party*. In connection with internal controversies regarding the nomination of the KMT's candidate for the presidential elections in 2000, James Soong, the (former) KMT secretary general, founded the *People First Party* (PFP). Whilst the PFP only ranked second in the presidential elections, it succeeded in winning a comparatively large share of seats in the legislative yuan in 2001. The winner of the 2000 presidential elections was the DPP candidate Chen Shui-bian – a fervent supporter of the idea of Taiwanese independence. Chen even announced holding a referendum and, expecting a majority of supporting votes for his idea, planned to formally declare Taiwan's independence as a sovereign state.

Beijing responded by passing the Anti-Secession Law (2005), which allows the use of "non-peaceful" means in case of a formal "secession" of Taiwan. However, in March 2008, the KMT candidate won the presidential elections and modified Taiwan's position towards mainland China. Moreover, given that the KMT also succeeded in securing the majority in the legislative yuan, open conflict could be avoided.

Free and fair elections are the basic preconditions to subsume a political regime into the category of democracies. For ranking a democracy as a robust and consolidated one, the condition is that elections can (and did) lead to the replacement of the ruling coalition by the political opposition. In Taiwan, presidential elections resulted in three electoral victories of the former opposition, which is seen as a clear indicator for the stability and functioning of the system's democratic institutions.

In January 2016, the DPP's candidate, Tsai Ing-wen won 56 % of all votes in the (direct) presidential elections. The KMT, which had supplied the president from 2008 to 2016, suffered a traumatic electoral defeat by just winning 31 % of votes. For the first time in history, it also lost its majority in the parliament, and ended up with only 35 seats in the legislative yuan (compared to 64 in the previous election). The DPP managed to increase the number of the 113 parliamentary seats from 40 to 68. Once again, with the DPP the pro-autonomy Pan-Green camp took over – generating fears and threat scenarios of a formal farewell to Beijing's concept of "one China". This explicates why, in November 2015 (i.e., in the run up to the elections) the Chinese state president met with the Taiwanese president, Ma Ying-jeou, to symbolise Beijing's support for and willingness to cooperate with the Pan-Blue camp. However, in order to avoid the impression that this would be a formal recognition of Taiwan as an independent, sovereign political unit, the meeting took place in Singapore. Both sides abstained from using official political titles and national ensigns. During Ma Ying-jeou's office term, a partial rapprochement between the two sides of the Taiwan Strait and a deepening of trade cooperation had occurred. The Economic Cooperation Framework Agreement (ECFA), concluded in summer 2010, paved the way for a further opening of Taiwan's economic and trade sectors, including the service sector. The agreement was signed by two associations – the mainland China-based Association for Relations Across the Taiwan Straits (ARATS) and the Taiwanese Straits Exchange Foundation (SEF) – that, officially, did not speak or sign on behalf of the two sides' governments. Protesting against a "selling off" of Taiwan and opposing the ratification of a sub-agreement on the opening of the service sector – the Cross-Strait Service Trade Agreement (CSSTA) was pursued notwithstanding the publicly voiced concerns and reservations of the Taiwanese society – students flooded the streets, built barricades and finally occupied the parliament. This contestation movement – taking place from 18 March to 10 April 2014 – used a sunflower as its symbol, thus bearing obvious allusions to Taiwan's wild lily student protests in 1990. The Sunflower Movement first asked for a clause-by-clause review of the agreement, and later demanded a cancellation of all trade and service sector concessions made by the Taiwanese authorities towards Beijing, and requested additional monitoring measures to oversee Taiwan's agreements and arrangements with the mainland. When a legislative monitoring of the agreement clauses and a postponement of the ratification process was announced, the student protestors vacated the parliament. In sum, the protests as well as their resolution were classified as peaceful ones (Rowen 2015).

Tsai Ing-wen's landslide victory in the 2016 presidential elections thus might be due partly to people's distrust in the KMT's policy towards the mainland and their fear of being integrated in and controlled by Beijing's state-led economy. In January 2020, Tsai was re-elected as president (DPP: 57.13 %; KMT: 38.61 %; PFP: 4.26 %).[28] This reversed the previous trend: prior to this landslide victory, the DPP had faced major losses in the local elections of 2018. In the aftermath of this event, Tsai resigned from her position as DDP chair(wo)man. The Hong Kong Umbrella Protests and Beijing's efforts to restore order by promoting the formulation of a revised Hong Kong security law might have had a direct impact on the 2020 elections in Taiwan. On 10 October 2019, in her speech on the Republic of China's national day, Tsai stated that the "chaos" in Hong Kong would have resulted from the "failure of 'One Country, Two Systems'". She continued by postulating that China was "still threatening to impose its one country, two systems model for Taiwan".[29]

---

28 On the results of the presidential elections in Taiwan, see the summary on the webpage of the Central Election Commission (Republic of China): https://web.cec.gov.tw/english/cms/es.
29 For the full (English) version of her speech, see: https://focustaiwan.tw/politics/201910100004.

3.3.2. Hong Kong

The former British Crown Colony Hong Kong has, as well as the former Portuguese protectorate Macao, the status of a Special Administrative Region (SAR). According to the formula of One Country, Two Systems, created by Deng Xiaoping in the early 1980s, the economic and administrative system settings of the two Chinese SARs, Hong Kong and Macao, would be upheld and guaranteed for 50 years, i.e., until 2047 (Hong Kong) and 2049 (Macao).

The One Country, Two Systems formula was part of the bilateral talks between the PRC and Great Britain to prepare for the planned handover of Hong Kong. On 19 December 1984, Zhao Ziyang and Margaret Thatcher signed a Joint Declaration that included this formula and the related Chinese concessions regarding the preservation of Hong Kong's special system patterns. Later, the formula was also inscribed into Hong Kong's Basic Law. This came into force on 1 July 1997, the day of the handover of Hong Kong to the PRC. Article 5 of Hong Kong's Basic Law states that "the socialist system and policies shall not be practised in the Hong Kong Special Administrative Region, and the previous capitalist system and way of life shall remain unchanged for 50 years". The method to (s)elect the head of Hong Kong's local administration, the Chief Executive, are outlined in article 45:

"The Chief Executive of the Hong Kong Special Administrative Region shall be selected by election or through consultations held locally and be appointed by the Central People's Government.
The method for selecting the Chief Executive shall be specified in the light of the actual situation in the Hong Kong Special Administrative Region and in accordance with the principle of gradual and orderly progress. The ultimate aim is the selection of the Chief Executive by universal suffrage upon nomination by a broadly representative nominating committee in accordance with democratic procedures.
The specific method for selecting the Chief Executive is prescribed in "Annex I: Method for the Selection of the Chief Executive of the Hong Kong Special Administrative Region".[30]

The Basic Law does not contain any exact schedule for the (potential) transition from selection to direct elections. In 2007, the Standing Committee of the PRC's National People's Congress, tasked with evaluating the development of Hong Kong, decided that the 2012 elections would not be based on universal suffrage, but rather announced they would re-evaluate Hong Kong's development and then decide on the election method for the 2017 elections. When, in 2014, the Standing Committee of the NPC ruled that a nomination committee would decide upon a list of potential candidates, and further specified that the Chief Executive would have to be "a person who loves the country and loves Hong Kong" (Xinhua 2014c), street protests erupted in Hong Kong. Whilst these protests brought together a number of different actor groups, the movement became known as a pro-

---

30 Hong Kong Basic Law: https://www.basiclaw.gov.hk/en/basiclawtext/chapter_4.html.

democracy "Umbrella Revolution" demanding universal suffrage for the 2017 elections of Hong Kong's Chief Executive. As Hong Kong's Legislative Council rejected the proposed amendments of the 2017 (s)election process, the selection method of Hong Kong's Chief Executive ultimately remained unchanged. The pro-democracy activists' lost dream of universal suffrage led to a radicalisation of the street protests, with more activist groups – including the Hong Kong Occupy movement – joining in. The latter supported the call for democracy but also engaged in their own crusade against global capitalism and their critical evaluation of socio-economic developments under Hong Kong's Chief Executive Leung Chun-ying. The adherents of the Occupy Central with Love and Peace movement blocked the streets in Hong Kong's financial and banking district. Parallelly, the Hong Kong Federation of Students, led by Alex Chow, and Joshua Wong's Scholarism movement – later reorganised as a political party, known as Demosistō – not only insisted on free and direct elections but also demanded the resignation of Leung Chun-ying, whom they accused of having betrayed Hong Kong. In 2019, several waves of (increasingly radical) street protests followed, reaching another peak with the Hong Kong protests against the plan to pass an extradition law that would have allowed the transferal of Hong Kong citizens to outside courts for investigation and trial. Facing heated protests, the (draft) law was first officially suspended and then finally withdrawn. The withdrawal of the extradition bill had been only one out of five major demands of the student protests ("five demands, not one less"). The four remaining demands comprised the demand for an official "retraction of the riot characterisation" of the protests, for the release and amnesty of the arrested demonstrators, for the instalment of an independent commission for inquiring policy violence, and for the resignation of Carrie Lam and the implementation of universal suffrage.

Emotions reached a new peak when, in November 2019, one of the student protest leaders, Alex Chow, was found unconscious in a car park, and finally passed away after several unsuccessful surgeries. Protesters accused the police of having been responsible for his injuries and eventual death. This triggered a series of university sieges; on 19 November 2019, the Hong Kong police forces finally stormed the campus of the Hong Kong Polytechnic University. The siege ended on 29 November, when most students had finally surrendered.

Beijing did not directly interfere in the Hong Kong's administration's efforts to stop the protests and to restore order. In 2014, the PRC released a White Paper on the One Country, Two Systems principle and the status of Hong Kong (Xinhua 2014b) – outlining and reconfirming Beijing's official position. This could have been planned as an attempt to calm down the protests in Hong Kong and defuse rumours about hidden attempts by Beijing to change the special administrative region's status quo.

Table 8: Chief Executives of Hong Kong SAR

Chief Executive	Office Term
Tung Chee-hwa	1997–2002
	2002–2005
Donald Tsang	2005–2007
	2007–2012
Leung Chun-ying	2012–2017
Carrie Lam	2017–

The non-granting of the right of universal suffrage for the elections in Hong Kong (2016/2017) was simply the final spark that ignited the fire. Those involved in the protests have been growing up in a rapidly transforming Hong Kong economy, where, step by step, large shares of the local economy were taken over by mainland companies and investors. With the opening of mainland Chinese free trade pilot zones, serving also as onshore renminbi hubs, Hong Kong seemed to lose its special financial status and its gateway function for trade and financial transaction directly settled in renminbi. Moreover, living costs multiplied – causing distrust in the Chief Executive's socio-economic development agenda.

Hong Kong's party landscape can roughly be divided into pro-democracy parties and the pro-Beijing camp.[31] The Democratic Alliance for the Betterment and Progress of Hong Kong (DABP),[32] established in 1992 by pro-Beijing politicians, is Hong Kong's largest political party. In 1993, the Liberal Party was founded,[33] which, one the one hand, sides with Beijing, whilst, on the other, supports a liberal economic model. The most powerful democratic parties in Hong Kong include the Civic Party[34] and the Democratic Party[35].

Hong Kong's Chief Executives are known for their pro-Beijing orientation. This is hardly surprising as the election committee reportedly has a majority of Beijing loyalists or, at least, supporters. In March 2018, with the election of Carrie Lam, Hong Kong was ruled by a female Chief Executive for the first time in its history. This did, however, not imply any major revision of the SAR's relations with the mainland.

The ability of the Chief Executive to initiate new pro-Beijing laws and regulations depends on the power constellations of the two party camps in the Legislative Council. According to Hong Kong's Basic Law, one half of Legislative Council members is elected by direct votes (through 5 geographic constituencies), the other half is elected through interest-group based functional constituencies. In

---

31 On Hong Kong's fragmented party landscape that also includes business associations as well as civil society organisations, see: Lau/Kuan (2002).
32 https://www.eng.dab.org.hk.
33 http://liberal.org.hk/en.
34 https://www.civicparty.hk/?q=en.
35 http://dphk.org/index.php?route=information/information/eng.

2012, the pro-Beijing camp won two thirds of all seats. Nonetheless, the one-third minority share still empowered the democratic parties with a veto right.[36] In November 2019, in the aftermath of the protests against the planned extradition law, local district elections were held in Hong Kong that resulted in a major victory of the pro-democracy camp which increased its number of seats from 124 to 388. The pro-democracy camp also won the majority in 17 of Hong Kong's 18 district councils.

In early 2020, Beijing reorganised its Hong Kong-related party personnel. Wang Zhimin, serving as director of China's liaison office in Hong Kong, was replaced by Luo Huining, the former party secretary of Shanxi province. The director of the Hong Kong and Macao Affairs Office, Zhang Xiaoming, was succeeded by Xia Baolong, former party secretary of Zhejiang province. Beijing's two new representatives in Hong Kong openly asked the Hong Kong authorities to initiate laws and regulations to restore national security (*China Daily* 2020). These regulations included the implementation of a new national security law, as prescribed in Article 23 of Hong Kong's Basic Law. Finally, in June 2020, the PRC's National People's Congress passed its own National Security Law (but not Hong Kong's Legislative Council). The new law targets crimes of "secession, subversion, terrorism and collusion with foreign forces" as crimes that can be punished by a maximum sentence of life in prison. The ultimate power to interpret the National Security Law lies in the hands of the Standing Committee of the PRC's National People's Congress.

3.4. PRC: Mirror Structures and Intertwined Institutions of the Party-State

The CCP operates with a hierarchical organisation of the party-state and instruments that allow the party to coordinate the composition of its core leading groups as well as to control the administrative party and state apparatus. The two main control instruments are the nomenklatura system, which the PRC copied from the Soviet Union in the 1950s, and the *bianzhi* system.[37] Both instruments underwent several rounds of modifications and readjustments, and, over the past few decades, were even temporally abandoned. During the high point of the Maoist mass campaigns, local units had more or less independently decided upon the staffing of institutions and the selection of personnel. In the early reform period, the party-state undertook several reform attempts to professionalise the state administration and the selection of qualified state officials. In this vein, the escalations of the contestation movement of 1989 and factional struggles between hardliners and reformers within the party has been interpreted as a response and counter-action to Zhao Ziyang's 1988 attempt to dissolve the party groups (*dangzu*) within the government and state apparatus, which had reduced and limited the Central Committee's power to supervise and control the implementation of the nomenklatura system. Only the highest 1 % of top positions should be coordinated by the party-state, whilst the state administration should rely on its

---

36 See the official webpage of Hong Kong's Electoral Affairs Commission: http://www.eac.gov.hk/en/about/c hairman.htm.
37 Brødsgaard (2012); Burns (1989, 1994); Chan (2004); Edin (2003a); Edin (2003b); Manion (1985).

autonomous mechanisms for the selection of qualified personnel (Burns 1994: 461–462). Zhao's reform attempt was in line with Deng Xiaoping's concept of a separation between party and state (*dang zheng fenkai*), but broke with the formerly practised gradualist, incremental reform mode.

After the crack-down on the 1989 demonstrations, the party tightened its grip and re-strengthened its control mechanisms. The Central Committee's Organisation Department has thus remained the party-state's core management centre for human resources. The nomenklatura lists several thousand of the PRC's top positions, ranging from ministerial positions to chancellors and presidents of universities and the national academies of sciences. As a complement, the *bianzhi* list covers further positions in the state administration, state enterprises and service organisations. The appointment of cadres to top positions is reserved for the organisation department; lower level positions can be staffed based on the decision of lower level organs of the party-state, but this requires the final consent of the Central Committee.

The Chinese debates on restauration and re-strengthening versus the reform and liberalisation of the nomenklatura system illustrate the ongoing power struggles between the central level authorities and the provincial administration and party organs. Via the nomenklatura system the central party leaders are able to fill positions at the provincial level and to decide upon cadres' promotion and demotion. This implies that the inclusion of provincial leaders into the Central Committee would generally enable them to influence the party's nomenklatura and cadre evaluation procedures and to counter attempts by the central party authorities to curb the power of China's provincial leaders. Under the reform-oriented politicians Deng Xiaoping and Zhao Ziyang, the number of provincial leaders present in the party-state's core organs and institutions had been increased; and even the fifth generation sought to co-opt influential provincial leaders by offering them key positions in the party's central organs.

Reforms initiated in 1998, aimed at erecting a small state and setting up a professional state administration, did not lead to the expected results. The general idea had been to outsource duties and responsibilities of the state to the (private) economy and local society. Market mechanisms should allow a self-optimising organisation of these units, the (party-)state would only define the legal framework and outline overarching goals of macro-economic development. Whilst reforms of the nomenklatura system were limited to the highest positions of the (party-)state, the 1998 reforms also reflected modifications of the *bianzhi* system targeting the coordination of open state official positions and personnel appointments at all levels of the administration, and also involving the state business sector and the military. The *bianzhi* system is administered by the organisation departments of the civil sector, not by the Central Committee (Brødsgaard 2002).

In addition to the nomenklatura and *bianzhi* systems, the CCP also defined criteria to evaluate cadres' performance and made a positive performance report a necessary precondition for the promotion of state officials. In July 2002, the Central Committee promulgated the "Regulations for the Selection and Appointment of Leading Party and Government Cadres". Cadres should be promoted based on merit, and, according to this document, taking into account their "character and ability, with emphasis given to character". As part of the reform of the PRC's cadre personnel system, elements of democratic participation have been introduced. Apart from output efficiency, cadres are evaluated and ranked according to their level of loyalty to the party-state and local society's perception and evaluation of their performance. Performance is no longer just measured in quantitative terms of regional economic growth, but also takes into account how these growth rates have been achieved (Shambaugh 2008a: 142). Accordingly, local protests against the negative socio-ecological side effects of high-speed economic growth or people's resistance against illegal land-grabbing and power abuse might relativise or even end local cadres' promotion prospects. Meanwhile, in the 1980s, evaluation criteria shifted from ideology and loyalty to the party to professional performance and management skills. Under the fourth generation, accountability and responsivity were defined as core values; the Central Committee also amended the cadre responsibility system (Edin 2003b).

Whilst Deng Xiaoping and Zhao Ziyang had tried to separate the party from the state (*dang zheng fenkai*) and to reduce the party's control over the company sector (*dang qi fenkai*), under the fifth generation, new instruments of top-down coordinated centralised control have been set up. However, prior to this step, the former post-1989 political party elite had already sought to reinstall party control: in 1992, the 14th National Party Congress put forward the formula of "administration with unified party leadership" (*yi dang ling zheng*), catalysing the re-establishment of party leading groups within state institutions. In the economic and financial sector, efforts to separate the party-state from companies and businesses were continued. In 2015, the CCP initiated a feasibility study on nationwide institutional reform. The Third Plenum of the CCP's 19th Central Committee therefore finally approved the proposal for a reform of party and state institutions. The fourth plenary session, convening in October 2019, added to this top-down orchestrated reform path by passing its decision on measures for the modernisation of China's governance system and for re-strengthening state capacity.

3.5. Reform and Restructuring of the PRC's Administrative Apparatus

Chen Yun once described the planned integration of select market mechanisms with the formula "bird in a cage", with the bird representing capitalism encaged and controlled by the PRC's centrally planned socialist economy. Whilst (modest) liberalisation of the economy was seen as a steppingstone for the realisation of China's catch-up modernisation plans, the "cage" should prevent any unintentional liberalisation effects spilling over into China's political system settings and state–society relations. Nonetheless, the gradual transition to market socialism and the turn to a high-speed economic growth strategy had visible socio-ecological repercussions and created unforeseen new developmental challenges. The rise of a new middle class and the formation of (business) elite networks outside the party implied a reorganisation and partial adaptation of the party-state's steering mechanisms and the opening of additional channels of citizen participation (and additional modes of societal self-organisation).

In 2013, the Third Plenum of the 18th Central Commission addressed long-pending reforms of China's political economy and redefined the country's development strategy. The plenum's 60-point reform package responded to the negative side-effects of the 1978 reforms, such as environmental degradation and socio-economic stratification. These long-term effects had been classified as destabilising factors, aggravating inner-societal tensions and causing the formation of contestation movements. The Fifth Plenum, convening from 26–29 October 2015 in Beijing, outlined the framework of the 13th Five-Year Plan that defined socio-economic core targets for the years 2016 to 2020. The final version of China's five-year plan must be passed by the National People's Congress at its annual plenary meeting in March. The NPC generally follows the lines set by the CCP at its plenary sessions – with the adoption of the 13th Five-Year Plan in March 2016 being no exception.

The 13th Five-Year Plan (2016–2020) prescribes a shift from imitation to innovation. Moreover, the plan underlines the idea of a green and sustainable growth model. It sets the target of doubling China's 2010 per capita income until 2020 – of urban residents as well as of the inhabitants of China's remote, often less-developed rural areas.

According to Xinhua, the PRC's state-owned news agency, eight core points, reflecting Xi Jinping's speeches on governance modernisation within China's one-party system, serve as the 13th Five-Year Plan's invisible backbones (Xinhua 2015):

- Common prosperity (and the upgrading of people's living standards);
- Economic development;
- Improvement of people's livelihood;
- Poverty reduction;
- Ecological civilisation;
- Regional development;
- Reform and innovation;
- International cooperation.

Until its final collapse, the Soviet Union operated with five-year plans – amounting to 12 plans in total. That the PRC managed to stabilise its economy and to avoid a regime transformation thus has symbolic significance, and the passing of the 13th Five-Year Plan marked a major milestone in the PRC's political history. The check dates for goal attainment (of those core targets outlined in the 13th Five-Year Plan) are thus chosen accordingly: the year 2021 stands for the centennial of the CCP; the year 2049 would mark the hundredth anniversary of the founding of the PRC.

In most simplified terms, the reform decisions inscribed into the 13th Five-Year Plan can be summarized as follows:

→ Reforms of the Administrative System and of the State Bureaucracy

To increase the state administration's efficiency, various duties and responsibilities should be outsourced and transferred to the local level administration (subsidiarity principle). Related decentralisation measures had already been introduced by the Hu–Wen administration. The goal is to create professionalised local administrative structures guided by the principles of transparency, accountability and responsivity. An outsourcing of duties and responsibilities might, however, also require a re-bargaining of tax redistributions, which could trigger distribution conflicts and competition for resources. The distribution of resources is coordinated by the central government – which might be facing increased demands from local administrations but will undoubtedly seek to defend its coordination and steering monopoly. Under Xi Jinping, additional rules and regulations, as well as control and supervision mechanisms, have been introduced to secure the correct spending of public funds. These include the recent revisions of the cadre management system's evaluation criteria. Via these evaluations, the party-state seeks to prevent power abuse and to fight corruption.

→ Reforms of the Economic Development Model

The Fifth Plenum (2015) reduced the annual growth target from 7 to 6.5 %. This slowing-down of national economic growth should reduce the risk of an uncontrollable overheating of the Chinese economy and prevent the formation of hidden financial bubbles. The reform decisions ascribe the market a central role in the allocation of resources. The privileges of the state-owned sector should be reduced and some state-owned companies should be transferred to other forms of ownership, for example by allowing private investors and company employees to become shareholders. In general, the reform decisions ask all state-owned companies to increase their transparency and to disclose their financial reports and budget plans to the public. Moreover, the 2013/2015 reform ideas included the break-up of China's state-owned companies' monopolies in the sectors of energy, telecommunication and transportation in order to increase competition and efficiency. As these companies had been (indirectly) subsidised by the state, the liberalisation turn might cause an increase in prices for consumers.

As part of liberalisation pilot experimentations in the PRC's new free trade zone in Shanghai, the party-state introduced "negative lists" for investment. These list everything that is banned or forbidden – implying that everything not listed is allowed. Additional sectors and fields that had formerly been closed for foreign investors have been opened – including the fields of finance, insurance and telecommunication. The step from positive to negative lists catches the Chinese administration flat-footed. All parties involved – private investors as well as the local administration – are uncertain how to read and implement these new lists and how to cope with the withdrawal of former regulations. By limiting these new procedures to pilot zones, the system runs local test runs. As the history of China's special economic zones demonstrates, if these measures are deemed successful, they will eventually be implemented nation-wide.

To secure sustainable growth, additional taxes for products that cause high emissions and consume a comparatively high amount of energy should be introduced. As a consumption-related tax, it would target consumers and force them to change their consumption behaviour. This would, in the long run, cause changes of the production mode and enforce clean and green industries. Chinese economists voiced their concerns and predicted a decline in sales. However, there have been successful examples of similar measures in the past: since the introduction of a small additional fee for plastic bags in supermarkets, litter pollution – also known as white bag pollution (*baise wuran*) – has been efficiently reduced.

Reforms also targeted the income gap and socio-economic discrepancies between urban and rural areas. In this vein, the reform of land-use rights, allowing rural inhabitants to sub-let or mortgage their land, would provide them with the financial backing to pursue a career outside of their home village. Furthermore, additional mechanisms were added to stop illegal land-grabbing and land expropriation by local officials.

→ Reforms of the Financial System

The reform package further included a strengthening of market-based competition via the opening of additional banks and financial institutes. Interest rates should become more flexible and deposits should be guaranteed to make sure people would not turn to the shadow banking sector. As there are no supervision and control mechanisms of informal capital flows in this grey sector, informal money lending poses an incalculable risk to China's financial system. Local communes had resorted to the shadow banking sector to finance local infrastructure projects they had been asked to launch to buffer the spill-over effects of the financial turbulences in the US and parts of Europe in 2007/2008. The measures formulated to reform the financial sector are designed to strengthen the "regular" banking sector and to reduce the system's vulnerability by privately-run lending systems. Additional steps of renminbi liberalisation and exchange rates were also announced.

→ Reforms of the Social Insurance Systems

The public insurance systems (health insurance, pension insurance etc.) shall be reformed and expanded. To finance these services, state-owned companies have been asked to provide the state with 30 % of their surpluses. In the course of the general liberalisation trend and the turn to market mechanisms, private insurance products will be promoted simultaneously.

→ Reforms of (Maoist) Social Steering Instruments

On 1 January 2016, the PRC's One-Child Policy was replaced by a Two-Children Policy. This decision resulted from economic calculations: the enforced shrinking of China's population has caused a hyper-aging process and loss of available labour forces. According to analysts, without the One-Child Policy, in 2015 the PRC's population would not have been 1.37 billion but almost two billion. Whilst the prescribed slowing-down of population growth did allow the PRC to avoid the trap of overpopulation, widespread poverty and malnutrition, the system is now facing the unexpected negative implications of demographic change. Nonetheless, even in the era of the One-Child Policy, some families had more children – even though there were financial sanctions. In the countryside, informally, families often had more children. But these did not have any official documents and thus could never get access to the education system or the social insurance system. As "illegal" people they could not sign a work contract, not rent or buy an apartment, nor marry. According to estimations, there might be about 13 million children without a *hukou* document. Tentative reform proposals include the ex post legalisation of this group. But even these additional millions could not close the gap between demand and availability of Chinese labour forces. Whether the re-steering towards a Two-Children Policy is going to work remains to be seen. China's urban society seems rather sceptical whether they have the financial resources to raise a second child. A general relaxation of the PRC's family planning regulations and policies is rather unlikely to occur. In March 2013, the National Population and Family Planning Commission was substituted by the National Health and Family Planning Commission. The commission is a department under the State Council with the status of a ministry. Despite the renaming of the commission, personnel continuity – Li Bin, a high-ranked party cadre and member of the Central Committee – guaranteed a general continuation of China's demographic control.

Additional reforms of the PRC's social control mechanisms focused on rural–urban labour migration and the *hukou* system. Some tentative reforms were launched; a national consensus for *hukou* transversion was sketched, mainly limited, however, to small- and medium-sized cities.

Both reforms do not stand for any all-encompassing liberalisation of the political regime. They rather mirror the system's focus on economic growth and the regime's calculation that the one-party state needs a stable economic growth rate in order to generate trust and followership based on output legitimation.

Simultaneously, under the fifth generation, new mechanisms of surveillance and control have been introduced, seeking to secure domestic stability. The National Security Commission is tasked with fighting the three evils of terrorism, separatism and extremism. The commission has ties to the police, the military, legal institutions and the secret service. Furthermore, additional structures and control mechanisms in the fields of cyber security were established, under the direct leadership of Xi Jinping. Registration procedures for NGOs were amended and standardised; regulations and restrictions for Chinese and international NGOs were tightened.

→ Reforms of the Legal System

As part of the post-2013 reforms, the labour camp system (*laogai*) has officially been abolished. These labour (and re-education) camps had been criticised by international human rights organisations, as they allowed the detainment of people for several years without any formal trial or court hearing.

Moreover, the reform package included a general strengthening of law- and rule-based governance, adherence to the constitution and the protection of human rights. The petition system should be reformed and decentralised. This step reflected reports about local cadres who had sought to prevent civilians from getting to Beijing to submit a petition so as to silence critical voices and negative feedback that would have had implications for their eventual promotion. Local checks and balances, as well as local channels to report mismanagement or power abuse, would allow local investigation of reported cases. The persistent intertwined relationship between party organs and state institutions, as well as cadres' dual roles in these mirror structures, might, however, impact on these supervision and control mechanisms' autonomy and independence.

→ Urbanisation

In March 2014, the Chinese government released its urbanisation strategy for the years 2014 to 2020.[38] The plan was that by 2020 60 % of Chinese people would live in cities. By 2018, China's urbanisation ratio already reached 59.15 % (a steep increase compared to 2008: 46.54 %). The 2014 urbanisation strategy promotes the formation of metropolitan regions and the founding of new cities in rural regions. The architect behind this urbanisation strategy is Li Keqiang, who did his research on the situation of Chinese peasants and sustainable modernisation strategies under the supervision of Peking University's star economist Li Yining. Li also coined the formula of the New Four Modernisations – of agriculture, industry, information technologies and urbanisation. He thus translated the Four Modernisations (agriculture, industry, defence, science and technology), defined in the early post-Maoist reform period and associated with Zhou Enlai, into the 21st century. Furthermore, already back in the 1990s, Li had warned of the long-term effects of informal migration, the "illegal" flooding of migrant workers into China's megacities. As a countermeasure, Li opted for the construction of small- and medium-sized cities and the gradual urbanisation of the rural areas.

→ Sustainability, Green Growth

The concept of urbanisation seems to be opposed to the overarching goal of sustainability – but only at first glance. Li's "new type of urbanisation" (*xin xing chengzhenhua*), however, favours the construction of modern urban spaces that are characterised by a high quality of life, as they are designed without the negative hyper-urbanisation problems (traffic jams, air pollution, exploding living costs, overload of the public service sector) that haunt China's megacities and

---

38 The Chinese version of the urbanisation plan is available online: http://www.gov.cn/zhengce/2014-03/16/content_2640075.htm.

industrial city clusters. The guiding idea of new urbanisation is the construction of smart eco-cities that entirely rely on e-mobility and smart traffic solutions.

3.6. Summary

Since the decisions on reform and opening (*gaige kaifang*) and the liberalisation of the Chinese economy, the central government has outsourced more and more duties and responsibilities to the lower levels of its bureaucratic state apparatus. By allowing for local policy experimentation and by strengthening societal self-organisation at the grass-roots level, the party-state attempted to increase the administrative system's efficiency. Simultaneously, by opening new channels of indirect participation and by encouraging local self-organisation, the party sought to increase people's trust in and support for the political regime. These decentralisation measures, however, also implied a lingering loss of control of the central level party-state authorities. The setting up of new leading groups, later upgraded to reform commissions, under Xi Jinping illustrates the party-state's awareness of the detrimental repercussions of decentralisation. Centrifugal tendencies and power gains at the provincial level might threaten the survival of the centralist top-down organised one-party system.

Without the post-Maoist decentralisation and the legalisation of the private economy sector, the PRC's rise to the world's second largest economy would probably not have happened. Thus no one in China opts for abolishing local self-administration or private businesses, as they are the mainspring of economic growth. China's central government henceforth operates with a mix of centralist control by the party-state – seeking to control and supervise cadres' work style via incentives and sanctions – and elements of market-based self-organisation.

By setting the concept of top-level design (*dingceng sheji*) as the PRC's new guideline, the Third Plenum of 2013 (re-)confirmed the central authorities' claim to exert control over all levels and sectors. The pooling of power in Beijing and the central supervision of the implementation of the 2013 reforms are expected to secure nation-wide socio-economic cohesion. The need for coordinated reforms of interconnected sectors (e.g., of the economic, the societal and the ecological segment) had been included in the 12th Five-Year Plan, passed in 2011. Like the small (and central) leading teams for reform, the recentralisation of political power and the top-down management of reform implementation is not a new phenomenon of the Xi administration. This said, the proclamation of the top-level design did not break with the previously established practice of local level policy experimentation. Likewise, the coordination between the national five-year plan and local five-year plans reveals a continuing interaction between the various levels of the party-state administration. In order to calculate local development conditions, the central organs depend on information from the lower levels of the state administration. Besides, development goals and strategies for goal attainment reflect the outcome of local level policy innovation and experimentation. Rich and powerful provinces might be tempted to inscribe their distinct policy solutions into the national five-year plan, as this would allow them to make other provinces copy their solutions whilst avoiding additional institutional adjustments and to save adaptation costs. The central party-state authorities are conscious of the power of the provincial level elites – and actively sought to co-opt them by providing them with positions in the Central Committee and other core organs and institutions at the central level.

Despite major reforms of the PRC's economic development model in the post-Maoist reform era, the basic political institutional settings remained unchanged – until the year 2018, when the National Supervisory Commission was added to China's core state institutions. However, this did not imply any general redefinition of China's regime type settings. The PRC continues to be a centrally organised one-party state ruled by a Communist party. After a short intermezzo in the 1980s, when reformist leaders tried to decouple the state from the party, the system switched back to the basic patterns of centralist Leninist organisational principles. Party decisions precede formal decisions by state organs; personal unions and mirror structures of the Communist party and the state apparatus guarantee the party's ultimate leadership authority.

The restructuring of disciplinary control under Xi Jinping and the staffing of the National Supervisory Commission with his cadres ensures the implementation of central reform ideas of the fifth generation and minimises the risk of opposition movements forming.

The majority of resolutions passed since the ascent of the fifth generation in 2012/2013 target power abuse and corruption of party cadres in all three pillars of the system – the party, the state and the military. Factional networks have been dissolved and persecuted; key positions have been re-staffed.

To initiate and enforce institutional reforms, the Xi administration operated based on special commissions and leading groups that act outside of the established institutional settings of the state apparatus. The re-steering of the Chinese political economy in the era of the "new normal" (*xin changtai*), symbolising a formal farewell to double-digit high-speed economic growth, and the active turn to socio-ecological sustainability require the closing or transformation of China's heavy industry sector. Any restructuring of China's state-owned companies will unavoidably trigger contestation and opposition movements. The same holds true for China's state bureaucracy, as political institutions are expected to oppose any changes that might reduce their (political and economic) power. Via special groups and commissions – accompanied by political mobilisation and mass campaigns – the Xi administration seeks to overcome the deadlock of the reform attempts launched by previous leadership generations. Informal structures and internal bargaining processes continue to be the real drivers of the Chinese governance process. The re-steering of the PRC's growth model is coordinated and designed by the CCP and its advisers and enforced via leading groups and commissions. The Third Plenum (2013) did not adopt the 383 reform plan developed by the National Development and Reform Commission but added major changes – to document the party's intellectual leadership.

Interactions with Hong Kong and Macao as well with China's border provinces Xinjiang and Tibet pose a major challenge to the one-party state. The Umbrella

Movement in Hong Kong as well as the Sunflower Protests in Taiwan indicate a growing distrust by these two communities in Beijing's One Country, Two Systems formula. The ongoing political protests in Hong Kong stand for far more than just a regime-type competition between a multi-party system and the PRC's one-party state. With the further liberalisation of the mainland Chinese economy and the establishment of onshore renminbi hubs, Hong Kong's special role as a centre for financial transactions with the West has been weakened. In the first stage of the Hong Kong protests, Beijing reflected the socio-economic dimension of the movement and announced to ascribe Hong Kong a special role in international renminbi transactions. In the second stage, in late 2019/early 2020, Beijing finally sharpened its tone and issued new security regulations to persecute "separatist" movements and local rebellions in Hong Kong.

In a nutshell, the developments and transformations of Chinese politics, summarised above, indicate that governance processes and state-society or state-economy interactions are highly fragmented and dynamically evolving. Instead of taking system patterns and institutions as monolithic structures designed for eternity, the interpretation of governance processes requires a circumspect analysis of the policy paradigms and development ideas promoted by competing factions within (and beyond) the CCP. And, as quite a number of reform decisions made by the fifth generation are inspired by governance ideas developed and discussed in the early 1980s, the interpretation of contemporary politics benefits from background knowledge of China's political history and state philosophy.

Questions for Discussion

- What does the concept of the "party-state" stand for? What kind of mechanisms and steering tools does the party use to secure control over the administrative state apparatus and state officials?
- What does the slogan "bird in a cage" describe? Does this formula still guide and determine the PRC's political economy in the 21st century?
- Does the PRC have a bicameral parliament? What is the role of the Political Consultative Conference in Chinese politics?
- Is the NPC still a "rubber stamp" institution? What are its main functions according to the official state constitution? How did its role and status develop over time, did its institutional autonomy increase since China's entry into the post-Maoist reform era?
- What are the main organisational principles of the CCP? How does the principle of "democratic centralism" work in political practice?
- Which societal groups does the CCP government represent according to the constitution? What are the implications of the CCP's transformation into a "governing" (catch-all) party?
- What is the main content of the One Country, Two Systems formula? When was it developed, what are its legal implications?

References

Brødsgaard, Kjeld Erik (2002), "Institutional Reform and the bianzhi System in China", *The China Quarterly*, 170, 361–386.

Brødsgaard, Kjeld Erik (2006), "Bianzhi and Cadre Management in China: The Case of Yangpu", in Brødsgaard, Kjeld Erik/Zheng, Yongnian (eds.) (2006), *The Chinese Communist Party in Reform*. London; New York: Routledge, 103–121.

Brødsgaard, Kjeld Erik (2012), "Cadre and Personnel Management in the CPC", *China: An International Journal*, 10:2, 69–83.

Burns, John P. (1989), *The Chinese Communist Party's Nomenklatura System: A Documentary Study of Party Control of Leadership Selection, 1979–1984*. Armonk: M.E. Sharpe.

Burns, John P. (1994), "Strengthening Central CCP Control of Leadership Selection: The 1990 Nomenklatura", *The China Quarterly*, 138, 458–491.

Chan, Hon S. (2004), "Cadre Personnel Management in China: The Nomenklatura System, 1990–1998", *The China Quarterly*, 179, 703–734.

China Daily (2017), "CPC Has Nearly 89.5m Members", 30 June 2017, http://www.china daily.com.cn/china/2017-06/30/content_29952238.htm.

China Daily (2020), "Top Official Warns of HK as 'Weak Link'", https://www.chinadaily.c om.cn/a/202004/16/WS5e97ada8a3105d50a3d16899.html.

Edin, Maria (2003a), "State Capacity and Local Agent Control in China: CCP Cadre Management from a Township Perspective", *The China Quarterly*, 173, 35–52.

Edin, Maria (2003b), "Remaking the Communist Party-State: The Cadre Responsibility System at the Local Level in China", *China: An International Journal*, 1:1, 1–15.

Fenby, Jonathan (2013 [2008]), *The Penguin History of Modern China: The Fall and Rise of a Great Power 1850 to the Present*. London: Penguin Books.

Global Times (2015), "Beidaihe Meeting Reportedly Cancelled", 6 August 2015, http://ww w.globaltimes.cn/content/935728.shtml.

Gong, Ting (2008), "The Party Discipline Inspection in China: Its Evolving Trajectory and Embedded Dilemmas", *Crime, Law and Social Change*, 49:2, 139–152.

Guo, Xuezhi (2014), "Controlling Corruption in the Party: China's Central Discipline Inspection Commission", *The China Quarterly*, 219, 597–624.

Huang, Chin-Hao/James, Patrick (2014), "Blue, Green or Aquamarine? Taiwan and the Status Quo Preference in Cross-strait Relations", *The China Quarterly*, 219, 670–692.

Hui, Victoria Tin-Bor (2015), "The Protests and Beyond", *Journal of Democracy*, 26:2, 111–121.

Johnson, Christopher K./Kennedy, Scott (2015), "China's Un-Separation of Powers: The Blurred Lines of Party and Government", *Foreign Policy*, https://www.foreignaffairs.co m/articles/china/2015-07-24/chinas-un-separation-powers.

Johnson, Christopher K./Kennedy, Scott/Qiu, Mingda (2017), "Xi's Signature Governance Innovation: The Rise of Leading Small Groups", https://www.csis.org/analysis/xis-signat ure-governance-innovation-rise-leading-small-groups.

Kan, Shirley A. (2014), "China/Taiwan: Evolution of the 'One China' Policy—Key Statements from Washington, Beijing, and Taipei", https://fas.org/sgp/crs/row/RL30341.pdf.

Kuhfus, Peter (1985), "Chen Duxiu and Leon Trotzky: New Light on their Relationship", *The China Quarterly*, 102, 253–276.

Lam, Willy Wo-Lap (2015), "Growing CCDI Power Brings Questions of Politically-motivated Purge", *China Brief*, 15:3, 7–9.

Lau, Siu-kai/ Kuan, Hsin-chi (2002), "Hong Kong's Stunted Political Party System", *The China Quarterly*, 172, 1010–1028.

Li, Cheng (2008), "A Pivotal Stepping-stone: Local Leaders' Representation on the 17th Central Committee", *China Leadership Monitor*, 23, http://www.brookings.edu/researc h/articles/2008/01/winter-china-li.

Li, Cheng (2012), "Leadership Transition in the CPC: Promising Progress and Potential Problems", *China: An International Journal*, 10:2, 23–33.

Lieberthal, Kenneth G./Oksenberg, Michel (ed.) (1988), *Policy Making in China: Leaders, Structures, and Processes*. Princeton: Princeton UP.

Lieberthal, Kenneth G./Lampton, David M. (eds.) (1992), *Bureaucracy, Politics, and Decision Making in Post-Mao China*. Berkeley: University of California Press.

Lieberthal, Kenneth G. (1992), "Introduction: The 'Fragmented Authoritarianism' Model and its Limitations, in: Lieberthal, Kenneth G./Lampton, David M. (eds.) (1992), *Bureaucracy, Politics, and Decision Making in Post-Mao China*. Berkeley: University of California Press, 1–30.

Liu, Alan P. L. (2009), "Rebirth and Secularization of the Central Party School in China", *The China Journal*, 62, 105–125.

Manion, Melanie (1985), "The Cadre Management System, Post-Mao: The Appointment, Promotion, Transfer and Removal of Party and State Leaders", *The China Quarterly*, 102, 203–233.

McDougall, Bonnie S. (1980), *Talks at the Yan'an Conference on Literature and Art*. Ann Arbor: Michigan Papers in Chinese Studies.

Mertha, Andrew (2005), "China's 'Soft' Centralization: Shifting tiao/kuai Authority Relations", *The China Quarterly*, 184, 791–810.

Mertha Andrew (2009), "'Fragmented Authoritarianism 2.0': Political Pluralization in the Chinese Policy Process", *The China Quarterly*, 200, 995–1012.

Miller, Alice (2008), "The CCP Central Committee's Leading Small Groups", *China Leadership Monitor*, 26, http://www.hoover.org/publications/china-leadership-monitor.

Miller, Alice (2014), "More Already on the Central Committee's Leading Small Groups", *China Leadership Monitor*, 44, http://www.hoover.org/publications/china-leadership-monitor.

Naughton, Barry (2014), "'Deepening Reform': The Organization and the Emerging Strategy", *China Leadership Monitor*, 44, http://www.hoover.org/publications/china-leadership-monitor.

Pantsov, Alexander (2000), *The Bolsheviks and the Chinese Revolution 1919–1927*. London; New York: Routledge.

Renmin Ribao (2014), Zhonggong Zhongyang guanyu quanmian tuijin yi fa zhi guo ruogan zhongda wenti de jueding (Resolution of the Central Committee on Some Major Issues Regarding the Promotion of Rule-based Governance), 29 October 2014, http://politics.people.com.cn/n/2014/1029/c1001-25926893.html.

Rowen, Ian (2015), "Inside Taiwan's Sunflower Movement: Twenty-four Days in a Student-occupied Parliament, and the Future of the Region", *The Journal of Asian Studies*, 74:1, 1–15.

Shambaugh, David (2008a), *China's Communist Party: Atrophy and Adaptation*. Washington: Woodrow Wilson Center Press.

Shambaugh, David (2008b), "Training China's Political Elite: The Party School System", *The China Quarterly*, 196, 827–844.

Sina (2015), Guan mei: Bie deng le, Beidaihe jinnian wu hui (Official Media: No Meeting in Beidaihe this Year), 5 August 2015, http://news.sina.com.cn/c/2015-08-05/174832176559.shtml.

Womack, Brantly (2005), "Democracy and the Governing Party: A Theoretical Perspective", *Journal of Chinese Political Science*, 10:1, 23–42.

Xinhua (2014a), "CPC Graft Watchdog Stronger and Cleaner", 19 March 2014, http://news.xinhuanet.com/english/china/2014-03/19/c_133198413.htm.

Xinhua (2014b), "Full Text: 'The Practice of the 'One Country, Two Systems' Policy in the HKSAR'", www.chinadaily.com.cn/china/2014-06/10/content_17576281.htm.

Xinhua (2014c), "Full Text of NPC Decision on Universal Suffrage for HK Chief Executive Selection", 31 August 2014, http://www.china.org.cn/china/2014-08/31/content_333903 88.htm.

Xinhua (2015), "Eight Key Words in Economic Blueprint that Reflect Xi's Thinking, 27 November 2015, http://www.chinadaily.com.cn/china/2015cpcplenarysession/2015-11/2 7/content_22522883.htm.

Xinhua (2018a), "CPC Releases Plan on Deepening Reform of Party and State Institutions", 21 March 2018, http://www.xinhuanet.com/english/2018-03/21/c_137055471.ht m.

Xinhua (2018b), "Xi Presides over 1st Meeting of Central Committee for Deepening Overall Reform", 28 March 2018, http://www.xinhuanet.com/english/2018-03/28/c_137072 674.htm.

Yang, Zhenjie (2013), "'Fragmented Authoritarianism' – The Facilitator behind the Chinese Reform Miracle: A Case Study in Central China", *China Journal of Social Work*, 6:1, 4–13.

Zarrow, Peter (2005), *China in War and Revolution 1895–1949*. London; New York: Routledge.

Recommended Reading

CCP

Brodsgaard, Kjeld Erik/Zheng, Yongnian (eds.) (2006), *The Chinese Communist Party in Reform*. London; New York: Routledge.

Dickson, Bruce J. (2010), "Dilemmas of Party Adaptation: The CCP's Strategies for Survival", in: Gries, Peter Hays/Rosen, Stanley (eds.) (2010), *Chinese Politics: State, Society, and the Market*. London; New York: Routledge, 22–40.

Zheng, Yongnian (2010), *The Chinese Communist Party as Organizational Emperor: Culture, Reproduction and Transformation*. London; New York: Routledge.

Resilience, Regime Survival, Reform

Dimitrov, Martin K. (ed.) (2013), *Why Communism Did Not Collapse: Understanding Authoritarian Regime Resilience in Asia and Europe*. New York: Cambridge UP.

Guo, Sujian/Stradiotto, Gary A. (2018), Prospects for Democratic Transition in China, *Journal of Chinese Political Science*, 23, 47–61.

Koss, Daniel (2018), *Where the Party Rules: The Rank and File of China's Communist State*.
New York: Cambridge UP.

Li, He (2014), Chinese Intellectual Discourse on Democracy, *Journal of Chinese Political Science*, 19, 289–314.

Li, Yao (2019), *Playing by the Informal Rules: Why the Chinese Regime Remains Stable despite Rising Protests*. Cambridge: Cambridge UP.

Tang, Wenfang (2016), *Populist Authoritarianism: Chinese Political Culture and Regime Sustainability*. Oxford; New York: Oxford UP.

Zhao, Suisheng (ed.) (2006), *Debating Political Reform in China: Rule of Law vs. Democratization*. London; New York: Routledge.

Hong Kong

Gu, Yu (2015), *Hong Kong's Legislature under China's Sovereignty, 1998–2013*. Leiden; Boston: Brill Nijhoff.

Jones, Brian Christopher (2017), *Law and Politics of the Taiwan Sunflower and Hong Kong Umbrella Movements*. Abingdon; New York: Routledge.

Lam, Wai-man (ed.) (2007), *Contemporary Hong Kong Politics: Governance in the Post-1997 Era*. Hongkong: Hongkong UP.

Lee, Ching-Kwan/Sing, Ming (eds.) (2019), *Take Back Our Future: An Eventful Sociology of the Hong Kong Umbrella Movement*. Ithaca; London: ILR Press.

Lo, Shiu-Hing (ed.) (2017), *Interest Groups and the New Democracy Movement in Hong Kong*. London; New York: Routledge.

Wong, Stan Hok-Wui (2015), *Electoral Politics in Post-1997 Hong Kong: Protest, Patronage, and the Media*. Singapore: Springer.

Wong, Yiu-chung (2004), *"One Country, Two Systems" in Crisis: Hong Kong's Transformation since the Handover*. Lanham: Lexington.

Zheng, Yongnian/Yew, Chiew Ping (eds.) (eds.) (2013), *Hong Kong under Chinese Rule: Economic Integration and Political Gridlock*. Singapore: World Scientific.

Taiwan

Blanchard, Jean-Marc F./Hickey, Dennis V. (eds.) (2012), *New Thinking about the Taiwan Issue: Theoretical Insights into its Origins, Dynamics, and Prospects*. London; New York: Routledge.

Copper, John Franklin (2018), *Taiwan at a Tipping Point: The Democratic Progressive Party's Return to Power*. Lanham: Lexington.

Fell, Dafydd (2012), *Government and Politics in Taiwan*. London; New York: Routledge.

Goldstein, Steven M. (2015), *China and Taiwan*. Cambridge: Polity Press.

Guo, Baogang/Teng, Chung-chian (eds.) (2012), *Taiwan and the Rise of China: Cross-Strait Relations in the Twenty-first Century*. Lanham: Lexington.

Hu, Shaohua (2018), *Foreign Policies Toward Taiwan*. London: Routledge.

Lin, Gang (2019), Taiwan's Party Politics and Cross-strait Relations in Evolution (2008-2018). Singapore: Palgrave Macmillan.

Strauss, Julia C. (2019), *State Formation in China and Taiwan: Bureaucracy, Campaign and Performance*. Cambridge: Cambridge UP.

Sullivan, Jonathan/Lee, Chun-Yi (eds.) (2018), *A New Era in Democratic Taiwan: Trajectories and Turning Points in Politics and Cross-Strait Relations*. London; New York: Routledge.

Tok, Sow Keat (2013), *Managing China's Sovereignty in Hong Kong and Taiwan*. London: Palgrave Macmillan.

Macao

Hao, Yufan/Sheng, Li/Pan, Guanjin (eds.) (2017), Political Economy of Macao since 1999: The Dilemma of Success. Singapore: Palgrave Macmillan.

Lo, Shiu-Hing (2008), *Political Change in Macao*. London: Routledge.

One-Child Policy

Fong, Vanessa L. (2004), *Only Hope: Coming of Age under China's One-Child Policy*. Stanford: Stanford UP.

Greenhalgh, Susan (2008), *Just One Child: Science and Policy in Deng's China*. Berkeley: University of California Press.

Whyte, Martin King/Feng, Wang/Cai, Yong (2015), "Challenging Myths about China's One-Child Policy", *The China Journal*, 74, 144–159.

Third Plenum (2013)

Lubman, Stanley (2013), "China Will Struggle to Walk the Talk on Legal Reform", *ChinaRealTime*, http://blogs.wsj.com/chinarealtime/2013/12/03/china-will-struggle-to-walk-the-talk-on-legal-reform/.

Naughton, Barry (2014), "After the Third Plenum: Economic Reform Revival Moves Toward Implementation", *China Leadership Monitor*, 43, http://www.hoover.org/sites/default/files/uploads/documents/CLM43BN.pdf.

Shambaugh, David (2013), "The Third Plenum: Initial Disappointment", www.chinausfocus.com/political-social-development/the-third-plenum-initial-disappointment.

Xi, Jinping (2013), Guanyu "Zhonggong Zhongyang quanmian shenhua gaige ruogan zhongda wenti de jueding de shuoming (Explanation of the Central Committee's Resolution on Some Major Issues Regarding the Comprehensive Deepening of Reforms), 15 November 2013, http://news.xinhuanet.com/politics/2013-11/15/c_118164294.htm.

4. Politics, Law, Political Economy: The (Late) Chinese Empire – The Republic of China – The People's Republic of China

Key Content and Learning Goals

- Introduction to the philosophical and ideational underpinnings of the Chinese legal system
- Overview of processes of constitutionalisation in China, the role of the (socialist) constitution in the context of Chinese governance, and efforts to practice a "rule-" or "law-based" mode of governance
- Introduction to the Chinese Variety of Capitalism and core patterns of the post-Maoist PRC's political economy

State administration, legal system, economy – these are three of the five sectors for which Xi Jinping announced the initiation of reforms that would not be limited to just one isolated sector but be designed as intertwined, simultaneously enforced restructuring processes. The decisions made by the Fourth Plenum of the 18th Central Committee (2014) sought to strengthen rule- and law-based modes of governance in order to further promote the modernisation and professionalisation of the PRC's administrative system. Five years later, the Fourth Plenum of the 19th Central Committee, convening in late October 2019, reconfirmed this development by passing a bundle of reform decisions designed to "uphold and improve the system of Socialism with Chinese characteristics" and "to promote the modernisation of China's governance system and governance capacities".

The PRC's joining of international institutions and its integration into global trade and financial transactions triggered a transformation of national institutions and the adoption of international laws and regulatory frameworks. Nonetheless, the PRC's legal system has not been harmonised with international legal standards but contains regime-specific elements and mirrors fragments of China's (ancient) state philosophy. Likewise, whilst the PRC amended its socialist, centrally planned economy by select features and streams of capitalist market economy, it did not subscribe to the liberal conception of Western capitalism.

The processes of constitutionalisation that China has been undergoing from the late imperial period until now document the tensions between internationalisation and indigenisation (Sinicization) as well as China's oscillations between copying "external" foreign models and the configuration of a Chinese model sui generis.

This chapter sketches China's state-building process based on the drafting and revision processes of state constitutions in the final years of the Qing dynasty, in the decades of the Republic of China, and since the founding of the PRC. The various versions, revisions and amendments of the constitution mirror the ruling elite's views on legitimate rule, the organisation of the state, and its domestic economy and China's development roadmap. For example, a closer look at the first constitution(s) of the Republic of China demonstrates that the Republican state constitution reflected the patterns of the GMD's authoritarian one-party regime. The consecutive passing of follow-up versions of the Republic's constitution mirrored Sun Yat-sen's three-step transition towards a modern state with democratic elements. After an interim period of military dictatorship, the system would enter a stage of political tutelage, before, finally, democratic elements would be gradually introduced at the grass-roots level. Under Chiang Kai-shek, the constitutional settings did not pursue this threefold evolution but erected a presidential-authoritarian one-party regime. The democratisation process of the Republic of China only started in the second half of the 1980s in Taiwan, to where the GMD/KMT government had fled after their lost war against the Chinese communists.

After a short overview of the Republican constitutions, this chapter undertakes a discussion of the main contents and functions of the PRC's state constitution and its revisions, amendments and reinterpretations. In the 1980s, the PRC passed a reform constitution that reiterated the chapters and articles of the PRC's Maoist state constitution. Revisions and amendments mainly addressed the passages on China's political economy. The revisions during the 1990s legalised private ownership, which one would generally see as incompatible with the core fundaments of a socialist planned economy. Elaborating on this paradox, this chapter concludes with some reflections on the redefinition and reconfiguration of the correct interplay between politics and economics under the PRC's fifth leadership generation.

4.1. Constitutionalisation Processes: Philosophical Underpinnings, Historical Evolution, Recent Transformations

The PRC's legal system is inspired by three streams of legal philosophy and legal history consisting of …

- China's premodern state philosophy (and philosophical reflections on the role of law in governing a state);
- Marxist legal philosophy, which served as dominant paradigm in the early years of the PRC, when Beijing was "leaning to one side" (i.e., towards the SU) and copying Soviet institutions and ideology;
- Select elements of international law and legal philosophy imported from the West, especially in the sectors of economic cooperation, global trade, and finance; the compliance with international legal standards was one condition the PRC had to accept when joining international institutions such as the World Trade Organization.

The PRC's oscillations between copying foreign legal traditions and formulating a distinct Chinese definition of law and legal norms can be divided into three historical phases: the Unequal Treaties of the Opium Wars forced the Chinese Empire to adapt to Western treaty law; the Republic of China widely borrowed from European legal traditions and constitutional experiences, though adding some "Chinese" modifications; the Maoist PRC officially relied on Marxist ideas, whereas, since the initiation of economic reforms (1978), the post-Maoist ruling elites have taken inspiration both from Western law as well as from the country's own legal traditions.

The Chinese debates on the nature of law, on the distinction between positive law and natural law, and on the function of law in the steering and coordination of Chinese society are causally connected with the ongoing search for the "best" governance model and for designing the PRC's future development roadmap. In times of major crises (or short-term economic turbulences), these philosophical debates, conducted within China's academic circles, are taken up by the political elites and state-owned media seeking to cherry-pick from the plurality of existing possible governance approaches and governance solutions in order to restore and restabilise the one-party state. When analysing Chinese politics, therefore, one should look out for these turning points and critical junctures as the related "public" debates reveal ideas and concepts that might serve as future guiding principles. Even if the solution eventually passed by the government formally rejects some of these reform proposals, these ideas can be rediscovered and reactivated at a later point, as the fifth generation's rediscovery of select ideas of the early 1980s corroborates.

4.1.1. Late Qing Dynasty – Republic of China

With the Boxer Protocol (1901), the Eight-Nation Alliance – which successfully defeated the anti-foreign, anti-Christian Boxer Rebellion that had been backed by the Empress Dowager Cixi – requested not only the execution of all supporters of the Boxers (*yihetuan*) and provisions for foreign troops stationed on Chinese territory, but also huge war indemnities. As China's previous efforts to restore its national sovereignty and get rid of foreign control via self-strengthening and military modernisation were unsuccessful, the Qing government eventually decided to launch major institutional reforms and to prepare for China's transformation into a constitutional monarchy.

Japan's Meiji Restoration (1868) and the Meiji Constitution served as the constitutional reform's core orientation blueprint. In 1853, Commodore Perry arrived with his warships and forced Japan to open itself up for international trade. To restrengthen Japan, the Meiji reform not only pushed for the modernisation of Japan's military but also opted for a modernisation of political state institutions. The Meiji Constitution, proclaimed in 1889, borrowed from the Prussian and the British constitutions and designed a Japanese version of constitutional monarchy that confirmed the power and authority of the Japanese emperor (*tenno*) as outlined in Chapter 1 of the constitution. According to Article 11 (Meiji Constitution) the emperor commands the army and the navy. Article 13 further ascribes the emperor the exclusive right to "declare war, make peace, and conclude treaties". Borrowing from the British model, the Meiji Constitution established a bicameral parliament: "The Imperial Diet shall consist of two Houses, a House of Peers and a House of Representatives" (Meiji Constitution, Article 33).[39] The Meiji Constitution entered into force on 29 November 1890 and was replaced by a post-war constitution in 1947.

---

39 The full text of the Meiji Constitution can be found online at: https://history.hanover.edu/texts/1889con.html.

The Qing Empire did not translate and duplicate the Meiji Constitution but took it as a starting point for further investigations into foreign law and constitutional practices. In 1908, the Chinese emperor presented the "Outline of the Constitution". The Qing dynasty's preparations for a gradual transition towards a constitutional monarchy were finally disrupted by the outbreak of the Xinhai Revolution (1911). In the aftermath of the 1911 revolution, Sun Yat-sen proclaimed the formation of the Republic of China (1 January 1912). Sun only acted as the Republic of China's provisional president. When the Qing emperor resigned (12 February 1912), Sun ceded political power to Yuan Shikai, the head of China's Beiyang army in Northern China.

On 11 March 1912, the Provisional Constitution of the Republic of China was passed. This first constitution did not even last two years. In 1914, the Provisional Constitution was replaced by a Constitutional Compact. In 1915, Yuan Shikai undertook an attempt to restore the monarchy and to proclaim himself as China's new emperor. The constitution's core principle of power separation was hence never implemented. Yuan finally passed away in 1916 with China divided into spheres of influence and control by local warlords who ruled based on their own laws and regulations.

On 10 October 1923, the Chinese Nationalist Party (GMD/KMT) and the Chinese Communist Party (CCP) replaced Yuan Shikai's autocratic constitution with the Common Programme, drafted by a constitutional assembly. The joint goal stated in this constitutional document was to restore the power of the central government and to secure control over China's provinces.

In 1931, in the early years of the Nanking Decade, the GMD government, headed by Chiang Kai-shek, released a set of constitutional documents that reflected Sun Yat-sen's state philosophy. The 1931 constitution replaced the previous 1924 constitution – for the period of military dictatorship – with a new version explicitly designed for the transitional period of political tutelage.

In the section "General Principles", Article 1 of the 1931 (provisional) constitution stated: "The territory of the Republic of China consists of the various provinces and Mongolia and Tibet". However, even after the Northern Expedition (with the goal to defeat the local warlords) and the establishment of the Republic's new capital in Nanking, the GMD government's power was far from consolidated. Whilst the GMD controlled the cities,[40] the Communist Party continued to expand its influence in remote areas, and later, during the Second United Front and the Second Sino–Japanese War, also over large parts of the Chinese countryside. In addition, in 1932, Manchuria proclaimed itself independent and was transformed into a Japanese protectorate. Later, Japan set up the "independent" puppet state "Manchukuo" and reinstalled the last Chinese emperor, who had been forced to resign in 1912.

The preamble of the 1931 Constitution underlines the importance ascribed to Sun Yat-sen's state philosophy by stressing that the Republic should be based on the

---

40 On state-building processes during the Nanking Decade under Chiang Kai-shek, see: Bedeski (1992).

Three Principles of the People and uphold the principle of a five-fold separation of powers.[41]

The Three Principles of the People (*san min zhuyi*), developed by Sun Yat-sen, consist of "*minzu zhuyi, minquan zhuyi, minsheng zhuyi*" – commonly translated as the three principles of "nationalism, democracy and people's livelihood". The first principle, *minzu zhuyi*, stood for the idea to unite the Chinese people and to jointly oppose oppression and control by foreign powers. The formation of a common Chinese national identity was, according to Sun, the conditio sine qua non to overcome the Unequal Treaties and to restore China's status as an international player with the same rights as other great powers. Sun demanded the abolition of the principle of extraterritoriality, which meant that foreign concessions in China operated beyond the reach of the Chinese authorities. The second principle, *minquan zhuyi*, should strengthen people's political rights. The 1923 version of the Republic of China's constitution hence states: "The sovereignty of the Republic of China is vested in the people as a whole" (Article 2). The third principle, *minsheng zhuyi*, stands for an ambitious welfare state project. The state, as Sun outlined, should provide its citizens with services relating to the four sectors: clothing, food, housing and mobility.

Sun's five-fold separation of power, dealt with in his section on people's rights, is based on Montesquieu's separation of powers into the executive, the legislative and the judicative. Sun added two "Chinese" institutions, inherited from the imperial state bureaucracy. In addition to the three Western branches (or, in Chinese, *yuan*), Sun included the examination *yuan* and the control *yuan*.

Following the attack by Japan (1937) and the formation of the Second United Front between the GMD and the CCP, the young Chinese Republic once again entered a state of emergency and constitutional principles were annulled.

On 25 December 1946, the National Assembly of the Republic of China finally adopted the first non-provisional republican constitution. This event took place in Nanking, at the peak of China's power struggle between the GMD and the CCP. When the GMD government retreated to Taiwan – still referring to Nanking, based on the Chinese mainland, as the capital of the Republic – it remained internationally recognised as sole legitimate representation of "China" until the early 1970s. Having retreated to Taiwan, the 1946 constitution continued to serve as the Republic of China's official constitution. Since the 1990s, after the initiation of Taiwan's democratisation process, this has been further amended and revised.

The PRC, established in 1949, has its own and distinct constitutional history.

4.1.2. Socialism and Marxist Legal Thought

In 1949, the PRC first issued a provisional constitution (September 1949), followed by the First Mao Constitution in 1954. The Mao Constitution underwent

---

41 On Sun Yat-sen's constitutional thoughts and the Chinese Republic's constitutional history, see: Xiao-Planes (2009).

three rounds of revisions: in 1975 (Second Mao Constitution); in 1978, in connection with the decisions on reform and opening; and in 1982 (Peerenboom 2002: 88). The Mao Constitutions were inspired by the Soviet model and reflected the basic institutional settings of the Soviet party-state. The preamble of the Mao Constitution(s) outlines the revolutionary identity of Mao's PRC:

> "In the year 1949, after more than a century of heroic struggle, the Chinese people, led by the Communist Party of China, finally won their great victory in the people's revolution against imperialism, feudalism and bureaucrat-capitalism, and thereby brought to an end the history of the oppression and enslavement they had undergone for so long and founded the People's Republic of China – a people's democratic dictatorship. The system of people's democracy – the system of new democracy – of the People's Republic of China guarantees that our country can in a peaceful way eliminate exploitation and poverty and build a prosperous and happy socialist society..." (1954 Constitution, preamble).

The 1978 Constitution restored many of the checks and balances, courts and procuratorates, and term limits for party leaders that had been deactivated or abolished during the years of political radicalisation under Mao. Symbolically, the text of the constitution underlined the party-state's adherence to Mao and his politics, as the preamble paid tribute to the Cultural Revolution and also proclaimed to continue the revolution: "To persevere in continuing the revolution under the dictatorship of the proletariat, carry forward the three great revolutionary movements of class struggle (...)". But it also outlined a shift to science and (economic) pragmatism by adding the following passage: "(to carry forward...) the struggle for production and scientific experiment, and make China a great and powerful socialist country with modern agriculture, industry, national defence and science and technology by the end of the century". This revolutionary, dogmatic framing finally disappeared in the 1982 version of the PRC's state constitution. The 1982 preamble even makes reference to Sun Yat-sen (who is celebrated as the "father of the Chinese nation" both by the Chinese nationalists and the Chinese communists), arguing that Sun initiated the fight against feudalism and colonialism. The CCP, under Mao's leadership, "ultimately, in 1949, overthrew the rule of imperialism, feudalism and bureaucrat-capitalism" (1982 Constitution, preamble).

The 1982 version has been revised and amended five times (in 1988; 1993; 1999; 2004; 2018), mainly (ex post) legalising the changing modes of production and new ownership structures of China's socialist market economy. Moreover, the CCP transformed itself into a ruling "catch-all" party that represents all strata of the Chinese society.

One should not forget the fact that major adjustments of China's official development roadmap are decided at the National Party Congress (convening every five years in the autumn months) before being put on the agenda of the annual meeting of the National People's Congress (usually taking place in March, i.e., five to six months later). The 14th Party Congress (1992) marked the end of the internal factional struggles between hard-liners and soft-liners who had first clashed over the issue of how to handle the protests of 1989. Jiang Zemin opened the Party Congress with his report and statement "Accelerating the reform, the opening to the outside world and the drive for modernisation, so as to achieve greater successes in building Socialism with Chinese characteristics". With this speech, he introduced the concept of the "socialist market economy", paving the way for further liberalisation of the Chinese labour market and the establishment of free market structures. The main difference between China's market economy and those in the West was that the Chinese economy continued to see state-owned companies as the main players and referred to the private economic sector as a complementary element. The 1993 version of the PRC's state constitution updated the articles on China's economy accordingly.

The 1999 revisions of the state constitution added Deng Xiaoping Theory to the constitution's formal ideological canon (Marxism-Leninism, Mao Zedong Thought). This corresponded with the revision of the CCP's party constitution at the National Party Congress in 1997. The 1999 version of the state constitution once again stressed that the PRC was still in the "primary stage of socialism" and would remain there for another one hundred years. This legalised the PRC's capitalist experimentations as these were not classified as a deviation from the country's journey towards socialism but as a necessary transition phase. This phase is characterised by the coexistence of elements of socialist planned economy and market capitalism. The 1999 version of the constitution upgraded the private sector (Article 6; Article 8). Article 11 even formulated that the "non-public sector of the economy comprising self-employed and private businesses (…) is an important component of the country's socialist market economy".

An additional paragraph was added to Article 5, which anchored the principle of rule *by* law, not to be confused with "Western" rule *of* law, in the state constitution: "The People's Republic of China exercises the rule of law, building a socialist country governed according to law". A new third paragraph was added to Article 3, confirming that "the state respects and preserves human rights". Besides this, some frames and terms were also adjusted. In Article 28, the expression of counter-revolutionary activities was reframed as criminal activities, signalling a final farewell to the (Great Proletarian Cultural) Revolution.

In 2004, the revisions followed the lines sketched above, and thus updated the constitution's ideological underpinnings and fine-tuned the articles on China's economic development stage. The 16th Party Congress (2002) added Jiang Zemin's Three Represents (*san'ge daibiao*) to the party constitution. Even though Article 1 of the state constitution highlights the role of workers and peasants, with the revisions of the preamble, all socio-economic groups are now seen as belonging to the Chinese "people", including not only workers, peasants and soldiers but also capitalist entrepreneurs and intellectuals. In the Maoist years, the latter two had been treated and persecuted as "enemies" of the people. Before the backdrop of the CCP's adoption of the principle of the Three Represents, the 2004 version of the constitution formally empowered the group of private entrepreneurs and confirmed the protection of private property (Article 13). However, these revisions did not imply a replacement of the socialist state-owned economy with the private sector. Given that the iron rice bowl had been lost, Article 14 (new paragraph 4) announced that "the state establishes a sound social security system compatible with the level of economic development". Overall, the 2004 revisions and amendments stand for the party-state's dedication to a modernisation programme which heavily relies on the innovation capacities of the private economic sector but also seeks to balance rising socio-economic disparities.[42]

As the CCP continues to have the final say and to exercise ultimate authority and control, the function of the PRC's state constitution is obviously not to limit and control the party-state's power. Contrary to democratic (liberal) constitutions, socialist constitutions mainly document the system's current stage of economic development and (ex post) legalise the related ownership and production structures.

In March 2018, the National People's Congress passed the fifth revision and amendment of the 1982 constitution. For the first time in the PRC's post-Maoist history, revisions also targeted the institutional architecture of the Chinese state administration. Furthermore, reference to the CCP's ultimate leadership, so far limited to the preamble, was added to Article 1: "The People's Republic of China is a socialist state under the people's democratic dictatorship led by the working class and based on the alliance of workers and peasants. The socialist system is the basic system of the People's Republic of China. The defining feature of socialism with Chinese characteristics is *the leadership of the Communist Party of China...*" (emphasis added).

The revised Article 27 states that all "state functionaries shall take a public oath of allegiance to the constitution". These revisions clearly oppose the idea to separate party and state organs (*dang zheng fenkai*) in order to increase the administrative system's efficiency, an idea put forward by Deng Xiaoping. Not only has the party's grip on the state been tightened, but the 2018 revisions also changed the status and position of Xi Jinping. The term limit for the Chinese president and the vice president, prescribed in Article 79, was lifted. Whilst the post-Maoist constitutions had allowed the president and vice president to serve for two consecutive terms, this decision would allow Xi to act as life-long president. Xi also managed to re-employ one of his close allies and supporters, Wang Qishan, by having him appointed as vice president in March 2018. Previously, at the 19th Party Congress (2017) Wang had to retire from his positions in core party bodies due to the age limit. The preamble of the constitution also complemented the passage referring to Marxism-Leninism, Mao Zedong Thought, Deng Xiaoping Theory, the Three Represents (Jiang Zemin) and the Scientific Development Outlook (Hu Jintao) by "Xi Jinping Thought on Socialism with Chinese Characteristics for a New Era". Additional frames of core speeches on Chinese socialism – such as "socialist core values" or "ecological civilisation" – were also included in the revised version of the constitution. Reference was also made to

---

42 For an overview of the PRC's constitutional history and the revisions of the 1982 Constitution, see: Zhang (2012), Chapter 2.

"harmony" – a term generally associated with the fourth leadership generation and Hu Jintao's concepts of the Harmonious Society and the Harmonious World.

A major revision concerned the constitution's sections and articles on state organs and institutions. The revised version of the constitution contains a completely new Section 7 that establishes a National Supervisory Commission and regional sub-branches as a new pillar of the PRC's state administration (Articles 123–127). This commission does not have the status of a simple ministry but is located at the same level of the administration as the State Council. Over the past few years, test runs with supervisory commissions had been conducted in Beijing, Shanxi and Zhejiang.

4.1.3. Politics and Law: The Fourth Plenum of the 18th Central Committee (2014)

The Fourth Plenum, taking place in Beijing from 20–23 October 2014, focused on issues of party organisation, following the established tradition of all previous fourth plenary sessions. But it also broadened the meeting's agenda by focusing on ruling the country "according to the law" and the modernisation of China's legal system, which also involves the state apparatus and the Chinese military. These contemplations on the importance of law- and rule-based governance reflect the party-state's increased awareness of the rising societal discontent, and contestation movements against local cadres' power abuse and non-compliance with Chinese policies and legal frameworks. Socio-economic tensions have intensified. Online and offline protests against party cadres and local governments indicate a loss of people's trust in the government and its steering capacities.

The decisions made by the Fourth Plenum of the 18th Central Committee send a clear signal to party cadres and the general public that the central party authorities are not willing to accept or to tolerate cadres' misbehaviour and mismanagement. Apart from measures to combat corruption, reform ideas include the establishment of more "independent" legal institutions. Local cadres' attempts to influence local investigations and lawsuits against local level government officials shall be punished. Nonetheless, this does not mean that the entire party-state is subordinate to the law. The communiqué of the Fourth Plenum pointed out that all measures should be in line with the "socialist rule of law with Chinese characteristics". In this vein, the Chinese term *fazhi* is best translated as "rule by law" or "rule-based governance", and should be clearly distinguished from "rule of law".

The Fourth Plenum (2014) also discussed modes of disciplinary control and the restructuring of China's legal institutions. Normative reflections on the function of law and state philosophy were not part of the debates.

With the Four Comprehensives (*si ge quanmian*) Xi Jinping set rule-based governance as one of his four core points for the reform of Chinese governance. In his speeches, parallel to the concept of law (*fa*) he simultaneously stressed the central role of the constitution (*xianfa*) for strengthening governance efficiency. Chinese debates on the role and meaning of the Chinese constitution, as the controversies of the past few decades regarding the relationship between politics and law in the

PRC prove, are closely linked to the abstract configuration of China's governance model. Xi's reference to constitutionalism and constitutional governance could be read as a plaidoyer for political freedom and legal certainty, but also indicates an instrumentalisation of the law and the constitution to stabilise the CCP's power monopoly and to consolidate the political regime. On the 30th anniversary of the Chinese (state) constitution, Xi stated that everyone must abide by the constitution and that any violation of constitutional principles would be punished. In fact, Xi's statement was not a new interpretation of constitutional governance but based on the principles of constitution- and law-based governance as outlined in Article 5 of the Chinese state constitution:

> "The People's Republic of China shall practice law-based governance and build a socialist state under the rule of law.
>
> The state shall safeguard the unity and sanctity of the socialist legal system.
>
> No law, administrative regulation or local regulation shall be in conflict with the Constitution.
>
> All state organs and armed forces, all political parties and social organizations, and all enterprises and public institutions must abide by the Constitution and the law. Accountability must be enforced for all acts that violate the Constitution or laws.
>
> No organization or individual shall have any privilege beyond the Constitution or the law".

Xi's speech, delivered on 4 December 2012, also included passages on the importance of securing and supervising the implementation of the basic principles outlined in the constitution. He also formulated that "the constitution is the basic law of the country, it is the general charter to administer state affairs and ensure national security" and that the "implementation of the constitution" would be the necessary prerequisite for "ruling the country according to the law". Xi formulated four points to achieve these goals: to uphold the political development path of "Socialism with Chinese characteristics", to promote law-based governance and a socialist rule of law, to ascribe the people a central role and to guarantee their rights (the Hu–Wen administration operated with the concept of *minben*, literally understood as "putting people first") and to uphold party leadership. This last point makes clear that the party's ultimate authority and leadership position will not be weakened by Xi's turn to "constitution-based" governance. Celebrated by liberal Chinese scholars as a strengthening of the Chinese constitution and a "constitutionalisation" of Chinese politics, Xi's speech triggered wide-ranging discussions about political system reforms which were stopped before they could initiate a domino effect-like pro-reform movement or cause open factional struggles. Liberal scholars demanded that the party itself should accept the supremacy of the constitution and that there should be equality before the law. The party journal *Red Flag* (*Hongqi*) opposed these demands arguing that this would be a narrow Western-bourgeois, capitalist reading of the concept, incompatible with China's socialist system.

As has been mentioned earlier in this chapter, China's legal traditions also include elements of pre-modern political philosophy and the competition between the concept of "law-based governance" (*fazhi*) and "rule by men" (*renzhi*). The multiplicity of competing concepts of political rule and the function of law became visible during the legendary Spring and Autumn period and the Warring States period, when China's "one-hundred schools" presented their contending conceptions of political rule and political order. Confucian scholars and their idea of moral rule/rule by virtue and the rule of the educated, benevolent emperor (*renzhi*) was countered by Legalist scholars' idea of rule by law (*fazhi*) (and punishment in case of non-compliance). A major point of disagreement between these two camps is rooted in their views on human nature. Those, like Xunzi, who see human nature as "bad", argue in favour of laws in combination with sanctioning mechanisms and punishments. Confucian scholars, by contrast, are convinced of people's dedication to moral self-perfection. Accordingly, societies simply need moral and ethical guidelines instead of laws and penalties. In modern political science terminology, these two positions would best be described by Max Weber's legal-rational versus personalistic-charismatic authority.

The strengthening of rule-based governance does not stand for a democratisation of the PRC's political system. The fact that the term "democracy" can be found in almost every document of the Chinese party-state can be irritating; however, a second look reveals that the PRC operates with concepts of democracy that deviate from the Western-liberal understanding (e.g., "people's democratic dictatorship", "inner-party democracy").

The revisions of the constitution passed by the NPC in March 2018 are a masterpiece example of the CCP's thoughtful framing and wording. The term 法制 *fazhi* ("legal system") was replaced by the homophonous term 法治 *fazhi* – "rule by law"/ "law-based governance". The system operates with abstract terms on which the various factions and actor groups can project their own governance ideas and normative expectations. As these terms often lack a binding definition, the party-state can update its policy paradigms without officially giving up the narratives and core slogans created by previous leadership generations. The *fazhi* word play communicates both policy change (on paper, where readers can find the new characters) as well as continuity and path-dependency (as these two-character compositions are pronounced in exactly the same way).

4.2. Democracy Experimentations: Outdoor Tests and Incubator Labs at the Local Level

One-party systems without open and free elections gain legitimacy via output performance and their ability to provide basic social services and public goods. Whilst the PRC's ruling elites reject the idea of a transition towards free multi-party democracy, the integration of cautiously selected elements of democracy stabilises the system and rebalances state–society relations.

The 12th Party Congress (1982) announced the setting up of "socialist" democracy. "Grass-roots democracy", societal self-organisation at the lowest level of the state administration (at the village level, complemented later by resident committees of urban neighbourhoods) was defined as a core feature of China's "socialist" democracy. The 15th Party Congress (1997) stressed that self-administration at the grass-roots level should rely on democratic elections and general participatory rights. It also mentioned the importance of transparency and accountability of administrative processes at the village level and deliberated over whether to introduce instruments for local society to supervise and evaluate local cadres. The 16th Party Congress (2002) explicitly addressed the promotion of self-administration in both rural and urban areas. Under the fourth generation of Chinese political leaders, the principle of grass-roots democracy was finally inscribed into the party statute (CCP constitution) to complement the system of China's people's congresses, multi-party democracy (under the umbrella and guidance of the CCP) and the self-administration of the autonomous regions of China's national minorities (Yan 2014: 198–199). These conceptions of Chinese-style democracy are omnipresent in almost all official Chinese party documents.

This democratic reference system of the Chinese one-party state stands in sharp contrast to the perceptions of the Chinese system by outside observers. In Western political science research, "democracy" – defined as a system where people have the right to choose and replace their government via free and fair elections (added, in the broader definition, by general participatory rights and liberal freedoms as well as rule of law) – is generally not associated with authoritarian regimes. By contrast, the basic assumptions and classification of autocracies is that ultimate power is concentrated in the hands of the ruler or the ruling elite and that political power is exercised without any legal restrictions and without public participation or control by the public. According to this categorisation, any reference to democracy by the ruling autocrats would just be part of a window-dressing strategy to appease domestic opposition as well as international criticism.

However, one should take into account that the Chinese system operates with its own narratives on and imaginations of "democracy". Mao's speeches and writings reflect on people's democratic dictatorship as well as the principle of democratic centralism. The declarations by China's leading elites during the early reform era reconfirmed the idea of establishing a "socialist" democracy and oppose any transformation that would cause an end to one-party rule.

Elections and modes of local self-administration also exist in the PRC. The PRC's electoral law dates back to 1953; a revised version was passed in 1979 and entered into force in 1980. Members of provincial people's congresses and of the National People's Congress are elected by the people's congresses one level below. According to the (state) constitution, the NPC "elects" the president and the vice president of the PRC as well as the head of the Central Military Commission and the president of the Supreme People's Court. It also "elects" the premier upon nomination by the president. Since the 2018 amendments to the constitution, the NPC also "elects" the chairman of the National Supervisory Commission. Informally, most personnel decisions are made by the CCP, hence there is a continued discrepancy between formal procedures outlined in the constitution and the PRC's "living constitution" and informal constitutional practice.

Refined direct elections have been added to the constitution in the reform era:

> "The residents' committees and villagers' committees established among urban and rural residents on the basis of their place of residence are mass organizations of self-management at the grass-roots level. The chairman, vice-chairmen and members of each residents' or villagers' committee are elected by the residents. The relationship between the residents' and villagers' committees and the grass-roots organs of state power is prescribed by law. The residents' and villagers' committees establish committees for people's mediation, public security, public health and other matters in order to manage public affairs and social services in their areas, mediate civil disputes, help maintain public order and convey residents' opinions and demands and make suggestions to the people's government" (1982 Constitution, Article 111).

In 1988, after a short trial phase, the Organic Law of Village Committees was passed by the NPC. Another round of revisions and amendments followed in 1998. This law prescribes that the members of village committees should be elected by all village inhabitants aged 18 years or older. In bigger villages, they should be elected by the vote of one member per village household for an office term of three years. The duties and responsibilities of village committees are restricted to local village affairs. One fiercely disputed point of the law, causing its introduction on a trial basis, was the relationship between village committees and township governments as well as party units at the village level. The 1988 version of the law outlined the role of the CCP in Article 3: "The primary organization of the Communist Party of China in the countryside shall carry out its work in accordance with the Constitution of the Communist Party of China, playing its role as a leading nucleus; and, in accordance with the Constitution and laws, support the villagers and ensure that they carry out self-government activities and exercise their democratic rights directly" (Organic Law of Village Committees, 1988, Article 3). Moreover, Article 4 of the Organic Law emphasised that "the people's government of a township, a nationality township or a town shall guide, support and help the villagers committees in their work, but may not interfere with the affairs that lawfully fall within the scope of the villagers self-government" (Organic Law of Village Committees, 1988, Article 4).[43]

Elements of local self-administration had already been introduced under the late Qing dynasty, with the Chinese emperor transferring the governance of villages to local elites (merchants, businessmen). These local entrepreneurial brokers were tasked with local tax collection and the provision of soldiers upon the empire's request. All efforts undertaken during the Republican era to exert direct control over the village level were never completed, as the conflict between the GMD government and the Communists, and the imminent invasion by Japan, posed an abrupt end to the establishment of a modern Republican state administration. With the founding of the PRC, the collectivisation of the agricultural sector, com-

---

43 For a detailed discussion of the evolution of the PRC's Organic Law of Village Committees and village elections, see: Alpermann (2001); O'Brien/Han (2009).

plemented by land reform and the confiscation of land from Chinese landlords, changed the modes of party-state control at the village level. As a second step, from 1958 onwards, the PRC started with the instalment of people's communes. With the entrance into the reform era, the household responsibility principle replaced the Maoist collectivisation approach.

Even though the law ascribes the village committees a high degree of autonomy – they are not formally subordinated to any institution – interventions by organs of the party-state, by the township or by the provincial level authorities do occur. O'Brien and Han (2009: 371) stress that "the salary and bonuses of village committee members are determined by township authorities, and levels are set in accord with how well important assignments are carried out. Some localities, in the wake of the tax-for-fee reform, have gone so far as to list village cadres on the township or county level payroll", hence creating new dependencies and empowering the township level. Another challenge village self-governance faces is that not all elections are free, fair and transparent. Local party committees intervene in the process of nomination and (s)election of candidates via informal channels. However, not only the party units or township level governments but also clans and triads are part of local power struggles and interfere in governance processes at the village level.

The revised version of Organic Law (1998) granted the inhabitants of Chinese villages the right to nominate candidates, added regulations for secret balloting and open vote-counting, and also stipulated that "the number of candidates shall be greater than the number of persons to be elected" (Article 14) (see also Tan 2009).

In 2009 additional revisions of the Organic Law were formulated and finally passed by the NPC in 2010. Revisions concern the supreme role of the party:

> "The grassroots organizations of the Communist Party of China in the countryside shall work in accordance with the Constitution of the Communist Party of China, play its role as the leading core, guide and support villagers committees' exercise of functions and powers, and, under the Constitution and the law, provide support and security for villagers to conduct self-government activities and directly exercise their democratic rights". (Organic Law 2010, Article 4)

In addition, the revised version introduced additional checks-and-balances to increase the transparency of self-governance at the grassroots level and the accountability of officially elected village officials. Chapter V of the 2010 version of the Organic Law explicitly formulates that village committees have to "accept the supervision of villagers" and have to display information about their decisions, the implementation of central family planning, as well as the use of funds to the general public (Organic Law 2010, Article 30).

Moreover, the nomination and election process for village committees has become further institutionalised. The 2010 Organic Law also includes articles on the formal requirements and procedures to remove village committee officials from office. Article 16 specifies that a group of at least one-fifth of the village people or one-third of the village representatives is needed to formally recall a village committee official. It also ascribes the latter the right to present a statement and to defend his/her position. When removing someone from office, it is not the total number of votes that counts but the majority of votes cast by those registered for the elections. In addition, the vote is only valid if at least half of the villagers entitled to vote participate in the ballot (Organic Law 2010, Article 16).[44]

The formalisation and institutionalisation of elections at the village level does not imply a turn towards Western-style liberal democracy (O'Brien/Han 2009). The strengthening of local self-administration is a rational response by central level authorities to the regional diversity and specific local development challenges that cannot be ruled from distance. To prevent an overload and collapse of the administrative system, the central government has outsourced more and more duties and responsibilities to the lower levels of its state apparatus (O'Brien/Li 2000).

Participatory elements have also been introduced in urban areas. One of the first local test runs included direct elections at the city level. Nanjing was chosen as the incubator lab for policy experimentation. Prior to this step, direct elections had been tested in Buyun (Sichuan province) in 1998. What all these experimentations have in common is that the number of listed candidates is higher than the total number of seats available. These electoral processes are hence competitive and not just confirming any top-down prescribed decisions.

Since the 1990s, neighbourhood committees (*shequ*) as a nucleus of local societal self-organisation have been set up (Derleth/Koldyk 2004; Xu 2008). The introduction of these new formats of societal self-administration occurred parallel to the reform and restructuring of the *danwei* (work unit) system (Bray 2005). The *danwei* structure, established in the 1950s, organised and regulated urban society. Work units coordinated their members' access to housing, medical services and social welfare provisions (Lü/Perry 1997; Yan 2014: 197). Since the end of the iron rice bowl, many of these social services have been cut or outsourced and privatised.

In the context of the Chinese one-party state, village elections and urban self-administration are instruments of regime stabilisation. Participatory and deliberative elements are seen as essential elements for generating diffuse support. "Democratic" deliberation should, however, not be measured according to the categories of pluralist, liberal democracies. Deliberation refers to public hearings and discourses via which the Chinese public can gather information about political decisions and policy ideas – accompanied by processes of consultation and exchange between (party-)state and society (He 2014). Via these public deliberation loops, political decisions are no longer perceived as "imposed" but display a higher level of abstract legitimacy, as the groups targeted by these decisions have been indirectly involved in the policy-formulation process.

---

44 For a detailed analysis of the 2010 revisions, see: Alpermann (2010: 9–10).

Deliberative procedures are not applied where the basic patterns of China's one-party regime are concerned. When it comes to new laws and policy principles, it is the CCP who pulls the strings and who has the final say. Nonetheless, before a new national law or legal guideline is passed, in many cases, a draft version is first published on the webpage of the NPC, allowing netizens to leave a comment. At the lower system levels, meetings are held with local society to inform people about planned projects and to engage in additional rounds of "open" deliberation (Zhou 2012). In sum, deliberation takes place at all levels and layers of the Chinese one-party state. The 18th National Party Congress referred to deliberation in connection with the concept of socialist consultative democracy and community-level democracy. It is mentioned as a core element of people's democracy, though framed as "consultation" instead of "deliberation": "Socialist consultative democracy is an important form of people's democracy in our country" (Hu 2012). Deliberation is often referenced, especially in Chinese academic debates, as an imported framework inspired by Western political philosophy (inter alia Habermas). Consultative elements, by contrast, are seen as inherited, path-dependent element of Chinese politics. The Chinese People's Political Consultative Conference was one of the first formalised "state" institutions, dating back to the interim period of united front collaboration between the then still-ruling GMD government and the CCP. Whilst deliberation primarily took place as an exchange of views and opinions within the party, i.e., amongst the competing political factions and the party-state's institutions, public hearings and discussions between representatives of the (local) party-state and local (civil) society stand for a more recent development.

In representative democracies, deliberative elements are conceived as correction mechanisms. Deliberative democracy is understood as being a variety of democracy between representative democracy and direct democracy. Whilst, in representative systems, the elected representatives are not bound to the promises made during the election process, deliberation allows the electorate to participate in the policy-making process. Deliberation also allows minority groups to voice their interests, which, in majority-vote-based systems would otherwise remain unheard. In autocratic system settings, deliberation is classified as part of direct democracy (or grass-roots democracy) and hence preferable to liberal representative democracy.

Deliberation, the public discussion of planned regulatory frameworks and laws with select groups of local society, is expected to upgrade the system's governance efficiency and to increase people's support for and trust in the political regime and its institutions (He 2006; He/Warren 2011). Political reforms and institutional restructuring, as well as modifications of the governance process, do not indicate a silent erosion of the one-party state but stand for a re-bargaining of state-society interactions within the framework of the one-party state.

Studies that criticise the Chinese governance process for lacking democratic elements and participatory rights generally operate based on frameworks derived from the theory and practice of liberal democracy to be found in Western social systems. Studies on political culture approach the issue of Chinese democracy from a different angle, posing the question whether (liberal) democracy would generally be compatible with the historical foundations and psychological dimensions of Chinese society, and whether the Confucian heritage would favour the formation of distinct societal-political hierarchies and regime patterns (Nathan/Shi 1993). Shi and Lu (2010), who conducted a public survey to map and evaluate the Chinese understanding and imagination of democracy, concede that the PRC's Confucian traditions did result in a configuration of democracy best described by the Chinese term *minben*. Minben ("taking people first"/"taking people as the root") represents a benevolent mode of patrimonial governance for, not by, the people. Another finding of their survey was that 22 % of people in Taiwan as well as 42 % of people living in mainland China did not have any concrete idea of "democracy". Given that Taiwan is categorised as a democracy, this result is slightly surprising. With regard to the mainland, the survey clearly documents that a positive evaluation of a political regime and its performance does not require the existence of (Western liberal) democratic features. "Good" governance is defined according to principles outlined in premodern Chinese state philosophy and operates with "Chinese" frames and terminology.

The model of democracy as practised by the PRC relies on co-optation and deliberation. Via offline and online channels, the party-state seeks to indirectly involve people in local governance processes – without empowering them to directly impact on the one-party regime.

4.3. Socialism versus Capitalism

Continuing the scenario of Cold War system antagonism between socialism and capitalism, the PRC is officially classified as a "socialist" system and autocratic one-party regime. The Chinese economic system, however, no longer stands for the ideal type of a centrally planned socialist economy. In a planned economy, the production and allocation of goods is centrally coordinated and prescribed by national economic plans. All means of production are state-owned, private ownership modes do not exist. The price is not calculated based on free market demand-and-supply mechanisms but is set by a central authority. Likewise, the state also controls the financial system. State-owned companies do not seek to maximise profits but to fulfil the centrally prescribed production targets and official quota. By contrast, in (capitalist) market economies, production, investment and the distribution of products are self-regulated based on demand and supply. In "free" market economies, the state and the economy are separated, there is no regulatory steering of the economy by the state. Finally, the negative socio-economic side effects of laissez-faire minimal state capitalism led to the theorisation and practice of interventionist modes of market capitalism. In these, the state defines a flexible regulatory framework to guarantee free and fair market competition. In some of these conceptions of interventionist market capitalism, the state also fulfils redistributive functions and provides social welfare services. In the 21st century, the "night watchman" (or minimal) capitalist state is the rare exception. Most economic systems operate with a mixture of free market elements and regulatory frameworks (and economic development plans). The social market economy, to name just one example, combines a free market with elements of social welfare and redistribution measures. In this model, the state intervenes to secure high levels of production and economic growth as well as low levels of unemployment.

The PRC practises its own variety of socialist state-controlled capitalism. The Chinese economy is still coordinated by five-year plans, a concept of central economic planning borrowed from the Soviet Union. The First Five-Year Plan (1953–1957) focused on the collectivisation of the Chinese agricultural sector and the industrialisation of the PRC (supported by Soviet aid and technical assistance). The Second Five-Year Plan (1958–1962) set the target to increase agricultural production by 270 %, added by an ambitious industrialisation programme focusing on China's heavy industry. Mao's Great Leap Forward to surpass the industrialised world in terms of coal and steel production, however, did not result in a threefold rise of the PRC's economic growth rate but instead ended with a severe famine. The Third Five-Year Plan was delayed, covering the years from 1966 to 1970. Again, the focus was on the agricultural sector but, additionally, the plan also targeted the modernisation and upgrade of the PRC's national defence capacities. The formulated goals and proposed quota were far more moderate than the previous plan of the Great Leap years. The post-Maoist five-year plans in general prioritised stable economic growth. Under the fourth (Hu Jintao, Wen Jiabao) and fifth generation (Xi Jinping, Li Keqiang) of Chinese political leaders, sustainable (green) development and the fight against absolute poverty have been highlighted in the official development agenda.

The continued reliance on five-year plans might suggest categorising the PRC amongst command-style, centrally planned economies. However, the one-party state's experimentations with market economy and the formation of a private capitalist sector seem to contradict this classification. Chinese typologies and reflections on the symbiosis of planned economy and market capitalism solve this contraction by positioning the PRC in the "primary stage of socialism". This is conceived as one stage of the PRC's transition to communism and socialism. This classification mirrors the five stages of development (primitive societies, slavery, feudalism, capitalism and socialism). Formally, the notion "primary stage of socialism" was introduced at the 13th Party Congress in 1987. Even before this, however, scholars and political practitioners adopted the term "undeveloped socialism". As this term was perceived as bearing a rather negative view on the development of socialism in the PRC, it was dropped in favour of the "primary stage" (Schram 1988: 177–178). As Zhao Ziyang defined in his report at the 13th Party Congress:

> "Because our socialism has emerged from the womb of a semi-colonial, semi-feudal society, with the productive forces lagging far behind those of the developed capitalist countries we are destined to go through a very long primary stage. During this stage, we shall accomplish industrialization and the commercialization, socialization and modernization of production which many other countries have achieved under capitalist conditions" (Zhao 1987).

At this stage, the main development strategy consists in pursuing the Four Modernisations. Again, this notion was proclaimed in connection with the PRC's decisions on reform and opening. Its origins date back to debates in the early 1960s. But gradual, pragmatic modernisation was superseded by Mao's ideology-inspired catching-up vision of great leap-style modernisation.

After the successful completion of this stage – i.e., when the PRC will have caught up with capitalist, industrialised economies – the system will be deemed ready to enter the final stage of socialism. Deng Xiaoping justified the PRC's embrace of market capitalism with his famous allegoric saying: "It does not matter whether a cat is black or white, the only thing that counts is that it catches the mice". His dedication to a pragmatic orientation of Chinese politics (*shi shi qiu shi* – "seeking truth from facts") signals a clear breakaway from ideology-based political radicalism and utopianism, and dedication to a development model that should improve people's general living standards and reduce absolute poverty. The "primary stage", coined as a transitional period, is a long-lasting interim stage. In his reports at the National Party Congress, Jiang Zemin repeatedly stressed that the PRC would remain in this "primary stage of socialism" for about one hundred years. During these "exceptional" one hundred years, experimentations with capitalism are not only legal but regarded as a necessary step to prepare for entering the next stage.

Over the past four decades, the PRC's turn to its own variety of (state) capitalism has caused a re-emergence of social strata and a widening gap between China's capitalist entrepreneurs and those employed under precarious contract conditions. The Chinese Neo-Maoists, joined by the Chinese New Left, have heavily criticised this development and asked for state interventions and redistributive measures to correct these developments. In Deng Xiaoping's collected writings, these socioeconomic tensions appear to be a transitional phenomenon to be tolerated in order to set up an all-encompassing well-off society. Deng formulated that "some people would have to get rich first" in order to trigger economic growth and create spill-over effects that would trickle-down to all groups (and economic strata) of the Chinese society. The group of capitalist entrepreneurs was regarded as the pioneer force to catapult the PRC to the ranks of the world's leading economies. In this vein, following the reform decisions, capitalists were no longer labelled as "enemies of the people". Since 2002, they are allowed to become formal members of the CCP. To summarise, the transformation and transition of the Chinese economy, discussed above, would be best classified as a "socialist market economy", where overarching development goals are formulated in the central five-year plan. But, overall, implementation and quota achievement rely on the emerging and continuously growing private sector. Contrary to the Maoist years, the PRC's post-1978 development strategy ascribed the market a central role and defined cooperation with foreign companies via joint ventures as a steppingstone to attract investment and achieve an indirect transfer of technological know-how. In 2005, the private economic sector already accounted for about 70 % of the PRC's economic growth.

The combination of elements of planned economy and the market is not a genuine Chinese innovation nor an idea first developed by Deng Xiaoping. During the 1920s, the Soviet Union resorted to a strategy known as New Political Economy (NPE). Lenin's idea was to legalise free market and capitalism under the control and supervision of the party-state. By allowing state-owned companies to operate in a profit-oriented manner, he thought to foster economic productivity. This also included a more flexible tax system for farmers, payable in agricultural products. Farmers were encouraged to produce more grain and were allowed to sell part of their additional production on the market. The NPE experiments also included monetary reforms and initiatives to attract foreign investment. The key industries, however, remained firmly controlled by the party-state. Lenin viewed the NPE as an interim step needed to establish a modern industrial sector and to secure the SU's supply with agricultural products. Following Marx' writings, Lenin defined this move as the only way to secure the material preconditions to finally steer the country towards the final stage of socialism. Stalin ordered an end of the NPE approach and established a centrally coordinated command economy (Fitzpatrick et al. 1991).

Many economic steering patterns of the post-Maoist PRC reveal the persistence of central economic planning under the leadership of the CCP. Despite wide-ranging economic liberalisation and the strengthening of market elements, independent labour unions have not been legalised. Furthermore, many formal regulations of labour relations are unable to keep pace with the transformations of the Chinese labour market currently occurring:

In socialist command economies, unemployment literally does not exist. Nevertheless, the post-Maoist PRC compiles official records and statistics of unemployment. These figures document an unemployment quota of 4 %, which has strikingly remained constant over the years 2005 to 2015,[45] even though the global financial crisis (with its epicentres in the US and parts of Europe) of 2007/2008 caused a wave of job cuts in China. If one takes the official statistics seriously, the stimulus programme launched by the Chinese government would have succeeded in buffering the long-term negative spill-over effects.

Several groups are not included in the official statistics: those who have not yet joined the official labour market are labelled as people "waiting for employment" (*dai ye*). Workers of China's state-owned companies whose jobs were cut during the modernisation and restructuring of the state-owned sector after 1978 are referenced as "laid-off workers" (*xia gang*). They (often) receive a living stipend and have access to social welfare services via their (former) *danwei* (work unit). Moreover, peasants could per definitionem not be ranked as unemployed, as their rural *hukou* bound them to their land where they were expected to earn their own living. Large groups of workers hit by the global financial crisis and the declining international demand for Chinese-manufactured goods were migrant workers. Flooding Chinese megacities from the countryside, these labour migrants

---

45   See Statista: https://www.statista.com/statistics/270320/unemployment-rate-in-china/.

often worked without any formal contract and normally could not register as (temporary) urban employees.

Labour conditions in China underwent tremendous changes. The privatisation and liberalisation of the labour market, gaining momentum in the 1980s, meant that there was no longer any job guarantee or any centralised job appointment. The Chinese government responded by passing new laws to domesticate the spreading Manchester-style capitalism. In 1994, the Chinese Labour Law was promulgated, followed by the Labour Contract Law and the Law on Mediation and Arbitration of Labour Disputes (both entered into force in 2008, the former amended in 2013).[46] The Labour Contract Law stipulates equal rights for employees of state-owned and private companies and also includes the group of migrant workers. It sets a legal framework for labour contracts and prescribes that these contracts must be in written form. The law also rules that contracts have to contain a detailed description of the job and the place of work, and have to include binding regulations concerning the employee's number of working hours, rest and vacation, the renumeration of labour, social insurance as well as working conditions and occupational protection. Workers' arbitration rights have been strengthened. Final sentences are publicly available, so as to provide transparency and to allow workers (and their representatives) to learn more about the interpretation of labour laws and regulations.

The interests of Chinese workers are represented by the All-China Federation of Trade Unions (ACFTU), one of the CCP's mass organisations which was reinstalled in 1978, i.e. after the turbulent years of the Cultural Revolution (when the ACFTU was replaced by revolutionary committees). It is the country's only legal officially mandated trade union. During the Maoist years, the ACFTU mainly served as a "transmission belt" between the Chinese party-state and (factory) workers, simultaneously seeking to achieve an increase in industrial production and to upgrade social welfare provisions for Chinese workers. As salaries were fixed, wage negotiations were obsolete. Job appointments were top-down coordinated; the socialist command economy was based on people's life-long employment. Due to the restructuring of the PRC's state-owned enterprises in the 1990s, the ACFTU lost large shares of its members and, therefore, had to redefine its position and role under the framework of China's mixed economy by also taking the private sector into consideration. The major difference between the ACFTU and independent labour unions is that the former's members are not elected but selected and appointed via party channels. The wage regulations and legal frameworks of collective contracts bargained by the ACFTU are generally in line with the formal suggestions of the central party-state. The ACFTU is also involved in mediation processes of labour disputes. Given that the ACFTU is financed by (state) taxes, critical reviewers see the ACFTU more as fulfilling the functions of an employment (management) agency and not as an organisation fighting for the

---

46 Law of the People's Republic of China on Mediation and Arbitration of Labor Disputes, available online: http://tradeinservices.mofcom.gov.cn/en/b/2013-10-29/27880.shtml.
Labor Contract Law of the PRC, available online:
https://www.ilo.org/dyn/natlex/docs/ELECTRONIC/76384/108021/F755819546/CHN76384%20Eng.pdf.

rights and interests of Chinese workers and employees. In most labour conflicts, the ACFTU acted as a neutral broker and mediator between the conflict parties. The Trade Union Law of the PRC does not grant any formal right to strike but the right of short-term work stoppage or the slowing down of the labour process (Feng 2010).

4.3.1. Chinese Varieties of Capitalism

Comparative studies on political economy categorise the PRC's hybrid economic model as a distinct "Variety of Capitalism" (VoC). Since the beginning of the 2013 reform package passed by the Third Plenum of the 18th Central Committee, the PRC's economic model has once again been modified and adjusted. The market is ascribed a major role in the allocation of resources. Further to promote free market mechanisms and to increase competition, negative lists have been introduced. This should increase the transparency and (legal) reliability for both domestic as well as international investors. Everything not listed is formally allowed. The negative lists are comparatively short and simply confirm a couple of red lines that no one is allowed to cross. Whilst, on paper, this reads like a wholehearted commitment to free market capitalism, a closer look reveals that these lists leave a back door open for ex post readjustments and state intervention. This gap between proclaimed reform procedures and the implementation of reform ideas becomes obvious with regard to the PRC's decision to break up state monopolies and to foster open competition. The developments in China's railway transportation sector are diametrically opposed to this reform idea, as the formerly separated China Northern Locomotive & Rolling Stock Industry (Group) Corporation and the China South Locomotive & Rolling Stock Corporation were merged to form one powerful global player.

More open competition also signals a liberation of prices. Whether or not, in the future, the party-state might accept a market-based regulation of consumer prices is uncertain. Market-based competition does not always result in lower prices. Price spirals and the end of direct state subventions could, therefore, aggravate the existing socio-economic tensions and broaden the gap between the lower income groups and China's upper-middle class. Social justice (*shehui gongping*) is a topic fiercely debated amongst the competing factions within the CCP. Whilst the neo-liberal factions defend the idea of the minimal state, Neo-Maoists and adherents of the New Left opt for active intervention by the state and redistributive measures.

Even after the 2013 reforms and the dedication to market mechanisms, China's VoC still falls into the category of state capitalism, a hybrid economy where the market is loosely embedded into a (legal) framework centrally coordinated by the CCP government.

4.3.2. China's Contribution to Global Financial Governance: Transitions from Keynes to Lin Yifu?

In March 2009, the head of the People's Bank of China (PBoC), Zhou Xiaochuan, openly advocated the idea of replacing the US dollar as the anchor currency of the international financial system with a supranational currency unit. Thus the open power competition for global leadership between the US and China, as predicted by neorealist scholars, does not necessarily occur on the chessboard of military constellations but could also become manifest in the fields of monetary power. Zhou Xiaochuan presented his proposal not as a Chinese attempt to overthrow the US-centred post-World War II international order; he instead reactivated parts of the Keynes Plan, which had once been debated at the Bretton Woods Conference as an alternative to the White Plan. The latter was finally selected to serve as the conceptual backbone of the post-World War II international financial system. Reactivating Keynes' Bancor currency, Zhou proposed an upgrading of the IMF's special drawing rights and the creation of a supranational currency unit. This supranational currency would be based on a basket of national currencies and thus be more robust and not directly affected by financial crises in the country issuing and managing the world's main currency for trade settlement (Zhou 2009).

The Chinese debate on the reform and restructuring of the global financial system and the Bretton Woods institutions does not start with Zhou's 2009 statement. At an international conference in Shanghai in 2004, Li Guanghui outlined three core preconditions to secure a stable development of the international financial system: indirectly addressing the US, Li formulated that the state whose currency functioned as main reference and anchor unit of the international system would have to guarantee the relative stability of exchange rates with regard to the most relevant currencies of international trade and global financial transactions. This state would have to pursue an economic and financial strategy dedicated to building a robust and stable exchange rate system. This would imply that the US would not be able to prioritise domestic economic growth but would have to respond to global developments and reflect the interests of the world society (regardless of the state concerned, it is rather unlikely that any rationally acting government would be willing to sacrifice its own domestic interests for a balanced and stable global system that benefits the development of other, competing, economies). Secondly, with regard to the IMF, Li asked for a strengthening of the role and function of the special drawing rights in order to buffer liquidity shortages. The main task of IMF interventions should, according to Li, consist in the stabilisation of the global financial markets. Finally, Li reportedly underlined the importance of regional and bilateral financial cooperation for upgrading regional currencies to global ones (Li, quoted from Ren 2012:12).

Repeatedly, it was the People's Bank of China and not the Chinese government or party leadership that put forward reform plans to respond to the perceived destabilisation of the global financial system. Shortly before the start of the G20 summit in London, Hu Xiaolian, vice president of the PBoC, proposed to establish a multilateral crisis reaction fund to avoid spill-over effects of the "financial" crisis onto the world's developing countries (*The Wall Street Journal* 2009).

The contagiousness of the Euro-Atlantic financial turbulences of 2007/2008 has been repeatedly mentioned by the Chinese side to stress the need for robust crisis response mechanisms. At the international meeting of the heads of central banks and financial ministers in April 2013, Zhou Xiaochuan iterated the PRC's demand to implement the surveillance and monitoring mechanisms (Integrated Surveillance Decision, ISD) approved in 2011(Zhou 2013). The Chinese side symbolically counters the "patronising and dominant" behaviour of the international community vis-à-vis the states of the Global South in bargaining rounds on financial aid. Since their establishment, the IMF and the World Bank have asked recipients of loans and credits to restructure their socio-economic systems according to neo-liberal principles and to comply with good governance criteria, criticising these systems' economic and financial underperformance. By 2013, the positions and roles had obviously started to shift, with the Global South blaming neo-liberal capitalism for its weak performance and detrimental effects for the global system. Another frequently stressed point on China's agenda (also voiced by the BRICS network) was the implementation of the 2010 quota reform of the IMF. 6 % of the shares and voting rights should be shifted towards the under-represented countries of the Global South, with a special focus being put on the rising economies. In addition, two seats in the IMF Executive Council, held by European states, should be transferred to the group of rising economies. The quota reform was finally completed in 2016, making the PRC the third largest shareholder of the IMF.

The quota reform formed part of a strategic restructuring of international institutions to (symbolically) recognise the growing importance of the Global South – in exchange for these countries' support of the "old" institutional order. This tit-for-tat arrangement worked out: the PRC supported the candidature of Lagarde to become head of the IMF. In return, Zhu Min was announced as new deputy managing director of the IMF. For the first time in the fund's history, a Chinese representative took over this top position – to facilitate the inclusion of the Chinese representative, a fourth deputy position had to be created. Earlier, Strauss-Kahn had already employed Zhu Min as a special advisor to the IMF in Washington. Almost simultaneously, the PRC's status within the World Bank was upgraded. In 2008, Justin Yifu Lin was appointed as vice president of the World Bank. During his time at the World Bank (2008–2012), he managed to amend and reformulate several basic principles and development concepts of the World Bank by bringing in ideas and experiences drawn from the PRC's post-Maoist reform process (on his economic and financial ideas, see Lin 2011). However, the promotion of Chinese advisers and financial experts into the steering circles of the Bretton Woods institutions should not be overrated. In order to increase states' commitment to and support for these institutions, the main strategy has been to include more representatives beyond the world's leading capitalist industrialised economies (Ferdinand/Wang 2013).

Bancor and the Triffin dilemma were keywords of Zhou's 2009 statement. His reflections on the special drawing rights are inspired by the Keynes Plan but do not intend to go back to the 1944 document of the Bretton Woods conference.

In fact, some of his reform ideas are incompatible with Keynes' original plan. Keynes did not design the Bancor as an alternative to existing currencies but as an instrument to correct international balance of payment deficits. The Bancor was pegged to gold. The Bancor was based on a unidirectional convertibility: gold could be exchanged into Bancor, but Bancor could not be cashed in for gold. This measure was expected to prevent currency speculations as they had occurred during the times of bimetallism. Keynes also envisioned the establishment of an International Clearing Union (ICU) to function as the world's central bank. The most revolutionary part of the Keynes Plan was that both debtor states and creditor states should be involved in solving balance of payment issues to guarantee the stability of the international system and to secure global liquidity (Betz 2010: 40–41).

The special drawing right (SDR), which Zhou Xiaochuan invokes, was introduced in 1969, when the US dollar was still pegged to gold, to counter the lurking liquidity crisis of the international financial system. The SDR, a supplementary international reserve asset, is not a currency but a unit of account that – upon its introduction – augmented IMF member states' financial reserves. Originally, the SDR equalled 0.888671 grams of fine gold (equalling the value of one US dollar). When the fixed exchange rate regime was replaced by a system of floating exchange rates, the SDR became based on a basket of (national) currencies. Until 2016, this basket included the US dollar, the British pound, the Japanese yen and the euro. The SDR has gradually emerged as a supplementary global currency reserve unit. Consequently, at the G20 summit in 2009, participant states not only discussed the need to increase the IMF's financial resources by an additional 750 billion USD but also to increase the IMF's SDR to 283 billion USD. As the SDR is linked to a selection of national currencies, it still mirrors the development and financial management of a rather small number of related economies. Nonetheless, the Chinese side continued to highlight the importance of SDR – and, in 2016, the Chinese renminbi was finally added to the IMF's currency basket. Whilst Keynes had opted for "global" financial regulations, the SDR and the IMF currency basket are more in line with the PRC's vision of multipolarity and a world composed of nation-states. This multipolar world would, consequently, also need a multipolar currency system.

The restructuring of the IMF and the reflections on the role of the SDR are not the final outcome of the PRC's demands for reform. Internally, IMF working groups had been tasked with developing innovative solutions for quite some years. In 2010, according to IMF meeting minutes, these groups deliberated ideas for creating a "global currency unit". The 2010 concept papers mentioned two possible solutions: to upgrade the IMF's SDR or to introduce a completely new global currency that would be circulated parallel to national currencies and could, in the long run, ultimately substitute the latter (IMF 2010). In 2011, another IMF concept paper assessed issues of international financial stability and the role played by SDR. This paper already contained the idea of adding more national currencies to the IMF's SDR currency basket. But it also stressed that the free convertibility of a currency would be a necessary prerequisite to include it in the IMF's SDR, thus generally opposing the inclusion of the Chinese renminbi. Nevertheless, some passages of the 2011 paper argued that, due to the renminbi being loosely pegged to the US dollar, its integration into the IMF's monetary architecture would also contribute to the strengthening of US financial power (IMF 2011). So, in 2015/2016, the IMF finally decided to add the renminbi to its currency basket.

Zhou Xiaochuan's vision of a supranational currency unit reflects select streams of international financial theories and does not present a distinct Chinese master-plan for a reformed international (financial) order. It rather mirrors the hidden competition between the PRC and the US for global power status and seeks to overcome the unipolar power structure with the US acting as the coordination centre of world politics and world trade. The ongoing "internal" contemplations by Chinese scholars and politicians after 2009 have attracted much less attention than Zhou's 2009 statement. In April 2013, Yao Yudong (PBoC) presented the idea of setting up a "new" Bretton Woods system and outlined the strategic positioning options of the PRC (Yao 2013).

Whereas Yao's remarks appear rather vague and leave room for interpretation, in his monograph (English version published in 2013), Justin Yifu Lin presented his concrete reflections on a post-2007/2008, post-global financial crisis financial and monetary order. Lin suggested the creation of a supranational, gold-pegged currency unit which he calls "paper-gold". It would serve as a "store of value, medium of exchange, and unit of account for international transactions" (Lin 2013: 201).

None of the Chinese visions of global finance, summarised above, is mentioned in official government documents or statements by the PRC's ruling elites. Nonethe-less, all scholars and practitioners involved in these reflections on the future of the global system maintain close contact with the core institutions and organs of the Chinese party-state. This implies that their visions and recommendations are somehow perceived and deliberated, though not openly documented, in the readjustments to the PRC's domestic and international development strategy.

From 2009 onwards, the PRC intensified its efforts to produce and purchase gold. In May 2014, a stock market for gold was opened in Shanghai, serving as a Chinese counterpart to the stock markets in London and New York. In 2015, the PRC officially declared that it had successfully augmented its gold reserves by almost 60 % (from 1,054 to 1,658 tons). In the world-wide ranking (as of August 2020), in terms of absolute reserves, the PRC is still far behind the US (8,134 tons of gold) and Russia (2,3 tons of gold) and is listed sixth. The PRC thus possesses only about 3.4 % of the world's gold reserves – pegging the renminbi to gold is, therefore, not currently an option. To internationalise the renminbi, the PRC has concluded currency swap agreements with select central banks, and has signed agreements with its major trade partners to settle transactions directly in renminbi. With Angola as well as with Russia, the PRC has established oil-for-loans agreements and is seeking to set up a petroyuan as an alternative to the petrodollar. Whilst these steps strengthened the PRC's monetary power, they did not automatically establish the Chinese renminbi as an international anchor currency or reserve currency.

The background of Chinese dreams and concrete initiatives for a reform of the global monetary and financial systems (Zhou Xiaochuan's SDR concept and Justin Yifu Lin's paper-gold) is the PRC's strategic intention to reduce its reliance and dependence on the US and Washington's currency policies. Lin's monograph departs from the empirical evidence that the anchor currency of the global system is not set for eternity but bound to states' (relative) economic (and financial) power capacities. The rise of an alternative anchor currency or currency unit is possible – and will, most likely, occur again and again. As the historical evolution of the global financial system demonstrates, a uni-currency (and uni-polar) system is generally not immediately overthrown and replaced by a competing, rising alternative currency. Instead, a transition from a uni- to a bi-monetary global system is more likely. The bi-polarity and bi-monetarism of the Cold War years, according to Chinese scholars and analysts, did not stand for a stable unified global system, as the formation of two antagonistic camps caused tensions and overt competition. Chinese policy advisers also warn to not openly present the renminbi as an alternative to the US dollar, as this could make the US resort to containment measures that would prevent the further internationalisation of the Chinese currency. Nevertheless, Chinese scholars see the US-centred global financial system as unbalanced and caught in the Triffin trap: although the US dollar functions as global anchor currency, the US prioritise national development interests over the stability of the global (financial) system.

The strategic options deliberated by Chinese scholars often operate with theories and models developed by international scholars and practitioners – some of which have long since been forgotten in Western debates. Elements of these international debates are currently being recycled and merged with "Chinese" concepts and lessons drawn from the PRC's economic transformation process – and, reaching the "international" debate, are erroneously interpreted as "Chinese" reform ideas opposed to the normative and conceptual backbones of the liberal international order.

4.4. Summary

The modernisation programme of the CCP government and the debates of Chinese intellectuals regarding the correct relationship between politics, economy and law display multiple parallels and similarities to the reform debates of the final years of the Qing dynasty. Back in those days, the debates were centred on China's transition towards constitutional monarchy. In the 21st century, again, the constitutionalisation of Chinese politics lies at the heart of the ongoing reform discussions.

The formalisation of procedures and the consolidation of rule-based governance are referred to as indispensable steps to restabilise the Chinese one-party state. The evolution of the various drafts of the Chinese constitution and the revisions and amendments of the 1982 reform constitution, discussed above, document a shift from ideology-based charismatic rule to a legal-rational mode of transactional steering.

With regard to the PRC's variety of capitalism, market economic reforms and private ownership have been legalised ex post via their inclusion into the revised version of the official state constitution. Reforms have been limited to the PRC's sub-sectors of state administration and the economy; the most recent amendments to the PRC's state constitution (March 2018) have stressed that the one-party regime as such is not part of the reform and restructuring process. Reforms targeting the bureaucratic state apparatus should thus not be misread as "political" reforms.

Via the inclusion of Chinese scholars and advisers, some elements of China's theory and practice in the fields of political economy have been added to the development policies of international institutions such as the World Bank: during his years as vice president of the World Bank, Justin Yifu Lin promoted the idea that developing countries should not be forced to undertake an unconditional transition towards capitalism and to transform themselves into (neo-liberal) market economies. He instead suggested to allow mixed, hybrid formats of state-led economic planning and the economy's self-coordination via the free market. This proposal clearly reflects the PRC's gradual transformation and its distinct variety of capitalism, which is still run by five-year plans but recognises that the market plays a key role in the allocation of resources.

The fifth generation's formal confirmation of rule-based governance does not stand for a transition towards a democratic-pluralist law conception. Democracy and (civil) societal self-administration remain limited to the grass-roots level. The strengthening of rule-based governance is related to the formalisation of administrative procedures at the domestic level and reflects the adoption of rules and legal standards which the PRC agreed to implement when (re-)joining international treaty organisations such as the WTO.

The Republic of China, especially during the ten years of the Nanking Decade (1927–1937), took inspiration from Western systems and sought to establish a modern economic and financial system in line with international standards. The early Maoist PRC first copied the Soviet model and was inspired by Marxist legal philosophy. Already under Mao, the PRC started to define its own version of Marxism and socialist modernisation. In the 21st century, the PRC has once again started to coin its own interpretation of "imported" models by practising (and theorising) its own variety of (state) capitalism. At the global level, the PRC put forward ideas to reform the international (economic and financial) order – presenting solutions that reactivate select streams of the bargaining rounds conducted prior to the instalment of the post-World War II international institutional order. In this vein, the reform statements by the Chinese side do not aim at exporting any distinct "Chinese" ordering principles, as the reform proposals are formulated based on an in-depth reading and understanding of central models and theories that guide international research on the global political economy.

Questions for Discussion

■ What are the main functions of the (state) constitution in the socialist system context of the PRC? Does the constitution limit and control (political) power? Is the CCP bound by the state constitution?

■ What were the core decisions made by the Fourth Plenum (2014) with regard to the strengthening of China's socialist rule-based governance?

■ How can the censoring of articles elaborating on the concept of "constitution-based governance" – published in connection with Xi Jinping's related speeches – be explained? What does this imply for the CCP's general approach to rule-based governance and rule of/by law?

■ Does the liberalisation of the Chinese economic system also imply a liberalisation of the political regime and, in the long-term perspective, a democratisation of the one-party state?

■ Does the PRC operate with a distinct variety of capitalism?

■ Is there any "Chinese" vision for a reform of the international monetary system?

References

Alpermann, Björn (2001), "The Post-Election Administration of Chinese Villages", *The China Journal*, 46, 45–67.

Alpermann, Björn (2010), „Neue Regeln für Dorfwahlen: Revision des Gesetzes der VR China über die Organisation der Dorfkomitees 2009/2010", http://www.regiereninchina.de/uploads/media/Background_Paper_No.1_2010_01.pdf.

Bedeski, Robert E. (1992), "China's Wartime State", in: Hsiung, James C./Levine, Steven I. (eds.) (1992), *China's Bitter Victory: The War with Japan 1937–1945*. New York: M.E. Sharpe, 33–49.

Betz, Thomas (2010), "Keynes Bancor Plan Reloaded", *Zeitschrift für Sozialökonomie*, 47:164/165, 38–48.

Bray, David (2005), *Social Space and Governance in Urban China*. Stanford: Stanford UP.

Derleth, James/Koldyk, Daniel R. (2004), "The shequ Experiment: Grassroots Political Reform in Urban China", *Journal of Contemporary China*, 13:41, 747–777.

Feng, Chen (2010), "Trade Unions and the Quadripartite Interactions in Strike Settlement in China", *The China Quarterly*, 201, 104–124.

Ferdinand, Peter/Wang, Jue (2013), "From Mimicry towards Pragmatic International Institutional Pluralism", *International Affairs*, 89:4, 895–910.

Fitzpatrick, Sheila/Rabinowitch, Alexander/Stites, Richard (eds.) (1991), *Russia in the Era of NEP: Explorations in Soviet Society and Culture*. Bloomington; Indianapolis: Indiana UP.

He, Baogang/ Warren, Mark E. (2011), "Authoritarian Deliberation: The Deliberative Turn in Chinese Political Development", *Perspectives on Politics*, 9:2, 269–289.

He, Baogang (2006), "Participatory and Deliberative Institutions in China", in: Leib, Ethan J./He, Baogang (eds.) (2006), *The Search for Deliberative Democracy in China*. New York: Palgrave Macmillan, 175–196.

He, Baogang (2014), "From Village Election to Village Deliberation in Rural China: Case Study of a Deliberative Democracy Experiment", *Journal of Chinese Political Science*, 19:2, 133–150.

IMF (2010), "Reserve Accumulation and International Monetary Stability", http://www.imf.org/external/np/pp/eng/2010/041310.pdf.

IMF (2011), "Enhancing International Monetary Stability: A Role for the SDR?", http://www.imf.org/external/np/pp/eng/2011/010711.pdf.

Lin, Yifu (2011), "New Structural Economics: A Framework for Rethinking Development", *World Bank Research Observer*, 26:2, 193–221.

Lin, Yifu (2013), *Against the Consensus: Reflections on the Great Recession*. Cambridge: Cambridge UP.

Lü, Xiaobo/Perry, Elizabeth (eds.) (1997), *The Changing Chinese Workplace in Historical and Comparative Perspective*. London: M.E. Sharpe.

Nathan, Andrew J./Shi, Tianjian (1993), "Cultural Requisites for Democracy in China: Findings from a Survey", *Daedalus*, 122:2, 95–123.

O'Brien Kevin J./Li, Lianjiang (2000), "Accommodating 'Democracy' in a One-Party State: Introducing Village Elections in China", *The China Quarterly*, 162, 465–489.

O'Brien, Kevin J./Han, Rongbin (2009), "Path to Democracy? Assessing Village Elections in China", *Journal of Contemporary China*, 18:60, 359–378.

Peerenboom, Randall (2002), *China's Long March toward Rule of Law*. New York: Cambridge UP.

Ren, Xiao (2012), *A Reform-minded Status Quo Power? China, the G20, and Changes in the International Monetary System*. RCCPB Working Paper.

Schram, Stuart R. (1988), "China after the 13th Congress", *The China Quarterly*, 114, 177–197.

Shi, Tianjian/Lu, Jie (2010), "The Shadow of Confucianism", *Journal of Democracy*, 21:4, 123–130.

Tan, Qingshan (2009), "Building Democratic Infrastructure: Village Electoral Institutions", *Journal of Contemporary China*, 18:60, 411–420.

The Wall Street Journal (2009), "China Suggests G-20 Set Up International Wealth Fund", http://blogs.wsj.com/g20/2009/09/22/china-suggests-g-20-set-up-international-wealth-fund.

Xiao-Planes, Xiaohong (2009), "Of Constitutions and Constitutionalism: Trying to Build a New Political Order in China, 1908–1949", in: Balme, Stéphanie/Dowdle, Michael W. (eds.) (2009), *Building Constitutionalism in China*. New York: Palgrave Macmillian, 37–57.

Xu, Feng (2008), "New Modes of Urban Governance: Building Community/*shequ* in Post-*danwei* China", in: Laliberté, André/Lanteigne, Marc (eds.) (2008), *The Chinese Party-State in the 21st Century: Adaptation and the Reinvention of Legitimacy*. London; New York: Routledge.

Yan, Jirong (2014), "China's Experiments in Social Autonomy and Grassroots Democracy", in: Lieberthal, Kenneth/Cheng, Li/Yu, Keping (eds.) (2014), *China's Political Development: Chinese and American Perspectives*. Washington: Brookings Institution Press, 192–210.

Yao, Yudong (2013), "Goujian 'Xin Buleidun Senlin tixi' guanli quanqiu liudongxing zongyamen" (Setting up a "New Bretton-Woods-System" as a Central Organ for Global Liquidity Control), http://forex.jrj.com.cn/2013/08/05081415631403-c.shtml.

Zhang, Qianfan (2012), *The Constitution of China: A Contextual Analysis*. Oxford; Portland: Hart.

Zhao, Ziyang (1987), "Advance along the Road of Socialism with Chinese Characteristics", *Beijing Review*, 30:45, p. I-XXVII.

Zhou, Wei (2012), "In Search of Deliberative Democracy in China", *Journal of Public Deliberation*, 8:1, http://www.publicdeliberation.net/jpd/vol8/iss1/art8.

Zhou, Xiaochuan (2009), "Reform the International Financial System", http://www.bis.org/review/r090402c.pdf.

Zhou, Xiaochuan (2013), "Statement by the Honorable Zhou Xiaochuan, Governor of the IMF for China at the Twenty-Seventh Meeting of the International Monetary and

Financial Committee", (Washington, April 20, 2013), http://www.imf.org/external/sprin g/2013/imfc/statement/eng/chn.pdf.

Recommended Reading

Law, Constitutionalization

Balme, Stéphanie/Dowdle, Michael W. (eds.) (2009), *Building Constitutionalism in China*. New York: Palgrave Macmillian.

He, Weifang (2012), *In the Name of Justice: Striving for the Rule of Law in China*. Washington: Brookings Institution Press.

Wang, Yuhua (2015), *Tying the Autocrat's Hands: The Rise of the Rule of Law in China*. New York: Cambridge UP.

Zhao, Dingxin (2015), *The Confucian-Legalist State: A New Theory of Chinese History*. New York: Oxford UP.

Village Elections

Alpermann, Björn (2009), "Institutionalizing Village Governance in China", *Journal of Contemporary China*, 18:60, 397–409.

He, Baogang (2007), *Rural Democracy in China: The Role of Village Elections*. New York: Palgrave Macmillan.

Landry, Pierre F./Davis, Deborah/Wang, Shiru (2010), "Elections in Rural China: Competition without Parties", *Comparative Political Studies*, 43:6, 763–790.

Li, Lianjiang (2003), "The Empowering Effect of Village Elections in China", *Asian Survey*, 4, 648–662.

Manion, Melanie (2009), "How to Assess Village Elections in China", *Journal of Contemporary China*, 18:60, 379–383.

O'Brien, Kevin J./Zhao, Suisheng (eds.) (2011), *Grassroots Elections in China*. London; New York: Routledge.

Oi, Jean C./Rozelle, Scott (2000), "Elections and Power: The Locus of Decision-making in Chinese Villages", *The China Quarterly*, 162, 513–539.

Pastor, Robert A./Tan, Qingshan (2000), "The Meaning of China's Village Elections", *The China Quarterly*, 162, 490–512.

Sun, Xin (2014), "Autocrats' Dilemma: The Dual Impacts of Village Elections on Public Opinion in China", *The China Journal*, 71, 109–131.

China and Democracy

Bell, Daniel A. (2015), *The China Model: Political Meritocracy and the Limits of Democracy*. Princeton: Princeton UP.

Chen, Jie (2019), *The Overseas Chinese Democracy Movement: Assessing China's Only Open Political Opposition*. Cheltenham: Edward Elgar Publishing.

Ci, Jiwei (2019), *Democracy in China: The Coming Crisis*. Cambridge: Harvard UP.

Ogden, Suzanne (2002), *Inklings of Democracy in China*. Cambridge: Harvard UP.

Shi, Tianjian (2000), "Cultural Values and Democracy in the People's Republic of China", *The China Quarterly*, 162, 540–559.

Yu, Keping (2010), *Democracy and the Rule of Law in China*. Leiden; Boston: Brill.

Zhao, Suisheng (ed.) (2000), *China and Democracy: Reconsidering the Prospects for a Democratic China*. New York: Oxford.

Political Economy

Economy, Elizabeth C. (2019), *The Third Revolution: Xi Jinping and the New Chinese State*. New York: Oxford UP.

Naughton, Barry (1995), *Growing out of the Plan: Chinese Economic Reform, 1978–1993*. Cambridge: Cambridge UP.

Naughton, Barry (2007), *The Chinese Economy: Transitions and Growth*. Cambridge: MIT Press.

Naughton, Barry/Tsai, Kellee S. (eds.) (2015), *State Capitalism, Institutional Adaptation, and the Chinese Miracle*. New York: Cambridge UP.

Perry, Elizabeth/Wong, Christine (1985), *The Political Economy of Reform in Post-Mao China*. Cambridge: Harvard UP.

Ten Brink, Tobias (2019), *China's Capitalism: A Paradoxical Route to Economic Prosperity*. Philadelphia: University of Pennsylvania Press.

Zeng, Ka (ed.) (2019), *Handbook on the International Political Economy of China*. Cheltenham: Edward Elgar Publishing.

5. Actors and Interactions: Pluralisation and Fragmentation of State–Society Relations

Key Content and Learning Goals

- Overview of select (socio-economic) actor groups and their interactions with the Chinese party-state
- Introduction to modes of legitimate resistance and channels of indirect participation
- Critical evaluation of the role of the Internet in non-democratic systems

Analyses of processes of political decision-making tend to focus on the PRC's political elites and highlight the charismatic authority of Mao (as well as, most recently, of Xi Jinping). Factional struggles within the CCP, as well as the role of political advisers and party theoreticians in the drafting of policies and development strategies, are often treated as a peripheral phenomenon. Given that the PRC's decision-making process remains controlled by the party and information about background bargaining rounds is not publicly displayed, the ways to assess the role of the "invisible" architects of the PRC's governance approach are, indeed, rather labyrinthine. The posthumous release of Chinese politicians' autobiographies or the opening of archives only allows for ex post reconstruction of (past) actor constellations and internal policy debates. In retrospect, resulting from the critical evaluation of archival material, Mao is no longer seen as the PRC's ultimate chairman steering (and monopolising) the policy-making process. This hidden fragmentation of the Chinese governance process and the existence of a plurality of actors involved has become more even obvious since the PRC's entrance into the era of reform and opening.

The de-collectivisation and the mushrooming of the private sector were accompanied by a partial outsourcing of central level administration duties to provincial governments and by a general strengthening of local level self-administration. This led to an increasing fragmentation of the Chinese party-state and the emergence of a patchwork of policy experimentations by local governments. Furthermore, the legalisation of the private economic sector opened career opportunities outside the party sector. The PRC underwent a transition from totalitarian to authoritarian rule; the early 1980s were characterised by a pluralisation of actors and policy ideas. Instead of imposing top-down decisions, the party-state engaged in bargaining and deliberation processes with advisers and relevant socio-economic actors. Even though Xi Jinping launched a re-centralisation and re-personalisation of Chinese politics, state–society interactions are clearly evolving dynamically and are being continuously re-bargained.

The following chapter assesses select relevant actor groups and sheds light on their role in policy-making and policy-implementation. It provides the reader with an overview of factions and factionalism within the CCP, sketches the role of the Chinese military as a political actor and takes a closer look at China's competing socio-economic actor groups in urban and rural settings. Finally, it also addresses offline and online modes of (civil) society contestation movements and the phenomenon of rightful resistance. The Internet, initially expected to trigger the downfall of the world's remaining autocracies and to empower civil society, has turned out to have contributed to the stabilisation and re-legitimation of the Chinese party-state. It should, however, neither be reduced to a "weapon" of civil society to fight against a repressive one-party state *nor* to an instrument of political mobilisation and control – as the short literature review on the evolution and transformation of the Chinese Internet will show. Empirical research on the online dimension of Chinese politics and state–society interactions proves that the Internet is best regarded as an additional realm where state–society relations are re-bargained and modified. Cyberspace interactions reveal some of the hidden dynamics underlying the PRC's most recent policy innovations and reforms of inherited political institutions.

5.1. Competing Positions and Agendas within the CCP

5.1.1. Factions and "Democratic Parties"

Chinese "factions" are informal political wings – groups of people with shared interests and policy ideas – within the CCP. They may be united by shared experience and educational training, they can belong to the same institution and defend that institution's strategic interests, or they can simply adhere to one specific socio-economic development strategy. Often hierarchically structured as patron–client relations, factions function as invisible job ladders. The rise of a new generation of Chinese leaders is informally coordinated and managed by influential patrons. These are often members of the outgoing leadership generation who seek to secure power by promoting members of their own factional network. Jiang Zemin (belonging to the third generation of political leaders) is regarded as the patron of the so-called Shanghai Clique (*Shanghai bang*), a factional network dating back to Jiang's time as mayor and party secretary of Shanghai. Another influential faction is the Youth League of the CCP (*tuanpai*), positioning itself as a network advocating reform, supporting the ideas put forward by Hu Yaobang in the early 1980s. The power of this faction increased again with the promotion of Hu Jintao (belonging to the fourth generation) to the position of CCP general secretary in 2002. A more recent factional network is the group of princelings (*dangpai*), a label used for the children of high-ranked CCP cadres. Xi Jinping, who took the helm of the party-state in 2012/2013, is the son of Xi Zhongxun, belonging to the first generation of CCP revolutionaries.[47]

Aside from genealogy-based factions, informal networks are often built on shared educational backgrounds and institutional affiliations. Under the Hu–Wen administration, many alumni of the Tsinghua University in Beijing were promoted to the party-state's top positions. The Tsinghua Clique is regarded as standing for a moderate-reformist development path.

---

47 For a short biographic sketch, see: http://www.chinavitae.com.

Beyond the categorisation of interest groups along the lines of factions and patron–client networks, another approach operates with the concept of leadership generations. The first generation of CCP politicians, with Mao Zedong as its figurehead, was shaped by their shared experience of the Long March, the War of Resistance against Japan and the civil war between the Chinese Nationalists (GMD) and the CCP. This first generation eventually proclaimed the founding of the PRC and stands for the revolutionary restructuring and renewal of the Chinese society. Politics, as conducted by this first generation, was characterised by ideological radicalisation and iconoclasm. The main goal was to get rid of feudal, bourgeois values and to establish a centralised one-party state inspired by Soviet socialism.

The second generation of Chinese political leaders, associated with the reformist politician Deng Xiaoping, took part in the Long March but was itself amongst the victims and targets of the Maoist mass campaigns. Many of them were labelled as rightists or capitalist roaders and were persecuted and mistreated during the years of the Cultural Revolution. Under the aegis of this second generation, the PRC passed the decisions on reform and opening and initiated the cautious integration of market capitalist elements into China's socialist planned economy.

The third generation, centred around Jiang Zemin, rose to power in the early 1990s. This third generation is regarded as far more fragmented and heterogenous than the previous two. A number of third generation politicians were still inspired by Soviet ideas, some of them had even spent some years as exchange students in the SU. Members of this sub-group of the third generation are known as hardliners, iron defenders of the "old" centralist and totalitarian one-party state. Nonetheless, under their leadership, the opening of the PRC for foreign companies and foreign direct investment was continued. In 1992 most sanctions imposed on the PRC as a response and sanctioning of Beijing's crack-down on the demonstrations in Tian'anmen Square were finally lifted (except the arms embargo) and economic as well as diplomatic relations were restored.

With the rise of the fourth generation, represented by Hu Jintao and Wen Jiabao, the group of Chinese technocrats entered the Zhongnanhai, the central headquarters of the CCP and the State Council in Beijing. Those promoted to the top echelons of the party-state were mostly engineers without major revolutionary experience. Contrary to the previous generations, they cannot refer to their glorious contribution to the Chinese Revolution to symbolically justify and legitimate their rule. The fourth generation, therefore, relied not solely on ideological legitimation – by adhering to (sinicized) Marxism – but operated via output performance and output legitimation.

The fifth generation, centred around Xi Jinping (and, during the early years of the first office term, Li Keqiang), took over in 2012/2013. The composition of this generation differs significantly from all earlier ones. Members of this generation often have university degrees in law, economics or finance. Many of them also work in the private economic sector. Some have studied in Europe or the US;

all of them are familiar with Western political-economic theories and governance ideas.

The approach to reduce Chinese politics to the official speeches and written documents of the Chinese leadership creates the impression of a consistent and coherent development of Chinese politics. The focus lies on the elite level: socio-economic actor groups outside the party are generally not taken into account. The factionalism approach, by contrast, counters the assumption of a unified, monolithic one-party state and stresses the dimension of intra-elite competition. It opens the black box of the Chinese party-state by looking at central conflict lines and the main factions involved in these internal struggles. Examples of this approach include the struggle between two lines of the Mao era as well as the 2012 competition between the Chongqing Model and the Guangdong Model. The outbreak of the latter evidences that factional struggles still continue and, internally, the CCP remains divided into competing ideological camps. The 2012 controversy centred on the design of the future development path of the PRC and the relationship between socialist economic planning and capitalist market mechanisms. The Guangdong Model, associated with Wang Yang (2007–2013 party secretary of Guangdong province, located in the southeast of China), favoured a minimal state and prioritised the private economic sector. Even when facing the destabilising spill-over effects of the financial crisis in the US (and parts of Europe) in 2007/2008 that threatened the survival of small- and medium-sized enterprises and companies in Guangdong, Wang Yang opposed the stimulus plan and state intervention strategy propagated by the central government in Beijing. He instead stressed that the local economy would have to reposition and coordinate itself via market mechanisms. Wang Yang is not only known for his dedication to a neo-liberal development concept, but also for his promotion of moderate political reforms at the local (grass-roots) level. In 2011, protests erupted in Wukan, where villagers opposed the instalment of a new village committee and protested against illegal land grabs. These protests were not silenced by sending special police forces (or military units), but were solved diplomatically by an intervention of the provincial government of Guangdong. Whilst serving in Guangdong, Wang Yang also launched several campaigns against corruption, power abuse and nepotism – creating some tensions and frictions with elder cadres and the group of (local) princelings. In March 2013, Wang Yang was appointed as vice premier (serving under Li Keqiang). His responsibilities included the agricultural sector, water management, commerce, tourism and the reduction of absolute poverty. He was also a member of several working teams and leading groups tasked with formulating reform proposals, especially in the fields of poverty reduction, food safety, intellectual property and counterfeit products.

Wang Yang was also part of the leading groups coining China's New Silk Road strategy. At the 19th Party Congress (2017), Wang Yang entered the rows of the Standing Committee of the CCP's Politburo. Since March 2018, he is also the head of the CPPCC.

The counter-model to this neo-liberal development agenda, favoured by the PRC's Neo-Maoists and parts of the Chinese New Left, is known as Chongqing Model.

Bo Xilai – after having held positions as mayor of Dalian and governor of Liaoning province – served as minister of commerce from 2004 to 2007. In 2007, he became a member of the Central Committee and took over the position as party secretary of Chongqing. This lining-up of core positions in the party-state – and the fact that Bo Xilai's father, Bo Yibo, was one of the leading CCP cadres of the early Mao era, making Bo Xilai a member of the princeling faction – seemed to designate him for further promotion at the 18th Party Congress. Bo's efforts to revive Maoist red values and to propagate an economic model of state-controlled redistribution and economic steering was, ultimately, not capable of winning a strategic majority within the CCP (in the end, Bo Xilai and his wife were imprisoned and sentenced for the murder of a British businessman).

The eight democratic parties[48] operating under the umbrella of the CCP should not be confused with the concept of political factions introduced above. These parties came into existence during the Anti-Japanese War of Resistance and have been closely integrated into the CCP's "multi-party" autocracy.

5.1.2. The (New) Political Role of the Military

The forerunner organisation of the PRC's People's Liberation Army (PLA), established as third pillar of the Chinese party-state in October 1949, was the Chinese Red Army. Following the PRC's official party historiography, the Red Army was formed in connection with the Nanchang Uprising (August 1927), the CCP's answer to the massacre of Communist troops by GMD forces in Shanghai (February 1926). When the GMD quit the (First) United Front and turned against the Communists, the CCP intensified its efforts to set up a modern, powerful military branch. The Red Army was established as a party-army; the CCP demanded absolute loyalty and compliance with party ideology. At the conference in Gutian (Fujian province) in December 1929, Mao entrenched the party's ultimate control and leadership over the armed forces.

Following Japan's official capitulation and the formal end of the Second World War, an open military power struggle between the ruling GMD and the Communist opposition forces erupted. The Chinese communists pursued a guerrilla strategy, as summarised by Lin Biao's 1965 pamphlet "Long Live the Victory of People's War!" (Lin 1965). By encircling the cities (the power bases of the GMD) the CCP finally managed to control large areas of the mainland – with the GMD government retreating to Taiwan.

Up until today, Mao's formula "political power grows out of the barrel of the gun" still serves as one of the basic principles of the Chinese party-state. Even after the end of the Maoist period, which was followed by a professionalisation and de-ideologisation of the Chinese military, this basic principle is still non-negotiable.

---

48 China's eight democratic parties consist of: the Revolutionary Committee of the Chinese Guomindang, the China Democratic League, the China Democratic National Construction Association, the China Association for Promoting Democracy, the Chinese Peasants' and Workers' Democratic Party, the China Zhi Gong Party, the Jiusan Society (*jiusan* = 3 September), and the Taiwan Democratic Self-Governance League.

The Law on National Defence, as passed in 1997, constructs the PLA as party-army, as it includes the formulation that "the armed forces of the People's Republic of China are led by the Communist Party of China" (see also Shambaugh 2002: 21–22). The PLA fulfils two major functions: it secures the survival of the Chinese one-party state and is tasked with its national defence.

Under Mao, especially during the years of the Cultural Revolution, the PLA was instructed along the lines of official ideology and, during the 1960s, revolutionary and military committees even temporarily replaced official political institutions. In the 1980s, with the reformers around Deng Xiaoping taking over, the party decided to restructure and rebuild the PLA forces into a modern, technologically advanced army. Learning from observing the combat missions and military interventions by the US in the Middle East (the Gulf War), Kosovo, Afghanistan and Iran, the guiding principle of the PRC's military modernisation was to build up capacities to "win local wars under the conditions of informatization" (Miller 2007: 133). Deng Xiaoping's (or, more precisely, Zhou Enlai's) Four Modernisations comprised the sectors of agriculture, industry, science and technology – and the military.

The military background of the fourth and fifth generation of Chinese politicians is rather weak – at least when being compared to the first generation whose shared revolutionary-military experience is linked to the Long March and the revolutionary takeover of political power over the mainland. Nonetheless, the unwritten regulation that in order to enter the supreme institutions of the party-state one has to have held offices in all three pillars (party/state/military) is still valid. Overall, however, the party has undertaken steps to reduce the influence of the military in Chinese politics: out of the 25 members of the (then incoming) Politburo nominated at the 18th Party Congress, only 4 had a background in the military or in the military bureaucracy – the two vice chairmen of the Central Military Commission, the party secretary of Xinjiang province, Zhang Chunxian, and the then-newly nominated incoming general secretary, Xi Jinping (Miller 2013: 3–4).

The one who controls the army presumably commands the most powerful control centre of the Chinese party-state. Jiang Zemin, even after his retirement from his positions as general secretary and state president after two consecutive legislative terms (as prescribed by the constitution), continued to serve as chairman of the Central Military Commission until 2004. His successor, Hu Jintao, was thus regarded as a rather weak leader of the Chinese party-state, given that he lacked control over the military. In the run-up to the changing of the guard in 2012/2013, speculations ran high that this limited, step-by-step transfer of political (and military) power to the next generation could be repeated. Finally, in 2012/2013, Xi Jinping took over control of all three pillars of the party-state, including the chairmanship of the Central Military Commission. He also made sure to secure the loyalty and followership of the military – a step deemed crucial due to rumours of a planned *coup d'état* by paramilitary units of the Chinese police and the head of China's state security apparatus, Zhou Yongkang, in defence and support of Bo Xilai. Internet entries reported that tanks would have been spotted approaching Beijing. Although these reports were later classified as rumours lacking any empirical foundations, in 2013, official investigations were launched against Zhou Yongkang and his circle by the CCP's Central Commission for Discipline Inspection. Anti-corruption investigations also included the top ranks of the Chinese military. Official trials were opened against Xu Caihou – who had been a member of the Politburo and vice chairman of the Central Military Commission from 2007 to 2012 – as well as against a number of high-ranked PLA generals.

In addition to these purges, CCP cadres and military officials had to take part in seminars designed to rectify their work style and to educate them in official party ideology. One of Xi's first official inspection tours in his role as state president (and CMC chairman) led him to the naval forces stationed in the South of China. Stories circulated that not all of these forces' manoeuvres had been authorised by Beijing. The East China Sea and the South China Sea are those areas where Chinese interests clash with those of Japan (Senkaku/Diaoyu islands dispute) and with those of the Southeast Asian island states. The US is involved in these disputes via security alliances with Chinese neighbours. Unauthorised missions or manoeuvres could cause an escalation of these tensions and conflicts; measures of establishing ultimate control and securing loyalty of the troops are, therefore, of central importance for Beijing's foreign and security politics. In November 2014, at the occasion of the 85th anniversary of the Gutian conference (1929), Xi held a work conference with leading party politicians and PLA officers in Gutian, where Mao had once secured the followership of the revolutionary armed forces.

The PRC's official national defence strategy has been outlined in White Papers (available in English) released by the Information Office of the Chinese State Council. These papers are published as White Papers on "national defence" – only the 2015 White Paper broke with this tradition, as it was released as "Military Strategy". The most recent version was presented in July 2019, entitled "China's National Defence in the New Era".

5.1.3. Consultation and the Role of Policy Advisers: Study Sessions and Working Groups

Under the fourth and the fifth generation, processes of consultation and deliberation have become formalised and institutionalised. Since 2002, the rather sporadically convened informal meetings of the Politburo with external advisers have been transformed into "study sessions". One of the first of this kind took place in December 2002, shortly after the appointment of Hu Jintao as CCP general secretary (Glaser 2012: 108–109; Ma 2007).

Relatively few referees invited to join these study sessions have a pure academic background. Mapping the study sessions during Hu Jintao's first office term, Lu Yiyi finds that the majority of referees was affiliated with the Chinese Academy of Social Sciences, whilst others belonged to the research units of the State Council or to the NDRC. Renmin University sent far more referees than Peking University and Tsinghua University. Amongst the study sessions' participants were also members of the Central Party School (Beijing) and the Military Academy (Lu 2007).

Issues of economic steering and the political economy dominated the agenda of the study sessions of the Hu–Wen era, followed by sessions on ideology and party organisation. Socio-economic tensions or developmental challenges, formally addressed at the annual meetings of the NPC, were not (officially) included in these study sessions. Furthermore, international relations and national defence were seldomly discussed. Instead, core slogans such as the concept of Scientific Development were developed and refined during study session meetings (Health 2014: 207). The study sessions thus contribute to creating a joint reference scheme and political terminology shared by the political leadership. Chen Gang (2012) hence classifies these meetings as part of the CCP's consensus-based governance approach.

A closer glance at the chronology of topics covered by these study sessions reveals that the Politburo uses these meetings to discuss topical fields where tensions between political factions or between the three pillars of the party-state have become obvious. The 17th study session's focus on the modernisation of the PRC's armed forces and the broadening of their official mandate follows this logic – as this is a field were the positions of hardliners and reformers within the party and the military continue to clash.

5.2. Red Capitalists versus State Capitalists: Competition amongst China's Economic Elites

Transformation and modernisation theories often tend to see a country's economic elites as promoters of democratisation. The PRC, however, has so far managed to stabilise its one-party regime even after the initiation of economic reforms. One explanation for this paradox that seems to contradict some of the core assumptions and empirical observations of transformation studies in other world regions is that the party-state has managed to co-opt and incorporate the national economic elites, turning them into "red" (aka supporters of the CCP) capitalists (Dickson 2003, 2007, 2016; Tsai 2006).

During the 1980s and the early 1990s, following the Third Plenum's decisions (1978) on reform and opening, large parts of the PRC's state-owned companies were restructured and transformed. However, even four decades after the initiation of economic reforms, SOEs account for about 30 % of the PRC's GDP; their number amounts to 40 % of all registered enterprises. China's (reformed) SOEs are supervised and coordinated by the State-owned Assets Supervision and Administration Commission (SASAC), set up in 2003, or, when falling into the category of finance, managed directly by the Ministry of Finance or by Huijin, an investment company owned by the Chinese government. The 2013 reforms proclaimed by the Third Plenum envisioned a further privatisation of the state-owned sector. Via mergers and major restructuring rounds, the number of state-owned companies was planned to be reduced from 106 to 40. SOEs should be reorganised as modern, internationally competitive cooperations with mixed ownership –

as outlined in the decisions by the Third Plenum (2013) and reconfirmed in the Guidelines on SOE Reform (2015).

Since the late 1970s, joint ventures have been set up with the goal to attract foreign capital and to import foreign technological know-how. Besides this, the private economic sector began to mushroom, competing with the state-owned sector. These private companies were founded in close coordination with the party-state and entered a symbiotic relationship benefitting the development (and profit-maximising) interests of both sides.

The case of China's Internet service companies illustrates the strategic collaboration between the party-state and the private economic sector: the PRC's leading Internet service companies, Sina and Tencent, are listed on the stock market. Whilst foreign companies such as Google, Twitter and Facebook have been banned from the Chinese market (or temporarily kicked out), apps providing similar services (search engines, social media, messenger programmes, sharing platforms) programmed by Chinese companies are available for download and are used all over China (and beyond Chinese borders, as Chinese companies are reaching out to the global market). As these tools, such as social media and chat-rooms, allow people to connect and to exchange their views, one would expect to observe censorship and control or a final crack-down on these apps. Whilst cases of censorship have been reported at the content level, i.e., targeting conversation amongst Chinese netizens, the software solutions as such have not been banned. Given that the stock-market value of companies such as Sina and Tencent, as well as their large market shares in China (and also in other world regions), relies on their social media apps and mass communication tools, state intervention would reduce these apps' popularity and thus cause a severe drop in the PRC's tax revenues from the Internet-related service sector and AI companies. As the post-Maoist PRC operates with output-based legitimacy, it grants these sectors some special rights and liberties – at least as long as these apps are primarily used for entertainment and not for political mobilisation. Internet-related companies are only allowed to operate if they comply with the PRC's legal framework. To attract more users, companies offering social media applications are walking a tightrope, going as far as they can to provide "free" exchange of opinion but intervening before being in danger of exclusion from the Chinese market.

Chinese companies, including the reformed SOEs, are operating worldwide. Many of them belong to the world's leading companies in terms of annual revenue, as Forbes' Fortune Global 500 list documents.

5.3. Urban and Rural Actors: Multiple Identities

5.3.1. Peasants and Migrant Workers

In his strategy on the people's war, Lin Biao stated that by focusing on the Chinese peasants and by encircling the cities from the countryside, the CCP would be able to win the war. In fact, the Maoist PRC's first reform and restructuring approaches, after the founding of the PRC, all targeted the Chinese villages. A land reform was launched to distribute land to the Chinese peasants; landlords were persecuted in mass campaigns and show trials. Since the late 1920s, Mao had propagated the idea to mobilise the poor Chinese peasants and to win them over for the Chinese Communist revolution. In 1958, with the Three Red Banners, the PRC's strategy for transforming the countryside entered its next stage: the general line for socialist construction sought to simultaneously develop the industry and the agricultural sector (first banner); the Great Leap Forward should enable a high-speed modernisation (second banner); and people's communes should form the nucleus (and incubator lab) of this development (third banner). About 24,000 people's communes were installed, each consisting of around 5,000 households. Contrary to the euphoric plan of a joint modernisation of industry and agriculture, the Great Leap caused a one-sided prioritisation of steel production in unprofessional backyard steel furnaces. The production of agricultural products was neglected, causing a severe famine (1959–1961) with millions of people starving to death. The grain supply of urban areas and all major Chinese cities was upheld, meaning that, initially, the catastrophic developments in the countryside remained widely unnoticed.

In the aftermath of this policy failure, the PRC's economic development strategy was marginally readjusted. Collectivisation was not abolished but production was delegated to smaller production teams. A few years later, however, the quota set for the agricultural sector was, again, relatively high and hard to meet. Dazhai, a commune located in Shanxi province, was celebrated as a successful example of socialist rural modernisation. In 1963, Mao started his campaign "to learn from Dazhai in agriculture" and asked peasants to study and copy this approach. Despite unfavourable local conditions, peasants in Dazhai – according to official party narratives and party historiography – successfully built terraces and irrigation systems to increase crop production and to improve their members' working and living conditions. During the Cultural Revolution (1966–1976) numerous delegations visited Dazhai, hailed as a (revolutionary) textbook example of rural collectivisation.

Despite the positive reference to the peasants as main protagonists of the Chinese Revolution and socialist modernisation, the CCP's socialist transformation path was realised at the expense of this group. The *hukou* system aggravated their already precarious situation, degrading them to second-class citizens, limiting their mobility and barring them from the urban educational and social welfare systems.

The PRC's informal labour migration, with millions of peasants flooding into China's megacities and metropolitan clusters, bears some uncontrollable dangers for the country's social "harmony" and stability. Many migrant workers work without any formal contract or insurance. The central government has launched reforms and passed new laws, but the exploitation of the lower socio-economic strata seems to continue, especially since the mushrooming of the Chinese platform economy. Income disparities continue, and the gap between the *noveaux riches* and the peasants (and migrant workers) is widening. The groups of peasants and migrant workers are increasingly articulating their demands and fighting for their rights – which has been perceived by some Chinese observers as a possible second wave of open class struggle. The fourth generation of Chinese politicians (Hu Jintao/ Wen Jiabao) thus officially stated that a radical class struggle (as associated with the Cultural Revolution) would not be going to take place (i.e., it would neither be initiated nor tolerated by the CCP authorities).

5.3.2. Rightful Resistance and Contestation Movements

One of the widely-held assumptions regarding the role of civil society in non-democratic system settings is that this actor group is most likely to position itself in opposition to the authoritarian regime and to start a pro-democratic contestation movement. Along these lines, protests by civil (society) actors are expected to destabilise the political regime, leaving the ruling elites with (almost) no other choice than to end these upheavals.

With regard to the post-Maoist PRC, it is noticeable that not all forms of civil protest have been banned or persecuted. Under certain conditions, contestation movements are tolerated, at least as long as they don't question the legitimacy of the one-party regime. Sometimes, these contestation movements even trigger reforms and policy adjustments (within the setting of the one-party state).

These accepted modes of contestation display two characteristics: first and foremost, civil (society) actors are not acting against the system but collaborate with sub-groups of the political elites (often located at a level higher to the one where concrete contestation movements take place). Second, the protesters claim to contribute to the consolidation and persistence of the political system and, via their protests, to call the government's attention to potentially destabilising, regime-delegitimising developments at the local level. Thus they do not pursue particular individual interests but act as spokespersons of the (entire) Chinese society.

In China-focused studies by political scientists, this specific mode of contestation is referred to as "rightful resistance". Drawing on basic ideas of social movement theories, these studies define the phenomenon of rightful resistance as civil protest movements that actively make reference to central laws and regulation and political guidelines. They frame their demands by borrowing from the party-state's official terminology, using key terms and slogans coined by the ruling elites in connection with their efforts to enforce rule-based governance procedures. Rightful resistance is presented in line with the central government's core reform agenda and campaigns to correct mis-developments at the local level to restore order and social cohesion ("harmony").

Rightful resistance takes place as a cautiously planned and coordinated protest movement that distances itself from *coup d'états* and rebellions that are both clandestinely prepared and tend to overthrow the given regime patterns. Their demands generally stick to the rights and freedoms granted in official legal documents or signature speeches by the CCP. The ruling elites are provided with information about local developments and asked to intervene to resolve the issue – in most cases power abuse or mismanagement by local cadres. The organisers of contestation movements that fall into the category of rightful resistance are dedicated to peaceful protest and reject the use of force and violence by protesters. They seek to find allies and supporters from the political authorities at the next highest level of the party-state administration. In order not to be silenced and prevented from voicing their demands by local powerholders, rightful resistance movements try to get public attention – and often use the Internet or social media (O'Brien 1996; O'Brien/Li 2006).

In order to be treated as a legitimate contestation movement by the Chinese party-state, these protests have to meet the criteria of "mass incidents", i.e., the organisers must mobilise a rather large group of civilian protesters. By the rule of thumb, and based on the observation of past events, mass movements start with a minimum of 500 participants. From the years from 2003 to 2009, the majority of these mass incidents belonged to the category of labour protests, followed by protests against illegal land-grabbing and against environmental pollution. According to a study by Tong and Lei, the protagonists of these movements were laid-off workers and peasants (Tong/Lei 2010). In most cases, the authorities did not seek to suppress these movements but to engage in deescalating protest management (Tanner 2004). Reports about labour protests occurring from 2000 to 2002 were mainly circulated via informal online channels. Since 2003, these movements have also been covered by the Chinese state media (CLB 2012).

Not all protest and contestation movements are ranked as legitimate articulation of people's interests (and rights). Pro-democracy movements, plotting a transformation of the political system, are prohibited and would be persecuted as an act of intolerable subversion. Patriotic movements, by contrast – e.g., the May Fourth Movement of 1919, anti-Japanese demonstrations, patriotic protests after the (accidental) bombing of the Chinese embassy in Belgrade – are, up to a certain point, encouraged and accepted. People's protests against an external enemy allow the party-state to temporarily overcome the dividing lines running between the various local socio-economic interest groups and thus contribute to intra-societal cohesion and the formation of a unified "Chinese" identity. Again, the formation of religious societies or pro-autonomy movements by Chinese national minorities are continuously suppressed – as soon as they fall into the category of separatism or terrorism (Perry 2001: 174).

5.3.3. Urban and Rural Protest Movements

Research on rightful resistance originally looked at the village level, especially at those located in remote areas far away from the central authorities in Beijing. Peasant protests occurred to oppose illegal tax demands, land-grabbing without monetary compensation, power abuse, corruption or the manipulation of village elections (O'Brien 2008; Li/O'Brien 2008; O'Brien 2009). In the course of growing socio-economic tensions, culminating in labour protests, research on contestation and mass protests also turned to developments in urban areas (He/Huang 2015).

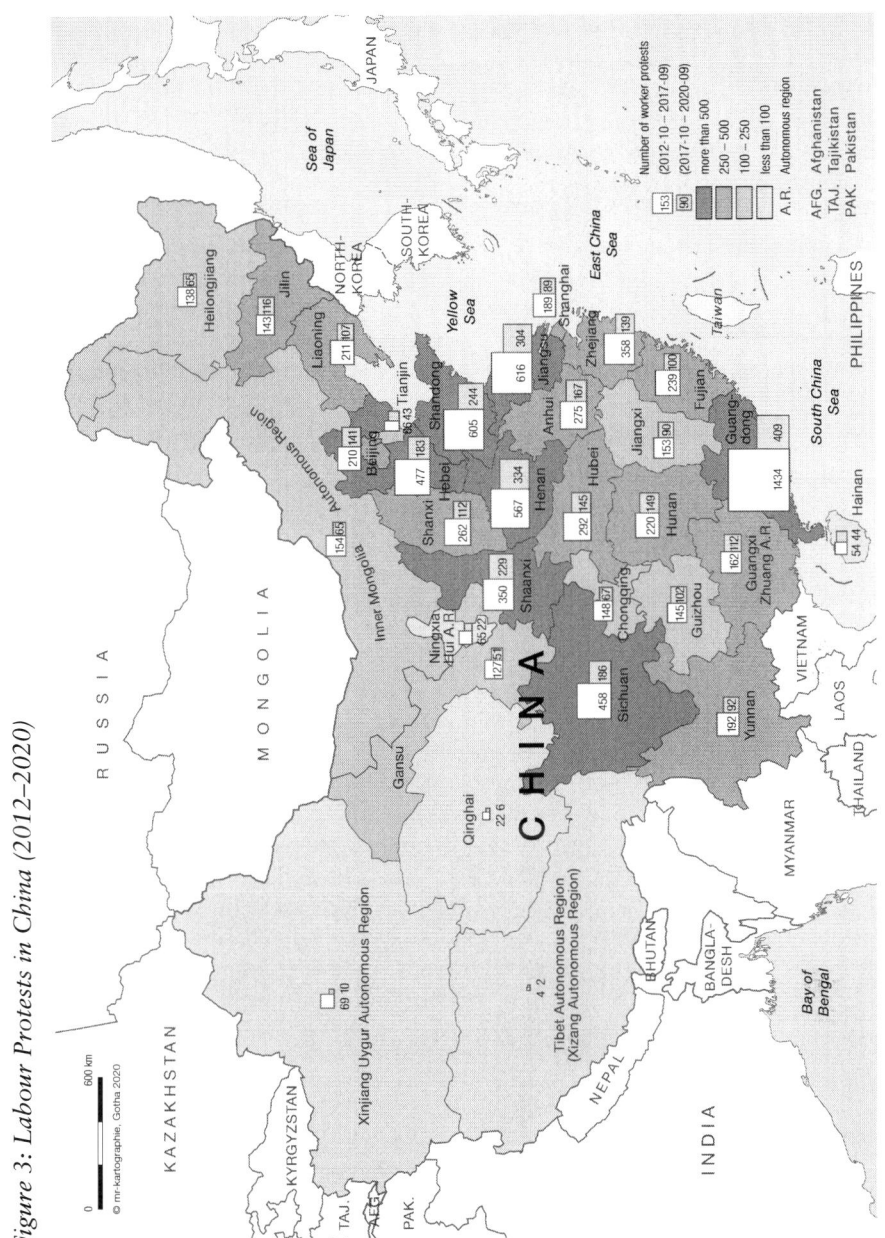

Figure 3: *Labour Protests in China (2012–2020)*

Source: http://strikemap.clb.org.hk/strikes/en

143

In 2010, a wave of strikes by Chinese workers reached the production sites of foreign companies (such as Foxconn, Honda, Toyota). The Honda strikes, which were mediated and finally resolved by wage increases, are illustrative of this new sub-type of labour contestation movements (Yang, Ray Ou 2015). In most of the protests targeting non-Chinese companies, the ACFTU intervened as mediator to represent the interests of the Chinese employees. In some cases, the (local) Chinese government expressed its support for the strikes. Many of these protests took place in Guangdong province, known for its rather neo-liberal development agenda and its high accumulation of private enterprises and foreign companies. Wang Yang, Guangdong's party secretary, reportedly sided with the Chinese workers and intervened in several local labour disputes (Xinhua 2010). This resonates with the provincial government's intervention in the Wukan protests (2011–2012), which ended with the removal of the self-proclaimed village committee and the holding of new elections (Vukovich 2015).

Scholars disagree over the question of whether the positioning of the party-state in the Honda and Toyota strikes might have been influenced by an anti-Western or anti-Japanese mood. At least, these protests ended without any violent escalation, neither the police nor the companies' security had to intervene. Apart from demands for higher wages and better working conditions, the protesters also wanted to be allowed to set up their own "independent" workers union – apart from the CCP's ACFTU. Another case that attracted international attention was the suicide cases and suicide attempts by Chinese workers employed by the (Taiwan-based) IT company Foxconn. Protests were sparked by working conditions, perceived as inhuman and unbearable. Protesters used the Internet and international social media channels to broadcast videos and pictures documenting the contestation movement (*The New York Times* 2010). Earlier labour protest waves were rather passive and often limited themselves to demanding the payment of agreed wages and adherence to the agreed contract clauses. The 2010 strikes and contestation movements document an increased legal awareness amongst Chinese workers (including the floating population). Workers do not only fight for the rise of their wages, but also for the reduction of over-time work or monetary compensation, respectful treatment and a better working environment (Elfstrom/Kuruvilla 2014).

5.3.4. Environmental Protests

Environmental Non-Government Organisations (ENGOs) operate under the protective umbrella of the central party-state. They report and denounce the violation of central environmental protection laws at the local level and thus provide the central level authorities with indispensable information about developments on the grounds. They often follow the practice of rightful resistance movements and wrap their reports and demands in official party rhetoric and refer to official legal frameworks (Yang, Guobin 2005). In connection with the PRC's entrance into the era of "new normal" – dedicated to a sustainable, green modernisation approach – Li Keqiang proclaimed the PRC's "war" against pollution. This might have been a reaction to the rising number of environmental movements, involving more and more actors that do not belong to any formally registered ENGO.

Not-In-My-Backyard (NIMBY) protests erupt(ed) as local contestation against the construction of emission-intense power plants or industries in people's immediate neighbourhood. As O'Brien and Deng have shown by assessing the closing of a major chemical plant in Zhejiang province, these NIMBY movements are extremely powerful and efficient – leaving the (local) government with no option but to agree to their demands (O'Brien/Deng 2015).

Pollutants classified as hazardous to health and the omnipresent degradation of the natural environment clearly function as powerful mobilising factors, with local movements winning adherents from all strata of Chinese society. These protesters do not fight for any long-term goals nor do they subscribe to any alternative ideology, but they are aware of the detrimental effects of China's high-speed economic transformation and the resulting immediate threats: smog and PM 2.5 particulate emissions in China's megacities, desertification and the loss of arable land, water pollution and the expected shortage of fresh water. Almost all major environmental protests ended with the (local) government formally giving in and accepting people's demands. Sometimes, however, these concessions remained rhetorical ones, as emission-intense production sites were, after some time had passed and protests had ebbed away, informally and silently re-opened (Hwang 2012).

One should, however, not take the emergence of NIMBY movements as empirical proof of a nation-wide ecological awareness. Evaluating local Chinese protests against the construction of hydropower plants and dams, Mertha concludes that the central government's initiatives to reduce emissions and to substitute coal with renewable energy is not always supported by the Chinese society – and rather generates new conflicts. Apart from protests by local ENGOs and local people voicing their concerns regarding the long-term effects of dams and hydropower plants on the local eco-system, protests also involve those whose villages are flooded to realise the central government's green energy dream (Mertha (2008 [2010]).

5.3.5. Weiquan Movements

Another type of protest is coordinated by Chinese lawyers and intellectuals, who protect and defend people's rights (e.g., property rights, housing rights) and individual freedoms (e.g., freedom of speech and expression). This mode of contestation is labelled as *weiquan* – "defence of rights" – movement. The *weiquan* lawyers operate as a civil corrective that formally seeks to assist the strengthening and enforcement of rule-based governance (Fu/Cullen 2008, 2011). They must operate within clearly defined limits: in 2007, Hu Jintao formulated his Three Supreme Principles (*san ge zhi shang*). These principles prescribe that courts (and lawyers) have to represent and protect the interests and the leadership role of the party, have to serve the interests of the Chinese people and, finally, have to respect the law. Lawyers (and courts) hence have to safeguard a balance between the principle of rule of law and the independence and autonomy of the legislative, on the one hand, and the party's guidelines for securing the stability of the political system on the other.

Not all *weiquan* activists are lawyers with a university degree. More and more migrant workers are informed about their legal rights and the central government's legal reforms; the Chinese society's legal consciousness has changed. Article 35 of the Chinese state constitution states: "Citizens of the People's Republic of China have the freedom of speech, of the press, of assembly, of association, of procession, and of demonstration". And Article 37 continues: "The freedom of the person of citizens of the People's Republic of China is inviolable. No citizen may be arrested except with the approval or by decision of a people's procuratorate or by decision of a people's court, and arrests must be made by a public security organ. Unlawful detention or deprivation or restriction of citizens' freedom of the person by other means is prohibited, and unlawful search of the person of citizens is prohibited". *Weiquan* activists claim to act as guardians of the Chinese constitution and hence to respect these Three Supremes. The dividing line between regime-supportive rightful resistance and subversive actions, which are persecuted, is not clearly demarcated. Contestation movements and petitions organised by *weiquan* actors have thus repeatedly come into conflict with the Chinese party-state, particularly when human rights, religious groups or ethnic minorities are addressed. In several cases of local mismanagement, the *weiquan* movement's intervention was quite successful – their petitions, just to name one prominent example, finally led to the launching of official investigations and enquiries into the cause of the collapse of school buildings during the earthquake in Sichuan province (March 2008). In the end, the report documented botched-up construction, poor quality building materials and miscalculations of the statics as the main cause of this house-of-card-like folding of the buildings. Local cadres were found guilty of corruption in connection with these cases of sloppy construction work.

The Internet plays a major role for collecting information about the background of local governance deficiencies. It also serves as the coordination platform of the *weiquan* activists. They reach out to local society to gain insight into local developments, and they use the Internet to start online discussions or to initiate online petitions (Teng 2012). China's *weiquan* activists are not part of any formal, institutionalised organisation. The *weiquan* label thus refers to a bundle of local actions and cases of contestation that are often spontaneous events at the local level. Given the movement's informality and ad hoc character, the Chinese government is only able to deal with this movement on a case-by-case basis. In her analysis of more recent contestation actions, Diana Fu thus postulates that a new type of informal networks might have emerged, which she labels as "disguised collective actions". She stresses that many contestation movements should neither be classified as spontaneous movements nor as temporary contestation by single actors or groups of actors (Fu 2016). Looking at the *weiquan* movement via her theoretical lenses, informal institutions managed by societal, non-state actors would thus have joined the power play between the party-state (and its formal institutions and mass organisations) and Chinese society. These power relations and the main patterns of interaction between (party-)state and society are not fixed but dynamically evolving, driven by both top-down regulation efforts and bottom-up counter-(re)actions.

5.3.6. Chinese Intellectuals between Internationalisation and Sinicization

The Chinese policy-formulation process oscillates between the two extremes of unconditional reception and internalisation of non-Chinese ideas versus the focusing on the formulation of distinct "Chinese" models. To understand these shifts and readjustments of the PRC's official policy images and policy paradigms, one has to undertake a retrospective analysis and reconstruction of the documented past oscillations against the backdrop of the historical evolution of Chinese politics and Chinese political science research.

In periods of internationalisation, Chinese political science reflected the international state of the art and relied upon imported (non-Chinese) theories and frameworks of analysis. Two streams of "international" policy ideas have to be distinguished: theories and concepts of Marxism-Leninism imported via the Soviet Union, and Western policy ideas and normative values. Western ideas reached the Chinese Empire via the ancient Silk Road as well as via missionaries based in China. Encounters with the West did not always play out in China's favour. After the Chinese Empire's traumatic defeat in the Opium Wars, some Chinese intellectuals preached to import (and master) the West's advanced weapon technologies in order to set up a powerful modern army and to restore China's sovereignty. Language schools and arsenals were opened in China. Since 1872, exchange programmes were initiated to send Chinese students to institutes of higher education in the US and Europe. The First Study Mission[49] was sent to the US (1872–1875). The plan was that the participants, upon their successful graduation, should return to China and contribute to the country's technological modernisation and the system's "self-strengthening". However, the mission was prematurely cancelled, and participants were ordered to return to China. Whilst the original mission was not completed, some participants later took over central positions in the state administration and contributed to China's infrastructure modernisation: Tang Shaoyi served as first premier of the then newly founded Chinese Republic; and Zhang Tianyou is known as the main "architect" of China's modern railway network. He was the chief engineer of the Peking–Zhangjiakou railway line, the first Chinese railway built without European assistance.

From 1877 onwards, a second wave of exchange students embarked for Europe and the US. They were part of a special programme for naval students that should prepare them for becoming the new Chinese navy's next generation of generals. But not all programme recruits respected the prescribed list of disciplines and fields of studies: Yan Fu is not known for his mastery of naval techniques but for his translations of Huxley's *Evolution and Ethics* as well as Adam Smith's *An Inquiry into the Nature and Causes of the Wealth of Nations* and other socio-po-

---

49   See also: La Fargue (1942); Rhoads (2011).

litical works. With his translations, Yan Fu added the ideas of Social Darwinism to the inner-Chinese reform debates (Schwartz 1969). Another destination of China's reform-oriented students was Japan. The founding fathers of the CCP, Chen Duxiu and Li Dazhao, both studied there. After the crack-down on the Hundred Days Reforms, the movement's figurehead, Kang Youwei, and his disciple, Liang Qichao, fled to Tokyo, where, a couple of years later, in 1905, Sun Yat-sen would found the Tongmenghui, the forerunner organisation of the GMD.

Starting in 1909, the Boxer Indemnity Funds offered scholarships to study in the US. The Tsinghua College was set up as an institute for preparatory training and for the coordination of the programme (Bieler 2004; Ye 2001). In 1915, a student work programme began, sending Chinese students to France where they came into contact with (European) Marxist ideas. Amongst these students was Deng Xiaoping, who later on would become the main initiator and intellectual architect of the PRC's reform and opening strategy. Zhou Enlai as well as Cai Hesen, who would later become high-ranked CCP officials, both spent some years of their studies in Paris.

From the 1920s onwards, Marxist ideas were not only imported from Europe but promoted via the Soviet Union which supported the formation of Marxist study groups in China. Many members of the first generation of CCP revolutionaries were trained in Moscow where they were introduced to the ideas of Marxism-Leninism. Apart from those who rose as party officials, the early PRC's groups of Marxist-realist writers also received their training in the SU. To counter the spread of Marxism, the GMD government supported Chinese students' exchange stays in Western Europe and the US. These students were expected to bring advanced Western knowledge back to China and to contribute to the state-building and modernisation process of the young Chinese Republic (Rhoads 2011).

After the proclamation of the PRC, the CCP government cancelled all exchange agreements with the capitalist West and relied exclusively on exchange programs with the SU and (select) Communist systems in Eastern Europe (Han 2013). During the Cultural Revolution (1966–1976), the PRC's institutes of higher education were "closed" or taken over by the red guards; exchange programmes were paused.

Study experience abroad did not always count as a necessary qualification for entering the upper ranks of the Chinese state bureaucracy. The Chinese Empire's civil servant examination system (*keju*), in power until 1904/1905, required the rememorating of the Confucian classics and their correct exegesis. Alternative selection criteria were only accepted when the Chinese Empire officially recognised its institutional faintness and thought to catch up with the West. The study programmes, summarised above, were officially designed to import technologies deemed necessary for the realisation of China's modernisation programme. The focus relied on science and technology. Only under Communist rule did the mastery of ideology – Marxism-Leninism – become a criterium for the selection (and promotion) of officials. During the Nanking decade, the import and diffusion of

Marxism via France and Japan was observed (by the GMD) as a rather negative (and unplanned) side effect of the exchange programmes.

As the above chronology of the Chinese encounters with foreign policy ideas and theories illustrates, the list of criteria decisive for the selection of political personnel and the official reference scheme underlying China's state-building process was defined by the ruling elites – and was readjusted in accordance with changing domestic and global transformations.

The tensions between internationalisation and indigenisation continue to shape the field of social science research in China. In the Maoist years, Marxist ideas were sinicized, adapting them to China's socio-economic conditions. After 1978, Western governance ideas were expected to allow a smooth, high-speed modernisation of the Chinese economy; however, already in the early 1980s, Western ideas were discredited once again and classified as a Trojan horse to trigger a democratic transformation of the PRC. In the late 20th/early 21st century, once the PRC had successfully re-joined international trade and global politics, political science research was characterised by conceptual and methodological pluralism and diversity: Marxist ideas no longer dominated the debate but were upheld by individual scholars or institutes closely related with the CCP. Western theories were widely discussed – though not accepted as a blueprint to be directly copied. Additionally, some scholars promoted the idea of setting up a Chinese School, of defining social science theories "with Chinese characteristics" (Noesselt 2010: 69–71).

Studies on the history of political science research in the PRC document a close relationship between politics and political science. Ideological radicalisation caused the closing of political science institutes in the 1950s. Institutes focusing on International Relations (IR) were, however, allowed to continue their research on Chinese foreign relations and the politics (and foreign strategies) of both Communist and Western-capitalist states. A decision passed by the Central Committee on strengthening research on international affairs established IR centres at the Peking University, the Renmin University and at the Fudan University in Shanghai. Earlier already, in 1955, a department for international politics had been installed under the roof of the Renmin University (Beijing). The Fudan University's IR department was the only one specialising in the politics of Western-capitalist systems – allowing them to lead the political science debates of the early reform years, when knowledge of these systems' theories and governance ideas was ranked higher than the mastery of Marxist(-Leninist) ideology.

Under Xi Jinping, a new campaign against Western values was launched, reaching its peak in 2014–2015. Efforts by scholars (and policy practitioners) to define "Chinese" governance solutions and policy paradigms have been officially encouraged. How far these approaches deviate from "international" governance solutions and to what degree they can be labelled as "Chinese" models remains to be seen. There is no definition of the criteria to be met in order to frame a theory as a "Chinese" one. Some scholars, involved in the search for a "Chinese" theory, have argued that this theory would have to use "Chinese" terminology, to refer to Chinese (premodern) state philosophy, and to reflect "Chinese" (development) interests.

Seen from the outside perspective, these three conditions could be read as a definition of a legitimation strategy that allows the system to justify its governance approach and to reject all alternative Western development blueprints as incompatible with China's historical-philosophical traditions and specific national conditions. Such a "theory" could most probably not be exported or added to global academic debates which require a more abstract terminology and theoretical assumptions not limited to the Chinese case. Whilst post-colonial, postmodern and post-structuralist streams of international political science research seek to include "non-Western" approaches and to pay attention to views from the so-called Global South, Chinese "theory" frames have, at least so far, not been ranked as equivalent to macro-theories of IR or of modern governance. Elements of "Chinese" theory formulations – Chinese scholars' reference to patterns of Chinese history and concepts of China's premodern state philosophy – might, however, find their way into the ongoing global meta-debates on IR theory (criticising the predominance of theory concepts coined by scholars based in the US). Scholars belonging to the English School (of IR research) tried to explain contemporary centre–periphery relations in the West by referring to basic patterns of interactions of the Chinese Empire and the wider *tianxia*. Most theory formulations by Chinese scholars remain, however, focused on Chinese foreign policy and the PRC's strategic positioning options. Thus, they often continue to be side-lined and remain in the shadow of macro-IR debates as the explanations and scenarios they develop are widely perceived as an effort (by the Chinese government) to counter conflict and power competition scenarios propelled by international neorealist analysts (e.g. Allison's "Thucydides' Trap").

5.4. Online – Offline Constellations: Re-bargaining State – Society Interactions via Cyberspace?

In the 1990s, the cyberspace was expected to become the breeding ground for pro-democratic movements worldwide. Whereas offline protests – such as the demonstration in Tian'anmen Square in 1989 – were put down, the widely-held belief was that the anonymity of netizens and the fragmented server architecture of the world-wide net would make it impossible to track civil society actors and their online contestation activities. In this scenario the Internet was imagined as a new type of virtual battleground from where pro-democratic civil society actors would engage in a guerrilla war against totalitarian despots. Over the past few decades, the initial Internet euphoria has calmed down, or, in some regards, switched completely, swinging to the other extreme: Internet activists world-wide have pointed at the hidden dangers of using the Internet for collective counter-actions – these activities remain archived in the world-wide web and can be traced back even several decades later. Videos of demonstrations, circulated online, can be used to identify critics and opponents to the political regime. Besides this, criminal organisations discovered the Internet, leading to a declining trust in the safety and security of the Internet amongst netizens. These dark sides obviously overshadow the rather positive development dreams associated with the Internet in the 1990s. Furthermore, all political systems – democracies as well as autocracies – have expanded their steering and regulation to the cyberspace. With regard to the case of Chinese politics, the continued dynamic transformation of state–society interactions via the cyberspace implies that one can observe emerging patterns and transformations that might have spill-over effects on offline politics and the PRC's political institutions. Offline politics are still bargained behind closed curtains. But by drawing parallels and examining the causal interplay between hidden offline and "visible" online dimensions of state–society relations, one might be able to identify core readjustments before they are officially proclaimed by the party-state.

The changing socio-economic system structures of the PRC force the government to modify and adapt its steering mechanisms in order to be capable of responding to the pluralisation of actors and their group-specific interests. Some of these new top-down defined steering patterns are first tested in the online realm. Even though the Chinese Internet is highly controlled and censored, it is also the agora to re-bargain party–society and state–society relations.

Research on the Chinese Internet is primarily guided by two diametrically opposed paradigms: when the PRC was first connected to the global Internet, international observers announced that the transformation and democratisation of China would simply be a matter of time, and that the CCP would be unable to stop this process. Later research, based on the empirical observation of the persistence of the one-party state, addressed the stabilisation of autocratic regimes via the Internet and also turned to these systems' successful supervision and control of the online sphere.

At first glance, that an autocracy should be willing to connect to the Internet (labelled by the pro-democracy movement as "liberation technology") appears highly paradoxical. The main calculations behind this step were not political but economic: in the reform and opening period, priority was given to economic and technological modernisation. The "going out" approach, i.e., the global outreach of Chinese companies and the active involvement of the PRC in global trade and financial transactions, meant that the country had to join the international channels of (online) communication. Besides, Chinese IT companies are quite successful in developing hardware and software solutions that are also sold to markets outside China – in parts of Africa and Latin America, these companies are the main partners of the local and regional economy and also provide package solutions for building these countries' e-government infrastructure. In sum, the Internet is the backbone of Chinese companies' quest for exploring the global market. The New Silk Road, proclaimed in autumn 2013, also includes a digital component. Chinese companies are not only constructing transportation corridors (cross-continental networks of railways, highways, airports, deep-water ports) but also setting up smart power supply and telecommunication grids. Responding to Germany's Industry 4.0, the PRC pursues a further digitisation of its production chains and AI-based innovation, as outlined in its "Internet Plus" strategy and the "Made in China 2025" strategy.

China's Internet service providers and AI start-ups do not operate against the one-party state but have entered a strategic symbiotic relationship (Jiang 2012). In 2014, Xi Jinping officially proclaimed that the PRC should transform itself into a "cyber great power" (*wangluo daguo*) (Xinhua 2014). This notion comprises an economic as well as a military component, as modern warfare includes the dimension of cyber warfare and the use of AI-based weapons.

Apart from economic development interests, the Internet also served the recentralisation of the PRC's highly fragmented administrative system. The economic transformation and administrative decentralisation of the post-Mao years resulted in the formation of "de facto federalist" system patterns (Zheng 2007). To regain control, the central government decided to invest in the expansion of its e-government capacities (Lagerkvist 2005). The local administration was asked to collect data and information that would be centrally stored and archived online. The e-government initiative also included the opening of an online service centre for public service applications (making long trips from remote areas to apply for or to submit documents unnecessary). The party-state sought to become more customer-oriented.

The rapid rise of the number of "civil" microblog users between August 2009, when Sina launched its microblog (*weibo*) application, and 2013 was applauded as the beginning of an era of increased freedom of (online) opinion. Between 2009 and 2012, microblog debates mushroomed – and censorship interventions were comparatively limited. The party-state's institutes for mapping public online opinion were attentively following these debates to learn more about people's demands, complaints and expectations. Based on the mapping results, the party-state was able to design policies that pre-empted (parts of) people's demands. Microblogs thus functioned as channel of indirect participation and feedback.

The strengthening of Internet regulation from 2013 onwards, however, caused the exodus of netizens from Sina Weibo. The long-announced real-name registration of user accounts was finally enforced, meaning that official ID cards were needed to confirm or open a microblog account (by the way, similar rules were, almost simultaneously, issued in democratic system settings in connection with data privacy and data security regulations). Fake accounts or non-confirmed accounts had to be closed.

Overall, the Internet in China is neither a liberation technology (Diamond 2010) that would empower China's civil society in their fight for their rights and freedoms nor simply a means of stabilising the PRC's autocratic rule – but rather a combination of both elements (see: Zheng 2008).

To end the party-state's passive observer role and rather defensive positioning in the cyberspace, the fourth generation of Chinese politicians proactively commenced a new format of exchange with Chinese netizens: real-time online chats with the PRC's core political elites. Since 2006, the party-state has used Internet blogs (and microblogs) to report about the annual sessions of the NPC and the CPPCC. The NPC also publishes draft versions of new laws online and invites people to comment and to submit feedback that can be reflected in the final versions of these laws and regulations. In connection with the boom of China's microblogging sector, party cadres were asked to increase their Internet literacy and to open government microblogs as well as "individual" accounts to directly provide Chinese netizens with information and to engage in direct exchange (countering the spread of rumours and information circulated by opponents to the one-party state). Most government microblogs, however, were not used for multidirectional exchange but rather as platforms to post updates about recent government decisions and government activities.

By March 2020, the number of Chinese Internet users reached 900 million and thus stands for a critical mass of people connected to the online sphere (Internet penetration rate 2020: 64.5 %). 99 % of users assess the Internet via their mobile phones. Rural netizens account for 28 % of Chinese netizens, implying that the Internet and Internet-based services are mainly focusing on the PRC's urban areas (see: CNNIC 2020).

The analysis of online debates (via microblogs and online fora) opens new insights into the internal debates on China's modernisation strategy, on institutional reforms, as well as on potential future development paths. Indirect and direct interactions between the party-state and Chinese netizens in cyberspace are closely connected to developments and readjustments of offline politics. "Reading" the Chinese cyberspace is, of course, not an easy undertaking: entries on Chinese microblogs often operate with abbreviations and neologisms not to be found in any official dictionary. Studying Internet slang and decrypting the coded statements by Internet activists, resorting to word plays to circumvent censorship, can be quite time-consuming. And, given the immense amount of entries, a qualitative entry-by-entry coding might be impossible. The quantitative analysis of big data in connection with Chinese politics and state–society relations is still under-theorised, and the existing tools and methods need to be adapted to the Chinese case. Some pioneer work has been done in these fields but is still in a very early stage.

With information spreading about China's Social Credit System, the meaning of big data for political steering, manipulation and control has become a hot topic in China studies as well as in research on autocracies. The PRC's Social Credit System was introduced gradually – starting with local pilot projects in 2009. A nation-wide plan, entitled "Planning Outline for the Construction of a Social Credit System", was presented in 2014.[50] Local test runs continued, with the most prominent ones launched in "model" cities (Chengdu, Hangzhou, Huizhou, Rongcheng, Suqian, Suzhou, Yiwu, Weihai, Weifang, Wenzhou). People's credit scores are measured based on about 400 indicators related to evaluating individual's social as well as financial performance. A negative scoring may, according to reports by human rights activists, result in travel bans or denial of access to public services. Scoring and credit systems are not unique to the PRC – banking institutes, (insurance) companies and the (platform) economy worldwide rely on big data and the algorithm-based evaluation of user/consumer behaviour. One

---

50   The Chinese document is available online: http://www.gov.cn/zhengce/content/2014-06/27/content_891 3.htm.

should also note that – contrary to the rather critical views on China's scoring system by international observers – acceptance of the social credit system in China is reportedly extremely high. It is not primarily perceived as a means of control or suppression but as a way to counter social misconduct (and the decline of moral standards, the loss of *suzhi*) and rampant corruption. Of course, all systems can be abused and distorted – that is why Internet activists in China demand more transparency and regulations on data privacy.

As the case of China's platform economy – an initially underregulated sector of the Chinese economy – evidences, Chinese consumers welcome the intervention of the party-state to regulate this mushrooming sector and to set national standards to guarantee people's safety and security. Again, big data and AI-based applications did not condemn people in China to a passive, powerless role: drivers working for Chinese sharing economy/sharing mobility sector have found their ways to escape AI-based tracking and monitoring. Moreover, even in the AI-assisted entertainment economy, Chinese netizens are increasingly demanding higher standards of data protection and data privacy. Thus the debates on big data and AI in China, within Chinese society as well as within the CCP, are dedicated to topics similar to those currently discussed in the West. Again, AI and big-data-related interactions between the party-state, the (private) economy and Chinese society illustrate that these relationships and actors' positions are not fixed but dynamically evolving – reflecting developments in and outside China.

5.5. Stability and Legitimacy: Scenarios of Decline versus Models of Regime Resilience

The classification and typology of political regimes date back to Greek and Roman state philosophy. These philosophical reflections still serve as invisible backbones of the contemporary mapping and cartography of the world's political systems. Aristotle (384–322 BC) compiled one of the oldest typologies of political systems based on a comparative analysis of 158 state constitutions. Looking at the number of people involved in ruling and their mode of governing the country, Aristotle distinguishes between three "good" types – monarchy/kingship, aristocracy, *politie* – and three degenerated ones, namely tyranny, oligarchy and democracy (the latter defined as rule by the uneducated and uncivilised masses). His reference model for reflecting on good governance is the *polis,* the Greek city-state.

Cicero transcribes these reflections to the Roman empire (*Imperium Romanum*). Cicero's utopian Republican state concept, the *res publica* understood as *res populi*, relies on the idea of shared benefits (*utilitatis communio*) and common agreement of the law (*iuris consensus*).

Contemplations on the motivations underlying people's setting-up of states and on the best way to organise these communities, therefore, are central philosophical topics with long historical roots. Whilst parts of these philosophical traditions have been inherited and reconfirmed, the content ascribed to core terms has evolved in line with the formation of "modern" societies. The *demos* of the

Athens city-state was limited to an elite circle of "full citizens", equalling less than 30 % of the adult population. Whilst Athenian democracy is still referenced as the origin of contemporary Western democracy, in later centuries, the concept of *demos* has become more inclusive, ascribing all residents the same rights and freedoms. Finally, following Max Weber's terminology, charismatic authority has become substituted by legal-rational authority based on free and fair elections.

During the years of the Cold War, the world's bipolar structure resulted in a black-and-white division of the world into totalitarian rule versus democracy (also framed, with regard to their economic systems, as socialism versus capitalism). In the 1980s, the concept of totalitarian rule, theorised by Arendt and Friedrich/Brezinski, was first broadened and then finally replaced by the concept of autocracy. Linz defined autocracy as a system characterised by centralised political authority and limited political freedoms. In contrast to totalitarian systems, autocracies display limited political pluralism and rather restrain from a mobilisation of society, as these developments could get out of control all too easily and threaten the stability and survival of the political regime. Instead of operating with an ossified ideology, autocratic regimes rather resort to mentalities and emotions (Linz 2000).

By the late-1990s, the assumption of an automatically occurring transformation of all political systems into democracies had proven wrong (Carothers 2002). And, at the beginning of the 21st century, about half of the world's political system could no longer be grouped into one of the ideal type/pure type categories of democracy versus autocracy (Diamond 2002). This observation supported the framing of sub-types – bearing the danger to end up with an over-fragmented matrix of individual sub-types of political regimes. The concept of hybrid regimes offered a way out of this fragmentation dilemma as it allowed the grouping of political systems in the grey zone between the two pure types.

Modern autocracies are – in certain regards similar to pluralist democracies – caught in a permanent, never ending re-stabilisation and re-legitimation modus. The PRC is one of the very few socialist one-party states that was not affected by the wave of 1989/1991 democratisation. Political power is centralised in the hand of the CCP – or, more precisely, since the proclamation of the top-level design (*dingceng sheji*), once again in the hands of the CCP general secretary. Nonetheless, the system still operates with elements of (indirect) participation and deliberation – and thus falls into the sub-category of learning autocracies characterised by a high degree of flexibility and adaptability.

The system's official self-classification is to be found in Deng Xiaoping's formula "Socialism with Chinese characteristics" (*you Zhongguo tese de shehuizhuyi*). As the PRC claims to pursue a model sui generis, it does not fall into the ideal type category of socialism. However, all attempts in defining this "Chinese Model" have so far ended in classifying the PRC's political system as a dynamically evolving construct that combines a mixture of centralist one-party rule with elements of market capitalism.[51]

Even reform-minded Chinese intellectuals warn that the PRC should avoid any big bang transformation of its political (or economic) system. Yu Keping, who headed the Central Compilation and Translation Department for many years before moving to Peking University (in 2015), compiled a number of studies on governance and potential blueprints for Chinese governance that also include the eclectic borrowing of democratic elements. He also points at the risks and uncontrollable effects of a radical democratisation of China and stresses that any re-steering would require the prior establishment of regulatory frameworks and would have to reflect the given socio-economic conditions. Without any protective mechanisms, democracy could easily deteriorate and transform into tyranny. He argues that certain elements of democratic governance would be compatible with China's socialist one-party regime, and that administrative modernisation and (Chinese-style) democratisation had already been out on the government's reform agenda by the Hu–Wen administration. In the 21st century, a remodelling of the PRC into a socialist democracy might be one possible development trajectory. Yu underlines the need to include the civil society in the implementation of certain administrative measures at the local levels of administration and, in general, advocates gradualist-explorative policy innovation (Yu 2002, 2009).

Another blueprint of China's future development is be found in Pan Wei's reflections on establishing a consultative rule of law regime in China (Pan 2003). His first conceptual drafts on this topic date back to the late 1990s. Pan decouples rule of law from the principle of democracy. He proposes to strengthen rule of law elements in order to re-stabilise the Chinese political regime and to prevent a regime transition towards multi-party democracy.

The reform ideas proposed by Yu Keping and Pan Wei indicate that developmental challenges and flaws of the Chinese governance system are not ignored but internally debated amongst social science scholars as well as amongst the party elites. The solutions proposed are not distinctively "Chinese". Chinese scholars take inspiration from historical as well as contemporary governance approaches developed and implemented in other political systems, including in Western democracies.

These debates centre on the negative socio-economic implications of the PRC's resource- and emission-intense catching-up modernisation strategy. All-encompassing democratic reforms are not regarded as a way out of this high-speed modernisation dilemma – as the "Five No" formula, proclaimed by Wu Bangguo (chairman of the NPC 2003–2013) in 2011, underlines. The Five No formula rejects multi-party democracy, diversified ideological principles, separation of power, federalism as well as privatisation (Wu 2013: 18).

All this raises the question of the direction in which the PRC might be heading. Many scholars concede that the PRC falls into the group of learning autocracies

---

51 For an excellent overview of the Chinese Modell debate, see: Zhao (2017).

(Nathan 2003) and has managed to re-stabilise the regime via pragmatic adaption and consultative elements (Teets 2013; Tsang 2009). Some scholars, however, classify the ongoing adaptation process not as sovereign steering but rather as passive crisis management that might not allow long-term stabilisation. Whilst, on paper, the Chinese party-state formally readjusted its institutions, these concessions should – according to critical observers – rather be seen as empty promises. Without a real enforcement of the officially proclaimed reforms, the assumed resilience capacities of the one-party state might soon be overstretched (Gilley 2003; Li 2013). In 2013, Nathan, adding to this debate, stated that the PRC's transformation process would not automatically result in a democratisation process – but could end up in a new mode of autocratic rule or even despotism (Nathan 2013). The "end-game of the CCP", however, predicted by Shambaugh in 2015, has so far not become reality.

Dimitrov, looking at the survival of modern communist autocracies from a comparative perspective, argues that their refocusing on the "people" would be the clue for their regime persistence. Neo-authoritarian political leaders, as Dimitrov explains, would no longer seek to secure their power monopoly based on the small group of the political elite but would have understood that they would have to win the support of the overall majority of the people. This approach opposes the assumptions of the theory of the selectorate. The selectorate approach argues that the continuity and robustness of autocratic systems would only formally rely on a rather huge selectorate – but that the political leadership would owe its power to an exclusive circle, the "winning coalition".[52] Moving beyond the selectorate paradigm, Dimitrov concludes that regime survival of communist autocracies relies on the combination of economic reforms, refined ideology, strategies to include and incorporate old and new socio-economic actor groups, and new modes of horizontal accountability (Dimitrov 2013: 20–34).

In the inner-Chinese debate, the decline and dissolution of the Soviet Union is rememorated as a warning example of uncoordinated reform and institutional restructuring. Chinese scholars thus, from time to time, undertake an ex post analysis of the drivers and determinants of decline of other political systems to formulate policy solutions that should not cause a transformation of the political regime (see also: Shambaugh 2011).

5.6. Summary

The stratification of Chinese society and the formation of new socio-economic actor groups poses a severe steering dilemma to the CCP government. The interests and demands of these competing actor groups are often not compatible. To cope with development and income disparities between the rich eastern coastal provinces and the remote, underdeveloped western regions, as well as with the rural/urban divide, the government might have to raise more taxes to finance

---

52 The selectorate is composed of three groups- the *nominal selectorate*, (s)electing the political leaders (the entirety of people formally entitled to vote), the *real selectorate* (those who are finally allowed to cast a vote), and the *winning coalition* (those whose vote is needed to win the election). See: Bueno de Mesquita et al. (2003).

redistributive measures to harmonise living standards and development opportunities all across the country. This could, however, destabilise the fragile consensus and symbiotic relationship between the party and the country's economic elites. Neo-liberal scholars stress that priority should be given to economic growth. China's New Left and Neo-Maoists, by contrast, are alerted by growing socioeconomic tensions and the loss of "social justice" and opt for state intervention and efforts to domesticate and regulate China's current variety of capitalism.

The 2013 reform decisions by the Third Plenum, ascribing the market a central role in the allocation of resources, seems to be inspired by a neo-liberal development strategy. Nonetheless, the formula *gongping zhengyi*, fairness and justice, runs like a golden thread through the party's reform documents. The term "inequality" is avoided – but a strengthening of social justice is repeatedly mentioned. This somehow continues Hu Jintao's slogan of the Harmonious Society, which was, however, not officially linked to concrete policies and steering initiatives.

So far, most contestation movements do not attack the political system as such. Protests are often driven by perceived corruption and power abuse by local cadres. The fifth generation presents its anti-corruption campaign as well as the rectification of party-cadres as an attempt to cope with these issues. The government also intervened as mediator in labour protests – legal frameworks to protect workers' rights have been amended and updated.

The rural/urban divide persists. Whilst the *hukou* system has not been formally abolished, some modest reforms have been launched to formalise *hukou* conversion. As surveys show, the number of rural inhabitants – even those belonging to the floating population – willing to change its *hukou* status to an urban one is rather small (given the growth of Chinese cities and the establishment of metropolitan clusters, the value of land has significantly increased, thus also changing people's views on the rights and obligations coming with a rural *hukou*). The policy experimentations started after the Third Plenum (2013) sought to further upgrade the options of China's rural population by allowing them to mortgage their (rural) land use rights.

Modern autocracies seek to implement reform decisions by securing a consensus with all actor groups involved instead of enforcing them by resorting to repression and coercion. This, however, might not always be an easy task. China's actor groups are highly fragmented, and instead of having to co-opt just one (monolithic) economic elite, the party-state has to coin policies that are acceptable for both the state-owned sector as well as for China's private economy sector.

Mass protests are commonly regarded as indicating a decline in people's support for and trust in the political regime and its institutions. The party-state observes and responds to mass movements – using them as seismographs for early warning, allowing the political elites to identify urgent reform needs and to come up with solutions that are designed to pre-empt people's demands.

The mode of cooperation between the (central) party-state and (local) (civil) society depends on the policy field concerned. With regard to environmental issues, the government has passed revisions of central laws and regulations that empower ENGOs and local pro-environment activists. When it comes to the Internet, the self-coordination of Chinese netizens and their freedom of expression is tolerated as long as they are not questioning the basic principles of the one-party regime.

Urban and rural actor groups continue to dream different "Chinese dreams". However, these two groups are not the only ones involved in the ongoing quest for formulating best practice solutions to inherited developmental challenges. The group of overseas Chinese also contributes to the coining of governance blueprints, and often maintains close ties to Chinese universities and research institutes. Some are also directly involved in rounds of internal consultation and policy advice.

Slogans such as the Harmonious Society or the Chinese Dream rememorate Chinese imaginations of peace and paradise (the Great Unity, *datong*, and the famous Peach Blossom Spring, *taohuayuan*). Whilst they promise a glorious future in the long run, the reform initiatives kicked-off since 2013 seek to provide visible short-term achievements. Whether the remaining (economic) tensions and conflicting interests within Chinese society will allow a successful implementation of the announced reforms remains to be seen.

Questions for Discussion

- What are the main drivers of social contestation movements in contemporary China?
- Under which conditions are these movements classified as "justified" actions? And what determines the party-state's decision to end or to support local social protests?
- Are the so-called mass movements coordinated by Chinese NGOs? If yes, what is there main role and agenda? If no, which other actors are involved?
- Do social movements and street protests signal a declining degree of legitimacy and opposition to one-party rule?
- The Internet and social media have widely been regarded as empowering civil society and as catalysing a democratic system transformation. Why, then, should an autocratic system allow the use of these technologies?
- How does the Chinese party-state integrate the Internet in its governance strategy? Are there any specific "Chinese" characteristics of state–society online interactions as compared to liberal democratic system settings?

References

Bieler, Stacey (2004), *"Patriots" or "Traitors"? A History of American-educated Chinese Students*. Armonk; New York: Sharpe.

Bueno de Mesquita, Bruce/Smith, Alastair/Siverson, Randolph M./Morrow, James D. (2003), *The Logic of Political Survival*. Cambridge: MIT Press.

Carothers, Thomas (2002), "The End of the Transition Paradigm", *Journal of Democracy*, 13:1, 5–21.

Chen, Gang (2012), "Politburo 'Group Study' Sessions: Is the Chinese Communist Party Becoming More Bureaucratic?", *EAI Background Brief*, 692, http://www.eai.nus.edu.sg/publications/files/BB692.pdf.

CLB (China Labour Bulletin) (2012), "A Decade of Change: The Workers' Movement in China 2000–2010", http://www.clb.org.hk/en/sites/default/files/File/research_reports/Decade%20of%20the%20Workers%20Movement%20final_0.pdf.

CNNIC (2020), "Zhongguo hulianwang fazhan zhuangkuang tongji baogao" (Statistical Report on the Development of the Internet in China).

Diamond, Larry (2002), "Thinking About Hybrid Regimes", *Journal of Democracy*, 13:2, 21–35.

Diamond, Larry (2010), "Liberation Technology", *Journal of Democracy*, 21:3, 69–83.

Dickson, Bruce (2003), *Red Capitalists in China: The Party, Private Entrepreneurs, and Prospects for Political Change*. Cambridge: Cambridge UP.

Dickson, Bruce (2007), "Integrating Wealth and Power in China: The Communist Party's Embrace of the Private Sector", *The China Quarterly*, 192, 827–854.

Dickson, Bruce (2016), *The Dictator's Dilemma: The Chinese Communist Party's Strategy for Survival*. New York: Oxford UP.

Dimitrov, Martin K. (2013), "Understanding Communist Collapse and Resilience", in: Dimitrov, Martin K. (ed.) (2013), *Why Communism Did Not Collapse: Understanding Authoritarian Regime Resilience in Asia and Europe*. New York: Cambridge UP, 3–39.

Elfstrom, Manfred/Kuruvilla, Sarosh (2014), "The Changing Nature of Labor Unrest in China", *Industrial & Labor Relations Review*, 67:2, 453–480.

Fu, Diana (2016), "Disguised Collective Action in China", *Comparative Political Studies*, https://doi.org/10.1177/0010414015626437.

Fu, Hualing/Cullen, Richard (2008), "*Weiquan* (Rights Protection) Lawyering in an Authoritarian State: Toward Critical Lawyering", *The China Journal*, 59, 111–127.

Fu, Hualing/Cullen, Richard (2011), "Climbing the *weiquan* Ladder: A Radicalizing Process for Rights-protection Lawyers", *The China Quarterly*, 205, 40–59.

Gilley, Bruce (2003), "The Limits of Authoritarian Resilience", *Journal of Democracy*, 14:1, 18–26.

Glaser, Bonnie S. (2012), "Chinese Foreign Policy Research Institutes and the Practice of Influence", in: Rozman, Gilbert (ed.) (2012), *China's Foreign Policy*. New York: Palgrave Macmillan, 88–124.

Han, Donglin (2013), "Returnees and their Political Impact: Evidence from Returned Students and Trainees from the Soviet Union in China, 1950–1966", *Journal of Contemporary China*, 84, 1106–1122.

He, Alex Jingwei/Huang, Genghua (2015), "Fighting for Migrant Labor Rights in the World's Factory: Legitimacy, Resource Constraints and Strategies of Grassroots Migrant Labor NGOs in South China", *Journal of Contemporary China*, 24:93, 471–492.

Health, Timothy R. (2014), *China's New Governing Party Paradigm: Political Renewal and the Pursuit of National Rejuvenation*. Farnham: Ashgate.

Hwang, Cindy (2012), "Not In My Backyard", *The Politic*, http://thepolitic.org/not-in-my-backyard-chinas-environmental-conscience-fights-back/.

Jiang, Min (2012), *Internet Companies in China: Dancing between the Party Line and the Bottom Line*. Paris: Ifri.

La Fargue, Thomas E. (1942), *China's First Hundred*. Washington: State College of Washington;

Lagerkvist, Johan (2005), "The Techno-cadre's Dream: Administrative Reform by Electronic Governance in China", *China Information*, 19:2, 189–216.

Li, Cheng (2012), "The End of the CCP's Resilient Authoritarianism? A Tripartite Assessment of Shifting Power in China", *The China Quarterly*, 211, 595–623.

Li, Lianjiang/O'Brien, Kevin J. (2008), "Protest Leadership in Rural China", *The China Quarterly*, 193, 1–23.

Lin, Biao (1965), "Long Live the Victory of People's War!", https://www.marxists.org/refer ence/archive/lin-biao/1965/09/peoples_war/index.htm.

Linz, Juan (2000), *Totalitarian and Authoritarian Regimes*. Boulder; London: Lynne Rienner.

Lu, Yiyi (2007), "The Collective Study Sessions of the Politburo: A Multipurpose Tool of China's Central Leadership", *University of Nottingham Briefing Series*, 27, https://www .nottingham.ac.uk/cpi/documents/briefings/briefing-27-collective-study-sessions-of-the-p olitburo.pdf.

Ma, Shiling (2007), "Jiexi Zhongyang jiti xuexi zhidu de liu ge mima" (Decyphering Six Secrets of the Collective Study Sessions), *Renmin Ribao*, http://politics.people.com.cn/G B/1026/5429770.html.

Mertha, Andrew (2008 [2010]), *China's Water Warriors: Citizen Action and Policy Change*. Ithaca; London: Cornell UP.

Miller, Lyman (2007), "The Political Implications of PLA Professionalism", in: Finkelstein, David Michael/Gunness, Kristen (eds.) (2007), *Civil-Military Relations in Today's China: Swimming in a New Sea*. New York: M. E. Sharpe, 131–145.

Miller, Alice L. (2013), "The New Party Politbureau Leadership", *China Leadership Monitor* 40.

Nathan, Andrew J. (2003), "Authoritarian Resilience", *Journal of Democracy*, 14:1, 6–17.

Nathan, Andrew (2013), "China at the Tipping Point? Foreseeing the Unforeseeable", *Journal of Democracy*, 24:1, 20–25.

Noesselt, Nele (2010), *Alternative Weltordnungsmodelle? IB-Diskurse in China* (Alternative Models of World Order? IR Debates in China). Wiesbaden: VS Verlag.

O'Brien, Kevin J./Li, Lianjiang (2006), *Rightful Resistance in Rural China*. Cambridge: Cambridge UP.

O'Brien, Kevin J. (1996), "Rightful Resistance", *World Politics*, 49:1, 31–55.

O'Brien, Kevin J. (ed.) (2008), *Popular Protest in China*. Cambridge: Harvard UP.

O'Brien, Kevin (2009), "Rural Protest", *Journal of Democracy*, 20:3, 25–28.

O'Brien, Kevin/Deng, Yanhua (2015), "Repression Backfires: Tactical Radicalization and Protest Spectacle in Rural China", *Journal of Contemporary China*, 24:93, 457–470.

Pan, Wei (2003), "Toward a Consultative Rule of Law Regime in China", *Journal of Contemporary China*, 12:34, 3–43.

Perry, Elizabeth J. (2001), "Challenging the Mandate of Heaven: Popular Protest in Modern China", *Critical Asian Studies*, 33:2, 163–180.

Rhoads, Edward J. M. (2011), *Stepping Forth into the World: The Chinese Educational Mission to the United States*. Hongkong: Hongkong UP.

Schwartz, Benjamin (1969), *In Search of Wealth and Power: Yen Fu and the West*. New York: Harper & Row.

Shambaugh, David (2002), "Civil-Military Relations in China: Party-Army or National Military?", *Copenhagen Journal of Asian Studies*, 16, 10–29.

Shambaugh, David (2011), "Learning from Abroad to Reinvent Itself: Explaining the Survival of the Chinese Communist Party after 1989", Conference Paper 2011.

Shambaugh, David (2015), "The Coming Chinese Crackup", https://www.wsj.com/articles/ the-coming-chinese-crack-up-1425659198.

Tanner, Murray Scott (2004), "China Rethinks Unrest", *The Washington Quarterly*, 27:3, 137–156.

Teets, Jessica C. (2013), "Let Many Civil Societies Bloom: The Rise of Consultative Authoritarianism in China", *The China Quarterly*, 213, 19–38.

Teng, Biao (2012), "Rights Defence (*weiquan*), Microblogs (*weibo*), and the Surrounding Gaze (*weiguan*): The Rights Defence Movement Online and Offline", *China Perspectives*, 3, 29–41.

The New York Times (2010), "In China, Labor Movement Enabled by Technology", *The New York Times* (written by Barboza and Bradsher), http://www.nytimes.com/2010/06/17/business/global/17strike.html?src=busln&_r=0.

Tong, Yanqi/Lei, Shaohua (2010), "Large-scale Mass Incidents and Government Responses in China", *International Journal of China Studies*, 1:2, 487–508.

Tsai, Kellee S. (2006), "Adaptive Informal Institutions and Endogenous Institutional Change in China", *World Politics*, 59, 116–141.

Tsang, Steve (2009), "Consultative Leninism: China's New Political Framework", *Journal of Contemporary China*, 18:62, 865–880.

Vukovich, Daniel (2015), "Illiberal China and Global Convergence: Thinking through Wukan and Hong Kong", *Third World Quarterly*, 36:11, 2130–2147.

Wu, Guoguang (2013), "Debating Political Reform: Societal Pressures and Party-State Responses", in: Wang, Gungwu/Zheng, Yongnian (eds.) (2013), *China: Development and Governance*. Singapore: World Scientific, 15–20.

Xinhua (2010), "Guangdong Party Chief Urges Companies to Care More for Employees after Foxconn Suicides", 29 May 2010, http://news.xinhuanet.com/english2010/china/2010-05/29/c_13322933.htm.

Xinhua (2014), "Xi Jinping: Ba wo guo cong wangluo daguo jianshe chengwei wangluo qiangguo "(Xi Jinping: Transforming China into a Cyber Great Power), 27 February 2014, http://news.xinhuanet.com/politics/2014-02/27/c_119538788.htm.

Yang, Guobin (2005), "Environmental NGOs and Institutional Dynamics in China", *The China Quarterly*, 181, 46–66.

Yang, Ray Ou (2015), "Political Process and Widespread Protests in China: The 2010 Labor Protest", *Journal of Contemporary China*, 24:91, 21–42.

Ye, Weili (2001), *Seeking Modernity in China's Name: Chinese Students in the United States, 1900–1927*. Stanford: Stanford UP.

Yu, Keping (2002), "Toward an Incremental Democracy and Governance: Chinese Theories and Assessment of Criteria", *New Political Science*, 24:2, 181–199.

Yu, Keping (2009), *Democracy is a Good Thing: Essays on Politics, Society, and Culture in Contemporary China*. Washington: Brookings.

Zhao, Suisheng (2017), "Whither the China Model: Revisiting the Debate", *Journal of Contemporary China*, 26: 103, 1–17.

Zheng, Yongnian (2007), *De Facto Federalism in China*. Singapore: World Scientific.

Zheng, Yongnian (2008), *Technological Empowerment: The Internet, State, and Society in China*. Stanford: Stanford University Press.

Recommended Reading

Social Movement Theories

Buechler, Steven M. (2011), *Understanding Social Movements: Theories from the Classical Era to the Present*. Boulder: Paradigm.

Della Porta, Donatella/Diani, Mario (eds.) (2015), *The Oxford Handbook of Social Movements*. Oxford: Oxford UP.

Tilly, Charles (2013), *Social Movements, 1768–2012*. Boulder: Paradigm.

Contestation and Mass Movements in China

Cai, Yongshu (2010), *Collective Resistance in China: Why Popular Protests Succeed or Fail*. Stanford: Stanford UP.

Chen, Xi (2012), *Social Protest and Contentious Authoritarianism in China*. Cambridge: Cambridge UP.

Perry, Elizabeth J. (2002), *Challenging the Mandate of Heaven: Social Protest and State Power in China*. Armonk: M. E. Sharpe.

Thornton, Patricia M. (2002), "Framing Dissent in Contemporary China: Irony, Ambiguity and Metonymy", *The China Quarterly*, 171, 661–681.

Tong, Yanqi/Lei, Shaohua (2014), *Social Protest in Contemporary China: 2003–2010*. London: Routledge.

Wasserstrom, Jeffrey N. (ed.) (1992), *Popular Protest and Political Culture: Learning from 1989*. Boulder: Westview Press.

Environmental Protests

Deng, Yanhua/Yang, Guobin (2013), "Pollution and Protest in China: Environmental Mobilization in Context", *The China Quarterly*, 214, 321–336.

Jing, Jun (2003), "Environmental Protest in Rural China", in: Perry, Elizabeth J./Selden, Mark (eds.) (2003) (2nd edition), *Chinese Society: Change, Conflict and Resistance*. New York; London: Routledge, 204–222.

Tong, Yanqi (2005), "Environmental Movements in Transitional Societies: A Comparative Study of Taiwan and China", *Comparative Politics*, 37: 2, 167–188.

Labour Protests

Becker, Jeffrey (2012), "The Knowledge to Act: Chinese Migrant Labor Protests in Comparative Perspective", *Comparative Political Studies*, 45:6, 1–26.

Chan, Chris King-Chi (2010), *The Challenge of Labour in China: Strikes and the Changing Labour Regime in Global Factories*. New York; London: Routledge.

Chan, Chris King-Chi/Pun, Ngai (2009), "The Making of a New Working Class? A Study of Collective Actions of Migrant Workers in South China", *The China Quarterly*, 198, 287–303.

Kuruvilla, Sarosh/Lee, Ching Kwan/Gallagher, Mary E. (eds.) (2011), *From Iron Rice Bowl to Informalization: Markets, Workers, and the State in a Changing China*. Ithaca: ILR Press.

Protests in the Rural Areas

Guo, Xiaolin (2001), "Land Expropriation and Villagers' Complaints in Northeast Yunnan", *The China Quarterly*, 166, 422–439.

Zweig, David (2003), "To the Courts or to the Barricades: Can New Political Institutions Manage Rural Conflicts?", in: Perry, Elizabeth J./Selden, Mark (eds.) (2003) (2nd edition), *Chinese Society: Change, Conflict and Resistance*. New York; London: Routledge, 113–135.

Internet

Chang, Xinyue (2013), "China's weibo: Political and Social Implications?", *Education About Asia*, 18:2, 16–18.

Chase, Michael S./Mulvenon James C. (2002), *You've Got Dissent! Chinese Dissident Use of the Internet and Beijing's Counter-strategies*. Santa Monica: RAND.

Chen, Wenhong (2014), "Taking Stock, Moving Forward: The Internet, Social Networks and Civic Engagement in Chinese Societies", *Information, Communication & Society*, 17:1, 1–6.

Ding, Sheng (2009), "Informing the Masses and Heeding Public Opinion: China's New Internet-related Policy Initiatives to Deal with its Governance Crisis", *Journal of Information Technology & Politics*, 6:1, 31–42.

Esarey, Ashley/Xiao, Qiang (2008), "Political Expression in the Chinese Blogosphere: Below the Radar", *Asian Survey*, 48:5, 752–772.

Esarey, Ashley/Xiao, Qiang (2011), "Digital Communication and Political Change in China", *International Journal of Communication*, 5, 298–319.

Lagerkvist, Johan (2012), "Principal-agent Dilemma in China's Social Media Sector? The Party-State and Industry Real-name Registration Waltz", *International Journal of Communication*, 6, 2628–2646.

Leibold, James (2011), "Blogging Alone: China, the Internet, and the Democratic Illusion?", *The Journal of Asian Studies*, 70:4, 1–18.

MacKinnon, Rebecca (2011), "China's 'Networked Authoritarianism'", *Journal of Democracy*, 22:2, 32–46.

Swaine, Michael (2013), "Chinese Views on Cybersecurity in Foreign Relations", *Chinese Leadership Monitor*, 42, 1–27.

Tong, Yanqi/Lei, Shaohua (2013), "War of Position and Microblogging in China", *Journal of Contemporary China*, 22:80, 292–311.

Yang, Guobin (2009), *The Power of the Internet in China: Citizen Activism Online.* New York: Columbia UP.

6. Global Dimensions: China's "New" Role in World Politics

Key Content and Learning Goals

- Overview of core theories and frameworks of analysis to assess the underlying multidimensional dynamics and main determinants of China's positioning in world affairs
- Introduction to the historical and cultural foundations of contemporary Chinese foreign relations
- Summary of Chinese world order views and think-tank debates on key concepts of world politics and global governance
- Illustrative case studies on China's changing positioning in global governance
- Theory-guided evaluation of China's "new" role in world politics: "norm taker", "norm maker" versus "norm innovator"

In the first decades following the PRC's entrance into the post-Mao reform era, the country's foreign policy decision-making process was readjusted and professionalised. Personalistic, charismatic leadership as practised by Mao was replaced by the principle of collective leadership. Instead of being (mis)guided by ideological visions and Maoist revolutionary dreams of the global spread of Chinese socialism, economic pragmatism became the predominant focus of Beijing's foreign relations. To achieve a critical, theory-guided assessment of China's regional and global environment and to calculate Beijing's options in bi- and multilateral bargaining rounds of international politics, the party-state intensified its deliberation with external advisors and promoted the formation of professional foreign policy think-tanks.

Informal institutions and informal consultations are far more powerful than the formal settings of China's foreign and security policy-making process. The PRC's foreign strategy has to accommodate the interests of a huge variety of actors, who sometimes even try to pursue their own foreign policy agenda beyond the PRC's officially proclaimed foreign and security strategy. As the case of China's engagement in Africa clearly illustrates, China's foreign relations with Africa are not so much coordinated by the Ministry of Foreign Affairs, but are clearly deeply influenced by the Ministry of Commerce and Chinese (state-owned) banks. On the ground, a plurality of state-owned as well as of private Chinese companies and investors is competing for market shares. Whilst there is still one unified, official foreign strategy of the PRC, activities by local (especially private) "Chinese" actors do not necessarily mirror the Chinese government's official agenda and vision of world order.

The following chapter introduces the reader to the main patterns and drivers underlying the PRC's foreign relations and Beijing's strategic positioning in global affairs. It reflects the PRC's national role claims as well as the roles ascribed to China by the international community. To document the (still ongoing) transformation of China's international actor identity, this chapter includes case studies on China's evolving role as a global investor and supporter of development in Africa and Latin America. Furthermore, additional case studies elaborate on the reconfiguration of the PRC's national and global security concept and China's efforts to explore and govern "new" areas – such as outer space, cyberspace or the Arctic region.

This chapter concludes with some reflections on China's role in international institutions and reassesses the main assumptions of socialisation theories. The original expectation had been that the integration of states in international (liberal) institutions and global capitalism would lead to these states' compliance with international norms, values and principles of interaction. The related policy diffusion and learning process was thought to occur from the Global North to the Global South, and from the West to the East. The PRC's rise to global power status does not seem to fit into this equation. Beijing is no longer a passive receiver of prescribed rules nor a submissive, accommodating member of international institutions. The PRC has (re-)started to articulate its own world order views and global governance concepts, and to ask for a reform of select international institutions. In addition to these reform initiatives targeting the "old" order, the PRC has also commenced to set up its "own" multilateral institutions such as the Asian Infrastructure Investment Bank (AIIB) and the BRICS New Development Bank (NDB). Whilst this move has widely been interpreted as a challenge to the "liberal" order and its institutional backbone(s), a closer and theory-guided evaluation of these "Chinese" institutions might, as the reader will see at the end of this chapter, lead to a more complex scenario beyond the black-and-white scenario of an overt power struggle and system antagonism between the "West" (the US) and the "East" (the PRC).

6.1. China's Self-Image as a Modern Great Power: Imperium or Pole in a Multipolar World?

"Theory is always for someone and for some purpose. All theories have a perspective. Perspectives derive from a position in time and space" – this statement by Robert Cox (1981: 128) highlights the impact of the analyst's location and socialisation on their interpretation of past and current international relations and the formulation of policy advice.

How the rise of China to global power status is evaluated and classified depends on the theoretical framework applied. Neo-realist scenarios and power transition theories postulate that the ascent of a novel player will never be peaceful and will lead to an inevitable war between the old hegemon and the rising power. Scholars inspired by liberal or globalist frameworks, by contrast, tend to stress the increased economic interdependencies and related mutual vulnerability and thus argue that most players will rather seek to avoid any open confrontation. Certain streams of socio-constructivism stress the role of interaction-induced identity-formation as well as the travelling and diffusion of norms and values, hoping that the integration of China will kick-off the internalisation of Western liberal norms and standards. Or, at least, secure compliance with international norms and institutions.

When assessing China's role in world politics, one has to differentiate between foreign policy analysis (FPA) and International Relations (IR) theories. FPA approaches look at the level of foreign policy decision-making, evaluating actors and their mind maps, structural determinants, abstract policy options as well as the final implementation of the foreign policy solutions. FPA thus targets one specific dimension of international relations. Theories of IR look at the level of interactions and often operate with scenarios derived from the analysis of historical cases. IR theories relying on the concept of "like units" start from the assumption that all actors will, given similar environmental conditions and structural settings, follow a unified pattern and resort to the same mode of interaction (and conflict behaviour). This implies that the categorisation of an actor as an "empire" or "great power" is directly linked to ideas regarding his positioning, strategic actions and long-term foreign policy goals.

Opposing the threat scenarios and conflict predictions put forward by neo-realist analysts, Chinese scholars and politicians are engaged in coining an alternative narrative on China's identity and strategic behaviour as a global power. The diversity of IR debates and world order contemplations within China indicates that the remodelling of China's national and global role is still an ongoing process. A critical decryption of the debates related to Chinese IR allows one to gain insight into the transformation and remaking of China's actor identity at the global stage.

This deciphering requires a context-based reading of think-tank publications combined with a frame analysis of the PRC's official diplomatic rhetoric. Transition and foreign policy adjustment processes can occur via a substitution of the official foreign policy master frames or by reiterating key frames but filling them with new content:

Whilst the international debate often tends to classify the PRC as an emerging revisionist and increasingly assertive "empire", the PRC itself operates with the self-image of being a pole in a multipolar world and a great power (*daguo*) in a world composed of one superpower and many great powers. Whilst the concept of multipolarity, coined back in the 1970s, continues to serve as the official reference scheme of China's diplomacy, the meaning ascribed to the concept of "pole" and *daguo* has silently been amended and adapted to the changes in China's regional and global environment. The PRC's official world politics rhetoric still iterates Deng Xiaoping's claim that China would never pursue any hegemonic power ambitions and would never seek to position itself as a global leader (*bu dang tou*). Moreover, the PRC has reconfirmed its dedication to the Five Principles of Peaceful Coexistence presented by China's foreign minister Zhou Enlai at the Bandung Conference back in 1955. Nonetheless, the PRC's conduct of its foreign relations is often overshadowed by tensions and contradictions between Beijing's abstract foreign policy principles and its actual foreign behaviour. Some inherited foreign policy principles, or "thinking sets", however, seem to be eternal, unchanging ones – such as the prioritisation of (national) economic development or the conviction that China's relationship with the US ranks highest on China's foreign strategy matrix, overshadowing and driving all other bi- and multilateral interactions (see also: Xu/Du 2015).

Given the existence of eternal, axiomatic principles of China's foreign and security strategy, the general expectation is that regular leadership changes are orchestrated as a handing over of the baton to the next generation of leaders who will follow in the footsteps of their predecessors. Nonetheless, the changing of the guard in 2012/2013 and the ascent of Xi Jinping to the top echelons of the Chinese party-state was accompanied by international debates expecting a formal modification and update to the PRC's official foreign strategy. Xi Jinping did, indeed, introduce novel formula such as the Chinese Dream (*Zhongguo meng*) and the Community of Shared Destiny (*renmin gongtong mingyunti*). A thoughtful decryption and excavation of these concepts' historical and philosophical underpinnings evidences that – at least at the content level – the PRC's old, inherited foreign strategy and world order narratives have been continued and reconfirmed. Sometimes, however, official frames might also be filled with "new" content, e.g., by reactivating and adapting strategies and world order ideas that had been temporarily put on ice (He/Feng 2013). Nonetheless, whether the PRC pursues a grand strategy or just undertakes ad hoc crisis management, implying punctual modifications to its foreign behaviour and positioning strategy, remains a question yet to be answered.

The PRC's rise to global power status has fuelled debates amongst scholars and intellectuals in China regarding the eventual need to reformulate the country's foreign strategy in order to reflect changing structural constraints as well as Beijing's upgraded bargaining power vis-à-vis other players in the international realm. The liberal, reform-oriented camp of Chinese scholars favours continuity and advises the government to avoid any actions that could be interpreted as an assertive move and thus catalyse the emergence of anti-Chinese containment coalitions. The hardliners, including certain groups within the Chinese military, by contrast, demand a more self-confident positioning and defence of Chinese national core interests. This internal conflict has become known to the wider public in and outside China in connection with the controversy over the correct reading and interpretation of Deng Xiaoping's *taoguang yanghui* formula.

As the Chinese political scientist Ye Zicheng explains, the formula *taoguang yanghui* – commonly translated as "keep a low profile and bide your time" – is taken from a 28-character statement by Deng Xiaoping back in the 1990s. Deng's statement reacted to continued international criticism directed against Chinese socialism and calculated ways to upgrade Beijing's diplomatic leverage and room of manoeuvre at the global stage. Deng's contemplations do, however, not condemn the PRC to a passive and obedient subordinate to demands and expectations put forward by the international community. The *taoguang yanghui* formula is directly followed by the four-character set *yousuo zuowei* – "to play an active role". Seen from a strategic point of view, *taoguang yanghui* formed part of camouflage tactics, aimed at defusing threat perceptions and preventing the formation of anti-Chinese containment coalitions. Following the end of the Cold War and the dissolution of the Soviet Union, the PRC, as the only remaining major socialist power, became the main target of global initiatives seeking to induce the transformation of the few remaining non-capitalist communist one-party states. These prevailing scenarios of system antagonisms were identified as adverse to Chinese economic development interests. To realise the modernisation of the Chinese economy and to boost economic growth, the PRC needed a stable and peaceful regional and global environment. The integration into global trade and finance ranked high on the post-Maoist modernisation roadmap (Ye 2002). In the run-up to the changing of the guard in 2012/2013, the "correct" definition and interpretation of the *taoguang yanghui* formula triggered a heated, controversial debate amongst Chinese scholars, think-tank researchers and factions within the CCP. Patriotic groups as well as hardliners from the military demanded that the PRC should undertake a more active and self-confident positioning in regional and global affairs, reflecting the country's upgraded power capacities and rising global economic status. They called for a substitution of the *taoguang yanghui* concept, stressing the tension and incompatibility between *taoguang yanghui* and *yousuo zuowei*. Rather liberal, globalist circles, by contrast, argued that Deng's statement would not a priori inhibit an active engagement and positioning of the PRC in world politics and economics. Scholars from this liberal-globalist group also voiced their concerns that a formal invalidation of *taoguang yanghui* would kick-off dangerous security spirals and arms races. As Yan Xuetong, IR specialist at Tsinghua University in Beijing, explains, Xi Jinping has added a novel frame to the debate on China's foreign and security strategy: *fenfa youwei* – which he translates as "striving for achievement" (Yan 2014).

The *taoguang yanghui* episode shows that the PRC is currently re-thinking and re-evaluating the basic principles of its foreign policy. Likewise, international IR analysts seem to be quite uncertain regarding Beijing's future strategic moves. These debates on China's evolving role in the global system are often guided by the core assumptions of neo-realism and power transition theories, predicting that rising powers will pursue an increasingly assertive foreign strategy and seek to achieve global hegemony. It is expected that the old power centre will try to defend its position, which implies overt confrontation or even the outbreak of war (Organski 1968; Organski/Kugler 1980).

Shaun Breslin, however, argues that the PRC does not actively strive for the overthrow of the existing system structures but rather asks for (modest) reforms – given that the "rise" of China took place embedded in the institutions set up after the Second World War. Any structural change or substitution of these institutions might have unpredictable implications for China's global status and development options (Breslin 2013).

Major critical junctures, such as the end of Cold War bipolarity and the restructuring of international institutions, neither generated a major readjustment of the PRC's foreign and security strategy nor kicked off a reformulation of the country's national role conception and related status and identity claims (Beylerian/Canivet 1997). As the *taoguang yanghui* debate evidences, it was not the external structural transformation of China's global environment as such, but the increase in the PRC's economic and monetary power capacities which has triggered a redefinition of the official Chinese national and global role set.

China operates with an inherited but highly fragmented set of national and global roles, combining the role of "great power" with a reference to "socialism" and the status of a "developing country". Since the PRC's entrance into the Xi Jinping era, the concept of "great power" has, undoubtedly, emerged as the predominant national role element. The official Chinese narrative constructs the notion of "great power" (*daguo*) as opposed to the idea of "empire" (*diguo*). The latter has a rather negative connotation and, dating back to the Cold War years, had been mainly used to classify both the US and the Soviet Union as "empire" and "imperial(ist) powers". The PRC's self-proclaimed national role identity is that of a "responsible great power". This term might remind the reader of the US's efforts to secure the PRC's compliance with international norms and standards by asking Beijing to behave as "responsible great power". The integration of this national role conception ascribed to – if not rhetorically "forced" on – the PRC by other players did, however, not result in compliance and passive role-taking. Instead, the Chinese side displayed an "as if" role-taking behaviour by borrowing a key term of the US debate and merging it with "Chinese" IR norms and world order conceptions.

Diplomatic statements and states' narratives of world politics generally do not allow any direct conclusions to be reached regarding these players' current and future international behaviour. Instead, the coining of official national roles can be understood as part of identity-building and symbolic legitimation. These legitimation narratives are often designed as indirect two-level games: they seek to present political decisions and actions as being in line with the country's historical and cultural traditions and the related value system – thus addressing a domestic audience. Targeting specific groups of cooperation partners at the international level, the official national role conceptions create a shared group identity – when reaching out to the states of the Global South and the developing world – or, in the case of Sino–US interactions, stress the PRC's claim for acceptance and to be treated as an equal partner.

National roles are regarded as dysfunctional if they are not accepted by the targeted audience. Furthermore, if a country's national role claims are perceived as standing in sharp contrast to its actual role behaviour, the continued reference to these internationally "questioned" role claims might be highly counterproductive, as this might ultimately fuel contestation movements. Reports about hidden debt traps attached to China's unconditional granting of loans and credits along its New Silk Road corridors caused the postponement or annulation of already signed investment and infrastructure construction deals by quite a number of states in Africa and Latin America. Whilst the PRC officially sticks to its self-defined identity as a "developing country", and thus promoter of win-win solutions with the Global South, counter-narratives have emerged, accusing China of being a "neo-colonial" power, exploiting these countries and expanding its (political-ideological) spheres of influence.

The perception of Chinese role claims and the interpretation of its actions on the ground do have a strong impact on China's national role conceptions and the coining of related narratives (Hu 2006). The concept of a Peaceful Rise, forming part of the PRC's national role conception narrative under Hu Jintao, was ultimately replaced by the formula of Peaceful Development, as the former notion had not been well-received by the international audience who doubted the feasibility of a "peaceful" redistribution of power capacities amongst the core players of world politics.

The configuration of Chinese national and global roles mirrors a strategic mapping of given global power constellations: the Chinese role conception of *daguo* is, first of all, a status claim and, in connection with the formula "new type of great power relations" coined by Xi Jinping, constructs a symbolic power parity between China and the US. *Daguo* as such remains an empty signifier, allowing the various (competing) societal actor groups to fill it with their own ideas and imaginations of China's future role in world politics and economics. The self-imagination of China as being a power centre and great power continues the old legacy of China's self-proclaimed identity of *tianxia*. *Tianxia* – all under heaven – is not only the Chinese term for the Chinese Empire, but also operates with the division of the world into the civilised space of the *tianxia* and the barbarian world beyond the imagined four oceans which separate the *tianxia* from these uncivilised parts of the world. *Tianxia* thus symbolises a cultural, civilisational community and is not bound to territorial borders (Zhang, Weiwei 2012). The forced opening of the Chinese Empire for international trade by the Unequal Treaties of the Opium Wars did, as Levenson, postulates, initiate a transformation of China from the status of empire/*tianxia* to the status of a nation-state. Tributary relations and the symbolic *kowtow* submission to the Chinese emperor were substituted by international law and treaty regulations of the Westphalian system composed of nation-states. Beyond this operational level, as Gerald Chan argues, China did not follow the role and identity of a nation-state but remained deeply inspired by its historical identity as a civilisation-state. Some irrational moves and overreactions in Chinese foreign relations could be the result of these internal role and identity tensions (Chan 2014: 280).

Despite international and domestic structural transformations, the PRC did not undertake any official readjustment of its national role conceptions at a terminological level. It did, however, adapt its foreign strategy and foreign policy behaviour (Chen, Yingchun 2007). When entering the post-Maoist reform era, the PRC officially changed its core foreign policy slogan from "war and revolution" (*zhanzheng yu geming*) into "peace and development" (*heping yu fazhan*), later adding the concept of cooperation (*hezuo*) (Liu 2013). Qin Yaqing, summarising this evolution, argues that the PRC underwent a transformation from being a revolutionary power to a rather conservative "status quo" actor. This transformation, according to Qin, was primarily driven by economic calculations. China's economic modernisation required the country's active involvement in the world economy. Integration into the international institutional settings implied a partial modification of China's system configurations and created structural interdependencies, thus forcing China to stabilise the institutional architecture of international trade and finance (Qin 2003). The modification of the PRC's national development strategy, implying a farewell to ideology-based revolutionary

171

foreign policy, also included a turn from the domestic to the global level. The government encouraged Chinese companies and banks to "go out" and to explore new markets.

Putting the historical evolution of the PRC's shifting strategy and role identity in a nutshell, Gerald Chan proposes the following periodisation: socialist state (1950s), developing state and part of the so-called Third World (1960s), revolutionary state (late 1960s to late 1970s), reform and opening state (1980s), peacefully rising state (1990s), responsible state (Chan 2014: 265). This list obviously merges elements of national role claims – such as the Chinese "peaceful rise" – with the country's economic development strategy.

The PRC actively coins auxiliary national role frames to oppose US debates – that classify the PRC as a "rogue state" and, jointly with Russia, as an "evil" state promoting the spread of illiberal, authoritarian regime patters. At the international level, the Chinese side seeks to counter threat scenarios by arguing that China's rise will not occur in an assertive way and will not result in an aggressive overthrow of the post-World War II international order.

China's national role remains highly fragmented. National role contestation – long since taken as being a unique feature of parliamentary debates in multi-party democracies (inter alia Cantir/Kaarbo 2012, 2016) – also occurs within China's party-state, though not being publicly displayed or documented. Along these lines, the *taoguang yanghui* controversy is not only about foreign strategy and global status, but is closely related to the ongoing efforts to come up with a more concrete definition of China's role as a *daguo* and related responsibilities at the global level.

Ideas and mind maps do not necessarily determine foreign policy decision-making, but they might impact on related strategic calculations and long-term plans. Given China's growing embeddedness in global trade and production chains, the vulnerability of China's domestic economy has multiplied. The global presence of Chinese companies and banks in addition to the multiple investment and infrastructure activities beyond Chinese borders imply that conflicts, wars and crises in other world regions have to be included in the PRC's "national" development agenda and its foreign and security strategy. Officially, the PRC sticks to the Five Principles of Peaceful Coexistence and the concept of non-interference into other countries' internal affairs. Crises and civil wars in African states might, however, require some actions to restore order and to protect Chinese investment and infrastructure initiatives. China's global activities hence entail a further update or partial modification of the PRC's official foreign policy principles – at least at the operational level.

The PRC moves to contribute to the governance of transnational challenges and to propose solutions for complex global governance dilemmas add more pressure on the system to update its official role frames and strategies. Under China's fourth generation of political leaders, research on global governance was still in its initial stage. World politics were designed as regulations and agreements bargained between national governments; transnational and global dimensions –

as well as actor constellations – were not taken into consideration. The introduction of refined Chinese IR concepts – the Chinese Dream, presented as a shared dream of peace and development across the globe, and the Community of Shared Destiny – signal a shift from Westphalian world order views to global IR.

The articulation of national role claims, self-images and world order conceptions does not mean that the PRC's international actions are determined and bound by these ideas. The official diplomatic narratives coined in China justify certain foreign policy decisions taken, add to the construction of a distinct Chinese identity and narrate the storylines of world politics from a "Chinese" perspective.

6.2. The Outside Perspective: China as "Status quo"-Actor or Revisionist Power

Following the renormalisation of diplomatic relations since 1992 – when most sanctions, except the arms embargo, imposed on China as international response to the crack-down on the protests in Tian'anmen Square (1989) were lifted – international China watchers developed two main competing scenarios regarding the country's future positioning and behavioural patterns. These can be clustered and categorised as studies featuring China's status quo orientation versus those predicting a turn to overt revisionism. Scenarios anticipating an inevitable conflict between the world's leading superpower US and the rapidly rising PRC (Bernstein/Munro 1997) would thus see containment measures and efforts to induce a regime transformation as the only way to secure the survival of the "liberal" order. China watchers, evaluating the drivers and motivations of China's foreign strategy, by contrast advocate active engagement instead of confrontation, stressing that Beijing is primarily interested in stability and economic prosperity, thus not pushing for any overt system change at the global level (Ross 1997). Along the same lines, Johnston, analysing China's foreign policy behaviour at the turn of the century, highlighted Beijing's cooperative behaviour and doubted that the PRC would actively choose to position itself in opposition to the US (Johnston 2003). Likewise, Kastner and Saunders, looking at the PRC's foreign interactions and the diplomatic travel activities of China's political leaders during the years 1998–2008, did not find any indication of a strategy or position change (Kastner/Saunders 2012).

Tracing China's changing role and strategic positioning in international institutions, Alastair Iain Johnston (2008) identifies three specific dimensions of engagement-related socialisation, describing China's participation in international politics as a learning process. Whilst newcomers to international institutions observe passively at first, trying to understand the given rules and organisational principles, they are expected to adapt their role(s) as soon as they have reached a certain power position and are familiar with internal procedures. In fact, coinciding with the outbreak of the global and financial crisis of 2007/2008, the Chinese government did show a more self-confident positioning in regional and global affairs. These rhetorical statements and China's (re)actions to conflicts and tensions in the South China Sea kicked off another round of China threat debates in the US, centring on the overarching theme of "new assertiveness" (Swaine 2010). The identification of an "assertive" turn in Chinese foreign relations did justify the US pivot to Asia, the renewal of security alliances in Asia and the increased US military presence in the region. Johnston, examining the examples quoted as empirical evidence for China's "new assertiveness", however, concludes that neither China's claims and positions in the territorial disputes in the South China Sea, nor the island dispute with Japan, nor the positioning of Beijing at the Copenhagen Conference would bear any measurable traces of policy change or increasingly aggressive behaviour. Johnston concludes, therefore, that China's post-2010 foreign policy did not undergo any major reorientation (Johnston 2013). Friedberg, again, postulates that China's bargaining strategy has been refined, arguing that the strategic turn to "assertive" behaviour – quoting the meeting between Xi and Abe in 2014 as well as China's bargaining stance in regional contexts – allows Beijing to push for the acceptance of Chinese demands. After a short period of apparently assertive rhetoric and symbolic escalation of the situation, the Chinese side finally accepted a conflict resolution – thus using assertive means only to increase its bargaining leverage (Friedberg 2014).

6.3. Power Shifts in the Global System: Economic and Monetary Dimensions

The steering and governance of world politics is increasingly done via multilateral fora and networks. The (power) positions of the actors involved depend on their access to the related deliberation and bargaining processes. Therefore, power in international relations cannot be measured in terms of economic or military capacities alone (Nolte 2006). One of the more nuanced categorisations of power at the level of global politics has been presented by Barnett and Duvall. They differentiate between compulsory power, institutional power, structural and productive power – combining the two levels of material and ideational power dimensions (Barnett/Duvall 2005).

Financial and monetary power dimensions are regarded as increasingly relevant for an actor's global positioning and bargaining options (Armijo et al. 2013; Cohen 2013; Eichengreen 2008). The PRC has noticeably managed to upgrade its power resources in the related sectors: it reportedly holds the world's largest US dollar reserves, has managed to install itself as a global investor (and main creditor to the US), has successfully internationalised its national currency and bargained its inclusion into the IMF SDR currency basket.

Andrews defined the related dimension of "monetary power" as follows:

> "Monetary power at the macro-level consists of the capacity either to delay payment of adjustment's continuing costs or to deflect its transitional costs on to others" (Andrews 2006: 6)

> "international monetary power can assume any of a number of different forms: the Power to Deflect the transitional costs of monetary adjustment, the Power to Delay payment of adjustment's continuing costs, the Power to Rearticulate actors' economic interests, and the Power to Reconstruct actors' social identities" (Andrews 2006: 16).

Benjamin J. Cohen reflected on this concept further by stating:

> "The Power to Delay is largely a function of a country's international liquidity position relative to others, comprising both owned reserves and borrowing capacity. The Power to Deflect has its source in more fundamental structural variables: the relative degree of openness and adaptability of the national economy" (Cohen 2006: 49).

Monetary power can be converted into structural power, the power to structure and design the basic patterns and institutional arrangements of international transactions – following the concept of "structural power", defined by Susan Strange as:

> "the power to shape and determine the structures of the global political economy within which other states, their political institutions, their economic enterprises, and (not least) their scientists and other professional people have to operate" (Strange 1988: 24)

Power, especially when materialising as structural power, is increasingly seen as being linked to and created (and reconfirmed) via bargaining processes. International law and regulations do not only limit states' freedom of action and seek to prevent arbitrary actions, but also cement power structure and power relations amongst those state-actors involved in the constitutionalisation process. Power in contemporary international relations is no longer conceptualised as power to impose and control, but rather as a complex interplay between authority and legitimacy. By granting formal recognition to the established order, states (and other players) also accept and iterate the underlying power distributions (Krisch 2005).

A broader definition of power thus displays certain connections to processes of constitutionalisation and norm-based regulation of world politics. In this context, legitimacy of the international order is measured in terms of efficiency and problem-solving capacities (output dimension) added by abstract, often normative-teleological elements. The existence of this, often overlooked, abstract dimension implies that the international order is facing a severe legitimacy crisis, not only in the case of underperformance or declining efficiency but even more so if the established institutional order and its normative, ethical foundations are perceived as incompatible with the value systems and normative principles of (the majority of) other relevant players. A considerable number of states in the Global South seem to be united by the observation that the international realm is, contrary to the starting assumption of mainstream IR theories, not characterised by anarchy and the absence of a supreme authority. By contrast, this group of unsatisfied states (and regional organisations) sees hierarchy and US supremacy as the main challenge to their development interests and is, therefore, susceptible to "alternative" world order settings.

6.3.1. China as a Global Investor: New Positioning in Europe and the US

The general turn to a more complex conceptualisation of power in international relations that also calculates non-military economic and monetary facets might explain the threat scenarios associated with the PRC's emergence as a worldwide investor and global creditor.

Whilst the PRC is still a major recipient of overseas foreign direct investment, Chinese banks have continuously expanded their financial activities (Chin/Helleiner 2008) – and not only in so-called developing regions of the Global South.

In 2009, Chinese foreign direct investment amounted to 43 billion USD. In 2013, this had been multiplied to 90 billion USD, making China the world's third largest investor after the US and Japan. Also, in 2013, the amount of FDI by state-owned companies equalled the FDI share of Chinese private companies; but their investment strategies diverged. Private companies were mainly investing in the US and parts of Europe, whilst state-owned companies focused on the African continent. In Europe, investment mainly targeted three countries: Great Britain, France and Germany (in 2019, the focus shifted to investment in Northern Europe). Chinese companies purchased shares of Heathrow Airport Holdings and Thames Water Utilities. Geely, which had taken over Volvo, also bought shares of the London Taxi Corporation. In 2018, Geely also secured a 10 % share of Daimler. A couple of years earlier, in 2016, the leading Chinese chemical company acquired the German machine manufacturer KraussMaffei for 925 million EUR; and China's Midea company purchased 95 % of the German industrial robot manufacturer Kuka. Major (and heavily disputed) investment deals with Southern Europe include Chinese investment in the port of Piraeus (Greece). The Budapest–Belgrade railway is one of China's major construction (and investment) deals with Eastern Europe.

Official figures released by China's National Bureau of Statistics document that, in 2013, the lion's share of Chinese financial transactions flowed in the direction of Hong Kong (58 %) and to offshore tax havens (such as the Cayman Islands and the Virgin Islands) (12 %). Europe received 6 % of Chinese OFDI, the US only 4 %. The 13 % OFDI share of Latin America points at an increased economic and strategic interest of the PRC in this region. With regard to the US, most investments were undertaken by private companies (2013: 80 % of all transactions; 70 % of the total investment volume).[53] One explanation might be that Chinese investors felt highly attracted by the US Visa Program EB-5, which offers Green Cards in exchange for foreign investment. The programme required a standard minimum investment of 500,000 USD and a minimum of 10 employment opportunities.[54] In 2006, 486 investors applied for this program, increasing to 10,000 in 2014 (with an estimated 85 % being private investors from China)

---

53 For the most recent dates and figures, see: China Investment Monitor (Rhodium Group): http://rhg.com/in teractive/china-investment-monitor.
54 US Citizenship and Immigration Service, Green Card through investment, https://www.uscis.gov/green-car d/green-card-through-job/green-card-through-investment.

(*Bloomberg* 2016). The requirements and regulations were eased in the years of the US subprime mortgage crisis, but revised and tightened in 2020.[55]

In early 2015, the PRC's Ministry of Commerce reported that in 2014, for the first time in the PRC's history, Chinese outbound foreign direct investment surpassed the total amount of foreign direct investment to China (Ministry of Commerce 2015). Moreover, in 2016, Chinese OFDI accounted for almost 200 billion USD, ranking second only to the US. Chinese FDI in the US from 1990 to December 2019 amounted to 150 billion USD. As the US have passed regulations to limit the access of Chinese companies and investors to the US market, Chinese investment in 2019 dropped remarkably. However, this might not only have been a result of US protectionism but also an effect of the new regulation passed by the PRC to reduce irrational global capital flows. In 2019, Chinese investment in Europe dropped from 18 billion EUR in 2018 to 12 billion EUR due to a combination of economic and political factors.

To encourage companies to invest abroad, the NDRC and the Chinese Ministry of Commerce (joined by the People's Bank of China and the Ministry of Foreign Affairs) have issued guidelines to "guide and regulate" the directions of outbound investment. The guidelines are revised and updated on a regular and frequent basis.

The PRC's focus on global investment stands for a readjustment of the PRC's global strategy. The idea is no longer to secure access to resources and agricultural products but also to position Chinese companies in strategic sectors of the global market and to upgrade these companies' technological innovation capacities. Infrastructure and investment deals are clustered along the (imagined) corridors of China's New Silk Road.

Chinese state-owned and private companies followed the government's "going out" (*zou chuqu*) call and have transformed themselves into competitive global players. This has been channelled and facilitated by the PRC's entry into the WTO (2000/2001) and its active involvement in global trade and global finance. With this has come the accumulation of foreign currency reserves, given the huge trade imbalances in favour of China. As of May 2020, the PRC owned 4 % of the US national debt, equalling about 1 trillion USD.[56] In 2014, the PRC held 58 % of its currency reserves in USD (2005: 79 %) – and its total foreign currency exchange reserves amounted to more than 3 trillion USD in 2020. Given the trade dispute with the US and the vulnerability of the Chinese economy by US financial policies, the PRC has continuously diversified its currency reserves, converting part of its USD reserves in euro, Japanese yen and British pound.

The drafting of regulations for foreign exchange market activities and the management of the foreign currency reserves of the People's Bank of China lies in

---

55 https://www.uscis.gov/working-in-the-united-states/permanent-workers/eb-5-immigrant-investor-program.

56 In 2018, the PRC was reportedly the main creditor of the US, holding 1.13 trillion USD of US debt. In 2020, Japan replaced China as the largest holder of US national debt.

the hands of the State Administration of Foreign Exchange (SAFE).[57] In 2007, the China Investment Corporation (CIC)[58] was established to manage parts of the PBoC's currency reserves. Reportedly, the CIC, starting with 200 billion USD, had to face speculation losses in connection with the downward spirals of the US economy (Blanchard 2011).

The diversification of China's investment and reserve currency strategies, mentioned above, did not reduce the country's financial vulnerability as originally planned as it has become dependent on the stability of not just one but a number of liberal economies, sharing similar democratic values and normative principles (i.e., opposing China's one-party state).

China also continued to internationalise its own currency, the Chinese renminbi. In 2020, the renminbi ranked fifth in global payment transactions by value, meaning a share of 1.86 % (USD: 38.77 %; euro: 36.46 %; British pound; 7 %, Japanese yen: 3.46 %).[59]

6.3.2. "Going out": China in Africa and Latin America

Relations between China and Africa, the states of Latin America and the Caribbean are falling into the category of South–South cooperation. In these bi- and multilateral settings, China plays its national role identity as a developing country and part of the "Third World", often pointing at the joint experience of having been colonialised and stressing the need for self-reliant economic development. Cooperation agreements are framed as win-win solutions amongst equals.

Whilst, for many states in Africa and Latin America, China has emerged as the most important trading partner and main creditor, the majority of them do not play a major role in Chinese foreign relations. In terms of trade volume, the US, Europe and Japan are far more important. The PRC's foreign relations still follow the old pattern of major power diplomacy. As Qin Yaqing, president of China's Foreign Affairs University in Beijing, outlined, "major powers are the core concern, priority is ascribed to China's immediate periphery, developing countries are seen as basis, and multilateral platforms as a new stage" (Qin 2007).[60]

6.3.2.1. ChinAfrica

When reaching out to Africa, the PRC symbolically distances itself from the colonial ambitions of former colonial powers and the good governance-based conditional developmental cooperation initiatives as financed by the IMF and the World Bank. Chinese diplomatic narratives also refer to the non-colonial historical traditions of China's "discovery" of Africa, as associated with the global voyages of the Chinese general Zheng He during the Ming Dynasty. As archived as part of China's account of historical diplomatic relations, the Chinese Empire

---

57 SAFE: http://www.safe.gov.cn/wps/portal/english/Home.
58 CIC: http://www.china-inv.cn.
59 For the most recent data, see: SWIFT RMB Tracker: https://www.swift.com/our-solutions/compliance-and -shared-services/business-intelligence/renminbi/rmb-tracker.
60 大国是关键，周边是首要，发展中国家是基础，多边是重要舞台.

not only restrained from colonialising other regions but also decided to stop the maintenance and dispatch of its global fleet. Even though critical scholarship on these episodes implies that this decision might have been caused by the emperor's lack of sufficient funding for further expeditions, the Zheng He paradigm remains reiterated in China's Africa diplomacy. When interacting with African states, the PRC also refers to its own experience of victimisation and humiliation by the colonial powers – Mao had categorised China as a semi-feudal, semi-colonial system – and, as a second element of joint identity with their African counterparts, used to stress its status as developing country.[61]

China's relations with African states are formally based on the Five Principles of Peaceful Coexistence: mutual respect for each other's territorial integrity and sovereignty; mutual non-aggression; mutual non-interference in each other's internal affairs; equality and mutual benefit; peaceful co-existence. According to the official historiography of the PRC's foreign relations, these principles were fixed as a binding code of conduct at the Bandung Conference, the first international conference of Asian and African states (hosted by Indonesia in April 1955), where they were presented by the Chinese Foreign Minister Zhou Enlai as a new mode of post-colonial relations between states. These five points had earlier been included in a treaty signed between China and India (Panchsheel Agreement, April 1954). They were finally included in the Ten Principles catalogue, issued at the end of the Bandung Conference. Ownership of the Five Principles remains, nonetheless, contested, as both India and Indonesia also see themselves as their original creators. On the side-line of the Bandung conference, Zhou Enlai bilaterally met with representatives of six African countries.[62]

During the 1960s, the Maoist PRC pursued an ideology-based foreign policy, aiming at the global diffusion of socialism. Beijing actively supported national liberation movements in Africa. Some of these African independence movements turned to "socialism" as an alternative to the structures imposed upon them by the colonial powers. Other African countries just sought to intensify ties with Moscow or Beijing to secure support and funding. The Soviet Union and Mao's PRC competed with the (former) European colonial powers and the US for securing and expanding their "socialist" spheres of influence across the African continent. Following the official Sino–Soviet split in the mid-1950s and these two "socialist" powers' controversy over the correct interpretation of "Marxist" development, Beijing's African charm offensive was redesigned to also limit the Soviet Union's grip on Africa. In 1963 and 1964, Zhou Enlai visited ten African states, outlining the PRC's development assistance offer in the "Eight Principles for Economic Aid and Technical Assistance". By proposing interest-free or low-interest loans in combination with material and technical equipment and the delegation of Chinese engineers without requesting the fulfilment of any "good governance" criteria and

---

61 For an overview of changing relations between the PRC and Africa, including both the international state of the art as well as Chinese scholars' views, see: Alden/Large (eds.) (2019).

62 On the PRC's support of Africa's national liberation movements against imperialism and colonialism and Zhou Enlai's legendary Africa journey, see: Shinn/Eisenman (2012), Chapter 2.

with no other strings attached, the PRC distanced itself from the initiatives and programmes offered by the US and the Soviet Union (Sun 2014: 3–4).

In the 1960s, most states granted diplomatic recognition to the GMD government which had been forced to withdraw to the island of Taiwan but claimed to speak for "all of China", including the mainland controlled by the CCP. However, some African states began to shift their official relations from the GMD government to the CCP government in Beijing. Due to internal factional struggles, *coup d'états* or regime transformations, some states switched recognition several times. Furthermore, during the 1990s, the GMD government on Taiwan quite successfully used its cheque-book diplomacy by granting loans and credits to restore contacts with a number of African states that had already deserted and joined sides with the CCP government. Gambia, which had established official diplomatic contacts with Beijing in 1975, turned back to Taiwan (and the Republic of China) in 1995, before finally subscribing to Beijing's One China Principle in November 2013. The latest round of diplomatic recognition of the PRC took place in the aftermath of the launching of China's New Silk Road Initiative – indicating the persuasive power of Beijing's global connectivity and development campaign. In 2016, Sao Tomé cancelled diplomatic relations with Taiwan, followed by Burkina Faso in 2018. The only African state not giving up the Republic of China (Taiwan) is Swaziland (Eswatini).

In 2006, Beijing outlined its vision of relations with Africa in a first White Paper. This paper speaks of Sino-Afro relations in terms of a new partnership amongst the states of the Global South, which should be rooted in solidarity and cooperation, dedicated to the shared goal of achieving joint development.[63] The document confirms political cooperation of China and Africa in the UN; the longest part of the paper concerns cooperation in the fields of trade, finance and investment. This also encompasses the exploitation of resources, the expansion of the agricultural sector and local infrastructure building. Joint projects are also announced for the sectors of education, healthcare, as well as science and technology. Economic assistance, as the document states, will be provided "with no strings attached"; debt relief is also announced. The concluding passages relate to peace and security issues in Africa and promise Chinese contributions to (UN) peacekeeping missions and support for African regional organisations.

China's "going global" initiative of the late 1990s and the resulting omnipresence of Chinese enterprises, banks, private companies and (micro-)traders all across the African continent – a development further speeded up by the inclusion of Africa into the New Silk Road Initiative – imply that Africa is ascribed an increasingly central relevance in the PRC's foreign strategy. Since 2014, Chinese FDI flows to Africa have surpassed those of the US.[64] However, according to UNCTAD data, the main investors in Africa throughout 2017 were France, followed – in numerical order – by the Netherlands, the US, Great Britain and China.[65]

---

63   China's African Policy (2006) is available online: http://en.people.cn/200601/12/eng20060112_234894.ht
     ml.
64   http://www.sais-cari.org/chinese-investment-in-africa.
65   https://unctad.org/en/pages/newsdetails.aspx?OriginalVersionID=2109.

In 2015, the Chinese state news agency Xinhua summarised China's African projects in quite impressive figures, stating that 1,046 projects had been concluded, 2,233 kilometres of railway networks and 3,350 kilometres of roads had been constructed. The PRC advertised this as proof of a successful South–South cooperation and furiously defended itself against accusations of practising a neo-colonial exploitation of its African counterparts. Chinese investment and trade activities are complemented by prestigious social projects, ranging from the construction of hospitals, schools, stadia or government buildings – including the construction of the headquarters of the African Union. Chinese state-owned companies have signed deals for the modernisation and expansion of Africa's railway connections. Railways have always played an important role in Sino–African cooperation. One of the first Chinese signature projects – and part of its Maoist image campaign to win the hearts and minds of African people and to outplay the Soviet Union – had been the construction of the "freedom railway" TAZARA, connecting Zambia to Tanzania's port city Dar es Salaam. In 1963, during his African journey, Zhou Enlai promised to provide an interest-free loan of 157 million USD and Chinese engineers for this trans-border connectivity endeavour. Prior to this, the World Bank and other banks had declined funding. The Maoist PRC reportedly sent 13,500 workers to realise the TAZARA line (Xinhua 2015a). Continuing along these lines, in the 21st century, the China Railway Group and the China Civil Engineering Construction Corporation were tasked with the modernisation of the railway network in Ethiopia – originally set up by France in 1917 –, the construction of a light railway in Addis Ababa, and a border-crossing railway connection to the port of Djibouti. These modern railways are electrified lines, (prospectively) fuelled by hydropower from power plants built by Chinese companies. Three Chinese banks fund these projects: the Chinese EXIM Bank, the China Development Bank (CDB) and the Industrial and Commercial Bank of China (ICBC).

In Nigeria, the state-owned China Railway Construction Corporation (CRCC) constructed a new railway between the capital city Lagos and Calabar, close to the border to Cameroon. In October 2017, Kenya reopened the old colonial railway connection from Nairobi to Mombasa. 90 % of the project (3.2 billion USD) was financed by the Chinese EXIM Bank. Additional railway connections to Uganda, Rwanda, Burundi and South Sudan are under construction or planned.

The PRC has become an important partner for the realisation of Africa's national (and regional) infrastructure-building and catching-up modernisation. Given that China's infrastructure modernisation programme has mostly been completed, Chinese companies – aided by the Chinese government – are seeking to secure contracts and to export overcapacities of the PRC's infrastructure-building sector. The scramble for contracts has increased competition amongst Chinese (state-owned as well as private) companies and banks. To avoid mutual undercutting in bidding processes, despite the announced crack-down on monopolies, some companies were (re)merged. As mentioned before, in 2015, the PRC's main manufacturer of locomotives, China CNR, merged with China South Locomotive and Rolling Stock Corporation to form the powerful CRRC.

China's economic and financial activities in Africa not only create jobs for Chinese workers, as Chinese state-owned companies often bring their own engineers, but also facilitate the further increase of China's monetary power. The loans and credit deals with Africa allow China to reinvest its foreign currency reserves or, via currency swap agreements, to install the Chinese renminbi as an international currency.

China's rise as creditor of and investor in Africa took place in the shadow of the financial crisis in the US and parts of Europe. The PRC reacted to the destabilisation of its traditional export markets by launching a stimulus package to increase domestic consumption, and by promoting a diversification of the PRC's global export destinations. These measures catapulted the PRC to the top ranks of Africa's trading partners, thus filling the void left when the US temporarily reduced trading and investment activities. In 1950, trade between China and Africa accounted for 121 million USD. By the year 2000, bilateral trade amounted to 10 billion USD; it is still growing exponentially with 300 billion USD reported for 2015 (Xinhua 2015b).

Albeit the PRC's White Paper constructs Africa as one unified actor, bilateral interactions with select African states do not seem to follow any unified pattern. Relations with South Africa, for example, are also embedded in the BRICS network. On top of bilateral interactions, cooperation via this network structure relates to policy coordination in fields of global governance. In the past, relations between the (Maoist) PRC and South Africa have been far from harmonious. During the years of the Cold War, South Africa maintained close cooperation with the Soviet Union, a key supporter of the African National Congress (ANC). The PRC acted as ally of the Pan African Congress (PAC), openly opposing the South African apartheid regime (see also: Shinn/Eisenmann 2012: Chapter 1). Triggered by the dissolution of the Soviet Union, South Africa began to readjust its foreign relations. In 1998, following the hand-over of Hong Kong to China (July 1997), South Africa established diplomatic contacts with Beijing. Since 2015, the PRC and South Africa officially maintain a strategic partnership; historical conflicts and ideological controversies are no longer mentioned.

The Darfur crisis and the war in Sudan were further test cases for the pragmatic flexibility of the PRC's foreign strategy. Diplomatic relations with the Republic of Sudan date back to January 1959. Since the imposing of international sanctions, the PRC has risen as one of Sudan's very few remaining trading partners and strategic allies. The PRC has been accused of acting against the UN's 2004/2005 arms embargo; in those years, however, the major share of weapons and armaments was shipped from Russia (SIPRI 2011).

Despite increased international pressure imposed on China to rethink its relations with the Republic of Sudan and to use its influence to push for an end to the continued human rights violations (Darfur crisis), the government in Beijing reiterated its unnegotiable adherence to the principle of non-interference. Beyond these abstract axiomatic foreign policy paradigms, China had a strong interest in Sudan's oil and other resources to fuel its resource-intense industry at home.

Chinese companies had invested in a railway connection running from Khartoum to Port Sudan as well as in the construction of power plants and oil refineries. Since 2005, the PRC has participated in UN peacekeeping missions in Sudan. In September 2014, under the Xi–Li administration, the PRC announced to send combat forces – indicating a silent readjustment to the country's foreign and security strategy, as Beijing had so far limited its contribution to sending engineers and medical personnel (Xinhua 2014). International analysts have argued that this unexpected move was caused by the experienced reduction or temporary interruption of Sudanese oil exports to China due to the escalation of the civil war and rising ethnic tensions. Domestic economic interests and the immediate security implications for Chinese entrepreneurs and businesspeople working in Sudan thus ultimately resulted in a reconfiguration of the PRC's security concept. Beijing actively condemns humanitarian interventions based on the principle of R2P as a violation of the national sovereignty and territorial integrity of sovereign nation-states. Terrorist attacks against Chinese citizens abroad or their exposure to (civil) war and related security threats have thus made the PRC support interventions and robust peacekeeping missions, albeit exclusively under a UN mandate. Beijing openly condemns unilateral interventions and joint actions taken by NATO coalitions.

Another challenge to Beijing's foreign policy principles was the referendum held in January 2011, with 98 % voting for the independence of South Sudan. The PRC, confronted with separatist, pro-autonomy movements in its own border provinces, is generally highly reluctant to grant formal recognition to any kind of segregation or separation initiatives. Nonetheless, between 2005 and 2008, the PRC had already commenced setting up informal ties with South Sudan, formally belonging to the Republic of Sudan, and, in 2008, finally opened a Chinese consulate in Juba (Large 2013). Sudan's oil resources are located in the southern parts of the country, which finally made Beijing choose a rather pragmatic solution by accepting the outcome of the referendum.

China's major oil supplier in Africa is, however, not Sudan/South Sudan. In 2014, oil deliveries from South Sudan amounted to only 2 % of Chinese oil imports, whilst 13 % were shipped from Angola (EAI 2015a). The PRC offered Angola, which set up diplomatic relations with Beijing in 1983, oil-backed, condition-free credit lines ("Angola model").

Not all resource-rich African states are exclusively dependent on exports to China to such an extent. Nigeria – with which the PRC had also maintained intense contacts during those years when Nigeria, ruled by a military regime, had been internationally isolated – ships major shares of its resources to Europe and the US. Amongst its main trading partners in Asia are India and Indonesia. The PRC, as this case evidences, is not only competing over market shares and resources with the US, but is also trapped in rivalries and economic competition with India and other Asian states.

Table 9: Nigeria's Energy Exports 2019

Direction	Country	Share
Europe		47 %
	The Netherlands	10 %
	Spain	11 %
	France	7 %
	Other	19 %
Asia-Pacific		30 %
	India	20 %
	China	3 %
	Other	7 %
America		13 %
	US	10 %
	Other	3 %
Africa		10 %
	South Africa	7 %
	Other	3 %

Source: https://www.eia.gov/international/analysis/country/NGA

The Nigeria case brings African agency back in. The country did manage to intensify strategic cooperation ties with the PRC despite its continued successful resource cooperation with Beijing's major regional and global contenders. The PRC supports Nigeria's bid for a permanent seat in the UN Security Council and provides training and technical assistance to the Nigerian military. Chinese IT companies have entered the Nigerian market, setting up modern telecommunication infrastructure. Beyond this, the PRC also backs the Nigerian space programme. In 2007, the Nigerian satellite NigComSat-1 was launched from a Chinese base. Seeking to secure a certain degree of independence and autonomy to advance its space programme, however, Nigeria simultaneously cooperates with Russia, the Ukraine and Great Britain.[66]

China's partnerships with Africa are not exclusively aimed at securing access to energy resources and raw materials. The group of African states holds one quarter of all votes in the UN General Assembly. The transfer of the permanent seat of China from the Republic of China (represented by the GMD government located in Taipei) to the PRC in 1972 would not have been possible without the coordinated support of African states. Most African states showed unrestrained support

---

66   For an overview of strategic cooperation between the PRC and Nigeria, see also: OECD (2011).

for Beijing, even during the years of political radicalisation under Mao, and did not subscribe to the condemnation of the PRC during the Cultural Revolution nor regarding the crackdown of the Tian'anmen movement in 1989 (Sun 2014: 4–5).

Since the formal establishment of the Forum on China–Africa Cooperation (FO-CAC) in the year 2000, ministerial meetings between the Chinese government and the heads of the African states – the only exception being Eswatini, which officially recognises Taiwan as the legitimate government and representative of "China" – have been convened every three years, with the summits alternating between China and Africa. At the FOCAC Summit 2015, Xi Jinping announced his intention to provide an additional 60 billion USD for infrastructure projects and regional development initiatives in Africa.[67] Chinese loans and credits are, however, often bound to infrastructure projects planned and realised by Chinese state-owned companies – with money granted never flowing out of the PRC but being reinvested into Chinese infrastructure-building companies. The PRC's approach to Africa has, however, become more varied and diversified. The second White Paper on the PRC's relations with the African continent, released in 2015, not only mentioned the importance of developmental cooperation but also reconfirmed Beijing's interest in strengthening cooperation in the fields of global governance.[68]

6.3.2.2. China and Latin America

Interactions with the states of Latin America did not rank too high on the PRC's foreign agenda. Even the publication of the PRC's White Paper on its relations with the Latin America states and the Caribbean in 2008[69] did not mark the opening of a new chapter in political and economic interactions. However, it signalled the PRC's interest in expanding cooperation and documented Beijing's awareness of the diversity of (state-)actors in Latin America. The PRC actively observed the emergence and transformation of regional organisations in Latin America and the related plans to set up integrated markets, custom unions or free trade areas.[70] The PRC also undertook efforts to strengthen its cooperation with the Unión de Naciones Suramericanas (Union of South American Nations, UNASUR).[71]

Beyond the PRC's White Paper on its relations with Latin America and the Caribbean states, in 2014, bilateral cooperation was further institutionalised via

---

67 The final summaries and declarations of the FOCAC summits are available online: http://www.focac.org/eng/.
68 China's second Africa policy paper (2015): http://news.xinhuanet.com/english/2015-12/04/c_134886545.htm.
69 The document (English version) is available online: http://www.gov.cn/english/official/2008-11/05/content_1140347.htm.
70 This includes, to name a few, the Comunidad Andina de Naciones (CAN); the Caribbean Community and Common Market (CARICOM); and the Rio Group.
71 In 2004, a founding treaty – the Cusco Declaration – was signed at a first constitutive summit held in Cusco (Peru). In 2018/2019, caused by the confrontation between the pro-Western Latin American countries, which jointly formed the Lima Group, and Latin America's new left regimes, most states formally cancelled their UNASUR membership.

the establishment of the China–CELAC[72] (Comunidad de Estados Latinoamericanos y Caribeños) Forum (CCF), marking a milestone agreement of the China–Latin America and the Caribbean Summit in Brasília (July 2014). At the CELAC Summit in Cuba (January 2014), Raúl Castro had actively pushed for deepening ties with the PRC to oppose US hegemony (and hegemonic ambitions in Latin America). At the summit in Brasília, Xi Jinping declared that the China–CELAC format would continue the tradition of South–South cooperation, respecting the principles of reciprocity and win-win solutions, and form part of the Community of Shared Destiny (Xi, Jinping 2014).[73]

The first China–CELAC meeting took place 8–9 January 2015 in Beijing. The joint declaration stressed the network's commitment to multilateralism, multipolarity and the promotion of a democratisation of international relations.[74] China announced an additional investment of 250 billion USD until 2025 in Latin America; the bilateral trade volume is expected to rise to 500 billion USD.[75] The inaugural meeting concluded with the passing of the Beijing Declaration of the First Ministerial Meeting of the China–CELAC Forum, the China–Latin American and Caribbean Countries Cooperation Plan (2015–2019) and the Institutional Arrangements and Operating Rules. The Santiago Declaration, issued at the second China–CELAC Forum, taking place in Santiago de Chile in January 2018, and the China–CELAC Action Plan (2019–2021) documented a further deepening and institutionalisation of the PRC's relations with this group of states (Xinhua 2018a). Xi Jinping sent a greeting statement to the summit, inviting the states of Latin America and the Caribbean to become formal partners of the Chinese Belt and Road Initiative. China's foreign minister Wang Yi also met with select Caribbean island states and offered them to become connected to China's maritime New Silk Road.[76]

In 2018/2019, however, disagreements between the pro-democratic CELAC member states and those expressing support for backsliding, re-autocratising political regimes in Latin America did not only cause the end of UNASUR integration but also lead to a deadlock of CELAC cooperation.

Since the 1990s, the PRC has intensified its bilateral relations with select states in Latin America and the Caribbean. In April 2001, Jiang Zemin undertook a 13-day trip to Latin America; in 2004, Hu Jintao visited Argentina, Brazil, Chile and

---

72 The founding treaty of CELAC was signed at the summit in Venezuela in 2011. It comprises all member states of the Organization of American States, except the US and Canada.

73 *Renmin Ribao* published some reading guidelines, explaining the meaning of Xi's Community of Shared Destiny: converging interests foster the formation of strategic coalitions. But one should make sure that those partnering in these coalitions are not going to foul each other and defect from cooperation to maximise their benefits. The Community of Shared Destiny implies that humankind as such is facing joint global challenges that no one can solve without the cooperation and contribution of others. It relies on solidarity but also has to reflect the strategic interests of the players involved in order to secure their willingness to contribute. See also: *Renmin Ribao* (2014).

74 *Beijing Declaration*: http://www.chinacelacforum.org/eng/zywj_3/t1230938.htm.

75 *Plan of Cooperation between China and the Latin American and Caribbean Countries* (2015–2019), available online: http://www.chinacelacforum.org/eng/zywj_3/t1230944.htm.

76 See the official press release of the PRC's Ministry of Foreign Affairs: http://www.fmprc.gov.cn/mfa_eng/z xxx_662805/t1528306.shtml.

Cuba.[77] Travel diplomacy was continued under the fifth generation. Xi Jinping's first trip to Latin America included stops in Costa Rica, Mexico and Trinidad and Tobago. In 2014, his second trip targeted Argentina, Brazil, Cuba and Venezuela. In November 2016, Xi visited Ecuador, Peru and Chile, and participated in the APEC meeting in Lima (Peru). Additional state visits to Argentina and Panama took place in 2018, followed by a trip to Brazil (BRICS summit) in 2019. Since 1993, the PRC has established strategic partnerships with nine states in Latin America and the Caribbean: Brazil, Mexico, Argentina, Venezuela, Peru, Chile, Ecuador, Costa Rica and Uruguay. Relations with Brazil, Mexico,[78] Argentina, Venezuela and Peru are ranked as "comprehensive strategic cooperative partnerships".

During these state visits to the US's strategic backyard, the PRC and their Latin American counterparts signed various cooperation and investment agreements. The more active positioning of the PRC occurred in the wake of the US's subprime mortgage crisis. Beijing managed to fill the opening void by providing urgently needed capital and investment. It did not enter into direct competition with existing US–Latin American treaties or business deals. In 2014, the China Development Bank provided 7.5 billion USD, which helped Argentina to escape a looming national bankruptcy. Besides this, the People's Bank of China and the Central Bank of Argentina signed additional currency swap agreements. China also invested in Argentina's energy sector: in 2015, China and Argentina signed an agreement to build additional nuclear power plants using Chinese investment; Chinese investors and (state-owned) companies are also setting up hydropower infrastructure and wind power stations in Patagonia, Argentina's southern region (Ray/Gallagher 2015; Xinhua 2019). On the sidelines of the G20 summit in Buenos Aires, Argentina and China agreed upon a five-year action plan (2019–2023).

Beijing's cooperation with Brazil combines bilateral as well as multilateral dimensions via the BRICS framework. In 2012, bilateral relations were upgraded by the formal establishment of a comprehensive strategic dialogue. Since 2009, the PRC has become Brazil's largest trading partner. Brazilian exports to China mainly consist of soybean products, iron ore and crude oil.[79] Chinese companies invest in the modernisation of Brazil's transportation infrastructure (construction of roads, railways and harbours). Beyond the fields of trade and finance, strategic cooperation includes a joint satellite program set up at the end of the 1980s. In 1999 and 2002, the first two (earth resource observation) satellites were injected into orbit.[80]

---

77 In addition to state visits by Chinese state presidents, travel diplomacy also included visits by Chinese vice presidents and ministers. In February 2009, two of these journeys even took place simultaneously but largely uncoordinated and independent from each other: Zhu, Zhiqun (2010: 94).

78 The upgrading of the PRC's "strategic partnership" with Mexico, established in 2003, to the status of a "comprehensive strategic partnership" happened after the ascent of China's fifth generation of political leaders. See also the summary of China–Mexico relations, provided by the Chinese Ministry of Foreign Affairs: http://www.fmprc.gov.cn/mfa_eng/wjb_663304/zzjg_663340/ldmzs_664952/gjlb_664956/3508_665108/.

79 For the most recent figures and data, see: http://comtrade.un.org/.

80 China–Brazil Earth Resources Satellite Program (CBERS): http://www.cbers.inpe.br.

China's changing global status and the strengthening of ties with Latin America – fuelling covert competition with the US – facilitated new modes of cooperation with the left-wing regimes in Latin America. After the election of Hugo Chávez, Venezuela, which had set up diplomatic relations with the PRC in 1974, proactively sought to rely on a "socialist" partnership with Beijing to reduce the country's dependency on the US. In 2004, during his third official state visit to China, Chávez delivered a speech at Beijing University presenting the Bolivarian Revolution as a continuation of Mao's legacy and interpretation of socialism (Domínguez 2006: 41). The PRC not only increased its investment in Venezuela, but also agreed to oil-for-debt swap solutions. The steep drop in oil (and gas) prices between 2013 and 2015 left Venezuela with no choice but to secure additional loans and credits from Chinese banks, driving it into an unsolvable debt trap. Chinese banks and companies have also contributed to the financing and implementation of Venezuela's national transportation infrastructure projects and the modernisation of its energy and resource sectors. Sinopec is involved in the exploration of the Orinoco Belt's oilfields; further joint projects and investment agreements include the sectors of petrochemistry and (gold) mining.

Credits and loans provided to Latin America and the Caribbean by Chinese banks – the Chinese EXIM Bank and the China Development Bank – are higher than the combined loans and credits granted to the region by the Inter-American Development Bank (IDB), the World Bank and the CAF Development Bank of Latin America. The largest share of the 137 billion USD loan commitment (2005–2019) targeted the infrastructure and energy sectors. The main recipients were Venezuela, Brazil, Ecuador and Argentina (Gallagher/Myers 2020). State-to-state finance and lending by the China EXIM Bank and China Development Bank dropped significantly after 2015, whilst Chinese (overseas) foreign direct investment reportedly increased exponentially.

China's lending and investment activities are not primarily inspired by ideological goals or anti-US sentiments. The PRC is practising a pragmatic and peaceful foreign policy, guided by the principle of peaceful coexistence. It is openly opposing the Latin American new left regimes' aggressive anti-US stance and hostile rhetoric. No cooperation agreement has been signed between the PRC and the ALBA states (ALBA = Alianza Bolivariana para los Pueblos de nuestro América), a network of new socialist regimes in Latin America and the Caribbean. Established in 2004 by Cuba and Venezuela, the ALBA group promoted regional economic cooperation and solidarity amongst the socialist and social democratic states of the region. In 2004, as part of intra-group solidarity, Venezuela and Cuba started a "(Venezuelan) oil for (Cuban) doctors" programme. The network was united in the joint goal to counter US hegemony and the US's idea to set up a (capitalist) free trade area. The ALBA group even introduced a virtual currency ("SUCRE") to replace the USD in bilateral trade deals. Following the turbulences and upheavals in Latin America, Ecuador left the ALBA network in August 2018, followed by the withdrawal of Bolivia in November 2019.

Despite its overall reluctance to side with the ALBA group, the government in Beijing expressed its support for Maduro, the (re-)elected successor of Venezuela's president Chávez who passed away in 2013. The 2018 presidential elections in Venezuela and Maduro's authoritarian crack-down on the political opposition was answered by international sanctions. The Organization of American States (OAS) criticised the mode and outcome of the elections; the US and many governments worldwide refused to recognise Maduro's re-election. In January 2019, the opposition-dominated National Assembly installed its head, Juan Guaidó, as acting president. In January 2019, the Chinese Ministry of Foreign Affairs formally condemned any interference of external powers into Venezuela's domestic affairs. In February 2019, at the regular press conference, the statement was amended to: "China has been in close contact and communication with all parties. We have been supportive of the efforts made by the international community to encourage Venezuela's government and opposition parties to seek out a political solution through dialogues under the framework of their Constitution. China stands ready to work with all parties and continue[s] to play a constructive role for the peaceful settlement of the Venezuelan issue" (MOFA 2019). The PRC and Russia, as well as Cuba and Bolivia, officially continued to express their support for Maduro and have vetoed the UN Security Council resolution demanding to hold new presidential elections. Nonetheless, given that Venezuela has been the main recipient of Chinese loans and credits and plays a key role for the PRC's supply of oil, Beijing obviously has a keen interest in restoring socio-economic stability and in securing the fulfilment of agreements and treaties once signed with the Maduro government. Venezuela's "interim president" Guaidó approached Beijing and Moscow, hoping to win their formal recognition, and expressed his wish to maintain and expand trade relations.

Whilst all political parties in Venezuela have underlined their interest in continuing cooperation with the PRC, the ousting of Bolivia's president Evo Morales in 2019 ended with the victory of the pro-US opposition. Under its new (interim) president, Jeanine Áñez, collaboration with "socialist" regimes in Latin America and the Caribbean was ended, ties with the PRC were symbolically cut.

Special socialist relations, however, continue to shape China's interactions with Cuba. Led by Fidel Castro, Cuba was the first Latin American country to recognise the CCP government in Beijing as early as 1960. Both countries continue their long tradition of party-to-party contacts. The reforms and modifications of Cuba's socio-economic development model under Raúl Castro have been discussed as reflecting and copying core ideas of the reforms introduced in China in 1978. Cuba continues to serve as China's advocate and bridge to the Latin American and Caribbean states (Hearn 2012). In January 2018, shortly prior to the transfer of political leadership from Raúl Castro to the former Cuban Vice President Díaz-Canel, the PRC sent a special envoy, expressing support for the internationally banned and isolated Cuban one-party system (Xinhua 2018b). In December 2018, Cuba's Chamber of Commerce and the China Council for the Promotion of International Trade signed a bilateral business cooperation plan. After the dissolution of the Soviet Union, the PRC had become Cuba's second-largest trading partner after Venezuela.

The PRC also successfully expanded its sphere of influence in the Caribbean. In May 2018, the Dominican Republic ended its diplomatic relationship with the Republic of China (Taiwan) and formally sided with Beijing; El Salvador followed in August 2018. The former's turn to Beijing means that the island of Hispaniola is divided into a pro-PRC (the Dominican Republic) and a pro-Taiwan (Haiti) camp.

Already in 2017, Panama had granted the PRC formal diplomatic recognition, which might allow Beijing to integrate the Panama Canal into its maritime New Silk Road dreams (the construction of the Nicaragua Canal as an alternative inter-oceanic passage, announced as a Chinese-financed infrastructure project, has so far not even been commenced – and might no longer be deemed necessary).

BOX V: US Responses to China's Charm Offensive in Latin America and the Caribbean

The increased presence of China in the US's strategic backyard has raised major concerns amongst international observers. Even more so as the Caribbean had once been a major stage for geostrategic calculations and competition over the past few centuries, causing an inclusion of the Caribbean region into Washington's foreign and security calculations. The threat perception vis-à-vis the entrepreneurial presence and economic power of European merchants operating right next door might have been a key driver of US interventionism and the formal expansion of its sphere of influence and direct control to the Caribbean. The Monroe Doctrine (1823) declared all colonial attempts by European powers in the (two) Americas as "acts of aggression" that would justify US intermediation. The Roosevelt Corollary, passed in December 1904, openly granted the US (the self-proclaimed) right to intervene in conflicts between Europe and the Americas.

During the Cold War, Cuba became a major hotspot in US-Caribbean relations – or, to be more precise, in the triangular power game between the US, Cuba and the Soviet Union. Anthony Payne, reviewing the literature on US hegemony in the Caribbean, convincingly argues that the symbolic maintenance of US predominance and control over the Caribbean was crucial for the recognition of that country as a global great power. Failure by the US to defend its strategic maritime backyard and third frontier would have been regarded as a sign of weakness and indicative of an inability to lead (Payne 1994: 158).

In 2017, observing China's emergence as a major creditor and thus strategic supporter of those CELAC states known for their anti-US orientation (especially Cuba, Venezuela and Nicaragua), the US Security Strategy identified China (and Russia) as the main opponent(s) to the US-based liberal world order:

"China and Russia challenge American power, influence, and interests, attempting to erode American security and prosperity. They are determined to make economies less free and less fair, to grow their militaries, and to control information and data to repress their societies and expand their influence" (The White House 2017: 2).

Investment (and the use of currencies other than the US dollar) was regarded as the main strategic weapon used to enlarge China's (and Russia's) spheres of domination:

"China and Russia target their investments in the developing world to expand influence and gain competitive advantages against the United States. China is investing billions of dollars in infrastructure across the globe" (The White House 2017: 38).

In February 2018, before embarking on his week-long trip to Latin America and the Caribbean – visiting Mexico, Argentina, Peru, Colombia and Jamaica – US Secretary of State Rex Tillerson gave a talk at the University of Austin in which he once again highlighted the unfair play of China. Further, addressing the two Americas, he commented that "our region must be diligent to guard against faraway powers who do not reflect the fundamental values shared in this region" (US Embassy 2018). He highlighted the shared "democratic" identity of the two Americas (hence dividing the LAC states into good democracies and hostile new left regimes):

> "We share an interwoven history, and importantly, we share democratic values [...] we share the same goals as the visionary leaders before us: to eliminate tyranny and to further the cause of economic and political freedom throughout our hemisphere" (US Embassy 2018).

As a response to shifting power constellations, in October 2018, US Secretary of State Mike Pompeo overtly criticised Panama's turn to the PRC, warning that Chinese investment in the Latin American country might not be in line with people's interests and society's development needs (Pompeo 2018). Earlier, also in October 2018, US Vice President Mike Pence had stated that the US would never give up on Taiwan and that the governance patterns of Taiwanese democracy would be the better option for the PRC – which he characterised as a repressive system and doubtful trading partner (Hudson Institute 2018).

The US Strategy for Engagement in the Caribbean, entitled "Caribbean 2020: A Multi-Year Strategy to Increase the Security, Prosperity, and Well-Being of the People of the United States and the Caribbean" (US Department of State 2019), lists six fields of cooperation with the Caribbean states: security, diplomacy, prosperity, energy, education and health. This links the specific interests of the US in limiting informal migration and stopping the trafficking of forbidden goods with the assumed development needs of the Caribbean island-states. The perceived growing influence of China could open a new window of opportunity for the small Caribbean island-states to re-bargain the terms of cooperation with the US.

Latin America and the Caribbean are central export destinations for Chinese IT infrastructure and smartphones. Chinese companies are also the main subcontractors for setting up the region's telecommunication grid architecture (Ellis 2014). Besides this, Chinese state-owned companies are involved in the energy sector, not only exporting nuclear and "green" power plants, but also modernising the electricity supply networks. In December 2010, the Chinese State Grid purchased seven Brazilian electricity distributing companies.[81] In 2019/2020 State Grid also entered the Chilean electricity grid sector.

Rumours about poor social and environmental standards of Chinese infrastructure projects have alerted local indigenous people as well as Latin American environmental activists. Local contestation has finally resulted in the cancellation or postponement of already agreed projects. Mexico, just to name one example, cancelled a contract on railway construction with China (Forbes 2015). More and more states are worried of being caught in a new debt trap.

---

81 See the official webpage of State Grid: https://www.internationalrivers.org/campaigns/state-grid-corpora tion.

Apart from economic and financial power competition, another area of friction between the US and the PRC is China's military and security cooperation with Latin America. This includes arms sales to Venezuela, Bolivia and Ecuador; the PRC also provided training for military officers and maintains close contacts with a number of military academies in Latin America (Ellis 2011). According to SIPRI (2019), China is ranked amongst the world's top-five arms exporters; Latin America, however, is not the main export destination.

6.4. Global Missions of the Chinese Military

China's exploration of new maritime trade routes – including the Arctic passage – and the globalisation of Chinese business activities (comprising not only state-owned companies and banks, but also private businesses and entrepreneurs) have added a global security dimension to the PRC's national development masterplan. Maritime terrorism and piracy are posing a direct threat to China's core interests, as the Chinese economy is highly export-oriented and relies on imports of energy and raw materials.

In 2013, under China's fifth generation of political leaders, the global deployment of China's armed forces was ex post legitimated and inscribed into the PRC's official security strategy. The White Paper entitled "The Diversified Employment of China's Armed Forces" (April 2013) opens with a statement that the world has entered into a "new situation" that brings "new challenges" and "new missions". The paper classifies the (re)adjustment of the US's Asia-Pacific security strategy and Japan's position in the Diaoyu/Senkaku island dispute as posing a major security threat and challenge to China. Apart from extremism, terrorism and separatism – mentioned with reference to the "Taiwan independence" movement – the White Paper lists maritime security, cyberspace and outer space security as key priorities of the PRC's national defence strategy. The White Paper reconfirms the PRC's commitment to the principle of "active defence": "We will not attack unless we are attacked; but we will surely counterattack if attacked" (State Council Information Office 2013). According to the official historiography of the Chinese party-state, the PRC never fought any wars nor pursued any expansionist ambitions. The conflict with Vietnam (1979) is thus framed as a "punitive expedition", as an act to defend Chinese interests and to protect Chinese citizens who had become under attack, rather than a war-like action. The border dispute with India in the early 1960s and the territorial disputes in the East China Sea and the South China Sea fall into the same category. The 2013 White Paper also reiterates the aim of "win[ning] local wars under the conditions of informatization and expanding and intensifying military preparedness". It also added a novel formula, by mentioning "military operations other than war (MOOTW)". The paper documents the modernisation and transformation of China's naval forces into a blue water navy – since 2008, the PLA has been involved in missions to combat piracy and maritime terrorism in the Gulf of Aden (Somalia). The PLA and its navy were also dispatched to evacuate and escort Chinese citizens trapped in the civil wars in Sudan and Libya (State Council Information Office 2013).

BOX VI: NEW SECURITY CONCEPT (*XIN ANQUAN GUAN*)

Since 1997, the PRC's diplomatic statements operate with the formula of a New Security Concept, associated with the readjustment of China's foreign and security strategy under Jiang Zemin in the second half of the 1990s. The concept was embedded in the 1998 National Defence White Paper. It stresses the importance of non-military means and states that international relations in the post-Cold War era should be based on negotiations and peaceful conflict resolutions. The New Security Concept has been interpreted as a continuation of the Five Principles of Peaceful Coexistence, presented by Zhou Enlai in 1954/1955.

At the Conference on Interactions and Confidence-Building Measures in Asia (CICA) in Shanghai (May 2014), Xi Jinping put forward an "Asian New Security Concept". This concept stresses that Asia must find its own way out of remaining or emerging security spirals, including non-traditional dimensions of complex security (Yan, Xuetong 2014). This comprises the further deepening of a multilateral regional security architecture and was obviously also inspired by the idea of a causal nexus between peace and development – thus making regional economic cooperation the precondition for peace and stability. Interference by external players – pointing at the US – and the formation of military alliances are categorically rejected.

The Chinese reflections on security, stability and peace, summarised above, have been once again addressed in the PRC's 2015 "military strategy"[82] – previous White Papers had been published on the overarching theme of national defence. For the first time in the PRC's history, maritime forces are ranked higher than conventional land forces. This mirrors the PRC's changing security environment. China's long maritime border is perceived as the Achilles heel of the PRC's defence architecture. The island disputes with Japan, reaching an unexpected level of escalation in 2012, the maritime resource disputes with China's South East Asian neighbours, and the patrolling of US military forces in areas regarded by Beijing as belonging to the PRC's territorial waters have aggravated the security dilemma in Asia – as the setting-up of a competitive Chinese blue-water navy indicates.

Seen from China's position, the Abe administration's efforts to revise Article 9 of the Japanese Peace Constitution and the modification of the Japanese defence doctrine appears as a revisionist and assertive turn. Tensions and rivalries escalated in 2012 triggered by the unsolved ownership dispute over the Diaoyu/Senkaku islands. Beijing and Taipei both base their claims on ancient maps dating back to the Ming dynasty, which, following Chinese claims, located the Diaoyu islands within the borders of the Chinese Empire. In 1894/1895, during the First Sino–Japanese War, the Japanese side proclaimed their control over (and ownership of) the Diaoyu/Senkaku archipelago. After the end of the Second World War, the 1951 San Francisco Peace Treaty transferred the islands and territories conquered by Japan back to "China" – explicitly mentioning Taiwan and the Ryukyu islands, but not the Diaoyu/Senkaku archipelago. Except Taiwan, those islands initially remained under US administration. The Republic of China, the internationally recognised government of "China", as well as Beijing, representing the PRC,

---

82 The English version of the PRC's White Papers is available online: http://eng.mod.gov.cn/Database/WhiteP apers/.

repeatedly referred to the post-war solutions agreed to in the Cairo Communiqué (1943) and the Potsdam Declaration (1945), calling for an immediate retransfer of the islands conquered by Japan in the First and Second Sino–Japanese Wars. During the years of the Cold War, as part of the Okinawa Reversion Treaty (1971), the US transferred the Diaoyu/Senkaku islands and Ryukyu to Japan – ignoring the fierce protests erupting in Beijing and Taipei (Swaine 2013).

In 2012, when the Japanese government stated that it had purchased the Diaoyu/ Senkaku islands from a private owner, this was perceived as a severe violation of the silent agreement to leave the final solution of this ownership dispute to "later generations", as proposed by Deng Xiaoping during his state visit to Japan in 1978. In November 2013, the PRC installed an Air Defence Identification Zone (ADIZ) covering large parts of the East China Sea, including the Diaoyu/Senkaku islands. Aeroplanes planning to cross this zone are expected to inform the Chinese Ministry of Foreign Affairs or the Civil Aviation Administration and to repeatedly report their flight coordinates. Air defence identification zones are not a unique Asian invention. The underlying idea is to avoid unexpected intrusions into a country's national airspace and to prevent unplanned confrontations as well as overreactions. The Chinese ADIZ largely overlaps with the Japanese ADIZ, created by the US in the 1940s. Japanese and US observers thus criticised China's move as an attempt to change the status quo and the security arrangements in the East China Sea (Kerry 2013). The PRC stated that the creation of the Chinese ADIZ would serve the stabilisation of the regional settings and represent a justified way to safeguard and protect China's national security interests. The US demanded that aeroplanes that only cross the Chinese ADIZ should not be bound to register and report their position. As well as other players, they undertook military flythrough manoeuvres.[83] The legacy and burden of unresolved territorial disputes between China and Japan and the remnants of the Cold War alliances in Asia could, as these episodes hint, all too easily fuel the tightening of security spirals. Mutual distrust and scrambles over concessions and access to resources might result in overt military confrontations.

Another potential source of overt confrontations is the South China Sea. Tensions with Vietnam over the Paracel and Spratly islands reached a new peak in 2014. When a Chinese oil platform was anchored close to the Paracel islands, Vietnam openly condemned this as disrespect for and violation of its "exclusive economic zone".

The Spratly case is far more complex than other territorial disputes, as a number of smaller island states claim (at least partial) ownership rights. Apart from Vietnam, the PRC and Taiwan (Republic of China), the Philippines, Malaysia and Brunei put forward their claims. The ownership dispute is driven by three strategic motives: access and control of the (untapped) oil and gas reserves, which, according to estimates and projections, could be found in the surrounding territorial waters of the Spratly islands; commercial fishing rights; control over strategic sea lanes connecting the Pacific and the Indian Ocean.

---

83 For an informed summary and discussion of the ADIZ controversy, see: Christensen (2015).

→ China's Defence Budget and the PRC's Military Modernisation

The PRC continues to upgrade its military defence capacities. China has the world's second largest defence budget – 1,189 billion yuan (178 billion USD) (2019) – although this is still far below the defence spending of the US (2019: 716 billion USD). The US announced an increase in their military expenditures in 2020 to 738 billion USD; the PRC, likewise, annually reports an increase of its defence budget – explained and justified as an adjustment due to inflation and to the long-postponed necessary modernisation of military equipment and installations. Nonetheless, China's global involvement in peacekeeping and its research in the fields of modern (prospectively AI-based) weaponry has catapulted the PRC to the position of the world's second largest producer of weaponry and armaments (SIPRI 2020). The reform of the military sector launched under Xi Jinping included a reduction of soldiers by 300,000 and a focus on training a specialised military elite instead of engaging in nation-wide large-scale recruiting (nonetheless, even after this reduction of personnel, amounting to about two million soldiers, the PLA would still remain the world's biggest army). In terms of weapon technology, experts see the PLA far behind the US. In 1998, the PRC purchased its first aircraft carrier – the old Soviet/Ukrainian carrier Varyag, which – after having been completely rebuilt – only started service as the Chinese aircraft carrier Liaoning in 2012. In 2015, the Chinese Ministry of Defence confirmed plans to design and construct additional "Chinese" aircraft carriers. In early 2020, the commissioning of the first "Chinese"-built aircraft carrier, the Shandong, was officially broadcast.

→ China against the IS

In November 2015, the PRC, which had so far remained silent on developments in Syria, was drawn into the global fight against the Islamic State (IS) when IS fighters kidnapped and, finally, executed a Chinese citizen – posting pictures online. Zhao Kejin, professor of international politics at Tsinghua University in Beijing, predicted that this would leave Beijing with no choice but to take a more active position in the crises and conflicts occurring in the Middle East. In his public statement, delivered on 19 November 2015, Xi Jinping stressed that "China firmly opposes all kinds of terrorist ideology and will resolutely fight any criminal terrorist activity that challenges the baseline of humanity". The speech as such does not stand for any deviation from the PRC's previous stance on terrorism and extremism. But Zhao convincingly argues that China's ambitious New Silk Road corridors crossing the Middle East will cause China to actively join the fight against the IS and religious extremism. On the one hand, the global activities of Chinese companies – supported and encouraged by the Chinese state – would necessitate Chinese diplomatic interference or even interventions in local as well as transregional conflicts beyond its own national borders. On the other hand, as Zhao points out, China itself might become a target for terrorist attacks, as IS ideology might spread to China's border province Xinjiang (Zhao, Kejin 2015). The issue turned viral on Chinese social media after the above-mentioned kidnapping and execution of a Chinese national in combination with aggressive

IS rhetoric directed at Beijing. Before online nationalism could get out of control, the name of the Chinese hostage, Fan Jinghui, was blocked and all related entries were deleted. A counterstrike by China, as called for by Chinese netizens, would have implied a departure from the PRC's axiomatic principle of non-interference and would not have been compatible with Beijing's resolute rejection of military interventions under the responsibility to protect (R2P) umbrella.

Responsibility to protect is a normative concept, reflecting the global debate on international human rights and global justice. It was discussed amongst UN member states and officially adopted at the 2005 World Summit. R2P stands for the moral obligation of the international community to intervene when national governments are unable or unwilling to stop genocide, ethnic cleansing and atrocities against humanity. In 2009, at the General Assembly of the UN, Ban Ki-moon presented a strategy to put the abstract R2P obligations into practice, dividing the implementation and enactment of R2P missions along the three pillars of "state responsibility; international assistance and capacity-building; and timely and decisive response". Not all governments supported the idea of R2P missions. Brazil criticised that previous UN missions conducted under the R2P label did not contribute to (re-)stabilisation nor stop human rights violations in the country or region targeted. Moreover, Brazil postulated that the R2P mandate had been overstretched and misused for political or economic goals. In November 2011, the Brazilian government presented a document outlining its own visionary idea of "Responsibility while Protecting" (RwP) as an alternative to the malfunctioning R2P concept. RwP stresses the responsibilities and moral obligations during operations and interventions, prescribing binding limits to multilateral actions jointly undertaken by the international community (or specific sub-groups empowered by a UN mandate).

In the past, the PRC had repeatedly supported, or at least tolerated, R2P-based UN missions – including those in Sudan and Libya. As one of the permanent members of the UN Security Council, the PRC would have been able to use its veto power to prevent UN interventions. However, already during the 1990s, the PRC had informally accepted that, under certain conditions, interventions would be inevitable and should not be stopped. In 2005, the PRC participated in the UN debates on the R2P principle and voted for UN Resolution 1674, which outlines the UN Security Council's general views and positions on the protection of civilians in armed conflicts. In 2012, Ruan Zongze, working at the China Institute of International Studies (CIIS), presented a "Chinese" variation of the R2P concept: "Responsible Protection" (RP). The focus of RP interventions lies on the protection of civilians but does not allow support for any political party or political actor group. The overarching goal is the restoring of peace and stability. Ruan stresses that the responsibility to protect local society against human rights violations and related atrocities lies with the national government. International RP interventions would have to be coordinated with the national government and require a UN mandate. Conflicts should be solved via diplomatic and peaceful means. International military interventions, even if they are undertaken in order to impose peace and to stop war atrocities, always cause civilian losses and can easily add huge damage to the local infrastructure – hence leading to an aggravation of the humanitarian emergency situation. Ruan emphasises that interventions should not leave the country in ruins. Interventions should neither aim at the overthrow of the ruler or the ruling elite nor actively promote a regime transformation. The RP mandate does not end when the war or human rights violations are stopped. The international community is, according to the RP principle, obligated to assist in post-conflict reconstruction (Ruan 2012).

6.5. Space Quest

The PRC's Military Strategy (2015) formally extended the action radius of China's armed forces to outer space. The Chinese space programme plays an important role in the PRC's national role conception as a great power and global leader in terms of technology and innovation capacities. The exploration of unknown spaces and the discovery of new details of the formation and dynamics of the universe contain a (hidden) symbolic positioning dimension. During the years of the Cold War, the arms race between the world's two superpowers, the US and the Soviet Union, included the launching of two ambitious national space programmes. Outer space became one of the arenas where the abstract competition for technological supremacy and global leadership was held.

Initially, the PRC had relied on cooperation with the Soviet Union to develop its satellite programme, which offered technology transfer, training of engineers and assistance by Soviet advisors. With the hardening of the Sino–Soviet dispute over ideology and the final Sino–Soviet split, Moscow called all Soviet engineers home and stopped the supply of technical equipment.

8 October 1956 is the date listed in the PRC's political history as the founding day of the "Chinese" space programme, as this is the day the Fifth Academy, the Chinese space research institute, was inaugurated under the Ministry of Defence. The Chinese space research programme was mainly driven by the work of two Chinese scholars, Qian Xuesen, a US-trained aerospace engineer who had worked at the California Institute of Technology (Caltech) in Pasadena, and Ren Xinmin, who had received his postgraduate training in astronautics and liquid rocket engine technology at the University of Michigan.

As a reaction to the Sputnik shock, in May 1958, Mao announced that the PRC would develop and launch a satellite weighing two tons, which would have surpassed the configuration and specifications of both the Soviet Union's Sputnik and the US's Explorer 1 satellites. For the announced launching of the satellite, China had to engage in research on rocket technology (Moltz 2012: 76). At the end of the 1960s, the first Chinese Dongfeng ("East Wind") rocket was successfully launched. China's first satellite was sent into space on 24 April 1970, launched from the PRC's launching centre in Jiuquan (Inner Mongolia).[84] This satellite, a flagship of Mao's catching-up modernisation programme, carried a political message: it was not only named after the PRC's de facto national anthem

---

84 Apart from the launching station in Jiuquan (Inner Mongolia), the PRC maintains spaceports in Taiyuan (Shanxi Province), in Wenchang (Hainan island) and Xichang (Sichuan Province).

"Dongfang hong" ("The East is Red") but also transmitted this national hymn back to receiving stations in China. With this step, China joined the ongoing space technology competition in Asia. In February 1970, Japan had released its first satellite (Ohsumi satellite) into orbit – and had thus become the world's fourth nation after the Soviet Union, the US and France to display its success in this sector of space technology.

The PRC's satellites following the Dongfanghong test launch were all designed for transmitting scientific data and images. This also explains the names given to this second generation of satellites: Shijian-1, Practice-1, and the Fanhuishi satellite – the "returning" (and recoverable) satellite, which not only transmitted but also archived data and images (Solomone 2013: 233–250).

Nixon's trip to China and the Sino–US rapprochement allowed Chinese aeronautic researchers to attend the Fourth International Aeronautics and Astronautics Exhibition as well as to enter in direct exchange with research teams in the US. In 1978, the US and the PRC signed several agreements on research on and cooperation in space technology. Two Chinese space experiments were taken aboard the US space expedition in 1992. Simultaneously, the PRC set up space cooperation agreements with several (Western) European countries. In February 1986, the PRC sent its communication satellite Dongfanghong 2 into orbit. Beijing also tried to acquire US satellite technology; after long rounds of bargaining with the US, the communication satellite AsiaSat 1 started operating in 1990 (Moltz 2012: 84). Finally, in October 2003, the PRC and the EU agreed upon the development of the Galileo programme as an alternative to the US GPS system (Johnson-Freese 2007: 1).

After the decline of the Soviet Union and the readjustment of relations between Beijing and Moscow, the PRC also purchased Russian space technology. A cooperation treaty was signed in 1994. The Russian space programme remained closely related to the country's military and defence apparatus, even though Moscow officially highlighted the importance ascribed to civilian use of the discovery of outer space. To defuse threat perceptions amongst its European cooperation partners, the PRC established a civilian branch of its space programme, the China National Space Administration (CNSA), founded in 1993.

In its initial stages, the Chinese space programme relied heavily on cooperation with those states regarded as leading in terms of space technology. Beijing's long-term plan, however, was to develop its own space fleet and to catch up in terms of technological innovation capacities. In November 1999, the PRC commenced a first test flight of its (unmanned) spacecraft Shenzhou ("magic vessel"), whose construction plan had been inspired by the Russian Soyuz. In 2001, Shenzhou 2 carried a monkey, a dog and a rabbit to check the spacecraft's life support functions; in March 2002, Shenzhou 3 carried an android test dummy. In December 2002, Shenzhou 4 was launched as the final test run to check the latest system modifications. The first manned Chinese space mission, Shenzhou 5, was launched on 15 October 2003. Similar to China's satellite and rocket launching programme, the space mission used distinct "Chinese" terms. To dissociate the

Chinese space journey from existing terminology, such as the Russian "cosmonaut" and the US "astronaut", the Chinese narrative is based on the Chinese term *yuhangyuan* ("space traveller") and the English term "taikonaut" (reflecting the Chinese expression for cosmos/universe (*taikong*)) (Seedhouse 2010: 184).

After the successful conclusion of the Shenzhou 5 mission, the PRC focused on its lunar exploration programme. So far, the US had been the only nation to send a manned mission to the moon. The (manned) Apollo programme formed part of the arms race and related technology competition between Washington and Moscow. Prior to the moon landing, the Soviet Union seemed to be winning the competition. In 1957, it had launched the first satellite (*Sputnik*) worldwide into orbit, completed the first space mission with Yuri Gagarin – and, already by 1959, had reported an unmanned landing on the moon.

The US Apollo programme has ended, but the dedication to the continued exploration of outer space, especially the Moon and Mars projects, was reconfirmed by the Obama administration (Obama 2010). Similar goals underly the Russian and the European space exploration programmes as coordinated by the Russian Roscosmos and the European Space Agency (ESA). These three main players – the US, Russia and the EU – have signed trilateral cooperation agreements. The International Space Station (ISS), permanently crewed since 2000, is a joint project that also involves Canada and Japan. The ISS replaced earlier single-nation space station projects – the Soviet/Russian *Salyut*, *Almaz* and *Mir* stations and the US's *Skylab*. In 1992, the Russian *Mir* space station – which had been in operation since 1986 – also hosted astronauts from Western nations. In March 2001, the *Mir* was deorbited; the remaining fragments fell into the South Pacific Ocean after the station's controlled and coordinated re-entry into the earth's atmosphere. The Russian *Mir* 2 project, as well as the counter initiative to build an independent Western *Freedom* space station, was never realised. Continuing along the previous lines of cooperation between Roscosmos and NASA, the construction of the five-nation ISS began in 1998.

In September 2011, the PRC started to set up its own space station. Tiangong-1 ("Heavenly Palace") more resembled a space laboratory than a space station. The Shenzhou 9 (2012) and Shenzhou 10 (2013) missions, docking to the Tiangong-1 station, conducted initial test runs and experiments to prepare for the construction of a large-scale space station (Harvey 2013: Chapter 1). With these test runs, China's manned space exploration programme entered in competition with the ISS – from which the PRC had been excluded, reportedly, due to the US's veto. The PRC did not reject the idea of the joint exploration of outer space and sticks to close cooperation and coordination with the ESA and Roscosmos in order to reduce the threat of an arms race in outer space and to promote the peaceful progress of non-military space flight.[85] In 2016, Tiangong-1, as the Chinese delegate to the UN confirmed, had ceased functioning, with its orbit decaying. When re-entering the atmosphere in April 2018, the station burnt up.

---

85 On the security implications of China's space program for the US, see: Liao (2005).

In September 2016, however, the PRC had already launched its next generation space station, Tiangong-2, which was deorbited – as planned – in July 2019.

The Chinese space programme has often been classified as bearing "techno-nationalistic" traits. Power in the fields of outer space relations is defined and measured in terms of technological innovation capacities (Johnson-Freese/Erickson 2006). This dimension of technological power is composed of two elements: an actor's ability to operationalise and adapt already existing technologies, and to catch up with other players in this field. Additionally, (technological) power in outer space depends on an actor's resources and capacities to engage (and lead) in unexplored new (sub-)fields: the ambitious Mars missions being just one example.

Since Xi Jinping's proclamation of the Chinese Dream, space exploration has become referred to as a central building brick for China's re-ascent to the position of one of the leading centres of world politics (and economics) (*China Daily* 2013). These contemplations continue the PRC's modernisation strategy as outlined in Deng Xiaoping's Four Modernisations and reiterate the legendary call for science (and technology) articulated by the May Fourth Movement of 1919. These programmes and movements were not dedicated to technological progress alone, they should also be understood as an expression of rising patriotic sentiments all across "China". Under the Trump administration, the US showed increased attention to the geostrategic and military dimensions of space technology and the exploration of outer space. When Donald Trump announced the formation of a specialised Space Force, science-fiction dystopia of space war scenarios seemed to have entered political reality.

The Chinese Chang'e lunar exploration programme was initiated in 2007, i.e., before the start of the Tiangong missions. In 2007 and 2010 the PRC launched two unmanned lunar-orbit spacecrafts (Chang'e-1 and Chang'e-2); Chang'e-3 (2013) finally transported an unmanned rover to the Moon, continuing the earlier Soviet Luna 24 mission of 1976 (Aliberti 2015). In January 2019, Chang'e-4 arrived at the backside of the Moon on the South Pole-Aitken Basin, dispatching a moon rover to explore and analyse spaces which, so far, had been mostly unknown. The next mission, Chang'e-5 (December 2020) brought Moon samples back to earth for further analysis (CGTN 2019).

The PRC's lunar mission mirrors the country's ambitions to leave a visible Chinese footprint on the Moon: the landing site of China's Chang'e-3 probe was later named *Guanghan gong* ("Moon Palace"), surrounding sites carry names related to China's moon mythology or are honouring leading Chinese scientists (Xinhua 2016). In Chinese mythology, the Moon is inhabited by the Moon goddess Chang'e. She shares her Moon palace with the jade rabbit (*yutu*). The Chang'e-3 Moon rover was, unsurprisingly, called "jade rabbit". The lunar programme, the space station and the spacecrafts are part of a national saga that is constructed parallel to those narrated by other space nations (whose narratives reflect Greek and Roman mythology – see the *Apollo* programme and the *Orion* project). The Soviet Union created its socialist-globalist saga by calling its space station *Mir* (peace; world). The early Maoist PRC connected the naming and labelling of its rockets and satellites to political ideology: the "East Wind", "The East is Red" and the "Long March" represented key concepts of Mao's socialist modernisation and national development path. The turn to Chinese mythology still presents the space and lunar projects as being distinctly "Chinese" but also as projects that could be connected to international space initiatives. The "jade rabbit" certainly enjoys a higher symbolic popularity than "The East is Red".

The Chinese Moon mission is not only motivated by the idea of leaving a Chinese footprint on the Moon by adding Chinese landmarks to the official cartography; the Chinese lunar programme seeks to go beyond the existing state of the art and to present new scientific findings to send the signal to the world that the PRC is no longer learning and imitating but has strong innovation capacities. In 2015, (Chinese) media reported the discovery of a new, so-far unknown type of basalt on the Moon (Ling et al. 2015).

6.6. Global Dimensions of the Cyberspace

Most studies on the Internet and China tend to exclusively look at the local, censored and controlled Internet within the walls of the Great Firewall. The global character of the world-wide web is treated marginally, often limited to the normative presumption that the "global" Internet generally puts additional pressure on the Chinese one-party system and, in the long run, would cause its decay. When China connected to the global Internet, Bill Clinton claimed that controlling the net would be like "nailing Jell-O to the wall". Contrary to expectations, the regulations and censorship mechanisms developed in China allowed the party-state not only to control and steer the Internet but also to use it as a tool to generate legitimacy and to upgrade the system's governance capacities. There is neither a transformation automatism inherent to the Internet and social media, nor is there a unilateral pressure exerted on China via the "global" Internet. The PRC developed local hardware and software solutions (sometimes even in collaboration with international, Western companies) that allow control and surveillance. But Chinese IT giants and AI start-ups also designed communication tools and applications that have a high popularity amongst Chinese netizens and amongst smartphone users all over the globe. The "Chinese" Internet is going global – exporting hardware, software and package solutions. The Chinese Internet and communication giants (e.g., Huawei, ZTE) are setting up ICT grids (and 5G infrastructure) in other countries and regions. Chinese ICT companies and AI start-ups also exported their smart (and safe) city solutions, tested in select Chinese cities, to a number of African capitals.

The global Internet has become a space, a new arena, of international relations (Choucri 2000, 2012; Eriksson/Giacomelli 2006). Cyberspace is not only a global platform for interactions amongst states, companies or (world) society, it is also a room created and shaped by their exchange and interactions. IR theory-guided approaches to the global dimension(s) of the world-wide web can be grouped into the following five categories of research:

1) Studies on the global cyberspace and global regulation efforts of online and offline politics via processes of constitutionalisation

2) Studies on the global cyberspace as a platform for interactions between states, focusing on cyber conflicts, cyber hacking and cyber manipulation

3) Studies on the global cyberspace as allowing a continuation of foreign politics with other means, focusing on cyber-warfare as a new mode of non-conventional combat

4) Studies on the global cyberspace as a space for (inter)actions and competition amongst IT and AI companies (Google, eBay, Twitter, Facebook in the US – or Baidu, Alibaba, Sina Weibo and WeChat on the Chinese side)

5) Studies on the global cyberspace as a hiding space for cyber terrorists, whose activities can target states as well as public and private security of civilian actors.

Whilst cyberspace has become a new arena of competition, joint challenges and security threats might pave the way for joint actions and regulations. The existence of national regulations and regional "great firewalls" indicates that the current "global" cyberspace is composed of various sub-realms and is highly fragmented.[86] IT and AI companies entering new markets are generally expected to comply with national laws and regulations – including regulations for data security and data privacy. Given the differences and contractions between certain national regulations – not to forget the tensions between the idea of a "free" Internet and the idea and practice of a censored and regulated "national" Internet – this raises a number of questions.

With regard to the regulatory backbones of the existing (global) cyberspace, NGOs and cyber activists have continuously expressed their criticism of the invisible hegemony and ultimate power of the US-based Internet Corporation for Assigned Names and Numbers (ICANN), coordinating the global Domaine Name System and managing Internet protocol numbers. ICANN, however, is not involved in content regulation nor engaged in the setting up of ethical, data-related standards. Likewise, the UN-sponsored World Summit on the Information Society did not succeed in establishing a global code of conduct, but set up a Working Group of Internet Governance (WGIG). The WGIG proposed the creation of a transregional Internet Governance Forum (IGF).[87]

The field of global Internet governance obviously is one of those where the PRC seeks to act as a norm-maker and coordinator. In 2014, the PRC opened a new format for the coordination of the future principles of global Internet governance: The World Internet Conference, also known as (annually held) Wuzhen Summit. At the inaugural conference, Xi Jinping outlined the principle of "cyber sovereignty", later on further defined in his speech at the second Wuzhen summit as follows:

---

86 O'Hara and Hall (2018) differentiate between "four" competing national/regional visions of the Internet and Internet regulation – the Silicon Valley's "open Internet", the EU's "bourgeois Internet", the PRC's "authoritarian Internet" and Washington's "commercial Internet".

87 http://www.internetsociety.org/igf.

"We should respect the right of individual countries to independently choose their own path of cyber development, model of cyber regulation and Internet public policies, and participate in international cyberspace governance on an equal footing. No country should pursue cyber hegemony, interfere in other countries' internal affairs or engage in, connive at or support cyber activities that undermine other countries' national security" (Xi Jinping, quoted from MOFA 2015).

A number of social media applications and Internet (entertainment) services provided by US companies are banned from the Chinese Internet as they are seen as Trojan horses that might be used to mobilise revolutionary upheavals or fuel local rebellions and separatist movements – an obvious threat to the PRC's (cyber) sovereignty. Following the outbreak of the 2007 riots in Xinjiang, Facebook, YouTube and Twitter have been blocked. Social media launched by China's IT giants in the years 2007–2009 – with Tencent's WeChat and Sina Weibo holding the largest market shares – are living in a symbiosis with the Chinese party-state. The number of Chinese microblog accounts increased exponentially from 2009 to 2012. Laws and regulations issued under the Xi administration, however, including the enforcement of real-name registration and the passing of the PRC's Cybersecurity Law (2016 – implemented on 1 June 2017)[88] caused a declining popularity of certain online applications and social media services. Under Xi Jinping, cyberspace has been identified as a core priority: in 2013/2014, a Central Leading Group for Cybersecurity and Informatisation was set up, directly headed by Xi Jinping. In 2018, as part of the reform and restructuring of state institutions, (most) leading groups were upgraded to the status of commission.

Beyond this national dimension of cybersecurity and cyber governance, at the 2015 Wuzhen Summit, Xi also elaborated on the need for global regulation and standardisation, stressing that "international cyberspace governance should feature a multilateral approach with multi-party participation" and claiming that the China-run World Internet Conference would provide the platform to achieve this purpose (Xi Jinping, quoted from MOFA 2015). In 2017, the Chinese Ministry released its "International Strategy of Cooperation on Cyberspace" (MOFA 2017), integrating the core frames and ideas outlined by Xi Jinping in a concrete roadmap for coordinated global cyberspace interactions.

China's New Silk Road includes a digital dimension, as Xi Jinping stated at the first BRI Summit in Beijing. Along the BRI trade corridors, Chinese companies are setting up digital connectivity networks (Shen 2018). This could mean a silent export of Chinese IT standards and related Internet governance concepts – the release of the China Standards 2035 strategy indicates that the PRC has started to design its own technological norms und legal regulations, which might not be in line with liberal Internet norms.[89]

---

88 The Chinese document is available online: "Zhonghua renmin gongheguo wangluo anquanfa" (Cybersecurity Law of the PRC), 2016, http://www.cac.gov.cn/2016-11/07/c_1119867116.htm.

89 Back in 2009, when Chinese Internet(-related) service companies designed their own social media applications, they had to comply with the PRC's national Internet laws and regulations. Tencent's smartphone app *Weixin* (WeChat) soon programmed an English-language user interface and won subscribers in almost

Xi Jinping's dream to build China into a "great cyber power" (*wangluo daguo*) is a multifaceted project, composed of centralized control over the domestic Internet, rule-making authority in the multilateral bargaining rounds on global Internet governance, the promotion of globally competitive Chinese IT and AI champions (supplying hardware, software, "smart" package solutions) – and the power to shape the debates and narratives on the global Internet. China's state news agency, online portals of Chinese newspapers, as well as the PRC's state television are offering information in various languages. The mid-range goal is to feed English-language news provided by Chinese agencies into global search engines and to secure that they are listed amongst the first research results. The global cyberspace is getting more Chinese, as a basic search will now include links to English-language Chinese views and Chinese interpretations of world politics (as well as developments in China).

6.7. Multilevel Interdependencies: Global Transformations and Domestic System Reforms

6.7.1. Environmental Protection and Measures to Combat Global Climate Change

China's changing position on issues of global climate change and environmental protection measures illustrates the country's development dilemma. Over the past few decades, the international community insisted that the PRC – as the world's largest CO2 emitter – should contribute to the global fight against climate change by changing its industrial production. At international conferences and fora on climate change, Beijing constantly stressed its role-identity as a developing country and refused to agree to any binding regulations. The Chinese government argued that China, being a developing country, would have the right to catch up by increasing its industrial output and that China should not be held responsible for its global emission footprint, as a large proportion of these emissions would have been caused by China's export-oriented production of goods for the US and the European markets. By outsourcing those parts of their production chains and thus causing heavy pollution to China, these states would have successfully reduced their emissions – but only at the national level. The PRC was, however, not the only actor refusing to reduce its emissions. The US as well as India likewise declined the ratification of international protocols that prescribe fixed emission reduction quota for states or groups of states. China, however, remained the main target of international criticism. Its national role claim to be treated as a developing country – repeatedly iterated at the annual meetings of the UN Climate Change Conference (UNCCC)[90] – was no longer accepted by most participating countries given China's rise to the world's second largest economy. China and India, the two rising Asian giants, were those held accountable for the "failure" of the Copenhagen Conference (December 2009). Contrary to hopes and expectations, the 2009 conference did not end with a configuration of a

---

all other world regions. As the company's servers were all based in the PRC, netizens were soon debating whether their private chats and short messages would automatically face censorship (Millward 2013).

90 Reports and background materials can be found on the official webpage of the UN IPCC: http://unfccc.int/2860.php.

follow-up treaty to the Kyoto Protocol. Nonetheless, the US also opposed the quota and mechanisms proposed by the European participants.

Whilst international media reports blamed Beijing's reluctance to take on more re-sponsibility in combatting climate change, Chinese media presented the outcome of the Copenhagen Conference as a diplomatic achievement. The Chinese govern-ment, according to Xinhua, successfully defended the PRC's national development interests and did not bow to international pressure. Furthermore, the Chinese accounts of the conference stated that China did agree to make a tangible contri-bution to the fight against global warming and climate change: Beijing proposed to reduce CO_2 emission by 40–45 % compared to 2005. This reduction would, however, not be measured in absolute terms but in GNP-related units (Xinhua 2009). How the final reduction equation would look like remained extremely vague.

At the APEC Summit in Beijing (2014), China and the US presented a joint declaration on climate protection measures. They stressed their commitment to (bilateral) cooperation in the renewable energy sector. The Chinese side also declared that it would not increase its emissions after the year 2030. By that time, non-fossil, renewable energy should account for approximately 20 % of China's total energy mix. The US gave even more concrete data for their own reduction plan: by 2025, emissions should be reduced by 25 % compared to 2005 (US–China Joint Statement on Climate Change 2014).

The 2014 statement did not trigger a U-turn of China's development strategy, as one could clearly observe at the following year's Paris Conference. The PRC continued to stress the "common but differentiated responsibilities" (CBDR) principle. One major demand voiced was to set a concrete red line for global warming. The Paris Agreement proclaimed to hold global average temperature increase well below 2 degrees Celsius above pre-industrial levels and to try to limit the average temperature increase to 1.5 degrees Celsius. The oil-producing and oil-selling OPEC countries, whose national wealth and economic growth relies on the export of their "black gold", are openly opposed to the idea of a carbon cut. Another controversial issue at the Paris Conference was the sharing of burdens of costs amongst the states of the developed and of the developing world. The old narrative had been that the industrialised nations caused the high emission rates that had triggered a degradation of the global climate and, there-fore, should shoulder the costs. The rapid economic rise of the BRICS countries and the catching-up modernisation of the states in Africa and Latin America did, however, change the global emission equation. To design a treaty without any binding obligations and quota for these groups of states and emerging economies was heavily opposed by Washington – as the US, belonging to the group of indus-trialised nations, would have been subject to fixed reduction quota and sanctions, in case of nonfulfillment. In 2018, the PRC accounted for 27.5 % of global fossil fuel CO_2 emissions, the US for 14.8 %, and India for 7.3 % (Figure 4).

Figure 4: The World's Top-ten CO2 Emitters

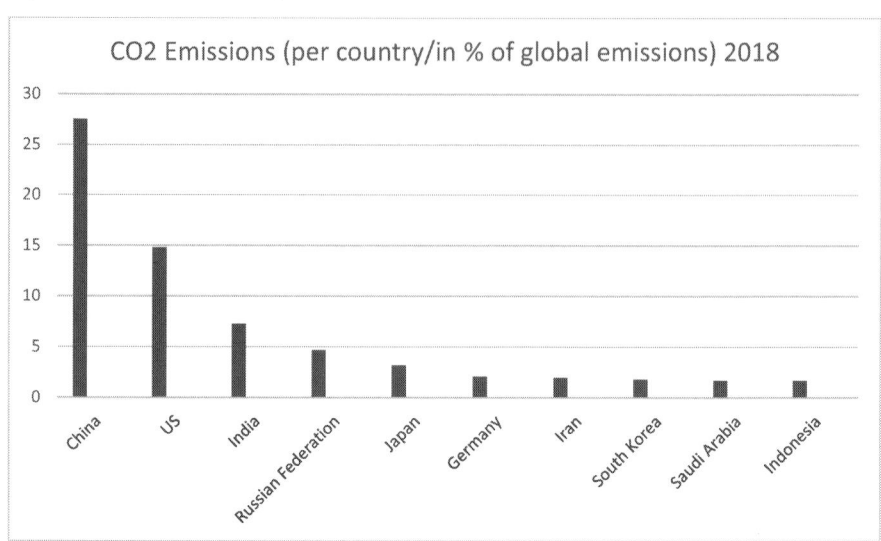

Source: Statista 2020

The final agreement reached at the Paris Conference was celebrated by Chinese media as a major breakthrough. Chinese media reports mentioned that the final agreement had been made possible due to Beijing's bilateral agreements bargained prior to the summit with the US, the EU, India, Brazil, France and other players. Xinhua reports stressed that China took a leadership role regarding the Paris Agreement on countering global climate change. The Chinese side stated that, according to calculations and projections, the PRC would reach its CO2 emissions peak by the year 2030, but would seek to cut emissions "per unit of GDP" by 60–65 percent measured compared to the year 2005 (Xinhua 2015d).

The Chinese representative at the Paris summit, Xie Zhenhua, outlined China's refined national role identity and strategic position as a promoter of global sustainability right from the beginning, underscoring that China would hope for a legally binding ambitious agreement (Xinhua 2015c). International media reports, by contrast, classified the PRC as a rather reluctant player, hindering the implementation of global regulations. The international documentation of China's role at the 2017 summit in Bonn was also rather critical (2017). Again, the Chinese narrative, as circulated via the state news agency, presented the PRC as a global green player and stressed that China would keep its promises and play an active role in combatting climate change, whilst the US under Trump had withdrawn from the Paris Agreement (Xinhua 2017). In September 2020, in his UN General Assembly address, Xi Jinping proclaimed that the PRC would achieve "carbon neutrality" by the year 2060 (UN News 2020).

The PRC's voluntary concessions in the fields of global climate change are caused by a combination of domestic and international factors. Over the past few years,

China has faced intensifying criticism regarding its "free rider" mentality in global politics. Given Beijing's increased concern over the country's international image and reputation, blaming and shaming might have been the constant dripping that wears away the stone. At the domestic level, the negative side effects of the post-Maoist resource-intense high-speed modernisation approach had become undeniable facts. Smog, desertification and the loss of arable land, as well as heavy water pollution (Economy 2006) were the undesirable hidden costs of China's rise to global economic power.

The Chinese government did not close its eyes to these developments. The government work reports, presented at the annual meeting of the National People's Congress, have addressed these issues for many years and asked for a more sustainable growth model. An impressive number of environmental protection regulations were passed by the NPC – but the main problem was the enforcement and supervision of their implementation at the local level. In 2005, the Chinese State Council published an overview of China's efforts, achievements and remaining challenges in the fields of environmental protection.[91]

Additional laws and regulations were passed, including the Cleaner Production Law (2002), the Environmental Information Disclosure Decree (2008) and the Law on Promoting Circular Economy (2009). In 2014, the NPC finally passed a revised and updated version of China's 1989 Environmental Protection Law (EPL), which entered into effect in 2015.[92] The new EPL allows sanctions and penalties to be imposed in case of violations: there is no upper limit for fines. Properties of polluters can be seized; the names of those found guilty will be made public, prison sentences can be issued. Emission data must be documented and transparently displayed; civil society organisations are given the power to sue polluters.

By updating these laws and regulations, the central government responded to social contestation movements sparked by the perceived threat for people's health and general quality of life caused by emission-intense industrial production. Many of these protesters did not address the abstract normative issue of environmental protection but ex ante opposed the construction of fossil power plants or chemical industry production sites in their immediate neighbourhood (e.g., protests in Heyuan, Guangdong province, opposing the opening of a new coal power plant). These movements fall into the category of NIMBY protests (Johnson 2010) but bear the potential of developing nationwide spill-over effects. Whilst (GO)NGOs and ENGOs are officially registered and monitored formal organisations, NIMBY movements are characterised by informal, spontaneous actions. Where they arise and how many people will join them is highly unpredictable. Johnson (2014) documents that these social environmental protection NIMBY movements are presenting themselves as acts of "rightful resistance", which means that these

---

protests are organised in accordance with central party-state regulations and not as an act of rebellion.

The revised Chinese Environmental Protection Law and related regulations also prescribe that local governments must make local environmental issues and emissions transparent and available to the public. The implementation and enforcement of environmental regulations by state agencies and local governments will be evaluated on a permanent basis. Cadres will be promoted or demoted from office based on their performance with regard to socio-ecological goal attainment. Likewise, everyone – not only party cadres – is reminded to pursue a frugal and sustainable lifestyle. Monitoring systems – the infamous social credit point system – might be used not only to monitor actions but also to reward certain behaviours.

In 2014, the number of environmental protests in China had risen by 33 % (measured against 2013). Environmental pollution ranked top on issues discussed by Chinese netizens. The Chinese journalist Chai Jing produced a documentary to map the current stage of environmental pollution and tried to devalue myths and fake news that the human body would be able to adapt to smog and air pollution and would not be damaged at all. This documentary, *Under the Dome*, was watched more than 200,000 times in just one week. State media featured Chai Jing's work. That the documentary was not censored until a week after its release and after it had been addressed and discussed by state news media indicates that it was supported (and maybe even initially approved) by influential groups within the Chinese party-state apparatus.

Chen Jie (2010) argues that the Chinese environmental protection movement became more powerful via networking with (trans)regional and international ENGOs. International models and reflections on sustainable and green development were hence merged with Chinese traditions and philosophical concepts of harmony between human society and nature. The latest revisions of the PRC's environmental protection laws and regulations are not the result of bottom-up pressure exerted by civilian protesters and NGOs,[93] nor should they be regarded as a re-steering and re-education campaign imposed from the top down by the government in Beijing. The combination of bottom-up and top-down dimensions reinforced each other. Both actors – the central government as well as local society – are united in their fight against local entrepreneurs seeking to lower production costs (and multiplying their profits) by disregarding social and environmental standards, and against local cadres who neither report nor sanction the violation of central government regulations (Shapiro (2016 [2012])).

The Hu–Wen administration introduced the notion of Scientific Development and discussed ways to secure a more sustainable development path. At the annual meeting of the National People's Congress in March 2014, the Chinese Prime Minister Li Keqiang declared a "war on pollution". This "war", as Li explained, should be conducted with the same intensity and engagement as the fight against

---

93 On the role and power of environmental NGOs in China, see: Cai, Yongshun (2010); Stalley/Yang (2006); Xie (2011).

absolute poverty (which had lifted millions of people out of more than precarious living conditions). Pollution-intense industries should be shut down; fossil energies should be replaced by renewable energies (Li, Keqiang 2014). Numerous crisis reports by Chinese ministries had previously documented the loss of arable land and the contamination of the air as well as China's groundwater.[94] Steps to push for an energy transition had been initiated long before the proclamation of a refined development model by China's fifth generation. Wind power generation had grown from one gigawatt (2005) to 77 gigawatts (2013). By 2020, wind power generation reached 280 gigawatts, while 250 gigawatts were generated by solar energy.

The war on pollution implies a readjustment of China's development and growth model. In the Mao era, the focus had been on Great Leap Forward modernisation at (almost) any price. The growth model was driven by ideology and often ignored the real conditions and constraints of the Chinese economy – still more agrarian than highly industrialised. In the early post-Mao reform era of the 1980s, renormalisation and re-stabilisation were defined as key priorities. At UN meetings and conferences, the Chinese side stressed that it would spare no effort to reduce absolute poverty and would not engage in any measures that could slow the country's high-speed economic growth.

The PRC's willingness to establish globally binding standards and regulations to combat environmental pollution and climate change deviates from this "old" development model. The PRC invests in the development of green energy technology and also tests local sustainable development solutions in urban as well as rural settings. The top-down regulation by the Chinese party-state has been labelled as "environmental authoritarianism" (Beeson 2010) or "authoritarian environmentalism" (Gilley 2012) – a concept which assumes that local (civil) actors only play a marginal role in the making of the PRC's green development agenda.

The drafting of a more sustainable development strategy is not an impulsive, short-term response by the party-state to the formation of a Chinese environmental movement. Carter and Mol indicate that China's participation in the UN Conference on the Human Environment in Stockholm (1972) initiated a paradigm change and a transition from the early-stage socialist model of development to a more controlled growth model assisted by mechanisms for pollution control. Already in 1974, a new state leading group – later upgraded to a state agency – for environmental protection was established, composed of a central level unit and regional sub-branches (Mol/Carter 2006: 152). Around 1998, this agency was reorganised to form the State Environmental Protection Agency (SEPA), a unit under the direct leadership of the State Council (Jahiel 1998: 758).

In 1979, the PRC passed the first Environmental Protection Law (updated in 1989 and, after several failed revision initiatives, once again in 2015). By 2006, the PRC's environmental protection was already highly formalised and regulated – on paper: the NPC had passed 20 environmental laws, about 140 executive

---

94 A summary of these reports published in 2014/2015 is available at: http://chinawaterrisk.org/resources/re search-reports/china-government-reports/ (titles are listed in English, the main documents are in Chinese).

regulations had been issued by the Chinese State Council, and a number of sector-specific regulations and environmental protection standards had been released by the Chinese SEPA (Mol/Carter 2006: 152). In the 1990s, the PRC installed working groups on climate change at the central level of the state administration. In 1998, a national coordination committee on climate change was set up and, in 2007, transformed into a national leading group on climate change, bringing together experts from 20 different ministries. In 2003, a national energy strategy was drafted, followed by the passing of the Renewable Energy Law in 2004. A national climate change programme was launched in 2007 (Gilley 2012: 289–290).

The Chinese government and its advisers do not pursue an ideological approach to modernisation, they actively monitor developmental strategies applied by other countries and evaluate their achievements as well as any backlashes. They also observe the development of the Chinese environmental sector, including the emergence of the civil environmental movement. Local environmental protests are tolerated, as they provide the central government with information about local developments and the failure of local government units to enforce laws and regulations. Kevin Lo (2015) therefore reasons that local mechanisms of self-coordination form a central part of the implementation and readjustment of the PRC's environmental protection programme – which goes beyond the paradigm of authoritarian environmentalism.

The turn to renewable energies, imposed from the top down, which generally corresponds to the UN's supreme goal of striving for decarbonisation, might create novel challenges and conflicts. For the construction of the Three Gorges Dam (Ho 2001) villages had to be flooded, requiring the (forced) relocation of local inhabitants. The long-term implications of large-scale dam construction for the ecosystem and the environment are also disputed. Ultimately, they might also contribute to the spread of vector-borne diseases, and, as waterpower projects in the Middle East illustrate, dam projects might also fuel conflicts between countries located at the upper streams of the river and those located at the lower streams. By shutting down coal plants and heavy industry, the government might manage to appease the rising environmental NIMBY movement. But the measures taken will create new rounds of protests by those groups whose rights and interests will be impacted by the turn to renewable and green development. The carbon cut will most likely destabilise the fragile symbiotic relationship between the party-state, business elites and entrepreneurs. Whilst the coal and steel industry, as well as the fossil energy sector, will be facing extreme cuts, the green energy sector and related start-ups will certainly profit from the top-down imposed reorientation. Given that many managers of state-owned companies rely on robust patron–client relations within the party, the enforcement of the carbon cut might fuel open factional struggles.

State subsidies allowed for the rapid growth of the Chinese green technology industry. The special state support for Chinese green start-ups also provided these companies with comparative advantages when entering global competition for market shares. In 2013, the EU introduced punitive tariffs and prescribed

minimum prices for renewable energy technologies to protect the European photovoltaic sector and to prevent price dumping (European Commission 2016). Similar trade wars in the fields of renewable energies and green technologies occurred
between the US and China (EAI 2015c).

Leadership in green energy innovation would not only augment the PRC's symbolic status as a modern global power. With cemented global power and status,
actors generally tend to establish their advanced national technologies as global
standards – creating additional costs for other state-actors that would have to
upgrade their systems (and might then have to purchase these most advanced
technology solutions from their former competitor who managed to redefine
the rules of the global green energy game). This scenario is inspired by lessons
drawn from previous energy transitions and related power shifts. The Industrial
Revolution relied on the use of water and steam power, allowing a transition from
hand-manufactured production to mechanised manufacturing during the late 18th
century. This was followed by a second industrial revolution fuelled by large-scale
electrification, based on the growth of the gas and oil sector. The third industrial
revolution, commencing in the second half of the 20th century, was fuelled by a
new type of energy: nuclear power. These three industrial revolutions spurred the
ascent of the centres of technology innovation to global power status. The rise
of green energies and related technologies is expected to decide upon the power
contributions and market shares amongst states and regions in the 21st century.

6.7.2. China and International Institutions

The international community's active integration of the PRC into international
institutions, established after the end of the Second World War, had been inspired
by core assumptions of socialisation theory. Rather than excluding and containing
the socialist one-party state, the main idea had been to change this regime via
active engagement. The inclusion into international organisations and multilateral
frameworks was expected to trigger an internalisation of liberal norms and values
and to erode Communist ideology.[95] The Chinese economic system of the Mao
era, built on the fundaments of a socialist planned economy, had been diametrically opposed to the basic principles of the international "capitalist" institutions
in the fields of global trade and finance – as represented by the Bretton Woods
institutions (IMF, World Bank) and the GATT.[96] In the late 1970s, the PRC
sought to reconnect with the global market and to attract foreign investment
(and technology). International companies and investors were eager to enter the
re-opened 1.3 billion-customers market. However, they needed formal regulations
and a reliable legal framework to protect their companies' interests and secure
long-term profit. The PRC's access to international organisations was based on
the condition that the country would adapt its national institutions and regulatory
frameworks and comply with international law. In the fields of trade and finance,

---

95 On socialisation theory and the PRC's changing role and behaviour in international institutions between
   1980 and 2000, see: Johnston (2008).
96 On the PRC's role in the IMF and the World Bank, and its efforts to become a treaty member of the GATT,
   see: Jacobson/Oksenberg (1990).

the PRC underwent a gradual transformation towards capitalist principles – though it never formally gave up its self-defined symbolic identity as a socialist planned economy.[97] The entry requirements to modify the legal frameworks and regulations of the PRC's banking and financial sectors allowed the Chinese party-state to enforce long-needed reforms – even against opposition from within the CCP and from the targeted sectors. The pro-reform factions inside the CCP played a multilevel bargaining game, presenting the restructuring as the necessary step to link the country and its economy to the global markets. Seen from the outside, these institutional readjustments and structural modifications seemed to confirm the transformation equation put forward by the adherents of the engagement approach.

In 1986, the PRC's application to be admitted to the GATT was declined. Finally, after two decades of preparations and bargaining rounds,[98] in 2001, the PRC was finally admitted to the World Trade Organization (WTO), the successor organisation to the GATT. The admission protocol contained a bundle of reform requests, such as the reduction of tariffs on industrial goods, the further liberalisation of the service sector, the elimination of quota and export subsidies for agricultural products, and an increase in overall transparency. The PRC joined the WTO with the status of a non-market economy – which enabled general anti-dumping investigations against Chinese companies. Most of the special regulations laid down in the accession documents were planned to expire by 2016/2017.

Since its entry into international organisations and institutions on world trade and finance, the PRC has developed its own distinct variety of capitalism. When, in 2007/2008, the US economy was hit by the subprime mortgage crisis that developed spill-over effects on the European financial markets, Chinese analysts started to talk about a failure of the Western variety of liberal capitalism and underlined the robustness of the Chinese economic model. However, even though the PRC was able to avoid a major infection of its domestic economy by starting a stimulus programme and developing measures to boost domestic consumption, the Chinese version of capitalism is not immune to all types of crises. The stimulus deal led to the mushrooming of China's shadow banking sector, creating dangerous financial bubbles. The PRC strategically made use of the crises in the US and Europe to call for a general reform of international institutions and organisations involved in the coordination of global trade and finance. This sharp criticism of Western capitalism serving as the foundational backbone of the world's international steering boards – the IMF, the World Bank and the WTO – was hardly new. The demand for building a new world order had been articulated again and again by developing countries, opposing the perceived hegemony of an exclusive circle of leading industrial countries in the regulation and constitutionalisation of global affairs.

---

97 Nonetheless, in the late 1990s, the PRC had not completed the adaptation of all sub-fields of banking and finance to international standards and regulations: Pearson (1999); Lardy (1999).

98 In 1999, the US and China reached an agreement on China's prospective WTO accession. The PRC's perspective on the related meetings and bargaining rounds has been compiled by the Chinese Ministry of Foreign Affairs, see: https://www.fmprc.gov.cn/mfa_eng/ziliao_665539/3602_665543/3604_665547/t18 051.shtml.

Since the formation of the G20, the PRC used this joint format as a strategic bargaining platform to rearticulate these demands, acting as dedicated advocate of the rising economies of the developing world (McKinney 2017). Finally, following the G20 bargaining rounds, the IMF's 14th quota review was concluded in 2010 and became effective in 2016. This reform implied that about 6 % of quota shares were shifted towards the emerging economies, upgrading the PRC's lending and voting shares. Nonetheless, the Chinese side continues to demand additional reforms, mainly targeting the overrepresentation of the US and its veto position at the IMF.

BOX VII: THE PRC's "INTERNATIONAL" INSTITUTIONS

Asian Infrastructure Investment Bank (AIIB)

The idea to set up the AIIB was first discussed at the 2009 Bo'ao Forum. At the APEC meeting in Bali, Xi Jinping further elaborated on this idea. The founding agreement of the AIIB was signed on 29 June 2015, counting 57 member states, including a number of European countries. The US and Japan refused to join the AIIB. In 2019/2020 100 states in total had joined the AIIB (75 countries) or were granted prospective membership (25 countries). The AIIB focuses on infrastructure and connectivity projects in the Asian region.[99] The AIIB was interpreted as a Chinese response to the postponement of the final implementation of the IMF quota reform, the underrepresentation of the PRC in the Asian Development Bank (ADB), and the perceived domination of the Bretton Woods organisations by the US and their allies. The AIIB headquarters are located in Beijing. Jin Liqun, AIIB president, had previous experience as chairman of the China International Capital Corporation, vice president of the ADB, as well as vice minister of finance of the PRC. The AIIB's highest decision-making body is the Board of Governors (one governor per AIIB member state) that convenes annually. Daily operations are handled by the Board of Directors, composed of 12 directors each representing one or more AIIB member states. Of these, 9 directors are from Asia and 3 are from outside the region. China holds 26 % of voting shares and thus has the power to veto decisions. However, as the AIIB's decisions require a two thirds majority of votes, Beijing must always secure followers amongst the AIIB member states. Germany is the AIIB's fourth largest lender (after the PRC, India and Russia).

BRICS New Development Bank (NDB)

The NDB, officially proposed by India in 2012, was established on 15 July 2014 by the five BRICS member states (Brazil, Russia, India, China, South Africa). The fact that this date symbolically marked the 70th anniversary of the Bretton Woods Conference (1944) – that concluded with the establishment of the IMF and the World Bank as anchor institutions of global trade and finance – signalled the initiative's critical views on the organisational patterns and principles of the post-1945 world order. The NDB, based in Shanghai, operates based on the principle of "one state, one vote". Voting shares are thus disconnected from member states' economic and financial power capacities. All five members are equally represented. Whilst the NDB's headquarters are based in China, Kundapur Vaman Kamath, who had founded and chaired India's largest private bank ICICI, was elected as the NDB's first president. He was succeeded (in 2020) by Marcos Prado Troyjo (Brazil).

---

99   See the summary provided by the AIIB: http://www.aiib.org/html/aboutus/introduction/history/.

Silk Road Funds

To finance projects along China's New Silk Road corridors, in December 2014, the PRC decided to set up a 40 billion USD fund. Amongst the first large-scale projects financed were the Karot Hydropower Project (Pakistan) and the liquid gas project Yamal LNG in Russia.

Shanghai Cooperation Organisation (SCO)

In 1996, in the aftermath of the dissolution of the Soviet Union, China, Russia, Kazakhstan, Kirgizstan and Tajikistan agreed to form the Shanghai Five to coordinate security and border issues in Central Asia. In 2001, when Uzbekistan joined the group, the multilateral coordination platform was renamed and restructured as the SCO. In 2017, India and Pakistan joined the SCO as full members. Afghanistan, Belarus, Iran and Mongolia have observer status. Armenia, Azerbaijan, Cambodia, Nepal, Sri Lanka and Turkey are listed as official dialogue partners. Turkey (granted dialogue partner status in 2012) is hence the only NATO member engaged in dialogue and exchange with the SCO and its member states. The SCO represents an exclusive Eurasian regional organisation. Official working languages are Chinese and Russian. Since 2015, Beijing and Moscow engage in joint military manoeuvres, sometimes also in cooperation with the organisation's Central Asian member states. From the perspective of the US and Taiwan, this is seen as the emergence of a new security alliance seeking to promote (and defend) Chinese and Russian power ambitions in the region.

The SCO has undergone a deepening and ramification of its regional cooperation agenda: in 2004, the five SCO founding member states agreed to establish the Regional Anti-Terrorist Structure (RATS) and to coordinate their fight against the three evils of terrorism, separatism and extremism. The SCO member states are further united by their joint interest in upholding regional stability to promote economic prosperity. Nonetheless, bi- and multilateral interactions are overshadowed by historical tensions and competing economic interests. The SCO had originally been installed as a platform to increase mutual trust and ensure peaceful regional conflict resolutions amongst its member states. Whilst security has remained its key focus, SCO members are also engaged in economic and financial cooperation.

China does not always act as a reformer of the international system. It signed numerous international treaties and agreements, including the treaty on non-proliferation of nuclear weapons and the biological weapons convention. The PRC's official no-first-use policy seems in line with the country's self-image as a peaceful and cooperative global power. In their assessment of China's activities in international arms control agreements published in the late 1990s, Swaine and Johnston come to the conclusion that the post-Maoist PRC's signing and ratification of these treaties and agreements was mainly driven by the idea to push for a disarmament in its immediate neighbourhood without making any concessions that would have resulted in a cut of China's own military capacities (Swaine/Johnston 1999: 118). In 2019, the Intermediate-Range Nuclear Forces Treaty (INF), originally signed between the US and the Soviet Union in 1988, was cancelled, as both sides accused each other of treaty violations. Moreover, international analysts had argued that the original treaty would not cover the new categories of weapon technology and AI-based warfare and that a follow-up treaty should also involve the PRC to secure Beijing's compliance and to avoid the formation of multi-actor security dilemmas.

In the fields of peace and security, the PRC obviously seeks to avoid any moves that could be interpreted as an act of aggression. In the areas of global climate change and environmental protection, the PRC, especially under its fifth generation, shows tendencies of a cautious reorientation to avoid being perceived as obstructing the development of global solutions for joint challenges. This diplomatic behaviour does not necessarily confirm the assumptions of socialisation and engagement theories, discussed above. The PRC's cooperative turn in global affairs might derive from rational cost-benefit equations and calculations. The reputational losses that Beijing might face if the PRC is perceived as a foot-dragger or free rider would be immense. When evaluating the development of the PRC's positioning in global climate change debates, one cannot quite avoid the impression that the political elites are playing a complex multi-level game by agreeing to global solutions that can be framed along the lines of both international demands as well as expectations (regarding green and sustainable development) of China's domestic society. In sum, the PRC appears to promote alternative ordering concepts and innovative norms in those subfields of world politics that are governed by principles incompatible with Chinese domestic institutions and regulatory frameworks. The overarching goal is to reduce transaction and adaptation costs at home. Only in those fields of the domestic economy where reforms are deemed overdue, did the political elites, ultimately, claim that participation in international institutions (such as the WTO) would leave them with no choice but to initiate institutional change at the domestic system level (with the reform of the banking sector being just one prominent example).

BOX VIII: CHINA AND THE ARCTIC

The melting of the polar ice means that the Northern Sea Route will become ice-free and passable year-round. This, added to projections that this region has huge untapped energy resources, has stirred the interests of those outside the Arctic countries. In 2012, the Chinese icebreaker vessel *Xuelong* (Snow Dragon) first traversed the passage on its polar research mission. In 2018, the PRC released its official Arctic Policy, positioning China as a "near Arctic state" and demanding to be included in the exploration and regulation of Arctic affairs.[100] The Arctic sea passage is also part of the PRC's global maritime Silk Road dreams, as it would offer an alternative to the passages running through the pirate-haunted South China Sea (and the Straits of Malacca and Hormuz). In 2009, the coordination of Chinese research on the Arctic and preparations to develop a Chinese Arctic strategy had been delegated to the Polar Research Institute of China (PRICS) (Jakobson/Peng 2012: 5). Whilst the PRC is involved in international initiatives and programmes for the scientific exploration of the Arctic, its demand to become a member of the Arctic Council was declined. The Arctic Council, founded in 1996, consists of Canada, Denmark, Finland, Iceland, Norway, Sweden, Russia and the US. In 2013, the PRC was granted observer status.

In addition to the PRC's efforts to establish "novel" international institutions – which do not automatically represent "Chinese" governance principles, but

---

100 Zhongguo de Beiji zhengce (China's Arctic Policy), http://news.sina.com.cn/c/nd/2018-01-26/doc-ifyqyqn i3132084.shtml.

instead rather express the PRC's quest for global status and recognition – Chinese political scientists are engaged in an ongoing debate on the theoretical underpinnings of global politics and the role of international institutions.

Out of the plurality of Chinese scholarly debates on International Relations (IR), one sub-stream strikes the eye: the search for a "Chinese School" of IR, sometimes also referenced as "IR theory with Chinese characteristics" (mirroring Deng Xiaoping's famous formula of practicing "Socialism with Chinese characteristics"). Articles falling into this subcategory range from critical reflections on the limits of explanatory power of "Western" IR frames when applied to the Chinese case to sinicized Marxist IR and reactivated premodern Chinese state philosophy. Only a few Chinese scholars are actively engaged in theory formulation, seeking to develop a Chinese alternative to Western IR theory. This includes the work by the Chinese philosopher Zhao Tingyang (Chinese Academy of Social Sciences); Qin Yaqing, president of the China Foreign Affairs University (CFAU) in Beijing, and Yan Xuetong, professor at the Tsinghua University in Beijing.

Zhao Tingyang postulates that China's concept of the *tianxia* not only shaped and regulated "international" relations in East Asia until the breakdown and forced transformation of the Chinese Empire, but could also be reactivated and modified to serve as a blueprint for global governance in the 21st century (Zhao, Tingyang 2005, 2006). Zhao contrasts the Western idea of the post-Westphalian global order, which would marginalise the role of the nation-state, with the hierarchical structure of the *tianxia*. According to Chinese political history and philosophy, the *tianxia* represented the civilised world ruled by the Chinese emperor, the son of heaven, positioned at the centre of this *tianxia* universe. The harmony and order of this system relied on everyone's willing recognition of and voluntary submission to the symbolic authority of the son of heaven. Despite being hierarchically organised, the *tianxia* system did not endorse despotism, as it was based on the mutual rights and obligations between the ruler and the ruled as laid down in the five Confucian relationships.

Zhao Tingyang's revived *tianxia* should not be mistaken as a revisionist intellectual endeavour aiming at restoring China's status as the centre of the (civilised) world. Zhao opposes the idea of global hegemony and unilateral solutions and highlights the fundamental principle of multipolarity, constructing the global *tianxia* as an integrative network composed of interconnected nodal points. This interwoven system is expected to have a symbolic centre and to operate based on a set of mutual rights and obligations. Elaborating on order and harmony under China's legendary Zhou dynasty, Zhao Tingyang identifies the maintenance of peace and stability as the world system's supreme goal. Should the system's universal principles be ignored or violated, order will have to be restored via punitive expeditions. In the (unlikely) case that the symbolic centre acts against the moral standards and legal norms upon which the *tianxia* is built, acts of resistance and even revolution by the sub-units are regarded as justified (Zhao, Tingyang 2009: 8). These reflections show that Zhao's reloading of the *tianxia* is deeply inspired by premodern Chinese state philosophy, especially by ancient Chinese contemplations on legitimacy as defined in the oeuvres of Confucius and Mencius. Zhao does not reflect the historical reality of Chinese dynastical rule and the challenges Chinese emperors were facing when seeking to maintain peace and stability. His focus lies on moral philosophy and the configuration of idealised political rule at a rather abstract level. He uses these reflections as a critical yardstick to measure the failure of the post-1945 international institutional arrangements. The UN, according to Zhao, did not act as a world government and neutral broker, but were mainly serving the interests (and power ambitions) of a rather small group of states. Borrowing core terms of "Western" IR, Zhao claims that the main challenge to global stability would not be "failed states" but the "failed world". In a nutshell, Zhao's philosophical reflections do not seek to replace one hegemonic world power and its institutions with another. Instead, he refers to Chinese state philosophy to make the point that the existing world order is not the only possible one. Zhao's reflections thus display certain connections to the (international) Critical School of IR.

Qin Yaqing, presenting himself as a realist IR scholar, engages in the deconstruction of US parochialism in IR research by pointing at certain misfits and contradictions of "Western" IR. In his essays on the concept of the PRC's peaceful rise (*heping jueqi*), Qin Yaqing argues that – contrary to predictions of an inevitable power struggle between old powers and ascending powers – the PRC's re-entrance into the global system and its new role as a global actor prove that a "peaceful rise" is possible. China's contribution to IR theory, filling this identified gap, would thus be a theory of peaceful power redistribution and changing actor constellation (see also: Qin, Yaqing 2005, 2012). Drawing inspiration from the five Confucian relationships, Qin constructs a Chinese counter-model to Western IR, hypothesising that the West would construct and theorise the world as based on interactions, whilst Chinese IR theory would focus on relationships and relationality. Given the specific mind maps and state philosophy underlying the PRC's international activities, Western IR theories would, consequently, be unable to identify the real drivers and ideas of China's positioning in world affairs. Whilst Qin starts from the idea of constructing a Chinese School of IR, his reflections do not target international politics and world order but are rather centred on China's foreign policy (thus linking up to models of foreign policy analysis).

Finally, Yan Xuetong and his team at Tsinghua University (Beijing) try to undertake a systematic mapping of premodern Chinese thought on inter-state relations in the pre-Qin era. The years prior to China's first national unification under Qin Shi Huang (221 BC) were characterised by heated debates amongst and within China's Hundred Schools of Thought on political rule and the meaning of laws versus the meaning of rites for the maintenance of political order. Yan's investigations start form the reading of the Chinese classics and canonical scripts of this period. He excavates a distinct Chinese typology of political rule and good governance, stressing that Chinese (foreign) politics would be guided by moral (philosophical) principles whilst Western IR would be rooted in (capitalist) cost-benefit calculations. The ideal Chinese emperor, as Yan outlines, is an enlightened one, basing his power and authority on benevolence to secure long-term stability and harmony (Yan, Xuetong 2011). Whilst Western IR operates with an understanding of good governance that requires democracy and the protection of human rights, Yan's typology illustrates that China has its own concepts and guiding principles that might lead to an alternative configuration of "good" governance. Yan's earlier work primarily focused on the inspiration to be drawn from ancient Chinese state philosophy for the conduct of contemporary (Chinese) politics. The follow-up publication turned to world politics and the drivers and determinants of the rise and fall of great powers (Yan, Xuetong 2019). Continuing along the lines of benevolent and moral governance, Yan develops the concept of "moral realism", arguing that moral leadership is the basis for any state to rise to global power status. China, following a moral approach to global governance and practising a benevolent foreign policy inspired by ancient Chinese philosophy, would, if one follows Yan's thought, be able to win followers and finally be accepted as a global leader without engaging in any direct military power competition with the US.

These three initiatives to excavate the cultural, philosophical foundations of Chinese politics and to blend these premodern thoughts into a "Chinese" IR theory do not represent the predominant stream of IR research in China. Most scholars tend to operate with (neo-)realist theories and rely on the master works of Western IR. Moreover, many scholars are rather unconvinced that elements of Chinese history and philosophy will allow for the formulation of a distinctly "Chinese" IR theory. Scholars working on Chinese history or premodern philosophy criticised the approaches discussed above as lacking historical-empirical foundations and as distorting the original meaning of the premodern philosophical writings to make them fit the authors' normative positions vis-à-vis contemporary (world) politics. The *tianxia*, as critics stress, was an imagined, utopian harmonious order, but never corresponded to political reality. As a utopian dream, the *tianxia* can only be revived on an abstract philosophical level but is not a concept to be used for political practice and real-world interactions. Furthermore, Victoria Hui points out that the iterated peaceful orientation associated with the *tianxia* contradicts the historical facts. The territorial expansion of the Chinese Empire, as her investigations show, was the result of wars and conquests (Hui 2010, 2012).

Nonetheless, some scholars of the English School reflected the claim put forward by the advocates of a (still-under-construction) Chinese School that Chinese IR can be traced back to the Zhou dynasty in their most recent works (inter alia Zhang/Buzan 2012). During that period, also referred to as the Spring and Autumn period (770–476 BC) and the Warring States period (475–221 BC), several small Chinese kingdoms contended for leadership and hegemony. Multiple philosophical schools presented their philosophical contemplations on the state, the ruler and modes of political rule. The interactions between the formally independent kingdoms, which later became unified under the emperor of the victorious Qin dynasty in 221 BC, are referred to as a historic example of premodern international relations in a regional context far from the West.

The internationalisation of these debates is a rather recent phenomenon. The post-modern, post-colonial turn in IR studies reactivated the controversial debates of the 1970s on (US) parochialism in IR and the limits of the explanatory power of frameworks and concepts derived from Western political history for developments in other "peripheral" world regions. Looking at international relations in Asia, Ikenberry and Mastanduno (2003: 19) come to the conclusion that Western IR theories are abstract enough to also cover the (East) Asian case and that one would not need to develop alternative frames in order to additionally reflect the specific cultural and historical context of the region. David Kang (2003) contradicts these findings and thematises the risk that the unmodified application of Western behavioural patterns and organisational principles, underlying these IR frameworks, to the analysis of Asian politics would lead to misinterpretations and misguided projections. Kang stresses the existence of Asia's distinct political culture and related value systems, which shape and determine culture-specific modes of interaction.

The assumption that China's political culture is unique and different from the West inspired a number of studies on China's theory of thought and the socio-cognitive underpinnings of Chinese foreign relations (Pye 1968; Shih 1990). These studies belong to the category of political psychology and are mainly dedicated to the explanation of visible irrational foreign policy behavioural patterns (e.g. Shih 1988; Huang/Shih 2014). Zhu Liqun's (2010) mapping of core frames of Chinese world order conceptions links this approach to the fields of IR. Zhu identifies *shi* (a Chinese term which describes the overall configuration and distribution of power) as a starting point for Chinese views on the world. Chinese foreign strategy, as Zhu outlines, is based on theory-guided perceptions of the PRC's external environment and its abstract developmental patterns. According to these contemplations, "Chinese" foreign policy analysis always was (and still remains) inspired by concepts and models inherited from ancient Chinese state philosophy and military strategy.

6.8. Summary

What kind of role China is going to play in the coming decades of the globally intertwined 21st century depends not only on the future structural transformations of the international system but also on socio-economic developments at the domestic level. Economic crises or financial bubbles could weaken China's bargaining power in bi-and multilateral contexts. Major modifications of the international system, which facilitated China's global rise, could have detrimental and incalculable spill-over effects on China's domestic economic development. This explains the widely observable confirmation of the existing international system structures by Beijing. Albeit the Chinese government demands reforms of the international institutions, it did not ask for their ultimate abolishment. Most reform demands are linked to recognition and reciprocity – defining itself as a (responsible) great power, the PRC wants to be treated and respected as an equal partner and refuses to maintain (or to enter) asymmetric relationships with other great powers.

The analysis of the foreign policy and foreign activities of non-democratic systems often operates with a rather monolithic conceptualisation of actors and agencies – limiting the focus to the political leaders. The growing pluralisation of actors involved in Chinese foreign diplomacy and foreign trade means that the analysis of "China" as an actor in regional and global affairs should not be reduced to the group of political leaders but should also reflect the role of relevant actors, including national ministries or transnational business networks. The examination of internal debates and bargaining rounds that occur prior to the official announcement of the outcome of political decision-making might provide additional information about the strategic positions of the multiple actors involved. When deciphering debates (and narratives) in the fields of Chinese politics, one should distinguish between debates and narratives that serve the justification and legitimation of political decisions (and the PRC's general political regime patterns) and those that contain concrete policy images that guide and determine China's foreign relations. Foreign policy change is not necessarily linked to the proclamation of novel policy frames in official diplomatic rhetoric. What is far more important is the policy image that dominates the horizontal intra-elite debates. The PRC formally adheres to the formula of *taoguang yanghui* – but has filled this notion with new content. This invisible adjustment of foreign policy-related slogans allows the PRC to signal role continuity and to avoid the impression of rising contradictions between the components of its national and global role identity. Whilst continuity is the message, at the operative level, the path to be followed reflects pragmatic interests and is based on rational choice calculations rather than on ideology.

The observation of domestic role contestation and of the changing ratio of ingredients in China's role conceptions thus offers one way out of the dilemma of static theories that are unable to assess the fluidity of Chinese (foreign) politics.

Questions for Discussion

- What are the core elements of the PRC's national and global role conceptions? Are these role conceptions stable or did they undergo major changes in connection with the transformation of the global system?
- What is the role of non-state, "private" actors in Chinese foreign policy?
- Is China's engagement in Africa and Latin America driven by mere economic interests? Or does Beijing seek to establish strategic coalitions with the states of the so-called Global South in order to overthrow the post-1945 international order?
- Is China's foreign strategy guided by hard power calculations? What is the "Chinese" definition of (global) power and leadership?
- Does the PRC's "military strategy" (released in 2015) indicate a U-turn in China's regional and global behaviour?
- How does China respond to global climate change? Does it support international regulations to achieve carbon neutrality?
- How does China act within international institutions and multilateral frameworks? Is it a status quo power or a revisionist one?

References

Alden, Chris/Large, Daniel (eds.) (2019), *New Directions in Africa–China Studies*. New York: Routledge.

Aliberti, Marco (2015), *When China Goes to the Moon*. Cham: Springer.

Andrews, David M. (2006), "Monetary Power and Monetary Statecraft", in: Andrews, David M. (ed.) (2006), *International Monetary Power*. New York: Cornell UP, 7–28.

Armijo, Leslie Elliott/Mühlich, Laurissa/Tirone, Daniel C. (2013), "The Systemic Financial Importance of Emerging Powers", http://www.leslieelliottarmijo.org/about/.

Barnett, Michael/Duvall, Raymond (2005), *Power in Global Governance*. Cambridge: Cambridge UP.

Beeson, Mark (2010), "The Coming of Environmental Authoritarianism", *Environmental Politics*, 19:2, 276–294.

Bernstein, Richard/Munro, Ross (1997), *The Coming Conflict with China*. New York: Knopf.

Beylerian, Onnig/Canivet, Christophe (1997), "China: Role Conceptions after the Cold War", in: Le Prestre, Philippe (ed.) (1997), *Role Quests in the Post-Cold War Era*. Montreal: McGil-Queen's UP, 187–224.

Blanchard, Jean-Marc F. (2011), "China's Grand Strategy and Money Muscle: The Potentialities and Pratfalls of China's Sovereign Wealth Fund and Renminbi Policies", *The Chinese Journal of International Politics*, 4, 31–53.

Bloomberg (2016), "Trump Tower Funded by Rich Chinese Who Invest Cash for Visas", 7 March 2016, http://www.bloomberg.com/politics/articles/2016-03-07/trump-tower-financed-by-rich-chinese-who-invest-cash-for-visas.

Breslin, Shaun (2013), "China and the Global Order: Signalling Threat or Friendship?", *International Affairs*, 89:3, 615–634.

Cai, Yongshun (2010), *Collective Resistance in China: Why Popular Protests Succeed or Fail*. Stanford: Stanford UP.

Cantir, Cristian/Kaarbo, Juliet (2012), "Contested Roles and Domestic Politics: Reflections on Role Theory in Foreign Policy Analysis and IR Theory", *Foreign Policy Analysis*, 8:1, 5–24.

Cantir, Cristian/Kaarbo, Juliet (eds.) (2016), *Domestic Role Contestation, Foreign Policy, and International Relations*. London; New York: Routledge.

CGTN (2019), "China to Launch Chang'e-5 Lunar Probe in 2020", 28 October 2019, https://news.cgtn.com/news/2019-10-28/China-to-launch-Chang-e-5-lunar-probe-in-2020-L9pRDXOQ1O/index.html.

Chan, Gerald (2014), "Capturing China's International Identity: Social Evolution and its Missing Links", *The Chinese Journal of International Politics*, 7:2, 261–281.

Chen, Jie (2010), "Transnational Environmental Movement: Impacts on the Green Civil Society in China", *Journal of Contemporary China*, 19:65, 503–523.

Chen, Yingchun (2007), Lun Zhongguo heping fazhan daolu lishi jincheng zhong de guoji juese zhuanxing (Transformation of China's Global Role in the Context of the Process of Peaceful Development), *Journal of Zhanjiang Normal College*, 28:4, 68–70.

Chin, Gregory/Helleiner, Eric (2008), "China as a Creditor: A Rising Financial Power?" *Journal of International Affairs*, 62:1, 87–102.

China's African Policy (2006), online unter: http://en.people.cn/200601/12/eng20060112_234894.html.

China's Second Africa Policy Paper (2015): http://news.xinhuanet.com/english/2015-12/04/c_134886545.htm.

China Daily (2013), "Exploration Part of Chinese Dream", 25 June 2013, http://europe.chinadaily.com.cn/china/2013-06/25/content_16653622.htm.

Christensen, Thomas J. (2015), *The China Challenge: Shaping the Choices of a Rising Power*. New York: W.W.Norton & Company.

Choucri, Nazli (2000), "Introduction: CyberPolitics in International Relations", *International Political Science Review*, 21:3, 243–263.

Choucri, Nazli (2012), *Cyberpolitics in International Relations*. Cambridge; London: MIT Press.

Cohen, Benjamin J. (2006), "The Macrofoundations of Monetary Power", in: Andrews, David M. (ed.) (2006), *International Monetary Power*. New York: Cornell UP, 31–50.

Cohen, Benjamin (2013), "Currency and State Power", in: Finnemore, Martha/Goldstein, Judith (eds.) (2013), *Back to Basics: State Power in a Contemporary World*. New York: Oxford UP, 159–176.

Cox, Robert W. (1981), "Social Forces, States and World Orders: Beyond International Relations Theory", *Millennium*, 10:2, 126–155.

Domínguez, Jorge I. (2006), "China's Relations with Latin America: Shared Gains, Asymmetric Hopes", https://wcfia.harvard.edu/files/wcfia/files/dominguez_chinas.pdf.

Economy, Elizabeth (2006), *The River Runs Black: The Environmental Challenges to China's Future*. London: Cornell UP.

EAI (2015a), "China: International Energy Data and Analysis", https://www.eia.gov/beta/international/analysis_includes/countries_long/China/china.pdf.

EAI (2015b), "Country Analysis Brief: Nigeria", http://www.eia.gov/beta/international/analysis_includes/countries_long/Nigeria/nigeria.pdf.

EIA (2015c), "Global Solar Photovoltaic Manufacturing Production Slows in Recent Years", https://www.eia.gov/todayinenergy/detail.cfm?id=22912.

Eichengreen, Barry (2008), *Globalizing Capital: A History of the International Monetary System*. Princeton; Oxford: Princeton UP.

Ellis, Evan R. (2011), "China–Latin America Military Engagement: Good Will, Good Business, and Strategic Position", http://www.strategicstudiesinstitute.army.mil/pdffiles/PUB1077.pdf.

Ellis, Evan R. (2014), *China on the Ground in Latin America: Challenges for the Chinese and Impacts on the Region*. New York: Palgrave.

Eriksson, Johan/Giacomello, Giampiero (2006), "The Information Revolution, Security, and International Relations: (IR)relevant Theory?", *International Political Science Review*, 27:3, 221–244.

European Commission (2016), "The European Union's Measures Against Dumped and Subsidised Imports of Solar Panels from China", http://trade.ec.europa.eu/doclib/docs/2015/july/tradoc_153587.pdf.

Forbes (2015), "Mexico Suspends Multibillion Dollar High-speed Rail Project at Center of Political Scandal", 10 February 2015, http://www.forbes.com/sites/doliaestevez/2015/02/10/mexico-suspends-multibillion-dollar-high-speed-rail-project-at-center-of-political-scandal/#157415212f12.

Friedberg, Aaron L. (2014), "The Sources of Chinese Conduct: Explaining Beijing's Assertiveness", *The Washington Quarterly*, 37:4, 133–150.

Gallagher, Kevin P./Myers, Margaret (2020), *China–Latin America Finance Database*. Washington: Inter-American Dialogue.

Gilley, Bruce (2012), "Authoritarian Environmentalism and China's Response to Climate Change", *Environmental Politics*, 21:2, 287–307.

Gregor, A. James (1967), "African Socialism, Socialism and Fascism: An Appraisal", *The Review of Politics*, 29:3, 324–353.

Harvey, Brian (2013), *China in Space: The Great Leap Forward*. New York: Springer

He, Kai/Feng, Huiyun (2013), "Xi Jinping's Operational Code Beliefs and China's Foreign Policy", *The Chinese Journal of International Politics*, 6, 209–231.

Hearn, Adrian H. (2012), "China, Global Governance and the Future of Cuba", *Journal of Current Chinese Affairs*, 41:1, 155–179.

Ho, Peter (2001), "Greening Without Conflict? Environmentalism, NGOs and Civil Society in China", *Development and Change*, 32, 893–921.

Hu, Jian (2006), Zhongguo guoji juese de zhuanhuan yu guoji shehui de renzhi (The Transformation of China's International Role and Its Recognition by International Society), *Xiandai Guoji Guanxi* (Contemporary International Relations), 8, 21–24+52.

Huang, Chiung-Chiu/Shih, Chih-yu (2014), *Harmonious Intervention: China's Quest for Relational Security*. London; New York: Routledge.

Hui, Victoria Tin-bor (2010), "Guojian 'Zhongguo Xuepai' bixu zhengshi lishi" (Chinese History Must Be Taken Seriously in the Construction of a Chinese School of International Relations), *Shijie Jingji yu Zhengzhi*, 5, 124–138.

Hui, Victoria Tin-bor (2012), "History and Thought in China's Traditions", *Journal of Chinese Political Science*, 17, 125–141.

Ikenberry, John G./Mastanduno, Michael (2003), "International Relations Theory and the Search for Regional Stability", in: Ikenberry, John G./Mastanduno, Michael (eds.) (2003), *International Relations Theory and the Asia-Pacific*. New York: Columbia UP, 1–21.

Jacobson, Harold K./Oksenberg, Michel (1990), *China's Participation in the IMF, World Bank, and GATT: Toward a Global Economic Order*. Ann Arbor: University of Michigan Press.

Jahiel, Abigail R. (1998), "The Organization of Environmental Protection in China", *The China Quarterly*, 156, 757–787.

Jakobson, Linda/ Peng, Jingchao (2012), *China's Arctic Aspirations*. Stockholm: SIPRI.

Johnson, Thomas (2010), "Environmentalism and NIMBYism in China: Promoting a Rules-based Approach to Public Participation", *Environmental Politics*, 19:3, 430–448.

Johnson, Thomas (2014), "Good Governance for Environmental Protection in China: Instrumentation, Strategic Interactions and Unintended Consequences", *Journal of Contemporary Asia*, 44:2, 241–258.

Johnson-Freese, Joan (2007), *Space as a Strategic Asset*. New York: Columbia UP.

Johnson-Freese, Joan/Erickson, Andrew S. (2006), "The Emerging China–EU Space Partnership: A Geotechnological Balancer", *Space Policy*, 22:1, 12–22.

Johnston, Alastair Iain (2003), "Is China a Status Quo Power?", *International Security*, 27:4, 5–56.

Johnston, Alastair Iain (2008), *Social States: China in International Institutions, 1980–2000*. Princeton: Princeton UP.

Johnston, Alastair Iain (2013), "How New and Assertive Is China's New Assertiveness?", *International Security*, 37:4, 7–48.

Kang, David (2003), "Getting Asia Wrong: The Need for New Analytical Frameworks", *International Security*, 27:4, 57–85.

Kastner, Scott L./Saunders, Phillip C. (2012), "Is China a Status Quo or Revisionist State? Leadership Travel as an Empirical Indicator of Foreign Policy Priorities", *International Studies Quarterly*, 56, 163–177.

Kerry, John (2013), "Statement on the East China Sea Air Defense Identification Zone", http://www.state.gov/secretary/remarks/2013/11/218013.htm.

Krisch, Nico (2005), "International Law in Times of Hegemony: Unequal Power and the Shaping of the International Legal Order", *The European Journal of International Law*, 16:3, 369–408.

Lardy, Nicholas R. (1999), "China and the International Financial System", in: Economy, Elizabeth/Oksenberg, Michel (eds.) (1999), *China Joins the World: Progress and Prospects*. New York: Council on Foreign Relations Press, 206–230.

Large, Daniel (2013), "China–South Sudan: Governance in Emerging Relations", *SAIIA Policy Briefing*, 77, http://www.saiia.org.za/doc_view/412-governance-in-emerging-relations.

Li, Keqiang (2014), "Zhengfu gongzuo baogao" (Government Work Report), http://www.gov.cn/guowuyuan/2014-03/14/content_2638989.htm.

Liao, Shu-Hsien (2005), "Will China Become a Military Space Superpower?", *Space Policy*, 21:3, 205–212.

Ling, Zongcheng et al. (2015), "Correlated Compositional and Mineralogical Investigations at the Chang'e Landing Site", *Nature Communications*, 6, http://www.nature.com/ncom ms/2015/151222/ncomms9880/full/ncomms9880.html.

Liu, Qiang (2013), "Weilai Zhongguo guoji juese dingwei de zhanlüe xuanze" (China's Future Strategic Choice Regarding the Configuration of its International Role), *Journal of PLA Nanjing Institute of Politics*, 2, 79–84.

Lo, Kevin (2015), "How Authoritarian Is the Environmental Governance of China?", *Environmental Science & Policy*, 54, 152–159.

McKinney, Jared (2017), "How Stalled Global Reform Is Fueling Regionalism: China's Engagement with the G20", *Third World Quarterly*, 39:4, 709–726.

Millward, Steve (2013), "Now China's WeChat App is Censoring its Users Globally", *TechInAsia*, https://www.techinasia.com/china-wechat-censoring-users-globally.

Ministry of Commerce (2015), "Regular Press Conference of Ministry of Commerce on January 21, 2015", 21 January 2015, http://english.mofcom.gov.cn/article/newsrelease/p ress/201501/20150100878729.shtml.

MOFA (2015), "Remarks by H.E. Xi Jinping President of the People's Republic of China at the Opening Ceremony of the Second World Internet Conference", 16 December 2015, https://www.fmprc.gov.cn/mfa_eng/wjdt_665385/zyjh_665391/t1327570.shtml.

MOFA (2017), "International Strategy of Cooperation on Cyberspace", https://www.fmprc .gov.cn/mfa_eng/wjb_663304/zzjg_663340/jks_665232/kjlc_665236/qtwt_665250/t144 2390.shtml.

MOFA (2019), "Foreign Ministry Spokesperson Hua Chunying's Regular Press Conference on 13 February 2019", https://www.fmprc.gov.cn/mfa_eng/xwfw_665399/s2510_66540 1/t1637635.shtml.

Mol, Arthur P. J./Carter, Neil T. (2006), "China's Environmental Governance in Transition", *Environmental Politics*, 15:02, 149–170.

Moltz, James Clay (2012), *Asia's Space Race: National Motivations, Regional Rivalries, and International Risks*. New York: Columbia UP.

Nolte, Detlef (2006), "Macht und Machthierarchien in den internationalen Beziehungen" (Power and Power Hierarchies in International Relations), Hamburg: GIGA Working Paper 29.

Obama, Barak (2010), "President Barack Obama on Space Exploration in the 21st Century", http://www.nasa.gov/news/media/trans/obama_ksc_trans.html.

OECD (2011), "China and Nigeria: A Powerful South-South Alliance", http://www.oecd.or g/china/49814032.pdf.

O'Hara, Kieron/Hall, Wendy (2018), "Four Internets: The Geopolitics of Digital Governance", *CIGI Paper*, 206, https://www.cigionline.org/publications/four-internets-geopoli tics-digital-governance.

Organski, A. F. K. (1968), *World Politics*. New York: Knopf.

Organski, A. F. K./Kugler, Jacek (1980), *The War Ledger*. Chicago: Chicago UP.

Payne, Anthony (1994), "US Hegemony and the Reconfiguration of the Caribbean", *Review of International Studies*, 20:2, 149–168.

Pearson, Margaret M. (1999), "China's Integration into the International Trade and Investment Regime", in: Economy, Elizabeth/Oksenberg, Michel (eds.) (1999), *China Joins the World: Progress and Prospects*. New York: Council on Foreign Relations Press, 161–205.

Pye, Lucian (1968), *The Spirit of Chinese Politics*. Cambridge: MIT.

Qin, Yaqing (2003), "Guojia shenfen, zhanlüe wenhua he anquan liyi" (National Identity, Strategic Culture and Security Interests), *Shijie Jingji yu Zhengzhi* (World Economics and Politics), 1, 10–15.

Qin, Yaqing (2005), "Guoji guanxi lilun de hexin wenti yu Zhongguo xuepai shengcheng de keneng he biran" (The Core Question of IR Theory and the Possibility and Necessity of Constructing a Chinese School), *Zhongguo Shehui Kexue* (Social Sciences in China), 26:3, 165–173.

Qin, Yaqing (2007), "Zhuanfang Qin Yaqing: Shiqida hou Zhongguo waijiao jiang geng zhongshi duobian wutai" (Interview with Qin Yaqing: After the 17th Party Congress, China will focus more on multilateralism), http://cpc.people.com.cn/GB/100804/6370470.html.

Qin, Yaqing (2012), "Culture and Global Thought. Chinese International Theory in the Making", *Revista CIBOP d'Afers Internacionals*, 100, 67–90.

Ray, Rebecca/Gallagher, Kevin (2015), "China–Latin America Economic Bulletin", http://www.bu.edu/pardeeschool/files/2015/02/Economic-Bulletin-2015.pdf.

Renmin Ribao (2014), "Xi Jinping waijiao xin zhanlüe: 'Mingyun gongtongti' zhu tui guoji geju xin zhixu" (Xi Jinping's New Foreign Strategy: The Community of Shared Destiny Leads to a New International Order), 23 July 2014, http://politics.people.com.cn/n/2014/0723/c1001-25328439.html.

Ross, Robert S. (1997), "Beijing as a Conservative Power", *Foreign Affairs*, 76:2, 33–44.

Ruan, Zongze (2012), "Responsible Protection: Building a Safer World", http://www.ciis.org.cn/english/2012-06/15/content_5090912.htm.

Seedhouse, Erik (2010), *The New Space Race: China vs. the United States*. Berlin; New York: Springer.

Shapiro, Judith (2016 [2012]), *China's Environmental Challenges*. Cambridge: Polity Press.

Shen, Hong (2018), "Building a Digital Silk Road? Situating the Internet in China's Belt and Road Initiative", *International Journal of Communication*, 12, 2683–2701.

Shih, Chih-yu (1988), "National Role Conception as Foreign Policy Motivation: The Psychocultural Bases of Chinese Diplomacy", *Political Psychology*, 9:4, 599–631.

Shih, Chih-yu (1990), *The Spirit of Chinese Foreign Policy: A Psychocultural View*. London: Palgrave Macmillan.

Shinn, David H./Eisenman, Joshua (2012), *China and Africa: A Century of Engagement*. Philadelphia: University of Pennsylvania Press.

SIPRI (2011), "Arms Flows to Sub-Saharan Africa", https://www.sipri.org/sites/default/files/files/PP/SIPRIPP30.pdf.

SIPRI (2019), "Trends in International Arms Transfers 2018", https://www.sipri.org/sites/default/files/2019-03/fs_1903_at_2018.pdf.

SIPRI (by Nan Tian/Fei Su) (2020), "Estimating the Arm Sales of Chinese Companies", SIPRI 20/02, https://sipri.org/sites/default/files/2020-01/sipriinsight2002_0_0.pdf.

Solomone, Stacey (2013), "Space for the People: China's Aerospace Industry and the Cultural Revolution", in: Wei, Chunyuan Nancy/Brock, Darryl E. (eds.) (2013), *Mr. Science and Chairman Mao's Cultural Revolution*. Lanham: Lexington, 233–250.

Stalley, Phillip/Yang, Dongning (2006), "An Emerging Environmental Movement in China?",
The China Quarterly, 186, 333–356.

State Council Information Office (2013), "The Diversified Employment of China's Armed Forces", http://english.gov.cn/archive/white_paper/2014/08/23/content_281474982986506.htm.

Strange, Susan (1988), *States and Markets*. London: Pinter.

Sun, Yun (2014), "Africa in China's Foreign Policy", http://www.brookings.edu/research/papers/2014/04/10-africa-china-foreign-policy-sun.

Swaine, Michael D./Johnston, Alastair Iain (1999), "China and Arms Control Institutions", in: Economy, Elizabeth/Oksenberg, Michel (eds.) (1999), *China Joins the World: Progress and Prospects*. New York: Council on Foreign Relations Press, 90–135.

Swaine, Michael D. (2010), "Perceptions of an Assertive China", *China Leadership Monitor*, 32, http://www.hoover.org/publications/china-leadership-monitor.

Swaine, Michael D. (2013), "Chinese Views Regarding the Senkaku/Diaoyu Islands Dispute", *China Leadership Monitor*, 41, http://www.hoover.org/publications/china-leaders hip-monitor.

The White House (2017), "National Security Strategy of the United States of America", December 2017, https://www.whitehouse.gov/wp-content/uploads/2017/12/NSS-Final-1 2-18-2017-0905.pdf.

UN News (2020), "'Enhance Solidarity' to fight COVID-19, Chinese President urges, also pledges carbon neutrality by 2060", 22 September 2020, https://news.un.org/en/story/20 20/09/1073052.

US–China Joint Announcement on Climate Change, https://www.whitehouse.gov/the-press -office/2014/11/11/us-china-joint-announcement-climate-change.

US Embassy (2018), "Remarks of Secretary of State Rex Tillerson on US Engagement in the Western Hemisphere", 1 February 2018, https://co.usembassy.gov/remarks-secretary-stat e-rex-tillerson-u-s-engagement-western-hemisphere/.

Xi, Jinping (2014), "Nuli goujian xieshou gongjin de mingyun gongtongti" (Joining Forces to Form a Community of Shared Destiny), 17 July 2014, http://www.chinacelacforum.or g/chn/zgtlgtgx/t1175807.htm.

Xie, Lei (2011), "China's Environmental Activism in the Age of Globalization", *Asian Politics & Policy*, 3:2, 205–222.

Xinhua (2009), "China Plays Key Role Making Copenhagen Talks Successful", 25 December 2009, http://news.xinhuanet.com/english/2009-12/25/content_12704224.htm.

Xinhua (2014), "China Sends First Infantry Battalion for UN Peacekeeping", 22 December 2014, http://news.xinhuanet.com/english/china/2014-12/22/c_133871006.htm.

Xinhua (2015a), "Commentary: China–Africa Relations: Something Besides Natural Resources", 2 March 2015, http://news.xinhuanet.com/english/2015-03/02/c_134030887.h tm.

Xinhua (2015b), "China–Africa Trade Approaches $300 Billion in 2015", 10 November 2015, http://www.chinadaily.com.cn/business/2015-11/10/content_22417707.htm.

Xinhua (2015c), "Backgrounder: China's Voices at Paris Climate Conference", 12 December 2015, http://news.xinhuanet.com/english/2015-12/12/c_134909275.htm.

Xinhua (2015d), "China Voice: China Takes Leading Role in Global Climate Deal", 14 December 2015, http://news.xinhuanet.com/english/2015-12/14/c_134916400.htm.

Xinhua (2016), "Chang'e-3 Landing Site Named Guang Han Gong", 5 January 2016, http://news.xinhuanet.com/english/2016-01/05/c_134980117.htm.

Xinhua (2017), "Spotlight: China Reasserts itself Responsible Player at Bonn Climate Talks", 18 November 2017, http://www.xinhuanet.com/english/2017-11/18/c_1367 62725.htm.

Xinhua (2018a), "2nd Ministerial Meeting of China-CELAC Forum Opens Up New Cooperation Areas, 23 January 2018, http://www.xinhuanet.com/english/2018-01/23/c_1369 18217.htm.

Xinhua (2018b), "Raul Castro Meets Xi's Special Envoy on Advancing Ties", 25 January 2018, http://www.xinhuanet.com/english/2018-01/2.5/c_136923530.htm.

Xinhua (2019), "Feature: China, Argentina Boost Green Energy Cooperation, 29 April 2019, http://www.xinhuanet.com/english/2019-04/29/c_138021701.htm.

Xu, Jin/Du, Zheyuan (2015), "The Dominant Thinking Sets in Chinese Foreign Policy Research: A Criticism", *The Chinese Journal of International Politics*, 8:3, 251–279.

Yan, Xuetong (2011), "A Comparative Study of Pre-Qin Interstate Political Philosophy", in: Bell, Daniel/Sun, Zhe (eds.) (2011), *Ancient Chinese Thought, Modern Chinese Power*. Princeton: Princeton UP, 21–69.

Yan, Xuetong (2014), "China's New Security Concept under Multilateral Diplomacy", http://carnegietsinghua.org/publications/?fa=56879.

Yan, Xuetong (2019), *Leadership and the Rise of Great Powers*. Princeton UP.

Ye, Zicheng (2002), "Guanyu taoguang yanghui he you suo zuowei: Zai tan Zhongguo de daguo waijiao xintai" (On *taoguang yanghui* and *you suo zuowei*), *Taipingyang Xuebao* (Pacific Journal), 1, 62–66.

Zhang, Weiwei (2012), *The China Wave: Rise of a Civilizational State*. Hackensack, NJ: World Century.

Zhang, Yongjin/Buzan, Barry (2012), "The Tributary System as International Society in Theory and Practice", *The Chinese Journal of International Politics*, 5:1, 3–36.

Zhao, Kejin (2015), "China Should Adopt Clear Attitude on ISIS", http://charhar.china.org .cn/2015-11/30/content_37196098.htm.

Zhao, Tingyang (2005), *Tianxia tixi: Shijie zhidu zhexue daolun* (The *tianxia* System: An Introduction to the Philosophy of a World Institution). Nanjing: Jiangsu Jiaoyu Chubanshe.

Zhao, Tingyang (2006), "Rethinking Empire from a Chinese Concept 'all-under-heaven' (tianxia)", *Social Identities*, 12:1, 29–41.

Zhao, Tingyang (2009), "A Political World Philosophy in Terms of all-under-heaven (tianxia)", *Diogenes*, 56, 5–18.

Zhu, Liqun (2010), *China's Foreign Policy Debates*. Paris: Chaillot Paper 121.

Zhu, Zhiqun (2010), *China's New Diplomacy: Rationale, Strategies and Significance*. Farnham: Ashgate.

Recommended Reading

Chinese Perspectives on World Politics

Chan, Gerald (2008), "Global Governance with Chinese Characteristics? A Preliminary Analysis", *The Copenhagen Journal of Asian Studies*, 26:2, 82–96.

Chan, Gerald/Lee, Pak K./Chan, Lai-Ha (2012), *China Engages Global Governance: A New World Order in the Making?* New York: Routledge.

Leonard, Mark (2008), *What Does China Think?* London: Fourth Estate.

Shao, Binhong (ed.) (2013), *China and the World: Balance, Rebalance and Imbalance*. Leiden: Brill.

Shao, Binhong (ed.) (2014), *The World in 2020 According to China*. Leiden: Brill.

Zhang, Yongjin/Zhang, Teng-chi (eds. (2016), *Constructing a Chinese School of International Relations*. London; New York: Routledge.

China, Monetary Power, Internationalization of the Renminbi

Cohen, Benjamin J. (1998), *The Geography of Money*. Ithaka; London: Cornell UP.

Eichengreen, Barry/Kawai, Masahiro (eds.) (2015), *Renminbi Internationalization: Achievements, Prospects, and Challenges*. Washington: Brookings Institution Press.

Lo, Chi (2013), *The Renminbi Rises: Myths, Hypes and Realities of RMB Internationalisation and Reforms in the Post-crisis World*. Basingstoke: Palgrave Macmillan.

China–Africa

Alden, Christopher/Large, Daniel/Soares de Oliveira, Ricardo (eds.) (2008), *China Returns to Africa: A Rising Power and a Continent Embrace*. New York: Columbia UP.

Alden, Chris/Alao, Abiodun/Zhang, Chun, Barber, Laura. (eds.) (2018), *China and Africa: Building Peace and Security Cooperation on the Continent*. London: Palgrave Macmillan.

Alden, Chris/Large, Daniel (eds.) (2019), *New Directions in China–Africa Studies*. New York: Routledge.

Bräutigam, Deborah (2009), *The Dragon's Gift: The Real Story of China in Africa*. Oxford: Oxford UP.

Gadzala, Aleksandra W. (ed.) (2015), *Africa and China: How Africans and their Governments Are Shaping Relations with China*. Lanham: Rowman & Littlefield.

Li, Xing (ed.) (2013), *China-Africa Relations in an Era of Great Transformations*. Farnham: Ashgate.

Taylor, Ian (2009), *China's New Role in Africa*. Boulder: Lynne Rienner.

Zhao, Suisheng (ed.) (2015), *China in Africa: Strategic Motives and Economic Interests*. London: Routledge.

China–Latin America

Ellis, Evan R. (2014), *China on the Ground in Latin America: Challenges for the Chinese and Impacts on the Region*. New York: Palgrave Macmillan.

Jenkins, Rhys (2012), "Latin America and China: A New Dependency?", *Third World Quarterly*, 33:7, 1337–1358.

Myers, Margaret/Wise, Carol (eds.) (2017), *China–Latin America Relations in the New Millennium: Brave New World*. London; New York: Routledge.

Paz, Gonzalo S. (2006), "Rising China's 'Offensive' in Latin America and the US Reaction", *Asian Perspective*, 30:4, 95–112.

Strauss, Julia C./Armony, Ariel C. (eds.) (2012), *From the Great Wall to the New World: China and Latin America in the 21st Century*. Cambridge: Cambridge UP.

Military and Security

Cheung, Tai Ming (2001), "The Influence of the Gun: China's Central Military Commission and its Relationship with the Military, Party and Decision-making System", in: Lampton, David M. (ed.) (2001), *The Making of Chinese Foreign and Security Policy in the Era of Reform*. Stanford: Stanford University Press, 61–90.

Graff, David A./Higham, Robin (eds.) (2012), *A Military History of China*. Lexington: University Press of Kentucky.

Ross, Robert (2009), *Chinese Security Policy: Structure, Power, and Politics*. New York: Routledge.

Scobell, Andrew (2003), *China's Use of Military Force: Beyond the Great Wall and the Long March*. Cambridge: Cambridge UP.

Shambaugh, David (2003), *Modernizing China's Military: Progress, Problems, and Prospects*. Berkeley: University of California Press.

China and Climate Change

Chen, Gang (2012), *China's Climate Policy*. London; New York: Routledge.

Li, Minqi (2014), *Peak Oil, Climate Change, and the Limits to China's Economic Growth*. London; New York: Routledge.

Wang, Weiguang et al. (2012), *China's Climate Change Policies*. London; New York: Routledge.

7. China in the Global System of the 21st Century

Key Content and Learning Goals

- Introduction to novel foreign policy trends under Xi Jinping: the New Silk Road and the PRC's interactions with the Arab world
- Overview of China's strategic positioning within the ("imagined") multipolar/pentapolar world order
- Critical assessment of the historical foundations and the evolution of China's relationship with the EU, Japan, Russia, and the US

It is quite remarkable that the PRC managed to undertake a twofold readjustment of its economic modernisation path – i.e., the turn to capitalism after Mao, followed by the proclaimed entrance into the era of "new normal" and socio-ecological sustainability under the Xi–Li administration – without formally giving up any of its axiomatic foreign policy principles. At the operational level, the PRC sped up the internationalisation of its domestic economy, starting with the reopening of the Chinese domestic markets for joint ventures and foreign direct investment, followed by the "going global" of Chinese companies and, finally, the outsourcing of parts of the Chinese production process to other world regions. Furthermore, the PRC diversified its foreign relations and started to explore (and develop) new markets in Africa and Latin America. The global expansion of Chinese economic activities has not been achieved via offensive competition. The rise of "China" to global economic and monetary power took place in the shadow of the global financial crisis, when the "old" investors and major trading powers reduced their global activities. Chinese banks and companies used this window of opportunity to fill this void. In addition, China's principles of peaceful coexistence and non-conditionality allowed Chinese investors and companies to interact with states sanctioned and isolated by the international community – such as in the case of Iran and Sudan. Moreover, under its fifth generation of political leaders, the PRC began to pursue a more sophisticated multi-level approach to international relations by not only cooperating with single states but by also intensifying its collaboration with regional organisations or regional sub-groupings. As the development of Sino–European relations evidences, the Chinese side has commenced to pay more attention to the mechanisms of the supranational decision-making procedures of the EU but also attentively observes the frictions and tensions within the EU (and the Schengen Area).

With the launching of the New Silk Road Initiative, Beijing positioned itself at the centre of a globe-spanning network of transportation and supply channels. The related connectivity initiatives create additional transnational and transregional interdependencies. Decisions made in Beijing will have direct implications for the future transformation and development of the global system. Vice versa, the reorientation of the US development model under the Trump administration, the readjustment of the US's economic strategy and Washington's re-joining of international agreements (such as the Paris Protocol) by the Biden/Harris Administration, as well as the restructuring of the EU's integrated market and customs union in connection with the Brexit are forcing the PRC to adapt its foreign strategy accordingly.

Changes and readjustments in a state's foreign (and security) strategy are often guesstimated rather than observed. Disruptive departures from inherited foreign policy principles are the rare exception in world diplomatic history – and normally occur in connection with regime transformations or in the early stages of regime-building. The PRC formally "cancelled" all treaties and cooperation agreements concluded by the GMD government of the Republic of China. Despite the fact that the Communist government in Beijing was not recognised as the official representation of China until the 1970s, it did exert power and control over the Chinese mainland and coordinate the mainland's foreign relations. In the first two decades under Mao, the PRC was "leaning to one side", i.e., copying the Soviet institutions and Soviet world order views. The Sino–Soviet split, the Sino–US rapprochement, and the reorientation of the Chinese political economy in the post-Mao years catalysed the PRC's transition towards a more pragmatic, cooperative foreign strategy, guided by the principle of peaceful coexistence.

The Cold War world is generally described as a bipolar power structure, dominated by the global system antagonism between the US and the Soviet Union. After the dissolution of the Soviet Union, a unipolar world order emerged centred on the US as the only remaining superpower. The PRC, joined by other rising economies and states located in the so-called Global South, promotes the formation of a multipolar world and openly opposes any world order dominated by just one or two superpowers. Multipolarity is both a vision for a future (post-US) global order and a pair of theoretical lenses through which China looks at the world. In the late 1970s and early 1980s, Chinese scholars broke the concept of multipolarity down to the idea of a pentapolar world system composed of five major power centres (the US, Russia, China, Europe/EU, Japan). The formula of multipolarity has never been deactivated and can still be found in Chinese diplomatic statements and joint declarations with Russia and the BRICS countries. There are, however, certain indications that the definition of multipolarity has changed and that the configurations of the model's core poles might have been silently modified. Likewise, the modes of interaction between poles and non-poles appear to have undergone a major revision – in theory as well as in political practice.

How can these changes and modifications be tracked and categorised? As, in most cases, the PRC reiterates the core foreign policy paradigms and terms coined in the Mao era – amended but not substituted by auxiliary follow-up concepts by each Chinese leadership generation – it is almost impossible to deduce these reorientations in Chinese foreign strategy directly from official speeches or diplomatic statements. As these reorientations occur gradually, they often start with the redefinition of core terms at the content level. It is thus important to undertake a critical analysis of the subtext of official diplomatic statements and speeches and to take the simultaneously occurring internal debates – within the party, Chinese think-tanks, across scholarly circles – into account.

Additionally, the launching of "new" initiatives or the proclaimed entrance into a "new" stage of development signals reform and renewal. Whilst stressing the path dependency of China's development model, the fifth generation seems to have proactively decided to enter "unknown" waters in domestic and global politics.

This chapter starts with a critical assessment of the PRC's 21st century New Silk Road initiative. The "re"-launch of the "old" Silk Road implies that Beijing will strive to deepen its relations with the Arab world. In 2016, the PRC released a first policy paper on its relations with the Arab world. Several corridors of the PRC's New Silk Road will run to or through the Middle East. Therefore, one could expect to see a more proactive positioning of China on issues related to regional peace and stability. Does Xi Jinping's visit to the region (Saudi Arabia, Egypt, Iran) in 2016 represent a farewell to the foreign strategy pursued by the fourth generation (Hu Jintao, Wen Jiabao)? Moreover, does the PRC's turn to the "East" and the Global South cause a declining interest in cooperation and interactions with the "old" poles of China's imagined pentapolar world order? This chapter thus continues with a retrospective assessment of the genesis and transformation of the PRC's relations and interactions with the US, Russia, Japan, as well as Europe.

7.1. China, the New Silk Road, and the Arab World

With the launching of the New Silk Road initiative, the PRC's relations with the Arab world have been upgraded. Whilst trade and economic transactions dominate bilateral exchanges, the Arab region is ascribed a central meaning for the realisation of China's long-term geostrategic goals. The diversity of the Arab region, the rivalries and tensions within the Arab world, and the revival of religious extremism do, however, pose unexpected challenges to the PRC's reiterated role identity and strategic positioning as a "neutral" partner without any political ambitions. So far, Beijing has refrained from siding with any of the conflict parties involved in territorial (or religious) disputes in the Middle East. The PRC's voting behaviour on issues related to UN interventions or the imposing of sanctions is principally driven by Chinese domestic development interests. Interventions in conflicts or crises are condemned as interference into the internal affairs of sovereign states. Besides, interventions by alliances of NATO states, even if backed by a UN mandate, are seen as a Trojan horse to silently induce a regime change and to replace the political elites by groups expected to comply with Western norms and demands.

China's cooperation with the OPEC states in the Arab world did not just take off with the New Silk Road but has been driven by the rising demand for oil and gas imports to fuel China's domestic economy. Initially, in the 1960s, the exploration of the Daqing oil field in Heilongjiang province, supported by Soviet expertise and technology, had made the young PRC self-sustaining in terms of energy. Due to the double-digit growth of the Chinese economy in the post-Mao decades, since 1993, the PRC has become a net oil importing country. Against this background, it is hardly surprising to observe a deepening and widening of cooperation between the PRC and the Middle East. Under the Hu–Wen administration, the PRC sought to set up ties with regional associations and organisations in the Arab world, including the Gulf Cooperation Council and the Arab League.

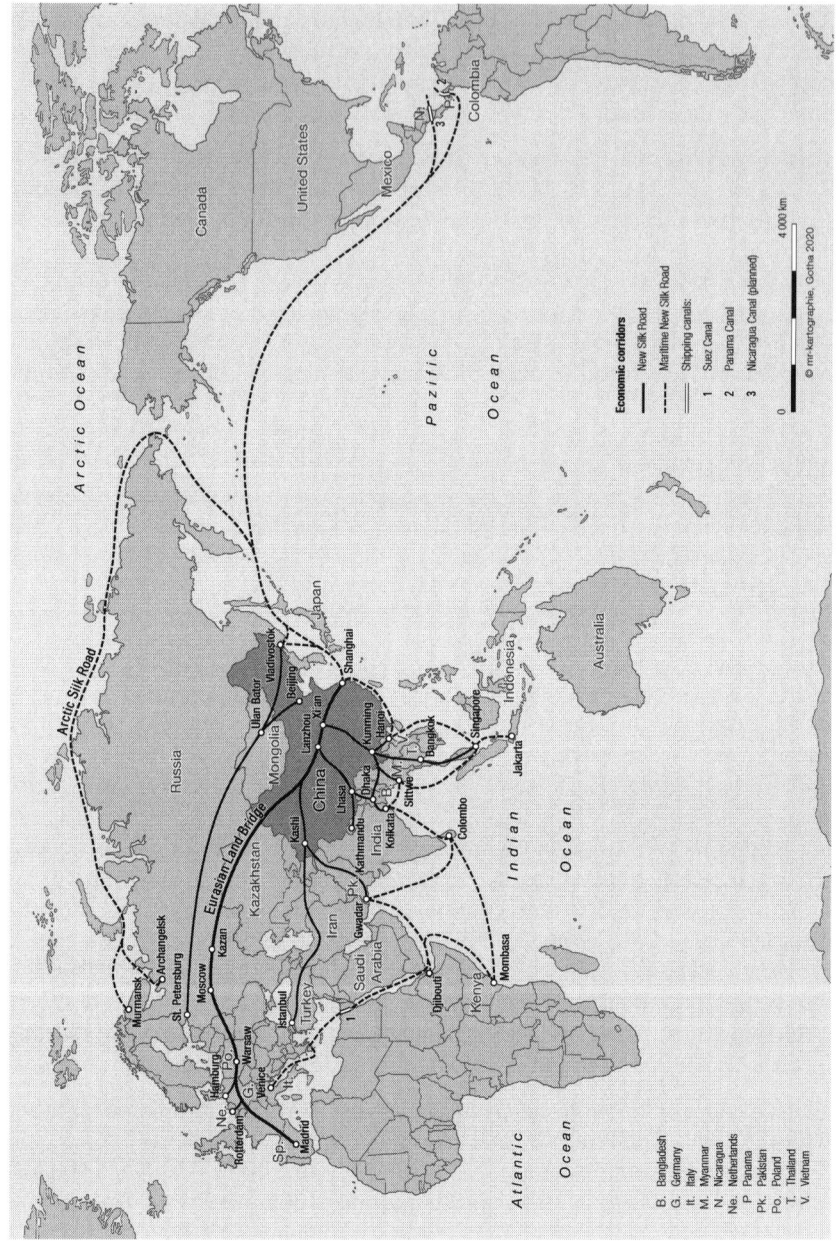

Figure 5: China's New Silk Road

Up until 2014, Saudi Arabia was listed as the PRC's most important oil supplier. In 2015, partly due to the introduction of the petroyuan, Russia outstripped the Arab world as China's top oil provider (*Bloomberg* 2015). After the end of the gold standard, the US had installed the petrodollar to settle oil trade with Saudi Arabia, cementing the related institutions and mechanisms of the global oil markets. The introduction of the petroyuan has thus been observed as an attempt to install alternative structures and to replace the OPEC system. In 2017, the PRC surpassed the US as the world's top crude oil importer. According to EIA, in 2019, the PRC's crude oil imports reached 10.1 million barrels per day (on average), an increase of about 0.9 barrels per day compared with the 2018 average (EIA 2020). In 2019, Saudi Arabia, once again, was listed on top of China's oil supplying trade partners.

Table 10: Chinese Oil Imports (2019)

Country	Share of total Chinese oil imports (%)
Saudi Arabia	16.8 %
Russia	15.3 %
Iraq	9.9 %
Angola	9.5 %
Brazil	7.8 %
Oman	6.9 %
Kuwait	4.5 %
United Arab Emirates	3.1 %
Iran	3 %
United Kingdom	2.7 %
Congo	2.3 %
Malaysia	2.3 %
Colombia	2.3 %
Libya	2 %
Venezuela	1.9 %

Source: EIA (2019/2020)

In January 2016, before Xi Jinping left for his first official state visit to the Middle East – touring Saudi Arabia, Egypt and Iran – the PRC released its first strategy paper on relations with the Arab world (Xinhua 2016a). In line with similar policy papers on the PRC's relations with other world regions (Latin America, Africa) or with regional organisations (EU), the 2016 paper does not just concentrate on state-to-state relations but also addresses China's cooperation with regional sub-units or regional organisations such as the Gulf Cooperation Council. Indirectly, however, the focus lies on the PRC's strategic trade and cooperation partners in the region, as reflected by the formula "1+2+3". The "1" defines energy cooperation as the "core". Infrastructure construction projects as well as trade and investment are referred to as "2 wings" carrying Sino–Arab cooperation, whilst the "3" symbolises the future-oriented "three breakthroughs" in the fields of nuclear energy, space (satellite) technology and new (renewable) energy. The main parts of the Chinese policy paper are dedicated to issues of trade and investment, but peace and security are also dealt with, even though in rather short paragraphs (China's Arab Policy Paper 2016, Xinhua 2016a). That these topics – traditionally following in the category of a state's "internal, domestic affairs" – are mentioned at all indicates that the negative spill-over effects of local crises in the Middle East are increasingly reflected in Chinese foreign and security calculations. As the Chinese economy is still heavily dependent on the import of oil and gas, despite the proclaimed carbon cut, the stability of its supply chains is of key importance. This is even more so the case as the Chinese party-state bases its legitimation strategy on output, measured in terms of economic performance, rising living standards, and the provision of public goods. The Arab world accounts for the largest shares of the PRC's total oil imports. Regional conflicts, civil wars, terrorism and religious extremism in the Middle East – despite occurring far beyond the PRC's national territorial borders – are perceived as a direct threat to Chinese development and socio-economic stability at home.[101]

In 2004, when Hu Jintao visited the headquarters of the Arab League in Cairo, the PRC and the Arab states agreed to set up the China–Arab States Cooperation Forum (CASCF).The CASCF is composed of four permanent dialogue formats: a ministerial meeting, convening every two years; a senior officials meetings (gathering on an annual basis); the liaison groups; and additional cooperation and coordination meetings. The CASCF also includes the group of African Arab states, which are simultaneously involved in the FOCAC summits. Trade issues are discussed at the China–Arab States Economic and Trade Forum (CASETF) (Xinhua 2015a).

In 2012, when the PRC and Russia used their veto power to stop the UN resolution on Syria, this move also caused some unexpected collateral damage on China's relations with parts of the Arab states. Beijing's opposition to any UN mission in Syria resulted from China's lessons learnt from the UN intervention in Libya: the dethroning of Gadhafi and the induced regime change was regarded, as the Chinese side stressed, as not in line with the original UN mandate. The Arab League openly expressed its anger over China's veto play (Zank 2014: 169). Nonetheless, the PRC and Russia did not change their views on the Syria case. In 2014, they used their veto power to prevent a referral of the Syrian case to the International Criminal Court (UN News Centre 2014).

The PRC's formal cooperation with the Arab League also brings up another local conflict: the PLO, representing the internationally unrecognised state of Palestine,

---

101   For an overview of economic interactions as based on Chinese sources: Sun /Zoubir (2015).

is a member of the Arab League. Beijing maintains close contacts with all members of the Arab League, but is also a close ally of Israel, which is one of the PRC's main arms suppliers and a major trade partner in the region.[102] In May 2013, Xi Jinping had tried to present himself as a neutral mediator in the Middle East conflict. Representatives of both conflict parties – Israel's Prime Minister Netanyahu, and Abbas (representing the Palestinian side) – were invited for official state visits to China. However, even though these two visits did overlap in time, a trilateral peace talk did not take place (*South China Morning Post* 2013). Xi Jinping even released a Chinese four-point plan for a peaceful conflict resolution, proposing a "two states" solution, meaning the formal diplomatic recognition of an independent and sovereign Palestine (Xinhua 2013). At the end, however, the PRC did not manage to convince the two conflict parties to join the relaunch of Camp David-style peace talks in Beijing.

Apart from China's support for a two states-solution, Beijing's special relations with the internationally isolated and sanctioned regime in Iran adds additional impediments to the further deepening of Sino–Israel relations. Iran is China's strategic partner in the Middle East; Beijing not only ignored the international sanctions and sustained permanent trade relations with the country, but also supports Iran's admission to the SCO. Under Xi Jinping, China's relations with Iran were lifted to the status of a comprehensive strategic partnership. Chinese state-owned companies are investing in the modernisation of Iran's oil and gas sector and also finance (and construct) pipelines linking Iran's ports to the Caspian Sea oil and gas fields.

The relaunch of relations with Iran in the post-Mao reform era had been overshadowed by a major loss of face for the Chinese side: Hua Guofeng, assigned the position of CCP chairman after the death of Mao (1976), had paid an official state visit to the Shah in Iran shortly before the latter's ousting. Given the PRC's official condemnation of anti-shah protests, it took years to set up relations with the successive regime in Iran (Garver 2013: 64). Contemporary bilateral relations are relatively smooth and without major tensions, displaying patterns of a symbiotic relationship. Over the past few decades, the PRC has been one of Iran's top three arms suppliers. During the Iran–Iraq war, the PRC supported Tehran, whilst the US, the Soviet Union and France sided with Iraq. In the following years, when Iran was banned and isolated by the international community, the PRC successfully started to explore the Iranian market and to secure its access to the country's oil and gas resources. In January 2016, the PRC announced to increase the trade volume to 600 billion USD until 2026 (Tiezzi 2016).

In May 2018, the US withdrew from the Joint Comprehensive Plan of Action – an agreement to cut Iran's nuclear programme in exchange for a (partial) lifting of economic sanctions reached in 2015 between Iran, the five permanent members of the UN Security Council, and Germany – and intensified pressure on Tehran. In January 2020, tensions between Washington and Tehran entered the next level of escalation, as the US drone strike that killed Iran's top military chief Qasem

---

102 On Israel's involvement in arms sales to the PRC: Bräuner/Bromley/Duchatel (2015).

Soleimani was answered by a retaliatory attack on US military bases in Iraq. Beijing condemned the US drone strike and tried to convince both sides of a peaceful conflict solution. The PRC is, obviously, quite careful when engaging in (oil) trade with Iran and is not willing to sacrifice the stability of Sino–US relations for its "special" relationship with Tehran. In fact, the latter's sable-rattling and assertive announcement to close the Straits of Hormuz poses a severe threat to China's export-oriented economy, which still relies on energy imports and raw materials shipped via these maritime corridors. The PRC did not oppose the UN resolutions responding to Iran's continued nuclear build-up. Whilst the PRC remains Iran's most important trading partner and investor, Chinese companies have started to diversify their activities in the Middle East and to look for alternative partners in order to satisfy China's growing demand for energy resources and raw materials. The share of oil imports from Iran has dropped significantly. And even though Iran, as a littoral state of the Caspian Sea, is a strategic nodal point of the PRC's New Silk Road, the New Silk Road corridor to Pakistan and the port of Gwadar seems to rank much higher in Beijing's strategic foreign and security contemplations.

The nevertheless still tight cooperation with Tehran threatens to cast a cloud over the PRC's relations with Saudi Arabia which – also via the Arab League – continues to criticise Iran's (nuclear) activities and its role and position in regional conflicts and crises. The PRC obviously attempts to maintain robust working relations with both countries and to stay out of the Saudi Arabia–Iran disputes in order to prepare the ground for the implementation of its transnational New Silk Road network that will span and connect all countries in the Middle East – regardless of their regime types or ideological orientations.

Rather unwillingly, the PRC has been drawn into the region's (religious) conflicts. In November 2015, the Islamic State kidnapped and executed a Chinese national – and reportedly tried to recruit followers not only from China's Uyghur population in Xinjiang but also from the rather liberal Muslim Hui minority. Under Xi Jinping, the PRC has actively put forward ideas and proposals for a peaceful resolution of the Syria conflict. In the run-up to the Geneva peace talks on Syria (January 2016), the Chinese minister of foreign affairs, Wang Yi, arranged meetings and talks with representatives of the Syrian government as well as members of the Syrian opposition – taking place in China.

In addition to these diplomatic efforts to restore peace and stability in the Middle East, the PRC also updated its security strategy: in January 2016 the Chinese new Anti-Terrorism Law entered into force. This law legitimates overseas military operations to counter terrorist actions – even without a UN mandate. Any mission, however, requires the consent of the targeted country, an official mandate by the Chinese State Council and, if the military is going to be deployed, by the Central Military Commission. The law operates with a rather broad definition of terrorism:

> "Any advocacy or activity that, by means of violence, sabotage, or threat, aims to create social panic, undermine public safety, infringe on personal

and property rights, or coerce a state organ or an international organization, in order to achieve political, ideological, or other objectives" (Xinhua
2015b)

A rather controversial novelty of the Anti-Terrorism Law is the attempt to
strengthen the party-state's control over the Internet to monitor and counter
potential terrorist activities. Telecommunication and Internet service companies
will have to provide technical support and assistance even including decryption
and backdoor options.

Beijing's way of dealing with upheavals and tensions in Xinjiang – since 9/11
labelled as a contribution to the global fight against terrorism and, once again,
justified by the passing of the new Anti-Terrorism Law in 2015 – has not been
well received by the Arab world, as it was seen as a crack-down on China's
Muslim minorities and a campaign again Islam. Whilst Beijing did sharpen its
tone towards its Uyghur minority, which created open tensions with parts of the
Arab world, it tried to involve the rather liberal Chinese Muslim minorities in
its strategic charm offensive towards the Middle East. In 2013, the China-Arab
States Expo was held in Ningxia, the autonomous region of China's (Muslim) Hui
minority (Zank 2014:170).

The PRC also announced its support for the Arab states' fight against terrorism
and extremism by granting financial and developmental assistance (300 billion
USD in 2016). The idea is that by offering development opportunities and by
reducing (absolute) poverty as well as precarious living conditions, people will
no longer have any economic incentives to join the IS. In his speech at the Arab
League in Cairo (January 2016), Xi Jinping underlined that the upheavals, unrests
and conflicts in the Middle East had been caused by developmental challenges and
lack of perspective. He avoided presenting China's own development path as a
model for the Middle East but highlighted the similarities and parallels between
China and the Arab world, classifying them as two (ancient) civilisations with
their specific value systems – incompatible with the Western modernisation path
(Xinhua 2016b).

The PRC's attempts to co-opt its national minorities by incorporating them into
the Chinese Dream of development and prosperity is based on the assumption
of a causal nexus between peace and development, depicted above. This abstract
idea – which did not always lead to the expected results, at least regarding the
situation in Tibet and Xinjiang – is repeatedly mentioned in Chinese official
diplomatic statements on conflicts and tensions in the Middle East. During his
visit to the Arab League headquarters, Xi also announced to promote the region's
integration into China's New Silk Road and to provide an additional 15 billion
USD for investment into electricity, infrastructure and transportation. Finally, the
PRC's relations with Egypt were upgraded to a comprehensive strategic partnership, and a five-year cooperation plan was drafted (Xinhua 2016d). China and
Egypt also signed a joint declaration on endorsing the PRC's New Silk Road
initiative (Xinhua 2016c).

Saudi Arabia – one of the three stops of Xi Jinping's visit to the Arab region in his function as state president (19–23 January 2016) – had been one of the very few Arab countries that, by the end of the 1980s, did not yet have any official diplomatic contacts with the PRC. In 1989, when Saudi Arabia did not join the international anti-CCP chorus and did not support the imposing of sanctions, relations started to ameliorate. Official diplomatic relations were established in 1990. In 1999, Jiang Zemin's trip to Saudi Arabia marked the PRC's first official state visit, which led to the signing of contracts in the oil and energy sector. In 2004, China's state-owned oil company Sinopec engaged in negotiations on the exploration of the Saudi Arabian oil fields in Rub' al Khali. In 2006 and 2009, Hu Jintao travelled to Saudi Arabia to support these talks and to pave the way for future energy cooperation (Al-Tamimi 2014).

The release of the Chinese White Paper on its relations with the Arab world and the first state visit by Xi Jinping in 2016 continue the legacy of Sino–Arab cooperation of the 1990s. The PRC tries to act as a neutral broker and to implement the trade and investment plans of its New Silk Road regardless of the region's unsolved, simmering conflicts and tensions. China's attempt to initiate peace talks between Israel and Palestine differs in scope and style from Beijing's earlier multilateral mediation initiatives – such as the Six-Party-Talks with North Korea – and signals China's new role identity as a powerful global player. As a side effect of the launching of the New Silk Road, the PRC's foreign and security policy has become increasingly multi-focal: the idea is to construct a global trade and transportation network that would still work even if one or two network nodes would temporarily prove dysfunctional. This network is not built from scratch but reiterates and upgrades already existing relationships and cooperation agreements.

7.2. Pentapolarity under the Microscope

Considering the PRC's active efforts to diversify and deepen its relationship with entire world regions, one might be tempted to assume a declining interest in cooperation with the old poles of China's pentapolar world order. In Latin America and the Arab world, Chinese players (unwillingly) enter into competition with the US, and not just in terms of trade and investment. Whilst pragmatic economic interests and domestic development concerns had been the main drivers of the PRC's "going out" campaign, the resulting increased interdependence and mutual vulnerabilities of markets and local industries have made the PRC turn to risk assessment and the coining of a more sophisticated multilevel security concept. The government in Beijing, however, avoids any actions that could be perceived as a preparation of forming anti-US alliances or coalitions. Beijing has not signed up to the overt anti-US rhetoric of the new socialist regimes in Latin America (but would, notwithstanding these diplomatic precautions, be accused by the Trump administration of siding with "evil" states). Since the turn of the century, the PRC's trade relations with the US and Europe have been intensified – as have related trade disputes and currency wars. Again, China's relations with Japan are heavily burdened by the unresolved, inherited remnants of the two Sino–Japanese wars and the two Asian states' regional and global economic, financial and technological competition. The relationship between Beijing and Moscow, even though they did not always have good chemistry, has blossomed over the past few years as a result of the containment measures and sanctions imposed by the US and their allies (in connection with the Crimea crisis and the heating disputes in the East and South China Sea).

7.2.1. China and the US

Relations with the US are still listed as the most important bilateral relationship of the PRC's foreign affairs. The PRC's interactions with other countries or regions are, indirectly, often modelled as triangular relations, taking the role of the US as an "invisible" third player in those bilateral constellations into full account and anticipating the US's strategic responses. Over the past three decades, Sino–US interdependencies have shifted in favour of China – which not only became the world's second largest economy but also the US's main creditor. This development took place in the years of the unexpected subprime mortgage crisis in the US (2007–2010). As the PRC's rapid rise to global creditor and investor status shows, power constellations – especially in the fields of trade and finance – are far from being stable and eternally fixed. Like the US, the PRC has also had to cope with some lurking financial bubbles at the domestic system level. The PRC's current global monetary power relies on the combination of USD foreign currency reserves and the successful internationalisation of the Chinese RMB. A stable domestic economic and financial system is one of the necessary preconditions to defend and secure this global monetary power status. The 2015/2016 stock market turbulences in China caused severe losses. China's foreign currency reserves, amounting to 4 trillion USD in early 2014, fell to about 3 trillion USD in 2019/2020.

The PRC's rise in the fields of trade and finance catalysed a readjustment of the patterns of interactions between Washington and Beijing. The continuously growing (and almost uncontrollable) interdependencies of production chains and trade relations led to the establishment of additional frameworks and fora for coordination and dialogue. Under the second Bush administration, with the Senior Dialogue and the Strategic Economic Dialogue, two new instruments for Sino–US coordination on issues related to economy and security had been installed. The agreement on establishing the Senior Dialogue was signed on the fringe of the APEC summit in 2004 between Hu Jintao and George Bush; the Strategic Economic Dialogue was inaugurated in 2006.

Under the Obama administration, in 2009, these two formats were merged and continued as US–China Strategic Economic Dialogue. This was composed of two elements: the strategic dialogue between the two countries' core representatives of foreign affairs (2009: Hilary Clinton and Dai Bingguo), and the economic dialogue conducted between the US minister of finance and the Chinese vice prime minister in charge of foreign trade (2009: US Treasury Secretary Timothy

Geithner and the Chinese Vice Prime Minister Wang Qishan).[103] The institutional-isation of these dialogue formats demonstrates both sides' increased awareness of the mutual vulnerabilities and dependencies, which Ferguson and Schularick try to describe by coining the term "Chimerica" (Ferguson/Schularick 2009).

Whilst the commercial activities and investment of Chinese banks and companies in the US did create new jobs, the PRC's large-scale market entrance was not welcome in all market (sub-)sectors. In 2005, CNOOC's attempt to purchase the US oil company Unocal was prevented and stopped by US Congress intervention. This was explained and justified by reference to US core national security interests (Wan/Wong 2009). After this failed acquisition attempt, CNOOC and Sinopec did, nevertheless, manage to acquire shares of US oil companies (inter alia Devon Energy; Chesapeake) and to set up joint ventures (*The Wall Street Journal* 2013). Whilst the PRC is forced to broaden and diversify its fossil energy supply chains, US companies, hit by the 2007/2008 financial crisis, have to find additional investors and shareholders.

Despite these economic interdependencies, Sino–US relations are not always conflict-free. During the 1990s, the US and China had been on the verge of an open, fierce trade war. Again, the Obama administration, similar to the previous US administrations, imposed punitive tariffs on Chinese products (car and light truck tires, solar panels, steel) and condemned the PRC's "assertive" export strategy. One major point of dispute, raised again and again, is the accusation of China manipulating its national currency. This and the PRC's illegal subventions of Chinese export products, according to Obama, was the main reason for the US's huge trade deficit with China. The US continue to urge China to stick to international law and to secure a level playing field, whilst the PRC accuses the US of trade protectionism and discrimination of Chinese companies. Following the principle of reciprocity, the PRC responded to the US's tariffs on Chinese products by imposing punitive tariffs on US brands. These moves underline Beijing's claim to be accepted and treated as an equal partner and demonstrate the Chinese government's promise to represent and defend Chinese "core" interests vis-à-vis the outside world.

The US's pivot to Asia, initiated already under the Obama administration, adds additional frictions to the Sino–US relationship. Moreover, US relations with Taiwan (and the Taiwan Relations Act) and Tibet represent, from Beijing's perspective, a plain violation of the PRC's One China Principle. Officially, the US recognise Beijing's definition of the One China Principle. Nonetheless, the diplomatic recognition of the CCP-ruled PRC and formal non-support of the "democratic" Republic of China (in Taiwan) generates a moral dilemma. The US stress their dedication to liberal democracy and human rights – which appears incompatible with the Sino–US rapprochement of the 1970s. A retrospective view on the US's role in Asia exemplifies the ambivalence of US–"China" relations. After the Pearl Harbour attack (1941), the US, which had so far remained neutral, entered the

---

103 This new dialogue format was discussed and agreed on at the G20 summit in London between Obama and Hu Jintao: The White House (2009).

Second World War, counting the Republic of China – ruled by Chiang Kai-Shek's GMD – as one of their allies. After the end of the Second World War, the GMD government faced severe losses in the civil war and retired "temporarily" to the island of Taiwan, where an interim government representing "all of China", including the Communist-controlled Chinese mainland, was established. The US, as well as most Western states, continued to support the GMD one-party state in Taiwan and assisted the island against the CCP's manoeuvres to "liberate" and reintegrate the "renegade" province of Taiwan. During the Korean War (1950–1955) the US even sent their seventh fleet to control (and defend) the Taiwan Strait.

US global politics were directed against the regional and global spread of social-ism. The PRC was seen as belonging to the (Soviet) socialist camp. The Sino–Soviet split and their border dispute at the Ussuri river (1969) facilitated a gradual rapprochement between Beijing and Washington during the 1970s. Starting with informal ping-pong diplomacy, the increased threat posed by Soviet militarism made the US search for partners from the "socialist" camp. In 1971, Kissinger embarked on an informal visit to China, followed by a first meeting between Nixon and Mao in 1972. The Shanghai Communiqué[104] (1972) outlined the roadmap of a step-by-step rapprochement, realised via the opening of liaison offices in Washington and Beijing. The joint communiqué also confirmed the US's acceptance of Beijing's One China Principle, which states that there is only "one" China (including Taiwan, which is ascribed the status of a Chinese province) represented by the CCP government in Beijing. Formal diplomatic relations be-tween the US and the PRC were established in 1979 (as documented by the Joint Communiqué).[105]

In combination with the recognition of the CCP government in Beijing as the sole legitimate representation of China, the US granted Taiwan extended security guarantees. In 1979, the US Congress passed the Taiwan Relations Act.[106] This document defines the non-diplomatic dimensions of US–Taiwan relations – using the formulation "governing authorities of Taiwan" instead of the former label "Republic of China", and covering only the island of Taiwan and the surrounding Pescadores – and grants US "defense articles and defense services" for Taiwan, which does not necessarily include military intervention by the US to defend Taiwan in case of an open conflict with Beijing. By passing the Taiwan Relation Act, the US abrogated the Sino–American Mutual Defense Treaty concluded be-tween the US and the Republic of China in 1955. The US arms deliveries to Taiwan, as confirmed by the Taiwan Relations Act, continued to infuriate the CCP government in Beijing. Only after Washington and Beijing had reached a formal agreement to reduce the US arms deliveries to Taiwan in exchange for the PRC's promise to pursue a peaceful approach towards Taiwan – as written down in the third Sino–US communiqué (1982) (Li, Jerry 2006) – did political and economic relations improve substantially. When Chen Shui-bian, in his role

---

104   *Shanghai Communiqué:* https://history.state.gov/historicaldocuments/frus1969-76v17/d203.
105   *Joint Communiqué:* http://www.china-embassy.org/eng/zmgx/doc/ctc/.
106   *Taiwan Relations Act:* https://www.congress.gov/bill/96th-congress/house-bill/2479.

as president of (the Republic of China) Taiwan, coined his "Four Nos, One Without" (*si bu, yi meiyou*) formula, which contains the confession that Taiwan would not declare itself independent, not only cross-strait relations but also the relationship between Washington and Beijing seemed to enter less choppy waters. Overall, there was the widely shared hope that all parties involved would silently agree to the status quo (with Taiwan being de jure treated as a province of China, whilst de facto being organised as an independent, self-administrated unit). Chen Shui-bian's announcement to hold a referendum on Taiwan's independence and Beijing's new Anti-Session Law (2005), which stated that the PRC would resort to non-peaceful means in case of Taiwan's "secession", forced the US to rethink its role and position on the Taiwan issue. The Taiwan lobby in the US and anti-communist activists still have a strong impact on US foreign politics – and, indirectly, also on the positioning of the EU. Whilst various EU member states had considered the lifting of the arms embargo – imposed on the PRC as a response to the crack-down of the Tian'anmen movement in 1989 – the EU finally bowed to the lobbying of the pro-Taiwan camp and sided with the US scenarios regarding the potential implications for the future security architecture and conflict constellations in East Asia.

The US never stopped criticising the PRC's human rights conduct. After the imposing of sanctions in 1989, Sino–US relations experienced a political ice age. In 1994, the Clinton administration decided to decouple the human rights issue from trade affairs. Political, regime-related frictions, nonetheless, persist and have remained unchanged. At (most) bilateral meetings, however, talks are dedicated to economic issues; politically sensitive topics are not openly addressed. The 2014 US visit by the Dalai Lama – as a religious leader, not as a political representative – and Obama's appeal, addressing the government in Beijing, to respect the rights of the Tibetans annoyed the PRC's political leaders, who regarded the bilateral meeting as a violation of the One China Principle and, even more severely, as interference into the PRC's domestic, internal affairs.[107] In the case of Xinjiang, the PRC used a rather smart diplomatic move to silence official US criticism. In 2001, immediately after the 9/11 attacks, Beijing offered the US unrestrained support in the global fight against terrorism and declared its actions against separatist movements by its Uighur minority in Xinjiang as being a contribution to combatting global terrorism.[108]

The US's "pivot to Asia" – the focus re-shift of the US foreign strategy under Obama towards Asia – resulting in a renewal of security alliances in the PRC's "strategic backyard", creates additional tensions. Already by 2005, the US had updated and reconfirmed its security alliance with Japan, including Taiwan in the security parameter, which is not listed as a contracting party (Wu 2005). The US post-9/11 military interventions in Iraq and Afghanistan, although accepted by Beijing, as well as the instalment of military bases in Asia, are perceived as forming part of a US encirclement and containment of the rising PRC (Zhao,

---

107 On the US positions on Tibet, see: Xu (1997); Cao/Xu (2015).
108 On the catalysing effect of 9/11 on the deepening of Sino–US (security) cooperation, see: Friedberg (2002); Jia (2003); Taylor (2005).

Suisheng 2015). The 21st century security spirals in Asia are, undoubtfully, a typical chicken/egg situation. The PRC claims to modernise its maritime forces in order to be able to defend its national core interests in the light of aggravating territorial disputes in the South and East China Sea and as a response to the US "rebalancing" to Asia. The US, on the other hand, argues that the pivot to Asia is a strategic reaction to the PRC's increased assertiveness that threatens the fragile security constellations in the region. The Trump administration outlined, once again, the US's dedication to the freedom of navigation at sea and open markets in its Free and Open Indo-Pacific Strategy. The main threat scenario, to be prevented at (almost) any price, would be the blocking of sea lanes and "access denial" by the Chinese navy. In the Diaoyu/Senkaku islands dispute (2012)[109] the US overtly opposed the PRC's claims and increased its visible presence by sending surveillance aircraft.[110] In April 2019, the US and Japan confirmed their security cooperation and joint dedication to a "free and open" Indo-Pacific.[111] Additionally, the US revived the quadrilateral security dialogue with Japan, India and Australia, which had been initiated in 2007/2008.

The US security cooperation with Japan opened old wounds, reminding the Chinese side of the losses and humiliation suffered during the wars with Japan. The controversy over the historiography of the Second World War in East Asia – between Japan and China, as well as Japan and Korea – and the outstanding post-war settlement of territorial disputes permanently refuels old antagonisms and rivalries. Japanese "provocations" – Shinzo Abe's quest to revise the Peace Constitution of Japan (and Article 9), the official visits to the Yasukuni shrine, the history textbook issue – triggered the rise of patriotism amongst the younger Chinese generations. The US's rebalancing, likewise, evoked mass movements and demonstrations, which not only bore patriotic traits, but also illustrated the revival and rising popularity of anti-Western, anti-US sentiments (the – reportedly accidental – bombing of the Chinese embassy in Belgrade (1999) and the collision of a US aircraft and a Chinese fighter jet near the island of Hainan (2001) sparked anti-US demonstrations all across China (Cheng/Ngok 2004)).

Whilst the Clinton administration had classified the PRC as a "strategic partner", the labelling changed under the second Bush administration. Since then, Sino–US relations have been categorised as relations between "strategic competitors" (Shambaugh 2000). Whilst both players practise their own variety of capitalism, their political system structures and their world order visions are regarded as incompatible. Analysts therefore predict increased competition over regional and global spheres of influence and a global scramble for access to resources.

When Xi Jinping visited the US in 2012, in his function as vice president of the PRC, he stressed the Chinese vision of Sino–US relations in the 21st century by framing them as a "new type of great power relations" (*xin xing daguo guanxi*) (Lampton 2013). This re-labelling notwithstanding, the old tensions and frictions

---

109 On the historical background of the Sino–Japanese island dispute and potential conflict solutions, see: Liao et al. (2015).
110 The Japan factor of Sino–US relations has been discussed by Christensen (2011), especially Chapter 7.
111 Joint Statement of the Security Consultative Committee, https://www.mofa.go.jp/files/000470738.pdf.

between Washington and Beijing did not disappear overnight. Whereas Obama's first year in office received a rather positive media response in the PRC, the blocking of Google search in mainland China, the reception of the Dalai Lama by Barack Obama and the scorching criticism of the PRC's backing of North Korea resulted in a deterioration of bilateral relations (Wu 2012). Besides this, mutual distrust continued to spread, with the US accusing China of engaging in cyber-attacks and undertaking preparations for a cyberwar. During Xi's trip to California in 2013, both sides, finally, reconfirmed their interests in avoiding any escalation or stalemate and in strengthening cooperation. Nonetheless, the US side continued to criticise cyber-attacks on servers of US companies and the US military (which were supposed to have been launched from servers based in China). Besides, the US expressed certain concerns about the security dilemmas in East Asia (East China Sea, South China Sea, North Korea's nuclear programme). The PRC reconfirmed its demand for setting up a "new" type of great power relations (based on equality and reciprocity), disapproved the continued US arms trade with Taiwan and asked for more transparency regarding Washington's plans for setting up free trade agreements in the Asia Pacific (categorically excluding the PRC from joining). After having made clear their positions and expectations, both sides finally confirmed their commitment to cooperation in the fields of regional and global security as well as in climate protection measures (The White House 2013). The Sunnylands meeting between Obama and Xi falls into the category of confidence-building diplomacy; it represents a joint attempt to restore the fragile symbiotic balance of Sino–US relations. Follow-up meetings and summits likewise stressed cooperation in regional and global affairs. The US's China strategy, followed by the Obama administration, referred to the PRC as a strategic cooperation partner and stressed the latter's role in the maintenance of world peace and the stabilisation of the international system (The White House 2015).

Coordination between Washington and Beijing in issues related to regional and global security did not just start with the agreements signed by Xi and Obama. Over the past two decades, the US reiterated their request that Beijing should use its special relations with Pyongyang to urge North Korea's ruling elite to end its (military) nuclear build-up. A resolution of the North Korea issue without the support and consent of Beijing would be a mission impossible. The US hence favoured a multilateral approach, such as the Six-Party-Talks (North Korea, South Korea, China, Japan, Russia, US). These talks, established in 2003 when North Korea withdrew from the Nuclear Non-Proliferation Treaty, were unilaterally cancelled by North Korea in 2009. After a meeting with North Korea's political leader Kim Jong-un in 2018, Xi Jinping stated that there might be a way to resume the denuclearisation talks. However, Beijing's means to "steer" North Korea into the envisioned direction are obviously limited. After taking office as the DPRK's supreme leader (2011), Kim Jong-un's sabre-rattling and assertive positioning included threat utterances addressed at Beijing. His first state visit to the PRC (in March 2018, i.e., seven (!) years later) seemed to signal a departure from his initial collision course.

The Trump administration's siding with Taiwan's DPP president Tsai Ing-wen – and the latter's direct phone call to congratulate Trump for his winning the presidential elections (2 December 2016) (*The Wall Street Journal* 2016) – as well as the US's deepening of security alliances with China's regional neighbours (and competitors), finally caused a reactivation of Beijing's cooperation with Moscow. The international response to the Crimea crisis and the sanctions imposed on Russia by the US and their allies in 2015 further catalysed this Sino–Russian rapprochement, reviving the old political camps and security alliances in Asia. In this vein, the joint military manoeuvre of the US and South Korea in March 2016 was interpreted – by China, Russia and North Korea – as a blunt attempt to challenge the status quo. The US–South Korea joint military drills simulate war on the Korean peninsula, and, in 2016, included the scenario of landing operations in North Korea. The 2016 military drills took place against the backdrop of North Korea's rocket launch and continued nuclear tests. The US security guarantees for its South Korean ally also include the installation of an anti-ballistic missile defence system (Terminal High Altitude Area Defense, THAAD), which was promoted as a necessary measure to protect South Korea against ballistic and nuclear missile attacks from Pyongyang. The PRC openly opposed the deployment of THAAD in South Korea, resorting to (informal) economic sanctions to urge the government in Seoul to cancel the security cooperation with the US.

Power competition and frictions between the US and China at the global level go far beyond trade issues and the scramble for access to fossil resources and raw materials. The internationalisation of the Chinese renminbi and its integration into the IMF currency basket (IMF 2015) could, on the one hand, contribute to the stabilisation of the global financial sector. On the other hand, the rise of the renminbi poses a direct challenge to the role and status of the USD as the global system's anchor currency. The outbreak of a currency war thus cannot be ruled out (Goldstein/Lardy 2008). Up until 2005, the Chinese renminbi had been pegged to the USD. Since then, the renminbi floats around a base rate linked to a basket of currencies, implying a transition to a managed floating exchange rate. However, even though in May 2015, the IMF came to the conclusion that the renminbi would no longer be undervalued (IMF Press Release 15/237 2015), the US continue to accuse the PRC of currency and exchange rate manipulation.

Under the Trump administration, the PRC was treated as a strategic competitor with both sides facing mutual vulnerabilities and strategic interdependencies in the fields of global trade and finance. However, even though the PRC opposes the US-dominated international system, Beijing is not, at least so far, constructing a G1 world order or seeking to replace the USD by an internationalised renminbi. Learning from the internationalisation of the Japanese yen and the potential risks for its domestic financial system resulting from the globalisation of a national currency, Beijing propagates the formation of a multipolar world and a multi-currency global financial system. Moreover, reassessing the history of Cold War power rivalries, the PRC's political leaders (and their advisers) clearly seek to avoid the spread of enemy images and the re-emergence of security spirals by increasing their efforts to export a "positive" image of China as a responsible (and reliable) cooperation partner. A closer look at the US perception and images of China, as well as scenarios associated with China's rise, indicates that this soft power campaign has not (yet) had the desired effect.

Figure 6: China-Image in the US (Pew)

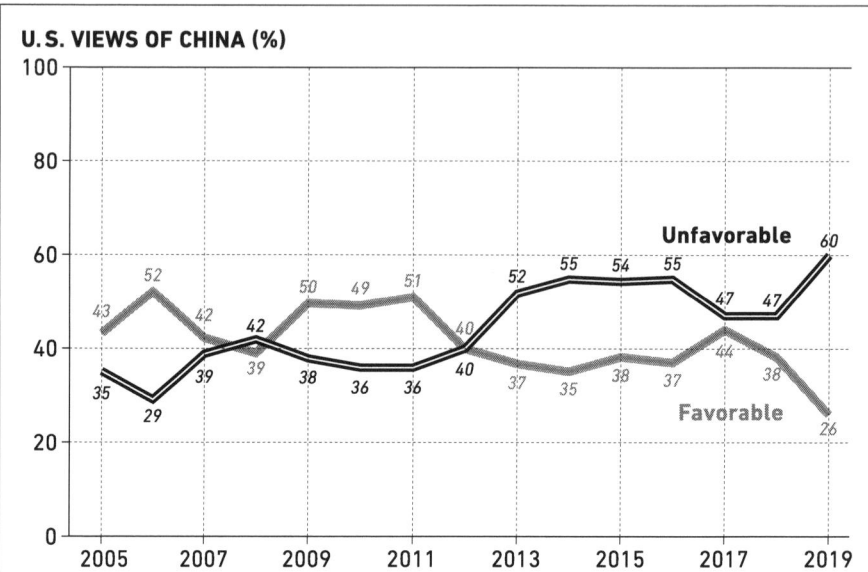

In February 2017, when visiting Japan, US Defence Secretary James Mattis underlined that the joint security agreement would also cover the Senkaku (Diaoyu) islands (US Department of Defense 2017). Besides, the US National Security Act 2017 allows the US navy to make port calls to Taiwan – observed by Beijing as a serious affront to the PRC's One China Principle and national security concerns.

Nonetheless, even after the Tsai–Trump phone call and the visible positioning of Washington in the territorial disputes in (East) Asia, travel diplomacy between Beijing and Washington was formally upheld. In April 2017, Xi Jinping travelled to Mar-a-Lago (Florida) for an informal meeting with Donald Trump; in November 2017, Trump visited Beijing during his Asian trip. In 2018, trade disputes added by the mutual imposing of punitive tariffs reached a historic high. The US Secure and Trusted Communications Act (2019) even prevents the use of US federal funds for telecommunications hardware or software solutions by Huawei or ZTE – China's two global champions in the fields of telecommunications technology. In November 2019, the US Federal Communications Commission declared that these two Chinese companies would pose a threat to US national security. In December 2018, Huawei's chief financial manager, the daughter of the company's founder, was arrested in Canada – obeying a request put forward by the US authorities condemning the company's bypassing of US sanctions imposed on Iran. In May 2019, Huawei was put on the US's blacklist, and a ban on delivering US software or hardware components to all "banned" Chinese ICT companies was announced. After several rounds of tit-for-tat tariffs and economic sanctions, on 15 January 2020 the US and China signed the Phase One Trade Deal, which refers trade disputes to a bilateral arbitration format. In the vein of the globally-spreading coronavirus – labelled by US President Trump as "China virus" – additional political and trade sanctions by the US led to a further cooling-down of cooperation and heating-up of the lurking "cold" power competition.

Under the Trump administration, relations with Taiwan have entered a new stage. In March 2018, US President Trump signed the Taiwan Travel Act (TTA) into law. The TTA legalises direct travels of high officials. In July 2019, Taiwan's DPP President Tsai Ing-wen thus, facilitated by the new law, travelled to New York and Denver meeting with UN delegations of those countries that still grant Taiwan diplomatic recognition (Gladstone 2019). In October 2019, the US Senate passed the Taiwan Allies International Protection and Enhancement Initiative (TAIPEI Act), which was confirmed and passed by the House of Representatives on 4 March 2020. This document expresses the US's support for Taiwan's efforts in securing and expanding its diplomatic recognition.[112]

As mentioned above, the narrative-based construction of China as "evil" rival to the US has been added by the narrative of China as being the one guilty of the emergence and global spread of the coronavirus. In August 2020, the US health secretary, Alex Azar, paid an official visit to Taiwan, praising the DPP government's transparent response to Covid-19. Azar was the highest ranked state official visiting the island since the formal recognition of Beijing's One-China formula. Zhao Lijian, spokesman of the PRC's Ministry of Foreign Affairs, reacted by urging Washington to stop high-level exchanges with Taiwan, formulating that "the US ha(d) seriously violated its commitments" (*The Diplomat* 2020).

Taiwan is not able to join any international organization that requires statehood. Its attempts to join the WHO as a full member have been opposed and blocked by Beijing. In the light of the corona crisis – especially given the appraisal of Taiwan's response to the pandemic by the US – the WHO issue has become part of the ongoing symbolic proxy battles between Washington and Beijing.

Again, in September 2020, Keith Krach (US Under-Secretary of State for Economic Growth, Energy, and the Environment), visited Taiwan (arriving on September 17, 2020) for the US–Taiwan Economic and Commercial Dialogue and to participate in a memorial service for Lee Teng-hui (president of Taiwan from 1988 to 2000) (Westcott 2020). Simultaneously, during the final years of the Trump administration, US politicians re-discovered Taiwan as democratic "alternative" to the CCP-ruled "China" (Box IX), openly attacking Beijing's one-party regime.

---

112 TAPEI Act: https://www.congress.gov/116/plaws/publ135/PLAW-116publ135.pdf.

Box IX: Washington's New China Threat Narrative(s)

Pompeo's speech entitled "Communist China and the Free World's Future", delivered on 23 July 2020, addresses the economic challenges posed to the US by the rise of China and also classifies the most recent events and transformations within the PRC as having direct regional and global implications:

> "We imagined engagement with China would produce a future with bright promise of comity and cooperation. But today – today we're all still wearing masks and watching the pandemic's body count rise because the CCP failed in its promises to the world. We're reading every morning new headlines of repression in Hong Kong and in Xinjiang (...) As President Trump has made very clear, we need a strategy that protects the American economy, and indeed our way of life. The free world must triumph over this new tyranny(...) We opened our arms to Chinese citizens, only to see the Chinese Communist Party exploit our free and open society (...) President Nixon once said he feared he had created a "Frankenstein" by opening the world to the CCP, and here we are (...)" (Pompeo 2020)

The rapprochement between the US and (communist) China in the 1970s and Washington's entering into diplomatic relations with Beijing is not presented as a major diplomatic mistake but as part of the US's past strategic calculations on inducing a regime transformation via integrating the PRC into the US-centered capitalist liberal market world economy. This, however, as Pompeo stresses, did not work out. Washington's refined China strategy is hence presented as a necessary response to the emergence of this "Frankenstein" monster. This goes hand in hand with Washington's strategic turn to Taiwan and Hong Kong. As Pompeo underlines, Asian democracy is in crisis or under attack, and the people are calling for US assistance:

> "We marginalized our friends in Taiwan, which later blossomed into a vigorous democracy (...) China ripped off our prized intellectual property and trade secrets, causing millions of jobs all across America (...) Look at the Hong Kongers clamoring to emigrate abroad as the CCP tightens its grip on that proud city. They wave American flags" (Pompeo 2020)

These threat narrations were not just a strategic move in the run up to the US presidential elections in 2020. On October 4, 2018, Vice President Mike Pence summarized the US administration's policy toward China as follows:

> "In our National Security Strategy that the President Trump released last December, he described a new era of "great power competition." Foreign nations have begun to, as we wrote, "reassert their influence regionally and globally," and they are "contesting [America's] geopolitical advantages and trying [in essence] to change the international order in their favor."

> In this strategy, President Trump made clear that the United States of America has adopted a new approach to China. We seek a relationship grounded in fairness, reciprocity, and respect for sovereignty, and we have taken strong and swift action to achieve that goal.

> After the fall of the Soviet Union, we assumed that a free China was inevitable. Heady with optimism at the turn of the 21st Century, America agreed to give Beijing open access to our economy, and we brought China into the World Trade Organization.

> Previous administrations made this choice in the hope that freedom in China would expand in all of its forms – not just economically, but politically, with a newfound

respect for classical liberal principles, private property, personal liberty, religious freedom — the entire family of human rights. But that hope has gone unfulfilled.

The dream of freedom remains distant for the Chinese people. And while Beijing still pays lip service to "reform and opening," Deng Xiaoping's famous policy now rings hollow."

"Within our own hemisphere, Beijing has extended a lifeline to the corrupt and incompetent Maduro regime in Venezuela that's been oppressing its own people. They pledged $5 billion in questionable loans to be repaid with oil. China is also that country's single largest creditor, saddling the Venezuelan people with more than $50 billion in debt, even as their democracy vanishes. Beijing is also impacting some nations' politics by providing direct support to parties and candidates who promise to accommodate China's strategic objectives.

And since last year alone, *the Chinese Communist Party has convinced three Latin American nations to sever ties with Taipei and recognize Beijing. These actions threaten the stability of the Taiwan Strait*, and the United States of America condemns these actions. And while our administration will continue to respect our One China Policy, as reflected in the three joint communiqués and the Taiwan Relations Act, *America will always believe that Taiwan's embrace of democracy shows a better path for all the Chinese people*" (Pence 2018) (emphasis added)

7.2.2. China and Japan

Formal diplomatic relations between the two Asian economic powerhouses – the PRC is ranked as the world's second, Japan as the third largest economy – date back to the 1970s. Informal interactions started slightly earlier, as the withdrawal of Soviet advisers and technical assistance made Beijing look for alternative partners. In the aftermath of the Sino–US rapprochement, the Japanese Prime Minister Kakuei Tanaka visited the PRC in September 1972, where the two governments signed a joint statement, by which Japan announced to grant the PRC full diplomatic recognition and to accept Beijing's One China Policy (official diplomatic relations were re-established in 1973).[113] Consecutive negotiations on a Sino–Japanese peace and friendship treaty were, however, paused in 1975 as no agreement could be reached on Beijing's demand for adding an anti-Soviet paragraph. Trade interactions intensified after the end of the Cultural Revolution and the PRC's entrance into the post-Maoist reform era. A treaty of peace and friendship was finally signed in 1978. Whilst Japan's concerns over the SU's military invasion of Afghanistan and its military presence in parts of South East Asia overlapped with the PRC's anti-Soviet stance, Sino–Japanese relations also entered more troubled waters due to disagreements on the coverage of Japan's role in the Second World War in Japan's history textbooks and visits to the Yasukuni shrine by leading government officials, a memorial where military officers responsible for war crimes committed in the Sino–Japanese war are also buried (and worshipped).

---

113 Joint Communiqué of the Government of Japan and the Government of the People's Republic of China (29 September 1972): https://www.mofa.go.jp/region/asia-paci/china/joint72.html.

The origins of the territorial disputes between China and Japan in the 21st century date back to the late 18th century. The First Sino–Japanese War (1894/1895), also known as the *Jiawu* War (*jiawu* standing for the year 1894 according to the traditional Chinese Stems-and-Branches system for recording time), represents a traumatic experience in Chinese political history. The Japanese Empire, which had been opened up for international trade by US gunboat diplomacy (Treaty of Kanagawa, 1854) a couple of years earlier than China, had embarked on an all-encompassing reform of its political system (Meiji Restoration, 1868) and also set up a modern navy. Furthermore, Japan, which had been following a policy of seclusion and isolation in the Edo period, started to expand its trade relations and spheres of influence in East Asia. Korea, the Chinese Empire's core tributary and vassal state, was caught between these two rivalling East Asian powers. When, in 1894, the Korean king asked the Qing Empire for assistance in repressing the local Donghak Rebellion, the Japanese side accused China of having violated the Convention of Tianjin by sending armed troops. Japanese troops were dispatched to Korea and a pro-Japanese Korean government was installed. After the defeat of the Chinese Beiyang fleet at the Yalu River Battle (September 1894), Japanese troops moved towards Manchuria, conquering the province's major cities including Port Arthur. Japanese troops also succeeded in occupying the Pescadores islands. On 17 April 1895 with the signing of the Treaty of Shimonoseki the Qing Empire officially recognised the independence of Korea and ceded the Liaodong peninsula in Northeast China, the Pescadores islands, as well as Taiwan to Japan. Moreover, the Senkaku/Diaoyu islands were annexed to Okinawa Prefecture (Japan). Japan's control over the Liaodong peninsula and Port Arthur – as included in the treaty – triggered an intervention by Russia, joined by France and Germany. This Triple Intervention (April 1895) finally made Japan resign from its territorial claims over Liaodong in exchange for an additional war indemnity from the Qing Empire.

The humiliation of the Qing Empire continued with the victory of Japan over Russia. For the Russian Empire, Manchuria and Port Arthur played a central (geo-)strategic role. The harbour of Vladivostok could only be operated during the summer months, so Russia had entered Manchuria and based its Pacific fleet in Port Arthur. This collided with Japanese territorial claims and interests in Manchuria, the Liaodong peninsula, as well as in Korea. After several battles during which the Japanese army proved its superiority, the war ended with the Treaty of Portsmouth (1905). Apart from the formal ceasefire, Russia had to withdraw from Manchuria and return Port Arthur and Dalian to China. Furthermore, Russia had to cede South Sakhalin to Japan.

Buoyed by its victory over an old "European" power, Japan formulated far-reaching demands vis-à-vis China. In January 1915, Japan presented a list of 21 demands to China, which would have degraded the formerly glorious Chinese Empire to a Japanese colony. These demands included the formalisation and expansion of Japan's control over large parts of the Shandong peninsula, Manchuria, Inner Mongolia and parts of the Yangzi River. Moreover, they contained the transferal of control over most areas of China's national administration to Japan.

All this happened in the context of the First World War, during which Japan had concluded secret arrangements with the allied forces according to which the former German colonies in Shandong would be given to Japan. During the peace negotiations in Versailles, the transferal of Shandong to the Japanese Empire was confirmed. China, which had also supported the allied forces, had to leave empty-handed. The news about the disrespectful treatment of the Chinese delegation in Versailles sparked a wave of patriotic movements all across China (see also: May Fourth Movement 1919).

After the Mukden Incident of 18 September 1931, a dynamite attack on the South Manchurian railway – potentially staged by the Japanese military based in Manchuria, according to the retrospect assessment by international historians – Japan occupied Manchuria and set up the puppet state Manchukuo. The latter existed from 1932 to 1945. The Japanese Empire promoted a pro-Japanese government and installed the ousted "last" Chinese emperor Puyi as the nominal regent of Manchukuo. Japanese troops continued their invasion and conquest of China, marching towards Beijing. The Marco Polo Bridge Incident (7 July 1937) marks the official begin of the Second Sino–Japanese War.

Japan's dealing with the war crimes committed by Japanese forces – the Nanking Massacre (Nanking/Nanjing was the capital of the Republic of China), the enslavement of Chinese women as "comfort women", lethal human experiments by the Japanese Unit 731 – and the silence of right-wing Japanese textbooks on this rather inglorious chapter of Japan's foreign politics enrages the Chinese public. Disagreements over the "correct" historiography of the two Sino–Japanese wars caused (and still do cause) anti-Japanese movements in China added by calls to boycott Japanese brands. Whiting thus argues that the textbook disputes of the 1980s and 1990s had been used to mobilise the younger Chinese generations. Those joining the anti-Japanese student protest of 1986 – a generation born long after the end of the war and without any personal memories of the Sino–Japanese war – were mobilised by negative reports on Japan (and Japan's dealing with its own past and war crimes) by the Chinese mass media (Whiting 1989: 19–20). Sino–Japanese relations are thus not just determined by contemporary constellations, but subject to manipulation and instrumentalization for political means. There is no fixed, stable image of Japan on the Chinese side – as images and perceptions are (re-)constructed linked to changing domestic and international power constellations.

After the end of the Second World War – the Republic of China had framed its war of resistance against Japan as a contribution to the allied forces' fight against fascism and the German–Italian–Japanese axis – Sino–Japanese relations slowly but steadily improved. With the normalisation of bilateral relations in the 1970s, Japan was no longer referred to by the PRC as China's "enemy" or "running dog" of the US but listed as "good neighbour" (Zhao, Quansheng 1996: 188). Chinese policy analysts actively observed the developments in Japan. The latter – for quite some time continuously ruled by one single party, the LDP, despite the holding of elections and the admission of opposition parties – not only served as a blueprint and source of inspiration for the transformation of South Korea and Taiwan, but also, informally, inspired the reform process of the PRC (Zhao, Suisheng 2004: 276).

Since the 1990s, historical (and ideological) cleavages have been complemented by geostrategic competition. This includes heated regional disputes over resources and raw materials, especially regarding the exploration of untapped oil and gas reserves in the South China Sea in the waters close to the Diaoyu, Paracel and Spratly islands (Yee 2011). In 2005, anti-Japanese protests in China were officially sparked by a new history textbook release in Japan. However, they also overlapped with Japan's application for a permanent seat in the UN Security Council (Gries 2005).

In August and September 2012, anti-Japanese protest emerged as a response to the Diaoyu/Senkaku island disputes (Reilly 2014). Similar to the 2005 protests, protests escalated, with Japanese shops and restaurants being attacked and Japanese flags being burnt by Chinese demonstrators. Parts of the movement somehow seemed to get completely out of control – from the perspective of the Chinese authorities – when sub-groups of the Chinese protestors carried Mao posters and propagated ideas of the Chinese New Left, demanding measures to be taken to respond to the rising socio-economic stratification and the widening gap between the upper and lower income classes within Chinese society. They not only disapproved of the PRC's (weak) position in the conflict and territorial disputes with Japan, but generally criticised the capitalist development path of the post-Mao era.[114]

Profound knowledge of the historical background of Sino–Japanese relations is, as the key events sketched above illustrate, a necessary precondition to understanding the current disputes and tensions – and the instrumentalization of history (and historiography) for domestic political means. In spite of these historic burdens and geostrategic conflicts, China and Japan maintain close economic ties. For Japan, the PRC has become its most important trading partner in East Asia. In a nutshell, the history and development of Sino–Japanese relations since the 1970s could also be told from a more optimistic perspective: in sum, four joint statements have since been signed, which have paved the way for close economic cooperation. The Joint Statement of 1972 marked the formal diplomatic recognition of the PRC by Japan; the Peace and Friendship Treaty finally followed in 1978. Whilst the first textbook issue (1982) and the Japanese prime minister's visit to the Yasukuni shrine (1985) did slightly slow down the renormalisation and deepening of relations, Japan's diplomatic response to the PRC's handling of the Tian'anmen protests (1989) set the course for close economic cooperation. Japan did not join the international (economic) sanctioning of Beijing but pursued a more conciliatory approach seeking to support the PRC's modernisation (and reform) process. In 1998, the Chinese State President Jiang Zemin visited Japan. The 1998 Sino–Japanese Joint Declaration reconfirmed both sides' commitment

---

114 Japanese media argued that the voicing of discontent regarding the PRC's post-1978 reforms was the main reason for the final termination of anti-Japanese protests by the Chinese authorities: *Asahi Shimbun* (2012).

to peaceful cooperation. In May 2008, Hu Jintao's trip to Tokyo included the signing of a fourth declaration – the joint statement on the "comprehensive promotion of a mutually beneficial relationship based on common strategic interests".

In the Xi–Abe era, tensions and open competition, once again, intensified. In 2010, with the collision between a Chinese fishing trawler and a Japanese coast guard patrol near the Diaoyu/Senkaku islands, bilateral interactions switched to a more offensive mode. The Japanese 2011 Defence White Paper's coverage of the PRC's military modernisation and assertive maritime activities enraged the Chinese side. In 2012, Japan's purchase of the Diaoyu/Senkaku islands, occurring in the run-up to the PRC's changing of the guard in autumn 2012, was regarded as an attempt to change the status quo and as a direct threat to Chinese security interests. Shinzo Abe's visits to the Yasukuni shrine and his attempt to revise Japan's Peace Constitution – and especially Article 9[115] – led to a further tightening of tensions and threat perceptions. Finally, in November 2014, the PRC's State Councillor Yang Jiechi and Japan's National Security Adviser Shotaro Yachi reached a Four Point Principled Agreement on Handling and Improving Bilateral Relations (7 November 2014). The agreement reconfirmed both sides' continued adherence to the four joint Sino–Japanese declarations, summarised above. China and Japan also formally mutually accepted the existence of divergent views and positions on the Diaoyu/Senkaku island dispute. Last but not least, the agreement highlighted the importance of re-building mutual trust.[116] A first official meeting between Xi and Abe took place on the fringe of the APEC summit on 10 November 2014 (Bai 2014). A second meeting followed during the Asia–Africa conference in Indonesia (April 2015). In November 2015, trilateral talks between China, Japan and South Korea – which targeted the setting-up of an integrated free trade area – were resumed. Similar to the frictions and cleavages between China and Japan, relations between Japan and South Korea are also hampered by unsettled disputes (and non-recompensated atrocities against humanity) dating back to the times of the Second World War in Asia. Shinzo Abe's speech on the occasion of the 70th anniversary of the end of the Second World War and Japan's final capitulation, including a direct mentioning of the deaths and suffering of "innocent people" in "China, Southeast Asia, the Pacific islands and elsewhere",[117] was not perceived as a formal confession of or apology for Japanese war crimes, neither by China nor by South Korea. Overlapping (regional) economic interests, shared concerns regarding Trump's "America First" strategy, and the nuclear

---

115 Article 9, listed under the title "Renunciation of War", confirms Japan's abstention from military actions other than self-defence: "1. Aspiring sincerely to an international peace based on justice and order, the Japanese people forever renounce war as a sovereign right of the nation and the threat or use of force as means of settling international disputes. 2. In order to accomplish the aim of the preceding paragraph, land, sea, and air forces, as well as other war potential, will never be maintained. The right of belligerency of the state will not be recognized."

116 Astoundingly, the "official" English versions of the 2014 declaration, as provided on Chinese and Japanese websites, are not 100 % identical. For the PRC's official English version, see: Xinhua (2014); for the Japanese version, see: Ministry of Foreign Affairs of Japan (2014).

117 Statement by Prime Minister Shinzo Abe (14 August 2015), https://japan.kantei.go.jp/97_abe/statement/201508/0814statement.html.

threat posed by North Korea, however, facilitated bargaining and coordination rounds despite the unresolved tensions and controversies – as the trilateral meeting in May 2018 demonstrated. With Shinzo Abe's unexpected retirement in 2020, Sino–Japanese relations might, finally, enter into a new era.

7.2.3. China and Russia

After the dissolution of the Soviet Union, bilateral relations between Beijing and Moscow entered a new modus operandi and catalysed coordination of political and economic strategies both at the regional as well as at the global level. In 1992, the two countries engaged in a "constructive partnership", which was upgraded to a "strategic partnership" in 1996. In the Jiang Zemin era, in 2001, a Treaty of Good Neighbourliness and Cooperation was signed.[118]

The ideological disputes and geostrategic contest between the two "socialist" powers – Mao's PRC and the Soviet Union in the era of Khrushchev – belong to the past and are no longer mentioned at all. In 1956, Khrushchev's secret speech, delivered at the 20th Congress of the Soviet Communist Party, had condemned Stalin's cult of personality (which had been copied by Mao). Moreover, the two systems also developed partly opposed interpretations of Marxism and related national development strategies. The PRC's continued Mao cult, as well as Mao's Great Leap Forward, were seen as unbearable and a deviation from Soviet Socialism; vice versa, in 1961, the PRC classified the Soviet leadership as "traitors" of the Socialist cause. The rift further widened when the SU sided with India in the Sino–Indian border dispute (1962). Likewise, Khrushchev's peaceful coexistence policy towards the US proved incompatible with Mao's idea of overt system antagonism and his support for national liberation movements worldwide. In March 1969, in the early years of the PRC's political radicalisation during the Cultural Revolution, a border conflict erupted at the Ussuri river, the north-eastern frontier of the PRC's Heilongjiang province; additional Sino–Soviet border clashes occurred in Xinjiang.[119]

Whilst a rapprochement between Washington and Beijing occurred in the early 1970s, even after the death of Mao and the pragmatic turn of the PRC's foreign relations, the two "socialist" states continued to regard each other with open distrust. In early 1979, the (post-Maoist) PRC launched a punitive mission against Vietnam which had signed a mutual defence treaty with the Soviet Union in November 1978. Moscow, however, did not directly intervene in this conflict but simply provided training, equipment and intelligence support to its Vietnamese allies.[120] The SU's invasion of Afghanistan, by contrast, was understood as part of Moscow's strategic efforts to encircle and contain the PRC – and was answered by Beijing's open siding with the US.

---

118 The English version of this document can be found on the webpage of the Chinese Ministry of Foreign Affairs: http://www.fmprc.gov.cn/mfa_eng/wjdt_665385/2649_665393/t15772.shtml.

119 For a concise overview of the Sino–Soviet split, see: Lüthi (2008).

120 On China's involvement in the Vietnam Wars and the role of the Soviet Union, see: Zhai (2000).

In the mid-1980s, Sino–Soviet relations improved at Gorbachev's initiative, who ordered the withdrawal of Soviet troops from the border regions close to China in (East) Russia, Afghanistan and Mongolia. In February 1989, the Soviet minister of foreign affairs, Eduard Shevardnadze, visited Beijing. In May 1989, the SU's reform-oriented state president, Mikhail Gorbachev, arrived in Beijing for a four-day Sino–Soviet summit with the PRC's government and core party officials – including a conversation with Deng Xiaoping, the intellectual architect of Chinese economic reforms. The Sino–Soviet summit and Gorbachev's visit to Beijing coincided with the student movement and protests that later culminated in the demonstrations in Tian'anmen square.

From 1989 to 1991, both systems underwent internal readjustments and structural reorientations. After the dissolution of the Soviet Union, bilateral talks on border issues between Beijing and Moscow were continued and ended with the passing of the Sino–Soviet Border Agreement (1991)[121] – the post-Soviet independent states in Central Asia concluded separate border treaties. With this step, the inglorious episode of the Unequal Treaties that the Russian Empire (joining the club of colonial powers) had once imposed on the Qing dynasty with the Treaty of Aigun (1858) and the Treaty of Beijing (1860) came to its end. The final demarcation process with regard to some islands located in the middle of the Sino–Soviet border rivers took another decade. In 2004, a complementary agreement was reached. In 2008, the formal transfer of several small islets located in the Amur river (including Heixiazi island) and the Argun river – together with the Ussuri river demarcating the eastern line of the Sino–Russian border – was officially orchestrated. Article 6 of the 2001 Sino–Russian Cooperation Treaty, mentioned above, states that unresolved boundary issues will be solved via dialogue and mutual consultation. Moscow's and Beijing's security concerns regarding Central Asia are coordinated via the multilateral formats of the SCO, which also involve the post-Soviet republics as sovereign participants.[122]

In 2009, Hu Jintao and Dmitry Medvedev bargained a five-point agreement and ratified the joint action plan on the implementation of the China–Russia Treaty of Friendship, Good-Neighbourliness and Cooperation (2009–2012).[123] Moscow reconfirmed its official position that Taiwan and Tibet are part of the PRC's state territory and expressed its support for Beijing's strategy of peaceful reunification with Taiwan. Beijing, in exchange, articulated its support for Russia's initiatives to secure peace and stability in the Caucasus region.

Xi Jinping's first state visit after taking office was his journey to Moscow (March 2013), which underlines the importance ascribed to Sino–Russian cooperation in the 21st century. Beyond additional oil and gas deals, China and Russia also announced to deepen their cooperation and coordination in international institutions and to promote the formation of a more just world order. In the following

---

121 The document is available via: https://www.peaceagreements.org/view/1740.
122 On the evolution and transformation of Sino–Soviet/Sino–Russian relations, see: Goldstein (1994); Garver (1998); Lukin (2015).
123 The English version is available online at: https://www.fmprc.gov.cn/mfa_eng/wjdt_665385/2649_6653 93/t15771.shtml.

years – against the backdrop of the Crimea crisis and the US's positioning in the territorial disputes between China and its neighbours in the East and South China sea – military and security cooperation were treated as a new core feature of Sino–Russian cooperation. In 2015, Xi Jinping was invited as a special guest of honour to join the military parade in Moscow held to celebrate and rememorate the 70th anniversary of the allied powers' victory and the end of the Second World War (TASS 2015). Vice versa, in September 2015, Vladimir Putin was standing next to Xi Jinping when the PRC held its military parade to celebrate the capitulation of Japan in the Second World War. This military parade sent a clear signal, especially as the PRC had so far only held (military) parades on its national day (1 October). Beijing presents itself – inspired by the slogan of the Self-Strengthening Movement – as a strong economic and powerful military player, joining forces with Russia. Since 2015, China and Russia have been conducting joint military manoeuvres, including joint military drills in the East China Sea (August 2015). After 1989, when the US and Europe issued an arms embargo in reaction to the 1989 crack-down on the Tian'anmen movement, Russia had become the PRC's main weapons and armament supplier. Since then, the PRC itself has modernised its arms industry and has risen to be the world's third largest arms exporting country. In 2015, only 11 % of Russian arms exports went to China (still the number 2 destination of Russian arms exports) – whilst 39 % were delivered to India (SIPRI 2015).

In 2019, the PRC celebrated the 70th anniversary of its founding – and 70 years of cooperation and partnership (not taking into account the years of the Sino–Soviet split) between Beijing and Moscow. Xi Jinping, during his three-day visit to Russia, called Putin "one of (his) closest friends and great colleague" and praised the two countries' cooperation in regional and global politics. He mentioned the successful implementation of joint projects in the fields of energy, investment, aerospace and aviation. Xi also sketched the idea of further coordination between Moscow's visions of Eurasian regionalism, and the Eurasian Economic Union, and Beijing's New Silk Road initiative.[124] Rather than constructing the New Silk Road as an alternative regional connectivity (and trade) initiative, the PRC's 2019 narrative highlighted shared interests and complementarities of the Chinese and Russian regional integration roadmaps. Moscow, however, would probably not accept the construction of a China-centred regional order with the renminbi serving as a regional anchor currency. The plans for the future of the Eurasian Economic Union go far beyond the idea of a customs union and a common market. In the long run, the Eurasian region might even introduce a joint currency unit. Nonetheless, with regard to the global dimension of Beijing's connectivity initiative, Beijing and Moscow have already expressed their willingness to cooperate and to jointly construct the "polar Silk Road" (Sorensen/Klimenko 2017).

---

124 For the English transcript of the remarks by Xi Jinping and Vladimir Putin on "70 years" of cooperation between Beijing and Moscow, see: FP Editors (2019).

7.2.4. China and the EU: Partners or Competitors?

→ The EU's China Strategy

The formal establishment of diplomatic relations between the PRC and the European Community (EC) – the precursor organisation to the European Union (EU) – took place in 1975, i.e., a couple of years after the UN Resolution 2758 (1971) had officially recognised the PRC as the only legitimate representation of "China". Immediately after the founding of the PRC, several Eastern European countries, belonging to the "socialist" camp, had recognised the PRC, as well as the "neutral" Northern European states Denmark, Finland, Norway, Sweden – and Switzerland. In the following years, the German Democratic Republic positioned itself as an independent socialist state and set up formal ties with Beijing. Great Britain, given its special relations with mainland China via its protectorate of Hong Kong, recognised the PRC in January 1950. The majority of (Western) European states maintained formal relations with the Republic of China (based on Taiwan) until the 1970s. In 1964, France changed its mind and turned to Beijing; followed by Italy (1970) and the German Federal Republic ("West Germany") (1972) (Cabestan 2008: 84–85).

Amongst the first treaties concluded between the European Community and the PRC were a trade agreement (1978) and a textile agreement (1985). In 1988, the EC opened a delegation office in Beijing. In 1989, the EC responded to the crack-down on the Tian'anmen protests by imposing economic sanctions and an arms embargo – which, up until now, has not yet been lifted. After Deng Xiaoping's symbolic "journey to the South" – where the PRC's first special economic zone had been opened – in 1992 and his confirmation to continue the reform and opening process, Sino–EC relations were "normalised".

The up and downs of Sino–EC/Sino–EU relations, gaining momentum in the mid-1990s, mirror both sides' internal reforms and modernisation efforts – as well as internal crises, spill-backs and reform deadlocks: with the Maastricht Treaty (1992), the European Union was set up, complementing European cooperation in the fields of trade and economy by the two additional pillars of a Common Foreign and Security Policy and Cooperation in the Fields of Justice and Home Affairs. In 1995, the European Commission released a first common EU China strategy, expressing its support for the PRC's modernisation process and the European interest in a further liberalisation of the Chinese (one-party) system. The document, entitled "A Long-term Policy for China–Europe Relations" (COM 1995 279), stressed the rising role of the PRC as an important player in international politics and articulated the EU's support for the PRC's transformation and transition, including the emergence of "a civil society based on the rule of law".[125]

The 1998 update of the EU's long-term China strategy (COM 1998 181) expanded bilateral cooperation beyond trade issues and formulated five action points:

---

125 This, and the following EU policy documents, are available online: http://eu-asiacentre.eu/links.php?ca t_id=24&level=0&tree=24&code=4. For a general overview of Sino–EU relations, see: Shambaugh et al. (2008).

(1) Engaging China further, through an upgraded political dialogue, in the international community;

(2) Supporting China's transition to an open society based upon the rule of law and the respect for human rights;

(3) Integrating China further in the world economy by bringing it more fully into the world trading system and by supporting the process of economic and social reform underway in the country;

(4) Making Europe's funding go further;

(5) Raising the EU's profile in China.

The 1998 strategy paper was published against the background of the British hand-over of Hong Kong (1997), the progress of the PRC's transition towards market capitalism and the deepening of European integration. One openly proclaimed goal of the EU's 1998 China strategy was the further "engagement" and the involvement of China in solving regional and global developmental challenges (also implying a sharing of financial burdens and responsibilities). The 1998 strategy coined the notion of a "comprehensive partnership", projecting the integration of the PRC as an "equal" partner in world trade under the condition of a further strengthening of free market principles, civil liberties and human rights, and, finally, the rule of law. On top of agreeing to deepen bilateral trade, the EU reinforced its support for the PRC's accession to the World Trade Organisation (WTO).

In 2003, the EU classified its relationship with Beijing as a "maturing partnership" (COM 2003 533). The document also evaluated the development of the political dialogue as a diplomatic coordination mechanism and outlined the basic institutional frameworks of (future) economic and political cooperation.

In 2006, the EU published a new trade and investment strategy that replaced the 1978 and 1985 agreements. It also presented a refined version of its China strategy, entitled "EU–China: Closer Partners, Growing Responsibilities" (COM 2006 632). The strategy paper opened with a chapter on the PRC's and the EU's economic power and their roles as core (rising) actors in global trade. The EU underlined its dedication to a combined approach of active engagement and partnership with the PRC, adding that any intensification of the partnership would imply growing mutual responsibilities and obligations. As a symbolic concession, the EU's 2006 strategy paper formally accepted Beijing's official foreign policy narrative by stressing that China's "re-emergence" – the PRC officially claims that China is re-rising to its old power status and centre position it had held prior to the Opium Wars – would be a "welcome phenomenon". In 2007, the EU further released a country strategy setting the official agenda for the years 2007 to 2013.[126] During this period (2007–2013), bilateral relations between China and select EU member states also witnessed a deepening and institutionalisation of cooperation. This includes, inter alia, the initiation of intergovernmental consultations between China and Germany in June 2011. At the intergovernmental con-

---

126 China Strategy Paper 2007–2013, http://eeas.europa.eu/china/csp/07_13_en.pdf.

sultations in 2014, a joint action plan, entitled "Shaping innovation together!", was adopted – depicting bilateral (research and development) cooperation as a "partnership on equal footing", a demand raised by the Chinese side shortly prior to the establishment of the consultation mechanism in 2011.

The EU–China Agenda 2020[127] (2013) documents the shift from unilateral strategy formulation to the joint drafting of regional and global development agendas. The Agenda 2020 commences with a section highlighting the complementarities between the PRC's 12th Five-Year Plan (and the "two one-hundred" goals coined by Xi Jinping) and the EU's 2020 Strategy. These synergies and win-win prospects are then further exemplified with regard to the fields of "peace and security", "prosperity", "sustainable development" and "people-to-people exchanges". Overall, the EU–China Agenda 2020 communicates both players' efforts to minimise the risks of open conflicts and mutual distrust.

Nonetheless, the PRC's special relations with 16 states (most of them EU member states) located in Central and Eastern Europe via the 16+1 format – with Greece joining in 2017 extended to 17+1 – created cracks and intensified tensions within the EU. The Visegrád group, seeking to decrease Eastern Europe's reliance on Brussels and to restrengthen national sovereignty, welcomed the PRC's New Silk Road investment offers with open arms. The PRC's 2013 agreement with Hungary to build a railway connecting Belgrade to Budapest and, potentially, being further expanded to the port of Piraeus, was delayed due to an official EU intervention. Hungary, a member state of the EU, was reminded to comply with the official competition laws and regulations. In 2017 and 2018, when the Hungarian government finally followed Brussels' requests and called for an open tender, the consortium winning the bid was a joint initiative of Chinese and Hungarian companies.

To avoid a division of the EU into competing regional blocs maintaining sub-regional relations with China, the EU sought to set up additional frameworks and channels for interest coordination between Brussels and Beijing. In 2015, the EU–China Connectivity Platform was created to coordinate investment and infrastructure activities in the Eurasian region (EEAS 2015). In 2017, the European Investment Fund and the PRC's Silk Road Fund signed a co-investment memorandum of understanding. Already back in 2016, the EU and China had concluded cooperation agreements in the fields of energy and climate change.[128] Furthermore, also in 2016, the EU once again updated its China strategy by publishing a Joint Communication of the EU Commission to the European Parliament and the Council (JOIN(2016) 30 final), followed by a response of the EU Council. The Joint Communication identified challenges and threats resulting from the ascent of the PRC to global power status:

---

127   EU–China 2020 Strategic Agenda for Cooperation (2013), https://eeas.europa.eu/delegations/china/1539
      8/eu-china-2020-strategic-agenda-cooperation_en.
128   The documents are available online: https://eeas.europa.eu/delegations/china/15394/china-and-eu_en.

"The EU will have to deal with a number of emerging trends:

- China's policy of 'going global' is accelerating. Its companies are being encouraged to trade, invest abroad, and find resources as never before. China's growing connection to global capital markets can generate benefits for all, provided that the right framework conditions are in place.
- China's growing global influence and interests lead to a corresponding demand for a greater say in global economic governance. In international relations, China is also engaging more (e.g. on development, climate action, and international security hotspots). In its region, it is becoming more assertive" (JOIN(2016) 30 final)

In March 2019, the EU Commission outlined its refined approach to China in its joint communication "EU-China: A Strategic Outlook" (JOIN(2019) 5 final). Whilst the document referred to the EU's 2016 China strategy as the "cornerstone" of its relationship with the PRC, it also addressed perceived imbalances and unfavourable development trends. The joint communication highlighted the need to speak with one voice and to restore the EU's "unity", especially when pushing for "more balanced and reciprocal conditions governing the economic relationship" with the PRC (JOIN(2019) 5 final). With the institutionalisation of the 16+1/17+1 summits between China and select states of Central and Eastern Europe (joined by Greece), the (short) era of casting unanimous critical EU votes on China has, clearly, come to an abrupt end. Hungary, as well as Greece, reportedly refused to sign EU positioning statements criticising China's regional and global assertiveness or shortcomings with regard to the protection of civil freedoms and human rights at the domestic system level. The terminology of the EU with regard to the roles ascribed to China has been adjusted to reflect the new power constellations:

"China is, simultaneously, in different policy areas, a cooperation partner with whom the EU has closely aligned objectives, a negotiating partner with whom the EU needs to find a balance of interests, an economic competitor in the pursuit of technological leadership, and a systemic rival promoting alternative models of governance" (JOIN(2019) 5 final)

Officially, the EU subscribes to Beijing's definition of the One China Principle and does not engage in diplomatic relations with Taiwan. Relations – as also confirmed on the EU's webpages – are limited to economic and cultural exchange. The European Economic and Trade Office (EETO) in Taipei was opened in 2003.

Due to the special historical ties between the UK and Hong Kong, as well as between Portugal and Macao, the EU maintains special relations with these two Chinese Special Administrative Regions. In connection with the hand-over of Hong Kong (1997) and the re-transferal of Macao (1999), the EU released separate position papers outlining its relations with these two special administrative units: "The European Union and Hong Kong: Beyond 1997" (COM 97 171) and "The European Union and Macau: Beyond 2000" (COM 1999 484). In 2006, when the EU outlined its China strategy for the years 2007 to 2013, it also updated its statements on cooperation with the two SARs: "The European Union, Hong Kong and Macao: Possibilities for cooperation 2007–2013" (COM 2006 648).

→ China's EU Strategy

Already in the early Maoist period, relations which Europe were ascribed a special role in China's foreign strategy. As the Maoist world-order models, dividing the world into two camps and "intermediate zones" or, later, into "three worlds", illustrate, the European states were seen as potential allies of the PRC. When entering the reform era, the PRC turned to a more pragmatic foreign and security strategy, seeking to overcome the Cold War system antagonism by opting for the construction of a multipolar world. The main idea is to set up a global order managed by several great powers – in the Chinese model referred to as "poles" – and to oppose power concentration in the hands of one hegemonic superpower. The bipolar system (US–SU) of the Cold War era and the emergence of a unipolar world order after 1989/1991 have a negative connotation, at least according to the official Chinese narrative on world politics.

Table 11: China's EU Strategy and World Order Conceptions

The Role of the EU in Chinese World-Order Conceptions	
Structure of the international system *(Chinese Perceptions)*	*Position ascribed to the EU* *(Chinese Imaginations)*
Two Camps (= as inspired by the Soviet world-order model)	Europe = Part of the capitalist camp; no differentiation between Eastern and Western Europe
Intermediate Zone(s)	European states located in the intermediate zone(s) in-between the US and the Soviet Union = potential allies and supporters of Chinese interests and world order visions
Three World Theory	First World: US, Soviet Union Second World: Europe, Canada, Japan Third World: Developing countries (Africa, Asia, Latin America) China acting as advocate (and symbolic leader) of the states of the Third World; cooperation with European states located in the Second World
Multipolarity	Pentapolarity: US, Russia, Japan, China ... and Europe

© Noesselt 2016, 2020

In 2003, the PRC put forward a "Chinese" vision of Sino–EU relations. China's EU policy paper was first celebrated as a symbolic upgrading of the bilateral partnership, given that this was the first Chinese policy paper dealing with relations vis-à-vis a regional organisation. Even though relations with the US were ascribed priority in China's foreign affairs, there was (and is) no similar Chinese policy paper on Sino–US interactions. The Chinese 2003 paper on its relations with the EU thus initially sparked speculations about the formation of a Sino–European axis in world affairs (Shambaugh 2004; Scott 2007a, 2007b; Holslag 2011). The 2003 policy paper stressed that Sino–EU relations were characterised by the absence of unresolved historical tensions or geostrategic competition. Both sides, as the document argued, would not pose any direct threat to each other. Nonetheless, the document mentioned differences with regard to the two actors' historical experiences, cultural foundations, as well as with respect to their political and economic system structures. The Chinese politics paper classifies divergent views and disagreements as a logical outcome of the historical and cultural background of China and Europe. It stresses that these disagreements would not threaten the future deepening of relations, at least as long as both sides would subscribe to the principle of symmetry/equality and mutual respect. The policy paper summarised the cornerstones of Sino–EU political relations in eight points:

(1) Strengthen the exchange of high-level visits and political dialogue
(2) Strictly abide by the One China principle
(3) Encourage Hong Kong and Macao's cooperation with EU
(4) Promote the EU's understanding of Tibet
(5) Continue the human rights dialogue
(6) Strengthen international cooperation
(7) Enhance mutual understanding between Chinese and European legislative organs
(8) Increase exchanges between political parties in China and the EU
 (China's EU Policy Paper (2003)).

The policy paper apparently presents a Chinese perspective on and vision of the Sino–EU partnership, underlining the axiomatic principles of Chinese politics and foreign relations (e.g., the One China principle). It formulates red lines and limits of cooperation and also outlines conditions and prerequisites for a deepening of cooperation. The central condition formulated in the Chinese policy paper is the elimination of "asymmetries" and inequalities in order to achieve a relationship on equal footing. The demands listed in the policy paper include the lifting of the EU's arms embargo (imposed in 1989), perceived by the Chinese side as "remnants" of the Cold War, the recognition of the PRC as a "market economy" and the unconditional compliance with Beijing's definition and interpretation of the "One China Principle" by the EU and its member states.

The PRC's 2003 policy paper on its relationship with the EU officially covered the next five years, i.e., until 2008. However, the next version was released in April 2014, one year after the fifth generation of Chinese political leaders had assumed office – even though none of the "asymmetries" listed above had been fixed. What has changed, according to the 2014 policy paper, is the status and global role of both China and the EU. The Chinese policy paper entitled "Deepen the China–EU Comprehensive Strategic Partnership for Mutual Benefit and Win-win Cooperation" is divided into ten chapters. The introduction states that China's first policy paper had been "implemented effectively" and that the "China–EU Comprehensive Strategic Partnership (had entered) its second decade" (China's Policy Paper on the EU (2014)).

Some months prior to the release of the Chinese policy paper, the EU and China had published a Joint Agenda 2020, outlining new fields of cooperation at the national, regional as well as global level.[129]Beyond these topics, the Chinese 2014 policy paper stresses the further deepening of high-level exchange and dialogue, but also goes beyond the level of government-to-government relations by, once again, highlighting the importance of exchange between Chinese and European legal bodies and political parties. The chapter on cooperation in the political field mainly reiterates the eight points formulated in the 2003 document. Whilst (symbolic) tensions and frictions remain, the 2014 document stresses the options for a deepening of cooperation and outlines the therefrom deriving mutual benefits.

The image ascribed to the EU by Chinese scholars (and politicians) has undergone a noticeable transformation. Had the PRC been perceived as "more European than the Europeans", given its optimistic views on European integration and the treatment of the EU as one unified actor, the current view is definitely more pragmatic and down to earth. One explanation for the emergence of a more differentiated view of the EU, perceived as being highly fragmented and composed of competing national and regional actor groups, might be the professionalisation of political science and EU Studies in China – assessing EU politics based on empirical data sets instead of being inspired by "Chinese" visions and imaginations of a (future) multipolar world order. An alternative explanation might be the bitter disappointment of the Chinese side when the prospective lifting of the EU's arms embargo – which had somehow been regarded as "granted" by Chinese observers – did not happen. Statements by single EU member countries had been interpreted as a statement on behalf of the EU. The fact that most decisions on the EU's common and security policy require (sometimes even double) majorities had, clearly, been ignored. Elections and the replacement of the government by a new coalition that also includes the (former) opposition parties might all too easily lead to the swinging of a pro-China foreign policy to a rather critical positioning vis-à-vis the PRC's debatable human rights conduct.[130] Moreover, the US also impacted the EU's decision not to lift the arms embargo, as the US government underlined the implication of such a decision for the fragile security constellations in Asia, especially in the East and South China Sea. The PRC's

---

129 EU–China 2020 Strategic Agenda for Cooperation (2013), http://eeas.europa.eu/china/docs/20131123_a genda_2020__en.pdf.

130 On the (divergent and sometimes competing) positions taken by EU member states towards China, see: Fox /Godement (2009).

Anti-Secession Law, released in 2005, was referred to as an indicator for a more assertive positioning of Beijing towards Taiwan (Tang 2005).

Since this diplomatic Cannae of 2005/2006, the Chinese side has started a critical re-evaluation of its relationship with the EU and is actively seeking to intensify its contacts with select member states, regional sub-groups of EU member states, as well as with the EU organs in Brussels. To promote special relations with Central and Eastern Europe, Beijing initiated the 16+1 format and formalised this multi-lateral meeting by opening a permanent 16+1 secretariat in Beijing.[131]The original 16+1 format involved EU member states as well as neighbouring European states located in Central or Eastern Europe. This signals a clear departure from the PRC's earlier treatment of the EU as a pole and unitary actor. Europe is no longer reduced to the European integration project; Beijing rather operates with a multi-dimensional strategy based on a new matrix of multiple types of actors (including groups of states as well as transnational business networks).

Special attention is now also payed to the voting system of the EU and the role (and responsibilities) of the various EU organs in Brussels. In March 2014, for the first time in the history of Sino–EU relations, the Chinese State President Xi Jinping travelled to Brussels, where he not only met with the EU Commission, but also visited the EU Council and the EU Parliament. The meeting in Brussels concluded with a joint statement that mainly reconfirmed the joint declaration of the 2013 summit meeting. The possibility of concluding a free trade agreement was mentioned as a long-term goal; the formulation of a joint EU–China investment (protection) agreement was listed as a short-term goal and precondition for the next bargaining rounds on a free trade agreement (European Commission 31 March 2014). Economic and financial relations between the EU and China likewise underwent a remarkable transformation: Chinese companies have emerged as new investors in Europe; transportation networks have been diversified (even long before the launching of the New Silk Road initiative (2013)).

In December 2016, some special clauses of China's Accession Protocol to the World Trade Organisation (WTO) finally expired, implying a prospective recognition of China as a "market economy". This would have complicated the initiation of antidumping investigations against the PRC. In meetings with the EU, the PRC repeatedly articulated its demand to be granted full market economy status. The EU, however, had always asked for institutional and legal framework readjustments. This mainly included the following four fields:

> "State influence: ensuring equal treatment of all companies by reducing state interference, which takes place either on an ad hoc basis or as a result of industrial policies, as well as through export and pricing restrictions on raw materials.

> Corporate governance: increasing the level of compliance with the existing Accounting Law in order to ensure in general the usability of accounting information for the purpose of trade defence investigations.

---

131 On Beijing's relations with the states of Central and Eastern Europe, see: Golonka (2012).

Property and bankruptcy law: ensuring equal treatment of all companies in bankruptcy procedures and in respect of property and intellectual property rights.

Financial sector: bringing the banking sector under market rules, i.a. by removing discriminatory barriers, in order to ensure rational allocation of capital by financial institutions". (MEMO/04/163 2004).

Finally, in December 2016, Beijing turned to the WTO, accusing the EU and the US of non-compliance with the accession protocol. The EU finally decided to give up the formal differentiation between market economies and non-market economies. Instead, the EU introduced a catalogue of antidumping measures to protect the common market against the inflow of (illegally) subsidised products sold below production costs.

Despite the release of the EU–China Strategic Agenda 2020 and both sides' confirmation to strive for a deepening of cooperation, political tensions and economic frictions do persist. Whilst the 2005 trade dispute focused on cheap manufactured textiles, current frictions and competition occur in the sector of high technology, including, inter alia, green (photovoltaic) energy solutions.

The PRC expects the EU to engage in an equal partnership and to respect China's axiomatic (foreign) policy principles. Beijing thus voiced its anger over the reception of the Dalai Lama (as religious head of the Tibetans, not as a political leader) in Germany (2007) and France (2008). Immediately after these receptions, bilateral trade dropped – a mode of informal sanctioning described by Fuchs and Klann as the "Dalai Lama effect" (Fuchs/Klann 2010).

In December 2018, the PRC released its third policy paper on its relationship with the EU (Xinhua 2018). The new version mainly integrated novel foreign policy concepts and terminology coined by Xi Jinping, highlighting the potential synergies between the BRI and the EU's connectivity strategy. It also underlined the global governance dimension of Sino–EU cooperation.

In a nutshell, the diversification of the PRC's approach to Europe and the EU indicates that Chinese foreign relations are no longer based on a pentapolar model of world politics. The PRC's activities in novel networks of rising powers, inter alia the BRICS (established in 2009/2010), illustrate that Beijing has commenced to identify strategic partners that could be used as strategic gateways to address (sub-)regions as well as transnational actor networks.

7.3. Summary and Outlook

Making any statements or predictions on the PRC's current and future role in the globalised world of the 21st century always implies undertaking a critical re-evaluation and reassessment of global power constellations, power shifts and power ambitions. The concept and definition of power that determines Chinese reflections on global politics is far more complex than the twofold categorisation of Hard Power as opposed to Soft Power. Symbolic dimensions – image and reputation, i.e., the recognition of Chinese national role claims and status positions – are essential building blocks of the Chinese definition of "power".

The global positioning strategy of China hence does not primarily rely on mere military power – the modernisation of the PRC's armed forces is defensive in nature – but is based on a combination of monetary and discursive power. Discursive power is linked to the PRC's claim to be involved in the (re-)bargaining and (re-)shaping of global institutions and to have its voice heard on issues relating to the constitutionalisation of "new" spaces (inter alia the Arctic region, outer space, cyberspace). The concept of discursive power (*huayuquan*) obviously draws inspiration from Foucault's post-structuralist reflections on language and framing processes in connection with the construction of political order and related hierarchies. Discursive power, as used in the (intra-)Chinese debate, includes two dimensions: access to participation in deliberation and bargaining processes, i.e., the right to articulate visions and demands. In addition, the choice of key terms and the framing of global politics is understood as a way to shape and steer world politics. The terminology used in official statements by international organisations and multilateral institutions is seen as setting certain normative (and ethical) standards, upon which world politics are evaluated. In this vein, by adding new terms and concepts to the global debate, states create (and legitimate) the international order and establish a (joint) vision of future global politics.

The perceived transformation of the PRC's role as a global actor is also debated amongst Chinese academic elites and within the groups acting as advisers to the central government. There seems to be a general consensus that the PRC should play a more pro-active role and voice Chinese core interests in regional and global affairs. Due to the global activities of Chinese companies and banks, China's security concerns and strategic development issues are no longer limited to the territory within the national borders of the PRC. Officially, Beijing pursues a peace-oriented foreign policy and seeks to avoid open territorial disputes and military confrontations. As the Diaoyu/Senkaku islands dispute, reaching a new level of escalation in 2012, evidences, historical cleavages and power rivalries with Japan and the US pose a challenge to the PRC's self-chosen conditional non-aggression clause of its foreign and security strategy.

The PRC's positioning in the Diaoyu/Senkaku dispute perpetuates "old" role claims – centred on the preservation of national sovereignty and the safeguarding of the country's territorial integrity. The reference to monetary issues and the Chinese renminbi in connection with the PRC's official "core interests" (*hexin liyi*) indicates that monetary and economic power are ascribed a central relevance in the country's global strategy. When, under Trump, the US withdrew from the Paris Agreement and turned to trade protectionism, Beijing responded by presenting itself as a "conservative" power, subscribing to the already reached global agreements on combatting climate change, and defending the concept of global economic liberalism and free trade. At multilateral fora, the Chinese side proposed models and ideas for a reformed global order. This increasingly self-confident articulation of "Chinese" views and concepts has been classified, by Chinese scholars, as a transformation of China's national role set from being a "rule taker" (*guize jieshouzhe*) to becoming a "rule participant" (*guize canyuzhe*) (Zhang, Liping 2013:1). The terminology used to categorise this transition clearly evidences that the political science debates in China avoid copying the "rule taker – rule maker" frame of Western IR debates. The term "rule participant" forms part of the official (national role) narrative that China wants to contribute to the ongoing bargaining processes on reforming the international institutional settings without overthrowing the existing order.

China's "new" national role conception as a global player must accommodate both the demands of patriotic movements as well as those of groups advocating a cooperative, dialogue-based enforcement of Chinese national interests. Whilst the development roadmaps proposed by patriotic-conservative and global-liberal groups are hardly compatible, all actors apparently agree that reforms of the global system structures must be implemented incrementally. A "big bang" approach is expected to generate "chaos" and anarchy, which would also have severe negative implications for the globally intertwined Chinese economy.

The Chinese economy's embeddedness into the global networks of trade and finance means that the PRC has to study national and international regulatory frameworks and legal norms in order to pursue a pragmatic and efficient development strategy that combines the national and the international level. China's transition from rule participant to rule innovator requires the coining of "Chinese" IR frames that are decoupled from "Chinese" regime patterns and thus universally applicable.

A closer look at the Chinese attempts to redefine its relationship with the old poles of the multipolar system suggests that Beijing is aware of its increased global bargaining power but is also afraid that its more active positioning might be perceived as "aggressive" or "assertive" and thus trigger the formation of anti-Chinese alliances. However, the concept of a Community of Shared Destiny, also used in China's soft power communication with the states of the so-called Global South, which are facing similar development and modernisation challenges, indicates a gradual reconfiguration of cooperation patterns in the multipolar world. Instead of zero-sum games, through which the gains of one state imply that its competitors loose (the total sum of gains and losses remains zero), the Community of Shared Destiny promises gains and benefits for all participants. Stability and development are defined by Beijing as shared goals of the world society, a move by which the "Chinese" triad "peace, development, cooperation" (*heping, fazhan, hezuo*) is transposed to the global level.

For all predictions regarding the future development trajectories of world politics, one general caveat should be kept in mind: these scenarios of the future are based on a linear extrapolation of contemporary constellations (or patterns derived from the analysis of past events). Unexpected turbulences – economic crises, stock market crashes – can cause short-term shifts of regional and global constellations and power distributions. Besides, the PRC has entered a new stage of state- and regime-building, and is currently redefining its national and global role conceptions and calculating its strategic positioning options. The post-2013 re-steering of China's economic system will – similar to the 1978 reforms – create new developmental challenges which must be answered by another set of counter-measures and reform initiatives. The PRC's trial-and-error approach to economic reforms at the domestic level is being continued in the context of global politics. The examples of the still-ongoing diversification of Chinese foreign relations, de-scribed above, mirror the plurality of foreign policy approaches and role concepts used depending on the significant other addressed. Rather than following a stat-ic-ossified, ideology-bound approach, the conduct of Chinese foreign relations is characterised by pragmatic flexibility – reflecting the transformation of its environment and position changes of its cooperation partners. Whilst certain ele-ments of China's national and global role claims appear to be non-negotiable iron principles – knowledge of China's historical and state-philosophical foundations hence remains important – one should always keep one's eyes open in order to be able to identify position changes.

The PRC's New Silk Road initiative, constructing Beijing as the centre of a global connectivity (and trade) network, brings back memories of the *tianxia* – and its reinterpretation by Zhao Tingyang as a model for the world of the 21st century. Symbolically, the governance models of the fifth generation of Chinese political leaders perpetuate elements of "Confucian" state philosophy – which constructs a correlation between the self-cultivation of the emperor, the stability and order of the state and the harmony of the cosmos (or *tianxia*). Read through the lenses of Chinese state philosophy, the Chinese concept of meritocracy – defined as the better alternative to liberal democracy – and the Chinese mode of governance are based on the morality and benevolence of the ruler. The ruler's virtue-based governance develops a magnetic effect, contributing to the cohesion of Chinese society (domestic level) and attracting followers and admirers amongst other states (global level). Allegorically, Confucius describes this model of harmony as stars grouping themselves around the polar star which, like the Chinese emperor, is at the centre of the universe and serves as the stability anchor of the system. This Confucian allegory has been quoted in political speeches of Xi Jinping. It outlines the parallelism between earthly and cosmological order – or, in more abstract terms, between national and global constellations and developments.[132]

References

Al-Tamimi, Naser M. (2014), *China–Saudi Arabia Relations, 1990–2012: Marriage of Convenience or Strategic Alliance*. New York: Routledge.

Asahi Shimbun (2012), "INSIGHT: Mao References in Anti-Japan Protests a Concern for Chinese Authorities", 18 September 2012, http://ajw.asahi.com/article/asia/china/AJ201209180053.

Bloomberg (2015), "Russia Pips Saudi Arabia in Race to Grab China Oil Market Share", 23 June 2015, http://www.bloomberg.com/news/articles/2015-06-23/russia-pips-saudi-arabia-in-race-to-grab-china-oil-market-share.

Bräuner, Oliver/Bromley, Mark/Duchatel, Mathieu (2015), *Western Arms Exports to China*. Stockholm: SIPRI Policy Paper 43, http://books.sipri.org/files/PP/SIPRIPP43.pdf.

---

132 See also the Chinese leitmotif at the opening of this textbook.

Cabestan, Jean-Pierre (2008), "The Taiwan Issue in Europe-China Relations, in: Shambaugh, David/Sandschneider, Eberhard/Zhou, Hong (eds.) (2008), *China–Europe Relations: Perceptions, Policies and Prospects*. London; New York: Routledge, 84–101.

Cao, Yongrong/Xu, Jian (2015), "The Tibet Problem in the Milieu of a Rising China: Findings from a Survey on Americans' Attitudes toward China", *Journal of Contemporary China*, 24:92, 240–259.

Cheng, Joseph Y. S./Ngok, King-Lun (2004), "The 2001 'Spy' Plane Incident Revisited: The Chinese Perspective", *Journal of Chinese Political Science*, 9:1, 63–83.

China's EU Policy Paper (2003), http://english.peopledaily.com.cn/200310/13/eng2003101 3_125906.shtml.

China's Policy Paper on the EU: Deepen the China–EU Comprehensive Strategic Partnership for Mutual Benefit and Win-Win Cooperation (2014), http://news.xinhuanet.com/english/china/2014-04/02/c_133230788.htm.

Christensen, Thomas (2011), *Worse than a Monolith: Alliance Politics and Problems of Coercive Diplomacy in Asia*. Princeton: Princeton UP.

EIA (2020), "China's Crude Oil Imports Surpassed 10 Million Barrels Per Day in 2019", 23 March 2020, https://www.eia.gov/todayinenergy/detail.php?id=43216.

Ferguson, Niall/Schularick, Moritz (2009), "The End of Chimerica", http://www.hbs.edu/faculty/Publication%20Files/10-037.pdf.

Fox, John/Godement, Francois (2009), *A Power Audit of EU–China Relations*. ECFR.

FP Editors (2019), "Xi and Putin, Best Friends Forever? A Transcript of the Two Leaders' Remarks in Moscow", 6 June 2019, https://foreignpolicy.com/2019/06/06/xi-and-putin-best-friends-forever/.

Friedberg, Aaron L. (2002), "11 September and the Future of Sino–American Relations", *Survival*, 44:1, 33–50.

Fuchs, Andreas/Klann, Nils-Hendrik (2010), "Paying a Visit: The Dalai Lama Effect on International Trade", http://www.econ.cam.ac.uk/dae/repec/cam/pdf/cwpe1103.pdf.

Garver, John W. (1998), "China–Russian Relations", in: Kim, Samuel S. (ed.) (1998), *China and the World: Chinese Foreign Policy Faces the New Millennium*. Boulder: Westview Press, 114–132.

Garver, John (2013), "China–Iran Relations: Cautious Friendship with America's Nemesis", *China Report*, 49:1, 69–88.

Gladstone, Rick (2019), "Taiwan President Risks Infuriating China with U.S. Visit", *The New York Times*, 11 July 2019, https://www.nytimes.com/2019/07/11/world/asia/taiwan-president-united-states-china.html.

Goldstein, Morris/Lardy, Nicholas R. (eds.) (2008), *Debating China's Exchange Rate Policy*. Washington: Peterson Institute for International Economics.

Goldstein, Steven M. (1994), "Nationalism and Internationalism: Sino–Soviet Relations", in: Robinson, Thomas W./Shambaugh, David (eds.) (1994), *Chinese Foreign Policy: Theory and Practice*. Oxford: Oxford UP, 224–265.

Golonka, Marta (2012), *Partners or Rivals? Chinese Investments in Central and Eastern Europe*. Warschau: CEED.

Gries, Peter (2005), "Nationalism, Indignation and China's Japan Policy", *SAIS Review*, 25:2, 105–114.

Holslag, Jonathan (2011), "The Elusive Axis: Assessing the EU–China Strategic Partnership", *Journal of Common Market Studies*, 49, 2, 293–313.

IMF (2015), "Chinese Renminbi to be Included in IMF's Special Drawing Right Basket", http://www.imf.org/external/pubs/ft/survey/so/2015/new120115a.htm.

IMF Press Release 15/237 (May 2015), "IMF Staff Completes the 2015 Article IV Consultation Mission to China", https://www.imf.org/external/np/sec/pr/2015/pr15237.htm.

Jia, Qingguo (2003), "The Impact of 9–11 on Sino–US Relations: A Preliminary Assessment", *International Relations of the Asia Pacific*, 3:2, 159–177.

Lampton, David M. (2013), "A New Type of Major-power Relationship: Seeking a Durable Foundation for U.S.–China Ties", *Asia Policy*, 16, 51–68.

Liao, Tim F./Hara, Kimie/Wiegand, Krista (eds.) (2015), *The China–Japan Border Dispute: Islands of Contention in Multidisciplinary Perspective*. Farnham: Ashgate.

Lukin, Alexander (2015), *The Bear Watches the Dragon: Russia's Perceptions of China and the Evolution of Russian–Chinese Relations since the Eighteenth Century*. London; New York: Routledge.

Lüthi, Lorenz M. (2008), *The Sino–Soviet Split: Cold War in the Communist World*. Princeton: Princeton UP.

MEMO/04/163= European Commission (2004), "CHINA – Market Economy Status in Trade Defence Investigations", https://ec.europa.eu/commission/presscorner/detail/en/MEMO_04_163.

Ministry of Foreign Affairs of Japan (2014), "Regarding Discussions Toward Improving Japan–China Relations", 7 November 2014, http://www.mofa.go.jp/a_o/c_m1/cn/page4e_000150.html.

Pompeo, Michael (2020), "Communist China and the Free World's Future", 23 July 2020, https://www.state.gov/communist-china-and-the-free-worlds-future/.

Reilly, James (2014), "A Wave to Worry About? Public Opinion, Foreign Policy and China's Anti-Japan Protests", *Journal of Contemporary China*, 23:86, 197–215.

Scott, David (2007a), "China and the EU: A Strategic Axis for the Twenty-first Century?", *International Relations*, 21:1, 23–45.

Scott, David (2007b), "China–EU Convergence 1957–2003: Towards a 'Strategic Partnership'", *Asia-Europe Journal*, 7, 217–233.

Shambaugh, David (2000), "Sino–American Strategic Relations: From Partners to Competitors", *Survival*, 42:1, 97–115.

Shambaugh, David (2004), "China and Europe: The Emerging Axis", *Current History*, 243–248.

Shambaugh, David/Sandschneider, Eberhard/Zhou, Hong (eds.) (2008), *China–Europe Relations: Perceptions, Policies and Prospects*. London; New York: Routledge, 84–101.

SIPRI (2015), "Trends in International Arms Transfers, 2014", http://books.sipri.org/files/FS/SIPRIFS1503.pdf.

Sorensen, Camilla T. N./Klimenko, Ekaterina (2017), *Emerging China-Russian cooperation in the Arctic: Possibilities and Constraints*. Stockholm: SIPRI.

South China Morning Post (2013), "Xi Proposes Four-point Plan to Resolve Palestinian Issue", 7 May 2013, http://www.scmp.com/news/china/article/1231358/palestinian-leader-mahmoud-abbas-meets-chinas-xi-jinping-ahead-netanyahu.

Sun, Degang/Zoubir, Yahia H. (2015), "China's Economic Diplomacy Towards the Arab Countries: Challenges Ahead?", *Journal of Contemporary China*, 24:95, 903–921.

Tang, Shao Cheng (2005), "The EU's Policy Towards China and the Arms Embargo", *Asia-Europe Journal*, 3, 313–321.

TASS (2015), "Chinese President to Visit Moscow for WWII Victory Day- Russia FM", 21 January 2015, http://tass.ru/en/russia/772365.

Taylor, Brendan (2005), "US-China Relations after 11 September: A Long Engagement or Marriage of Convenience?", *Australian Journal of International Affairs*, 59:2, 179–199.

The Diplomat (2020), "US Health Secretary Praises Taiwan's Covid-19 Response During Rare High-level Visit", 10 August 2020, https://www.theguardian.com/world/2020/aug/10/us-health-secretary-praises-taiwans-covid-19-response-during-rare-high-level-visit.

The Wall Street Journal (2013), "Sinopec to Buy Stake in Chesapeake Energy Asset", 25 February 2013, http://www.wsj.com/articles/SB10001424127887324338604578325901158645038.

The Wall Street Journal (2016), "Trump's Phone Call with Taiwan President Risks China's Wrath", 3 December 2016, https://www.theguardian.com/us-news/2016/dec/03/trump-angers-beijing-with-provocative-phone-call-to-taiwan-president.

The White House (2009), "Statement on Bilateral Meeting with President Hu of China", 1 April 2009, https://www.whitehouse.gov/the-press-office/statement-bilateral-meeting-with-president-hu-china.

The White House (2013), "Remarks by President Obama and President Xi Jinping of the People's Republic of China After Bilateral Meeting", 8 June 2013, https://www.whitehouse.gov/the-press-office/2013/06/08/remarks-president-obama-and-president-xi-jinping-peoples-republic-china-.

The White House (2015), "Remarks by President Obama and President Xi of the People's Republic of China in Joint Press Conference", 25 September 2015, https://www.whitehouse.gov/the-press-office/2015/09/25/remarks-president-obama-and-president-xi-peoples-republic-china-joint.

Tiezzi, Shannon (2016), "China's Balancing Act in Iran", *The Diplomat*, 16 January 2016, http://thediplomat.com/2016/01/chinas-balancing-act-in-iran/.

UN News Center (2014), "Russia, China Block Security Council Referral of Syria to International Criminal Court", http://www.un.org/apps/news/story.asp?NewsID=47860#.VtWoc8e-PVo.

US Department of Defense (2017), "Joint Press Briefing by Secretary Mattis and Minister Inada in Tokyo, Japan", 4 February 2017, https://www.defense.gov/News/Transcripts/Transcript-View/Article/1071436/joint-press-briefing-by-secretary-mattis-and-minister-inada-in-tokyo-japan/.

Wan, Kam-Ming/Wong, Ka-Fu (2009), "Economic Impact of Political Barriers to Cross-border Acquisitions: An Empirical Study of CNOOC's Unsuccessful Takeover of Unocal", *Journal of Corporate Finance*, 15:4, 447–468.

Westcott, Ben (2020), "US Holds Its Second High-profile Visit to Taiwan in Two Months as Beijing Escalates Military Pressure", *CNN*, 18 September 2020, https://edition.cnn.com/2020/09/17/asia/taiwan-us-china-keith-krach-intl-hnk/index.html.

Whiting, Allen S. (1989), *China Eyes Japan*. Berkeley; Los Angeles; London: University of California Press.

Wu, Xinbo (2005), "The End of the Silver Lining: A Chinese View of the US–Japanese Alliance", *The Washington Quarterly*, 29:1, 117–130.

Wu Xinbo (2012), "Forging Sino–US Partnership in the Twenty-first Century: Opportunities and Challenges", *Journal of Contemporary China*, 21:75, 391–407.

Xinhua (2013), "Chinese President Makes Four-point Proposal for Settlement of Palestinian Question", 6 May 2013, http://news.xinhuanet.com/english/china/2013-05/06/c_132363061.htm.

Xinhua (2014), "China, Japan Reach Four-point Agreement on Ties", 7 November 2014, http://news.xinhuanet.com/english/china/2014-11/07/c_133772952.htm.

Xinhua (2015a), "Arab League Says China–Arab Cooperation Historical, Deeply Rooted", 8 September 2015, http://news.xinhuanet.com/english/2015-09/09/c_134603747.htm.

Xinhua (2015b), "Zhonghua renmin gonghe guo fan kongbuzhuyi fa" (Anti-Terror Law of the PRC), 27 December 2015, http://news.xinhuanet.com/politics/2015-12/27/c_128571798.htm.

Xinhua (2016a), "China's Arab Policy Paper", 13 January 2016, http://news.xinhuanet.com/english/china/2016-01/13/c_135006619.htm.

Xinhua (2016b), "Xi Jinping zai Alabo guojia lianmeng zongbu de yanjiang" (Speech by Xi Jinpings at the Arab League), 21 January 2016, http://news.xinhuanet.com/politics/2016-01/22/c_1117855467.htm.

Xinhua (2016c), "Xi Jinping tong Aiji zongtong Saixi juxing hui tan" (Meeting between Xi Jinping and Egypt's President Al-Sisi), 21 January 2016, http://news.xinhuanet.com/world/2016-01/21/c_1117855156.htm.

Xinhua (2016d), "Zhonghua renmin gongheguo he Alabo Aiji gongheguo guanyu jiaqiang liang guo quanmian zhanlüe huoban guanxi de wu nian shishi gangyao" (Implementation Plan for the Strategic Partnership between China and Egypt for the Next Five

Years), 22 January 2016, http://news.xinhuanet.com/world/2016-01/22/c_1117855474.htm.

Xinhua (2018), "Zhongguo dui Oumeng zhengce wenjian" (China's EU Policy Paper), http://www.xinhuanet.com/world /2018–12/18/c_11238 68707.htm.

Xu, Guangqiu (1997), "The United States and the Tibet Issue", *Asian Survey*, 37:11, 1062–1077

Yee, Andy (2011), "Maritime Territorial Disputes in East Asia: A Comparative Analysis of the South China Sea and the East China Sea", *Journal of Current Chinese Affairs*, 40:2, 165–193.

Zank, Wolfgang (2014), "A 'New Silk Road' between China and the Arab World: A Problem for the US or the EU?", in: Li, Xing (ed.) (2014), *The BRICS and Beyond: The International Political Economy of a New World Order*. Farnham: Ashgate, 161–177.

Zhai, Qiang (2000), *China and the Vietnam Wars, 1950–1975*. Chapel Hill: University of North Carolina Press.

Zhang, Liping (2013), "Zhongguo zai guoji huobi tixi zhong de dingwei yu zuoyong" (China's Status and Function in the International Monetary System), *Chongqing Ligong Daxue Xuebao* (Journal of Chongqing University of Technology), 1, 1–7.

Zhao, Quansheng (1996), *Chinese Foreign Policy: The Micro-Macro Linkage Approach*. Oxford; New York: Oxford University Press.

Zhao, Suisheng (2004), "The Making of China's Periphery Policy", in: Zhao, Suisheng (ed.) (2004), *Chinese Foreign Policy: Pragmatism and Strategic Behavior*. New York; London: M.E. Sharpe, 256–275.

Zhao, Suisheng (2015), "A New Model of Big Power Relations? China–US Strategic Rivalry and Balance of Power in the Asia-Pacific", *Journal of Contemporary China*, 24:93, 377–397.

Recommended Reading

China–Arab World

Alterman, John B. (2013), *China's Balancing Act in the Gulf*. Washington: CSIS. http://csis.org/files/publication/130821_Alterman_ChinaGulf_Web.pdf.

Goldstein, Jonathan (ed.) (1999), *China and Israel, 1948–1998: A Fifty Year Retrospective*. Westport: Praeger Publishers.

Harold, Scott/Nader, Alireza (2012), *China and Iran: Economic, Military and Political Relations*. Santa Monica: RAND.

Olimat, Muhamad (2013), *China and the Middle East: From Silk Road to Arab Spring*. London; New York: Routledge.

China–US

Bachmann, David (2001), "The United States and China: Rhetoric and Reality", *Current History*, 100:647, 257–262.

Christensen, Thomas J. (1996), *Useful Adversaries: Grand Strategy, Domestic Mobilization, and Sino–American Conflict, 1947–1958*. Princeton: Princeton: UP.

Dreyer, June Teufel (2000), "US–China Security Relations: Past, Present and Future", *Issues and Studies*, 36:4, 33–65.

Sutter, Robert G. (2000), *Chinese Policy Priorities and their Implications for the United States*. Lanham: Rowman & Littlefield.

Sutter, Robert G. (2018), *China–US Relations: Perilous Past, Uncertain Present*. Lanham: Rowman & Littlefield.

Zhao Suisheng (2019) "Engagement on the Defensive: From the Mismatched Grand Bargain to the Emerging US–China Rivalry", *Journal of Contemporary China*, 28:118, 501–518.

China–Russia

Garver, John (1988), *Chinese–Soviet Relations, 1937–1945*. New York: Oxford UP.

Lukin, Alexander (2018), *China and Russia: The New Rapprochment*. Cambridge: Polity Press.

Rozman, Gilbert/Radchenko, Sergey (eds.) (2018), *International Relations and Asia's Northern Tier: Sino–Russia Relations, North Korea, and Mongolia*. Palgrave MacMillan.

China–Japan

Chang, Iris (1997), *The Rape of Nanking: The Hidden Holocaust of World War II*. New York: BasicBooks.

Mitter, Rana (2013), *China's War with Japan, 1937–1945: The Struggle for Survival*. London: Allen Lane.

Rose, Caroline (1998), *Interpreting History in Sino–Japanese Relations: A Case Study in Political Decision-making*. London; New York: Routledge.

Smith, Sheila A. (2015), *Intimate Rivals: Japanese Domestic Politics and a Rising China*. New York: Columbia UP.

Swanström, Niklas/Kokubun, Ryosei (eds.) (2013), *Sino–Japanese Relations: Rivals or Partners in Regional Cooperation?* Singapore: World Scientific.

Yahuda, Michael B. (2014), *Sino–Japanese Relations after the Cold War: Two Tigers Sharing a Mountain*. London: Routledge.

Sino–European Relations

Grant, Richard (ed.) (1995), *The European Union and China: A European Strategy for the Twenty-first Century*. London: The Royal Institute of International Affairs.

Kapur, Harish (1990), *Distant Neighbours: China and Europe*. London; New York: Pinter Publishers.

Kerr, David/Liu, Fei (eds.) (2007), *The International Politics of EU-China Relations*. Oxford: Oxford UP.

Shambaugh, David (1995), *China and Europe: 1949–95*. London: SOAS.

Shambaugh, David/Sandschneider, Eberhard/Zhou, Hong (eds. (2008), *China–Europe Relations: Perceptions, Policies and Prospects*. London; New York: Routledge.

Snyder, Francis (2009), *The European Union and China, 1949–2008: Basic Documents and Commentary*. Oxford: Hart.

Wiessala, Georg/Wilson, John/Taneja, Pradeep (eds.) (2009), *The European Union and China: Interests and Dilemmas*. Amsterdam; New York: Rodopi.

China and Soft Power

Li, Mingjiang (ed.) (2009), *Soft Power: China's Emerging Strategy in International Politics*. Lanham: Rowman & Littlefield.

Suzuki, Shogo (2009), "Chinese Soft Power, Insecurity Studies, Myopia and Fantasy", *Third World Quarterly*, 30:4, 779–793.

Wang, Hongying/Lu, Yeh-Chung (2008), "The Conception of Soft Power and its Policy Implications: A Comparative Study of China and Taiwan", *Journal of Contemporary China*, 17:56, 425–447.

Wang, Jian (ed.) (2011), *Soft Power in China: Public Diplomacy through Communication*. Palgrave Macmillan.

Appendix: Visualisation and Fictionalisation of Chinese Political History

The following list of semi-fictional films and documentaries on modern Chinese history does not claim to be exhaustive. The idea of this compilation is rather to support the reader in continuing their (self-)studies of the PRC's political history and its contemporary transformation. The chosen films and documentaries present highly complex historical evolutions in a condensed way, and often do so by looking at historical events from the perspective of Chinese society (thus reflecting a history-from-below approach). Some of the film scripts were written by Chinese authors living outside China, and some films were realised in co-production with a European partner. This selection thus allows a retrospect analysis and interpretation of Chinese political history as seen from the inside and outside perspective ...

To Live (alternative English title: *Lifetimes*) (Huozhe) (1994)

Based on a novel by the Chinese author Yu Hua, in his film adaptation of the story Zhang Yimou re-tells Chinese political history, starting with the end of the dynastical era up to the PRC's entry into the post-Maoist reform era. The film's main part focuses on the Mao years. The protagonist, Xu Fugui, offspring of a wealthy Chinese family in Peking, loses the family's property through gambling. Driven out of their mansion and bereft of their property, the family seems to be doomed to a life in poverty. However, Fugui's misstep unexpectedly turns out to have been a lifesaving one as the PRC launches campaigns and show trials against Chinese landlords and members of the "feudalist" upper class. Fugui is recruited by force by the Nationalist (Guomindang) army and becomes involved in its war against the Chinese Communists – who have started to encircle the cities from the countryside. After the defeat of his army subdivision, Fugui joins the Communist troops as a shadow puppet player. With the end of the war and the victory of the Communists, Fugui finally manages to return to his family – finding his daughter mute and partially deaf. The reunited family tries to live a life in peace and harmony but is haunted by additional strokes of fate. *To Live* sketches the impact of the Maoist mass campaigns – the disaster of the Great Leap Forward, the political radicalisation during the Cultural Revolution – on Chinese society. Neither of the family's two children survive the Mao years. The film ends with China's entrance into the reform era. The camera rests on Fugui's grandson putting chicks into the box in which Fugui once used to store his shadow puppets. Expectations regarding the (capitalist) future are high, and people appear partly disenchanted with communist modernisation experimentations. The future Fugui imagines for his grandson does not follow a utopian socialist design. It is based on economic growth and (technological) modernisation – guided by the formula "bird in a cage" that allowed the integration of market elements into China's socialist planned economy. Three generations, six stories, many sub-episodes – painted with images and colours (white is the colour of mourning) – provide additional invisible subtitles to the film's main story.

China: A Century of Revolution (1989–1997)

A six-hour documentary on Chinese history, divided into three episodes: "China in Revolution 1911–1949", "The Mao Years 1949–1976", "Born under the Red Flag 1976–1997". The documentary is based on archival images, archival film footage and interviews with eyewitnesses and Chinese historians. The documentary looks at events in China from an "outside" perspective, presenting core historical events in chronological order. Alternative interpretations of Chinese history or the political dimension of (party) historiography are not given much attention. Nonetheless, this compilation of archival records and retrospective reflections on Chinese history – even though presenting only one possible view – offer insights into China's political history which one would not gain via books or journal articles.

Shower (Xizao) (1999)

With *Shower*, the Chinese film director Zhang Yang describes the transformation of Chinese society in the post-Mao years, characterised by the loss of traditional family structures and the destruction of Chinese cities' old *hutong* quarters – demolished in order to make place for glamorous skyscrapers and capitalist enterprises. The story is set in Beijing, in one of the city's last few bathhouses. The film starts with a short scene presenting the replacement of these old-style bathhouses by fully-automized shower cabins, programmed like a car wash cabin. This is just one of the venturesome daydreams of one of the younger customers of the old Beijing bathhouse. The next scene opens with a snapshot of daily life in the old bathhouse, where the retired older generation of the neighbourhood spends their days drinking tea, playing mah-jong and watching their crickets fighting. The bathhouse is run by the Old Liu and his mentally handicapped younger son Erming. His older son, Liu Daming, is a successful businessman in Shenzhen, the PRC's modern and glamorous first special economic zone. The latter heads back to Beijing, alerted by a postcard he received from Erming – on which, as he learns upon his arrival, his younger brother did not paint his deceased father but his father sleeping.

The film not only depicts a conflict between the generations but also the tensions between the old socio-economic model (Old Liu, Erming) and the PRC's new capitalist development approach (Liu Daming). The district where the bathroom is located is going to be demolished – and, when the Old Liu catches a severe cold and finally passes away, the bathhouse is ultimately shut down. Zhang Yang sketches the bathhouse as a safe refuge, where conflicts are solved via mediation and where unscrupulous mafia-style debt collectors are denied entry. After the death of Old Liu, Liu Daming is torn between returning to his modern life in Shenzhen and taking on responsibility for his younger brother.

The film ends with a symbolic farewell to the old era – with a song that one of the bathhouse's daily guests used to sing under the shower on full blast – "O sole mio", re-echoed in the finally empty and dilapidated bathhouse.

The Cultural Revolution

There is certainly no lack of films, novels and modern art reflecting on and visualising the Cultural Revolution. The list below discusses one film of the early 1990s, another that is based on a novel written by a Chinese author based in France and filmed in the early 2000s, and one produced in 2014. All three of them look at specific aspects of the Cultural Revolution and their impact on society. The latter two also reflect people's long-lasting traumatisation and the open scars left by these ten "dark" years.

The Blue Kite (Lan fengzheng) (1993)

Tian Zhuangzhuang, like Zhang Yimou and Chen Kaige belonging to the fifth generation of Chinese filmmakers, tells the developments of the Maoist mass campaigns and the persecution of "capitalist roaders" and intellectuals from the perspective of a young boy, Tietou ("Iron Head"), growing up in Beijing. The symbolic leitmotif of the film is a blue kite Tietou is given by his father. This is one of the very few signs of continuity – not only Tietou's father but also his stepfathers fall victim to the Maoist mass campaigns that are running out of control, leading to political radicalisation and spreading violence. The film operates with short episodes and does not provide any historical-documentary explanation of the events. The protagonist of the film, as well as the audience, are left with many open questions, as some episodes – however, at first glance only – appear as disparate "fragments" not directly related to the film's main plot. *The Blue Kite* is a socio-psychological reading of the Cultural Revolution, showing the irritation, fascination and traumatisation of the younger generation facing the escalating violence of the Mao years.

Balzac and the Little Chinese Seamstress (2002)

Dai Sijie – born in Chengdu (Sichuan province) in 1954 and living and working in France since 1984 – tells the story of two teenage boys sent down to a rural village located in the mountains close to Tibet for re-education through labour during the Mao years. The unnamed narrator and his friend Luo find their own ways to cope with this situation – with Luo playing Mozart on his violin and disguising these banned pieces as hymns for praising Mao. The two friends find out that another teenage boy hides some books by French authors, including those by Balzac. They manage to borrow some of these books and read them secretly. They encounter the little Chinese seamstress, telling her the stories they have read. The camera jumps back and forth between the 1960s to the 1970s and present times, i.e., the post-Mao years, focusing on episodes in the village and the narrator's retrospect memories of these years. These episodes told by the narrator, shifting between times and perspectives, illustrate the impact of the partly romantic, partly traumatic memories of the Cultural Revolution (and the re-education through labour campaign) on the post-Maoist Chinese society.

Coming Home (Guilai) (2014)

Based on a novel by the Chinese author Yan Geling, in Coming Home Zhang Yimou addresses the radicalisation of the Chinese red guards, turning against their own parents, and addresses the failed renormalisation of people's lives in the aftermath of the Cultural Revolution. During the Maoist mass campaign, moral principles no longer guide and determine people's behaviour: Lu Yanshi, a Chinese professor persecuted as an enemy of the people during the Cultural Revolution, manages to escape from the labour camp and tries to re-join his family. It is his daughter, Dan Dan, who betrays him by informing the police. Due to her father's negative class background, she is not allowed to play the leading role in the Chinese ballet Red Detachment of Women. By denouncing her father, she hopes to change her fate. Years later, when Lu Yanshi finally returns home, he finds his wife living with amnesia. She does not recognise him and takes him for a stranger. His daughter, despite her betrayal, could not pursue her dream of acting as a ballerina and has instead become a textile worker. These (fictionalised) biographies illustrate the unpredictable ups and downs of the Mao years – during which those who tried to swim with the tide had to be fast enough in noting political changes in order not to be caught by the waves of the next mass movement. As in (almost) all of his films, Zhang Yimou uses colours as well as light and shadow to make the inner feelings and emotions of his protagonists visible. Coming Home is a multi-faceted, thoughtful reflection on the aftershocks of the Cultural Revolution.

Post-1989

Tiananmen 1989

The events of 1989, the demonstrations in Tian'anmen Square, are still regarded as a highly sensitive topic. The Gate of Heavenly Peace (Tiananmen) (1995) by Richard Gordon and Carma Hinton relies on archival news material – in June 1989, many international journalists were in China to document Gorbachev's state visit to Beijing and used the chance to conduct interviews with the student demonstrators and to film the protests. The documentary compares the 1989 protests to earlier Chinese demonstrations in Beijing – the May Fourth Movement, also used as a reference and source of inspiration for students' 1989 protests. Quite a number of former student leaders and student participants of the 1989 movement expressed their opposition to the documentary, criticising the selection of materials and excerpts from the interviews they had once given to journalists during the occupation of Tian'anmen square. The official webpage of The Gate of Heavenly Peace provides background information, additional documents, a full transcript of the documentary as well as video excerpts: http://ts quare.tv.

In Summer Palace (Yiheyuan) (2006) Lou Ye elaborates on student life in Beijing in the months prior to the demonstrations of 1989. Yu Hong (played by Hao Lei) leaves her home village to start her studies in Beijing in the late 1980s. At the universities in Beijing, these are the years of advanced individual freedoms and libertinage – the film documents the transformation of Chinese society and students' quest for liberty and independence, without focusing on politics. The film documents the disillusionment and students' panic when facing the crackdown of the protests. The story continues with three episodes taking place in the late 1990s that focus on the film's main protagonists: Yu Hong and her close friends and former fellow students. The camera follows Yu Hong – who, in summer 1989, quit her studies and left Beijing – to Shenzhen, Wuhan and finally Chongqing. These cities document the rapid transformation of China after the end of the Cold War – referenced in the film as a major historical turning point alongside the handover of Hong Kong (1997). Li Ti and Zhou Wei have both moved to Germany – but the latter is unable to forget China and his love affair with Yu Hong. He finally decides to go back – but when Zhou Wei finally meets Yu Hong, their empty, partly paralysed conversation – "what now?" – reflects the loss of orientation of the 1989 student generation, their ennui and memories of missed opportunities. The country's rapid economic growth and the spreading liberalisation offer multiple individual development opportunities, but the film's protagonists are no longer able to dream.

A Touch of Sin (Tian zhuding) (2013)

In *A Touch of Sin*, Jia Zhangke – belonging to the sixth generation of Chinese filmmakers and known for his underground documentary-style films – presents close-ups of the dark sides of China's economic reforms and the country's capitalist transformation. The film is composed of four main episodes that sketch the life of four individuals and their rebellion against exploitation, poor working conditions, sexual harassment or local officials' and company chiefs' corruption and power abuse. All four anti-heroes are solitary fighters, committing crimes as an act of defence, as an act to restore justice, or as an act just to earn their living. *A Touch of Sin* contrasts life in the backward rural countryside with living conditions and development opportunities in the booming industrial and financial centres in Southern China. The film's four main episodes reflect real stories about labour protests (and suicide attempts by Chinese contract workers), corrupt village chiefs and exploitation in Chinese coal mines that have also been covered by Chinese media over the past few years. The story the film tells about the current developments in China is a rather dark and dystopian one: despite the launching of legal reforms and the official persecution of cases of corruption, the protagonists see no way out of their precarious situation than self-justice. Two protagonists are turning from moral, rule-conforming people into murderers. By contrast, the only murderer, robbing and killing people to finance his family, is presented as a Buddhist believer adhering to Confucian values. *A Touch of Sin* does not judge the crimes and sins of these four protagonists – it is the bad "fate" of the protagonists that they can't escape.

Urban Centres and Remote, Backward Provinces

Beijing, being the capital of the PRC, is the central location of myriad Chinese films. Although the city often just functions as a coulisse, these films indirectly document the transformation of the city's architecture as well as people's changing lifestyle. Urbanity and urbanisation rank on top of the Chinese government's development agenda – as Li Keqiang's formula of the "new type of urbanisation" evidences. Metropolitan clusters have been set up, merging China's industrial centres with the villages and small townships of the neighbouring provinces. Nonetheless, the rural-urban divide persists and is even growing...

Beijing Bicycle (*Shiqi sui de dan che*) (2001) addresses the discrimination of labour migrants, their exploitation and treatment as underdogs by local residents. Guei, a peasant boy, takes on a job as bicycle courier. One day, the bicycle he was given by the company is stolen. If he does not manage to find the bike, he will lose his job and only source of income. As a parallel episode, the film tells the story of Jian, a high school student in Beijing, who is longing for a bike – and buys one on the second-hand market. Guei discovers that Jian is riding his bike and claims it back. The Salomonian solution is that the two boys share the bike. However, this does not work out and, in the end, Guei loses the bike and is heavily beaten up. Wang Xiaoshuai paints a dark and violent picture of the encounter between the different strata of Chinese society in the new capitalist era. His camera films both the new skyscraper towers of modern Beijing as well as the old *hutong* lanes. Labour migrants and the upper layers of urban society are next door to each other but in two separate worlds. The rapid economic growth of China has its price: Guei enters the wellness area of a luxury hotel to deliver a parcel, stunned and wide-eyed. Likewise, other rural migrants depicted in the film come into contact with luxury goods of a capitalist high society to which they will never belong. The gap between the haves and the have-nots is continuously growing, despite the one-party state's official narratives (and promises) of socialism.

Whilst the urban realms with the reflective glass facades of skyscrapers and office buildings allow people to escape in dream worlds and to believe in these illusions, Jia Zhangke's trilogy *The Pickpocket* (*Xiao Wu*) (1997), *Platform* (*Zhantai*) (2000) and *Unknown Pleasures* (*Ren xiao yao*) (2002) tells the story of the decay of his home village in Shanxi province, depicting the despair and lack of prospects of the local youth. Some of them are involved in semi-official jobs or just join pickpocket gangs, killing their time smoking and hanging out. The protagonist, a jobless local pickpocket, having experienced the rejection by his former friends and his family, becomes obsessed with the idea of robbing the local bank. With his arrest (and the final sentence), even this unrealistic dream, formed out of despair, is ultimately broken. The film, set in the late 1990s – the handover of Hong Kong is mentioned – shows the negative side effects of China's modernisation. The iron rice bowl is lost, people no longer enjoy a life-long employment guarantee. Even the military – once recruiting everyone willing to join – only accepts those who fulfil the army's new health requirements. Jia Zhangke's later work turns away from the remote villages and follows rural migrants to the Chinese megacities, depicting their inhumane working contracts and exploitation by merciless Chinese capitalists: *The World* (*Shijie*, 2004); *24 City* (*Ershisi chengji*, 2008).

Databases (selection)

China Brief

Jamestown Foundation

https://jamestown.org/programs/cb/

1–3 issues per month focusing on most recent developments in Chinese politics and economic as well as Chinese foreign relations.

China Digital Times

https://chinadigitaltimes.net

Bilingual online archive of articles and investigative background analyses, based in California. CDT was launched by Xiao Qiang (Graduate School of Journalism/University of California, Berkeley) in 2003. CDT archives news on recent developments in China with a focus on civil society and online contestation, but also covering most recent state-society interactions in general. Strong focus on Chinese online activism. Contains excerpts from and translations of select online debates.

China Leadership Monitor

https://www.prcleader.org

Initiated in 2002 under the editorial leadership of Alice Miller (Hoover Institution/Stanford University). In 2018, Minxin Pei (Claremont McKenna College) took over as main editor.

2–4 issues/per year. Covering domestic politics, party affairs, Chinese foreign relations as well as military and security dimensions. The short analyses also reference the inner-Chinese debate(s) and studies by Chinese scholars.

ECFR/Asia (and China Analysis)

https://www.ecfr.eu/publications/C11

Policy briefs as well as special issues (China Analysis) that cover select streams of the (ongoing) inner-Chinese debates on Chinese politics and international relations, based on articles published in the PRC's leading academic journals.

Newspaper Archives on Chinese Politics

The Diplomat

https://thediplomat.com/countries/china/

The Guardian

https://www.theguardian.com/world/china

The New York Times

https://www.nytimes.com/topic/destination/china

The South China Morning Post (Hong Kong)

https://www.scmp.com

Nanfang Zhoumo 南方周末(*Southern Weekly/Southern Weekend*)
(headquarters: Guangzhou; generally known as representing rather "liberal", critical views)

http://www.infzm.com

Renmin Ribao 人民日报(*People's Daily*)
(official newspaper of the Chinese party-state)

http://en.people.cn

Journals on Contemporary Chinese Political Developments

Journal of Chinese Governance

https://www.tandfonline.com/loi/rgov

Journal of Chinese Political Science

https://www.springer.com/journal/11366

Journal of Contemporary China

https://www.tandfonline.com/loi/cjcc

Index

Published in this series (since 2017)

Rechtsextremismus
Von Prof. Dr. Samuel Salzborn
4., überarbeitete und erweiterte Auflage 2020, 186 S., brosch., 22,- €,
ISBN 978-3-8487-6759-5

Entscheidungs- und Spieltheorie
Von Prof. Dr. Joachim Behnke
2., durchgesehene und aktualisierte Auflage 2020,
230 S., brosch., 24,- €, ISBN 978-3-8487-6254-5

Hispanoamerika
Von Prof. Dr. rer. pol. Hartmut Sangmeister
2019, 249 S., brosch., 21,90 €, ISBN 978-3-8487-5102-0

Internationale Politische Ökonomie
Von Prof. Dr. Stefan A. Schirm
4., unveränderte Auflage 2019, 290 S., brosch., 24,90 €,
ISBN 978-3-8487-5984-2

Theoretiker der Politik
Von Prof. em. Dr. Frank R. Pfetsch
3. Auflage 2019, 614 S., brosch., 29,90 €, ISBN 978-3-8487-5015-3

Chinesische Politik
Von Prof. Dr. Dr. Nele Noesselt
2., aktualisierte und überarbeitete Auflage 2018, 252 S., brosch., 24,90 €,
ISBN 978-3-8487-4238-7

Das politische System der Schweiz
Von Prof. Dr. Adrian Vatter
3., durchgesehene Auflage 2018, 608 S., brosch., 29,90€,
ISBN 978-3-8487-4806-8

Einführung in die Politikwissenschaft
Von Prof. Dr. Thomas Bernauer, Prof. Dr. Detlef Jahn, Dr. Patrick M. Kuhn und
Prof. Dr. Stefanie Walter
4., durchgesehene Auflage 2018, 566 S., brosch., 24,90 €,
ISBN 978-3-8487-4872-3

Internationale Sicherheit und Frieden
Von Prof. Dr. Heinz Gärtner
3., erweiterte und aktualisierte Auflage 2018, 338 S., brosch., 25,90 €,
ISBN 978-3-8487-4198-4

Methoden der Politikwissenschaft
Herausgegeben von Prof. Dr. Bettina Westle
2. Auflage 2018, 436 S., brosch., 24,90 €, ISBN 978-3-8487-3946-2

Parlamentarismus
Von Prof. Dr. Stefan Marschall
3., aktualisierte Auflage 2018, 265 S., brosch., 24,90 €, ISBN 978-3-8487-5231-7

Weltbilder und Weltordnung
Von Prof. Dr. Gert Krell und Prof. Dr. Peter Schlotter
5., überarbeitete und aktualisierte Auflage 2018, 462 S., brosch., 24,90 €,
ISBN 978-3-8487-4183-0

Grundbegriffe der Politik
Von Dr. Martin Schwarz, Prof. Dr. Karl-Heinz Breier und Prof. Dr. Peter Nitschke
2., aktualisierte und erweiterte Auflage 2017, 246 S., brosch., 22,90 €,
ISBN 978-3-8487-4197-7